BEFORE ENDEAVOURS FADE

A GUIDE TO THE BATTLEFIELDS OF THE FIRST WORLD WAR

BY ROSE E. B. COOMBS, MBE

AN
AFTER THE BATTLE
PUBLICATION

Thiepval: the majestic Memorial to the Missing stands amid fields still scarred with the trench lines of the Leipzig Redoubt.

© *After the Battle*, 1994

Paperback: ISBN 0 900913 85 1
Hardback: ISBN 0 900913 86 X

Printed in Great Britain

First published August 1976
Second edition November 1977
Third edition November 1979
Fourth edition March 1983
Fifth edition July 1986
Sixth edition April 1990
Seventh edition November 1994
Eight printing November 1998
Ninth printing February 2001

This edition prepared and completely revised by Karel Margry, European Editor, *After the Battle* magazine.

Designed and edited by Gordon Ramsey, Deputy Editor, *After the Battle* magazine

PUBLISHERS
Battle of Britain International Ltd.
Church House, Church Street,
London, E15 3JA
Telephone: (020) 8534 8833

PRINTERS
Heronsgate Ltd., Basildon, Essex

PHOTOGRAPHS
All photographs are the copyright of *After the Battle* except where indicated otherwise. RC – Author's collection; IWM – Imperial War Museum, London.

MAPS
All maps are copyright of the Michelin Company and are reproduced with their permission.

FRONT COVER
The 41st Division Memorial at Flers.

BACK COVER
Newfoundland Memorial at Gueudecourt.

ENDPAPERS
Trench maps of the period. **Front:** Hill 60 in the Ypres Salient from GSGS 3565, May 1917. **Rear:** The Somme battlefield in December 1916 reproduced from GSGS 3347.

PAGE 4
Dawn over Ypres. (RC)

PAGE 155
Desplanque Farm Cemetery located at La Chapelle d'Armentières. (RC)

ABOUT THE AUTHOR
'You haven't talked to THE expert on the Great War until you have talked to Miss Coombs.' So ran one letter received at the Imperial War Museum, London, where for 36 years, from 1946 until 1982, Rose Coombs worked — in latter years as Special Collections Officer.

Her interest in battlefields began at an early age, influenced largely by her father who served in the RAOC, but it was not until after the Second World War (in which she served as a Radar Operator with Nos. 10 and 11 Groups, RAF), that she was able to realise her ambition, through her position at the Imperial War Museum, to visit the battlefields of Europe.

During the years which followed, she had the opportunity to make hundreds of visits to the Western Front of 1914-18, on many occasions acting as guide to ex-Servicemen's groups returning to the battlefields. She accompanied authors writing on the period and lectured to groups of all ages, giving freely of her detailed knowledge of the terrain, its history, and the units and personalities involved.

In 1976, Miss Coombs combined years of study, travel and research into the production, with *After the Battle* magazine, of the first edition of *Before Endeavours Fade* — a name specially chosen by her to match the initial letters of the BEF — the acronym for the British Expeditionary Force which had set out for France in 1914. She constantly revised and updated 'BEF' through five editions until her death in January 1991.

For the seventh edition, *After the Battle*'s European Editor, Karel Margry, travelled every route during March-May 1994, checking and revising the text where necessary, and re-photographing every monument and memorial. Many new ones are included in this edition, yet we have striven to keep true to the flavour of Rose's original concept . . . before endeavours fade.

Contents

There will be voices whispering down these ways,
The while one wanderer is left to hear,
And the young life and laughter of old days,
Shall make undying echoes.

From *Looking Forward* by
Geoffrey Winthrop Young, 1909

Introduction by the Author

A visit to the battlefields should begin at one of the traditional entry ports for the BEF — Boulogne, Calais, Dieppe or Le Havre. However, the modern traveller can take advantage of other routes, by ferry or hovercraft, or now even travel beneath the waves! As it is the nearest port to the English coast, I have chosen Calais as the starting and departure point for this itinerary, but those of Boulogne, Dunkirk, Ostend and Zeebrugge are included in the relevant routes.

As regards war cemeteries, no effort has been made to include all of them, nor even to name all those that are passed along our route but details are given for many.

I have travelled all the routes described in an ordinary saloon car. On the whole, the main roads now have excellent surfaces but, here and there, the camber of the roads is not ideal and care should be taken to maintain a suitable speed to counter this. Total length of all routes combined is about 5,000 kms.

The motorways which now crisscross the old front line have access points to many of the areas covered in this book and views of parts of the battlefront can be obtained from them, but to really see the country it is necessary to keep to the old roads — the Routes Nationales (N); the Chemin Departmentals (D) or (CD), and the Vicinaux Ordinares (VO). Frequently, I have found these latter two categories are better surfaced than those nationally maintained roads, although narrower. Distances are in kilometres.

Maps are a necessity for any tour. Whilst the route is indicated on black and white extracts, I recommend the visitor to purchase the following Michelin 1:200 000 maps: Belgium Sheets 213 and 214; France Sheets 51, 52, 53, 56 and 57.

The new area sheets 236, 237 and 241 — Nord and Ile de France and Champagne respectively — are useful for forward planning, if a little large for use in the car. The scale is 1cm to 2 km (very approximately half-an-inch to one mile) and all the features are indicated in colour.

The renumbering of roads in Belgium and France is now complete, but variations may exist still. Those quoted in the text are based on the latest issues of Michelin maps. Autoroutes and international roads now carry 'E' numbers. In

THE LATE MISS ROSE COOMBS, MBE

Belgium, all main and secondary roads are numbered or named.

Another problem for the visitor today has been caused by the changes in place names due to the recent adoption of modern Flemish as opposed to the traditional spellings used for Belgian towns and villages as they were known to the BEF. For ease of navigation, I have indicated the version which is now to be found on signposts.

About this book

It is now over seventy years since war raged here. Thousands of soldiers died daily. Their relatives have visited their graves, their comrades also. Pilgrims have come from all parts of the world to say a prayer or bring flowers. An old soldier has tried vainly to find the trench he knew so well. But the old warriors — the majority of them — have disappeared; as have their loved ones. History is made but who will remember it? From far off, the descendants of those who fought here come to visit the villages whose names, for some four years, made people hold their breath. School children come with their teachers, coaches of tourists with guides, and the casual visitor. To all, this guide is indispensable.

The author spares no pains to attract your attention but she does not go in for melodrama. You will find all the details you need with the historic background to the events. As for the itinerary, you will find little is missed. All battle sites and monuments are included, even to the smallest or the most modest. Graves of the known and the unknown are pointed out and this is done with the utmost respect for all.

When the author asked me to write an introduction to her work, she recalled our many trips over the battlefields of France and Flanders. I would like to thank her for this expression of friendship and wish this guidebook every success.

Dr Alfred A. Caenepeel, OBE

Vice-Chairman, Last Post Committee
Founder & Curator, Ypres Salient Museum

THE LATE DR A. A. CAENEPEEL, OBE

In September 1989. the DOCUMENTATIE-CENTRUM DR ALFRED CAENEPEEL was opened as a public reference library, as an adjunct to the Ypres Salient 1914-18 Museum. This unique archive comprises books, maps, documents and photographs relative to every aspect of the Salient and of all the armies which fought there.

Demarcation Stones

In the decade following the Armistice, 119 small monuments were erected in Belgium and France, at intervals along the 960 kilometres of the Western Front, to mark the limit of the German advance in 1918. The Touring Club de France and the Touring Club de Belgique were the prime movers of this scheme which caught the imagination of the public.

Of pink granite, the monuments were no more than a metre in height. They were designed by the sculptor Paul Moreau Vauthier who produced three basic types, differing mainly in the helmet of the capstone. These were either of the British tin helmet or the French and Belgian 'Poilu's' helmet design. On the side of the stones were decorations consisting of a soldier's equipment — gas mask case, water bottle, etc., and each bore the inscription. 'Here the Invader was brought to a standstill' in either French, Flemish or English. On the front face, the

name of the place they were to stand in or near was inscribed.

The stones which became known as Demarcation Bornes or Stones were placed in positions where the battle line crossed a road or street, in town or country, at points decided by Maréchal Pétain and the General Staffs of France, Belgium, and Britain.

Funds to help in the erection of the monuments came from many sources beside the two Touring Clubs, which bore the main charge, and local authorities, ex-Servicemen's organisations and private people all contributed to their cost.

The number of stones remaining in-situ today is much depleted as many were destroyed or lost during the Second World War or have become the victims of the motor vehicle. For instance, of the seven donated by the Ypres League and erected in the Salient, only two or three have survived. Others have been broken up by the explosion of old ammunition which had been placed against them by farmers.

Where our itinerary passes a stone, I have usually drawn attention to it.

The Poppy Legend

The poppy legend originated in China. A white flower from which a potent drug was distilled was called the Flower of Forgetfulness. Ghengis Khan brought some of the seed westward but after a battle the flower became red. In the centre of each was a cross.

It was found that on many battlefields, when everything else had been laid waste,

the landscape was soon ablaze with the blood-red blooms. On the Somme battlefield in 1917 (and again after the war was over) the land burst forth in a blaze of scarlet with patches of yellow charlock and white chamomile. Many graves of those buried near the front line were soon marked by the charlock due to the seeds being released when the grave was dug.

Lord Macauley drew attention to the strange link of the poppy with battle and put forward the suggestion it should be regarded as the flower of sacrifice and memorial.

Battlefield Debris

The colossal expenditure in shell and ammunition during the First World War has left a dangerous legacy for the careless visitor today. Often, as the battle areas are traversed, small piles of rusting shells will be seen on the verge. These neat piles of ammunition are usually the result of a field being ploughed — the 'Iron Harvest' I call it — and still to this day, regular collections are made by the military authorities to take these dangerous objects away for safe demolition.

The sight of such things seems to turn many visitors into collectors and, with little thought of the danger of these seemingly inoffensive objects, they are bundled into the car. Please leave them where you see them — or, if it is within any of the memorial parks, draw the attention of the Superintendent to them. Explosives do not improve with age and many French children are still maimed and blinded by handling such objects.

Even the apparently innocent rusty bayonet or length of barbed wire carries with it the danger of tetanus if carelessly handled. Recently, scientists have been working on one aspect of the spread of the deadly disease rabies, as it has been realised that the

old battle-torn woods and shrublands are breeding grounds of the most frequent carrier — the fox. The French medical authorities have been investigating some of the untouched regions and have found evidence that careless wandering through dirty infectious ground can be dangerous.

Remember also that the removal of anything from private land is stealing. It is often possible to acquire material quite safely and legally for a small sum. However, always bear in mind the strict customs regulations concerning the importation of weapons and ammunition.

Accommodation

The traveller should be warned that, for the most part, the regions through which these routes pass are off the normal tourist track and, therefore, hotels are often few and far between. Beyond the coastal resorts or the cities of Amiens, Reims, or Arras, there is not a great deal of choice. The French and Belgian National Tourist Offices can supply lists of approved hotels in the area but few are of three or four star classification.

Ypres has a fairly good selection of moderately-priced hotels and out in the country, within easy access, there are some more expensive (but not outrageously so), country house type hostelleries. Usually in the small towns there are cafés with a few rooms.

Nowhere in France is one far from a good restaurant. In my travels, I have never failed to find the Buffets de la Gare of the larger or main-line stations of very good value. Amiens, Lille, Arras and Reims — all are good. Some stations have more than one restaurant on the premises catering for differing tastes or pockets. Often, if there is no

such café on the station, one will be found in the vicinity, for example, in Albert and Armentières.

For those doing their own catering, there is no village in France where bread cannot be bought daily (except between the hours of 12 and 2 p.m.). For reasonable prices I can highly recommend the hypermarkets on the outskirts of all major towns, frequently near motorway intersections. Parking is ample. This is important as in most towns parking meters have now been installed. They are expensive and the regulations are rigidly monitored by meter maids.

Calais. Hôtel de Ville Belfry.

Calais–Ypres
ROUTE I Via Bergues

Now a modern sprawling industrial area and busy port, **Calais** was a most important British base particularly for the ordnance services and the auxiliary units for the BEF. Hospitals, training camps and depots all grew up behind the town and, in February 1918, the train ferry link with the then new Richborough military harbour was established.

Little of the Calais the first BEF knew remains, and the new residential and industrial zones now spread over the flat land behind the sand dunes where the troops encamped. Here and there, however, little bungalows (originally temporary wooden huts) remain as residences.

During the Second World War, Calais was almost entirely destroyed in 1940; thereafter to be encircled by concrete bunkers of the German defences. Many of these were added to the old forts which had previously been its main defence.

The recommended route to leave the terminal for destinations other than Calais centre now takes the coast road. The road hugs the old moat up to the large roundabout where it is joined by the road from the hoverport. In the sand dunes around the hoverport a few bunkers remain.

To visit the town, follow the signs for 'Centre Ville'. From the hoverport roundabout, these lead through rue Mollien direct to the famous Hôtel de Ville and the Parc St Pierre; from the ferry terminal near the Gare Maritime, the route leads across the Pont Mobile, through the Place de Suède, the rue du Cdt Bonningue and the Place d'Armes, then left into the rue Royale and, past the Parc Richelieu, across the bridges to the park and town hall.

In the **Parc St Pierre** is the **Musée de la Guerre**. The exhibits are mainly related to the 1939-45 conflict. In front of the nearby **Hôtel de Ville**, a magnificent building in the Flemish Renaissance style with its famous Belfry, in the Place du Soldat Inconnu is the equally famous sculpture by Rodin of the Six Burghers of Calais.

From the hoverport roundabout, the new bypass now connects directly with the A16 and A26 motorways. With the opening of new parts of the motorway, the quickest route to Belgium and Ypres is via the new A16-E40 autoroute east to Dunkerque (32 kms), then the N225/A25-E42 south to Steenvoorde (20 kms), then the N38/N300 east to Poperinge and Ypres (26kms).

A more interesting route to Dunkerque and Ypres is via the D119. From the hoverport roundabout, turn right to the nearby smaller roundabout. Turn south here, into the rue du Nord, then after crossing the railway, take the second turning on the left, the route de Gravelines (D119). This road winds its way through the immediate hinterland of the sand dunes, through **Fort Vert** with a number of desolate bunkers, defences for the **airfield at Marck** which is on the right (8 kms), and for coastal artillery protecting both Calais and Fort Philippe, all of Second War vintage. Waldam is a small modern village passed through before the hamlets of Le Tap Cul and L'Étoile, part of Oye-Plage where the road rejoins the N1 on the modern outskirts of Gravelines. The nuclear power station and oil refinery at Petit Fort Philippe have caused considerable extension of the residential areas of both Grand Fort Philippe on the west bank of the River Aa and Gravelines. The N1 now curves round to the south of the ancient town.

During the Great War, **Gravelines** was a Belgian headquarters. It is possible to visualise the encampments located where light industry amid the workers' estates is now in view below the new road. There are still vestiges of the old fishing port with military connections dating back many centuries.

Within the crumbling walls and ramparts, largely designed by Vauban, the narrow and busy streets follow a spider's-web pattern. It is a quaint place and can be approached by a continuation of the D119 instead of turning right and then left onto the N1. The old road through the town centre with its attractive church tower rejoins the N1 at a new crossroad on the eastern side. The main road makes a sharp right-hand turn here. About 1 km further east is one of the **best preserved windmills** in Flanders, away to the right among the beet fields.

After 5 kms, Loon-Plage, a suburb of the ever-spreading complex of Dunkerque, is bypassed to the north. New roads have been constructed to carry the heavy traffic the new docks have caused and several further access routes are proposed to form a complete ring-road for the old port.

In 5 kms, at a major crossroad, the N1 swings to the left to enter **Dunkerque** (Duinkerken). Keep ahead on the N335 to the next major crossing where the N225, a fast dual carriageway, is the access road for the A25 autoroute. A short way along the N225, there is a lake for small craft and nearby there is a road sign which announces 'Zero altitude'.

If a visit to Dunkerque has been made, leave by the D916 which follows the Canal de Bergues for 9 kms, passing the old **Fort Vallières** about midway, to the quaint old town of Bergues. It can also be reached from the N225 by taking the left turn to Bierne and Bergues on the D352.

Bergues is a sleepy country town surrounded by fortifications designed in 1667 by one of France's illustrious sons, Sebastian le Prestre de Vauban, Marshal of France (1633-1707). He is remembered on the **Porte de Cassel** by a plain memorial plaque. This gate is one of the narrow gateways which gave entry to the town across the moat fed by the three canals whose junction is in the town. These canals were a vital asset to the BEF. The Inland Waterways Transportation units operated barges to carry stores and casualties over many miles through Flanders. Bergues was a staging post to and from the coast.

Belgian troops used the town as a rest centre during the Yser battles and, being only 25 kms behind the front line, it was bombarded in 1915. In 1940, it was badly damaged and many of the old houses were destroyed. Vauban's walls survived, as did the Port de Cassel with the emblem of the Sun King (Louis XIV) on the outer side (now removed), although the bridge over the moat did not and was replaced by a Bailey Bridge in 1944; now, this has gone too after many years' service.

The Porte de Cassel at Bergues. Until recent years, a Bailey Bridge, dating from the Second World War, straddled the moat at this spot.

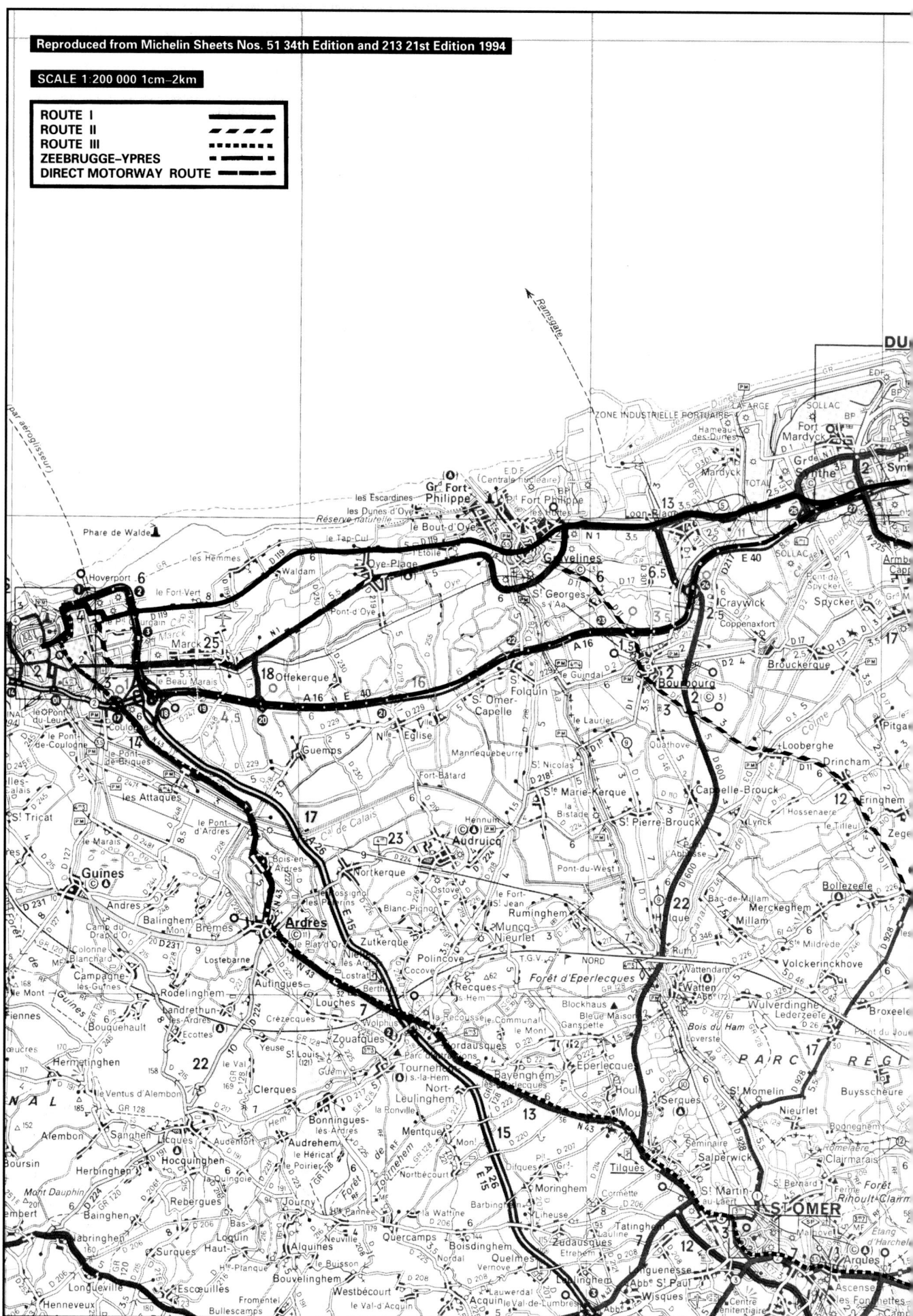

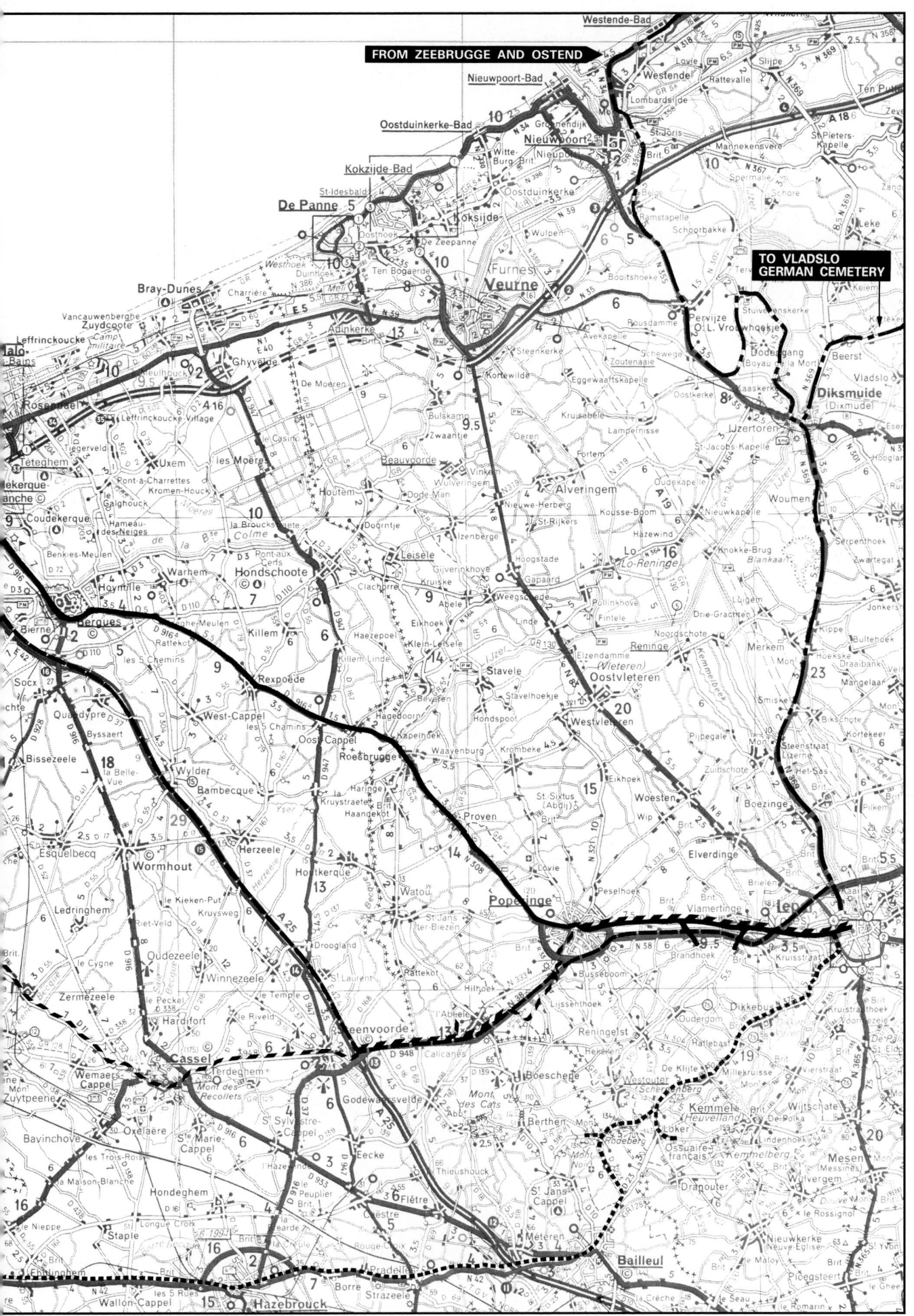

FROM ZEEBRUGGE AND OSTEND

TO VLADSLO GERMAN CEMETERY

Proven. La Lovie Château, headquarters for many BEF units and a base for King George V for his visit to the Western Front in July 1917.

The Germans captured Poperinge on October 4, 1914 but were driven out eleven days later. The photo of Scottish troops in the Grande Place was taken in 1917. (IWM)

The D916a, the road to the frontier at Oostcappel via Rexpoede, crosses the fertile agricultural plain with its tiny farmhouses set amid neat fields, and church spires of the villages dominate the landscape which was the southern boundary of the Belgian front.

After 13 kms, we reach Oostcappel frontier post — a small uninteresting hamlet. Driving straight on, the road has become the N308. Then, 7 kms further on, is **Proven**, well known to the BEF as a rail centre which, by 1916, was vast. Training areas and hospitals were set up all over the commune. **Mendinghem British Cemetery**, away on the right of the road just before the village, is one of a trio of cemeteries in the locality which served the hospitals and casualty clearing stations. The other two are **Dozinghem** (*see page 63*) and **Bandaghem**, all three names being coined by the British troops to sound like the local Flemish ones.

In the woods to the east of the village, the divisions grouped prior to the Third Battle of Ypres and, at **La Lovie Château**, on a side road on the left, 3¾ kms further down the road to Poperinge, was the Fifth Army Headquarters from June to November 1917. From May 1915, the house was commandeered as an Army headquarters. At that date, the VI Corps took the house over and the base set up by them remained until February 1916 when XIV Corps took over. In July, the VIII Corps took their place, being in residence until the advent of the Fifth Army, who were followed by II Corps, and from April 1918 the 34th, 41st and 49th Divisions each used the house until August when II Corps returned. In July 1917, King George V stayed here during his visit to the Front.

Return to the N308 and turn left for **Poperinge** (3½ kms). 'Pop' to every British soldier was the forward base for the Ypres Salient from the autumn of 1914 onwards. The town, briefly occupied by the Germans in October 1914, was recaptured on the 15th and soon became the venue for the military. Training camps, depots and hospitals sprang up amid the hop fields. Refugees from Ypres crowded in and the station became one of the most important behind the lines, as almost all troops going up to the front or returning on leave entered the area from its platforms.

The main square bustled with transport, horses, mules and men with lorries of all shapes converged here, as all the roads leading from it led to one facility or another. Restaurants and estaminets did a roaring trade, despite frequent bombardments, among the thousands who sought relief and relaxation from the rigours of trench life whilst 'out of the line'.

The square, now named Grote Markt in Flemish, with the graceful Stadhuis behind.

Toc H, Everyman's Club in Poperinge. Over 25,000 used the attic chapel.

Follow the signs for the centre and you will arrive in the pleasant **Grote Markt** with the elegant Gothic **Stadhuis** at the eastern end and nearby St Bertin's church. Gasthuisstraat curves away on the western side of the square with the old chapel on the right; a doorway beside it leads to the hospital which gives the street its name. Further along, at No. 43, a tall white house, perhaps the most famous in 'Pop', comes in view. The beautiful iron doors are the entrance to **Talbot House** or **Toc H**.

The Reverend Neville Talbot, senior chaplain of 6th Division, had been searching for a house which he could open as a church club for the division in 1915 when by chance the owner of No. 10 rue de l'Hôpital (as the street was then called) left to find less dangerous quarters — the house had been hit several times by artillery shells — and the Padre persuaded the Army to rent the house for the duration. In charge of the project he placed an old friend, the Reverend Philip Byard Clayton. A rotund little man in 'specs' with a contagious sense of devotion and fun, he had been padre at No. 16 General Hospital in Le Tréport earlier in 1915 and in November arrived at GHQ Montreuil expecting to be sent to the Guards Brigade but his tall friend (Talbot was 6 foot 7 inches tall) asked for him. And so 'Tubby' arrived in Pop and the house was opened on December 11, 1915 as a club for Everyman with rooms where men could relax and enjoy

Gilbert Talbot's temporary grave marker displayed today in Toc H chapel.

The forecourt of 'Pop' station was rarely devoid of soldiers during the war.

relative comfort and a delightful garden, but the most important place in the house was the Upper Room — the chapel in the old hop and fruit attic. It was named **Talbot House** after Neville Talbot's brother Lieutenant Gilbert Talbot who had been killed at Hooge on July 30, 1915 and who lies in Sanctuary Wood Cemetery (*see page 43*). The original marker from his grave is displayed at the top of the chapel stairs in Toc H.

The house remained open with few interruptions until, in May 1918, enemy bombardment forced its closure for a few months before re-opening on September 27, 1918. In January 1919, the owner reclaimed his house and the Club had to close but the spirit which had been born there did not die. In 1919, the Christian Movement Toc H was founded to help men and women who in the harsh days of peace searched vainly for employment and the 'brotherhood of the trenches'. Thus the name was perpetuated and the organisation grew worldwide. Branches sprang up in almost every country, all working to aid people through their life 'to think fairly, to love widely, to witness humbly and to build bravely'. This their founder did throughout his long life, travelling extensively from his base near the Tower of London until his death in December 1972. Each branch on formation was presented with a lamp, similar to those used in the time of Christ, to recall that which burned in the Upper Room at Pop.

In the years after the war, Tubby and other Toc H members made pilgrimages to the Salient but it was not until 1926 that they could persuade the owner of the Old House to allow visits. However, Lord Wakefield, who in 1928 had purchased the mine crater at Spanbroekmolen, the Pool of Peace (*see page 59*), bought the house in 1929 and soon once more its doors were open wide. During the German Occupation from 1940 to 1944, the people of Poperinge hid the treasures from the house which they had stripped as the Germans came; all were back in their familiar places when Tubby made his first post-war visit. It is still a venue for pilgrims, not necessarily Toc H members, and is presided over by a small staff helped by volunteers. There is always a cheerful welcome. A visitor's centre with a small exhibition has recently been opened in the garden in what was originally the bathhouse.

Further along the curve of the street, at No. 57, you will see another famous building. Now a private property, it was known the world over as **Skindles** — for years, the name sign was proudly worn above the front door, but it was taken down in 1990 when the rooms on the ground floor were turned into shops. Originally the **Café de la Commerce des Houblons**, it was opened under the direction of Madame Beutin and her two daughters. Their friendly welcome made it an extremely popular venue for the young army officers who crowded into Poperinge throughout the course of the war. When the Beutins opened at the then No. 43 rue de l'Hôpital, one young blade from Oxfordshire was reminded forcibly of a similar establish-

ment at Maidenhead, Berkshire — Skindles Hotel — and in time this name was adopted by Madame Beutin. It has been recorded that General Plumer was there the night before the Battle of Messines began and legend has it that ten seconds before the great arc of mines was detonated, he ordered a Vermouth!

Immediately after passing Skindles, take the next turning to the left and turn back into the Grote Markt skirting St Bertin's church. Across the T-junction and to the right, in Burgemeester Berten-Plein, is the **Collège Stanislas**, an episcopal establishment used as a hospital by the Friends' Ambulance Unit for civilian casualties from Ypres in 1915. Although the 1915 and 1918 bombardments caused much damage, there are many old houses in the town and, in spite of modern building going on everywhere, there is much of the town recognisable to those who knew it over 75 years ago.

Leave Poperinge by the N308 (Ieperstraat) and pass the real target for the enemy artillery — **the station**. It has been written that whenever a leave train was due to depart, the enemy artillery interfered, but this did not prevent the place being the most-popular and the most-loathed spot in the vicinity; always thronged with travellers waiting for the trains. Returning men, however, did not loiter with the same indifference. A rumour which took a great deal of scotching was that the stationmaster of Pop had been shot as a spy due to the suspicious regularity of the shelling.

The 12 kilometres along the straight road to Ypres were travelled by all not using the railway running parallel to it. The road was lined by encampments, hutted and tented, hospitals, dumps and offices. Today, all sign of these has gone with the passage of time. Across the railway now runs a great new

Hotel Skindles, the famous Officers' Club, now turned into shops.

highway which eventually will encircle the town as a bypass. Only the cemeteries remain to remind us of the thousands who passed this way. Even the tall trees which survived the bombardments have been felled to make way for the four-lane road and replenished with saplings.

On the outskirts of the town, the N308 crosses the ring-road which is now connected to Ypres by a fast dual carriageway bypass, the N38, which avoids Brandhoek and Vlamertinge and links with the motorway north of Ieper. The old road narrows at **Brandhoek** (2½ kms). On the left is **Red Farm Cemetery**, one of the smallest in the Salient. Here, in April-May 1918, 46 British soldiers and three civilians were buried.

Red Farm Cemetery, Brandhoek, with a headstone to three civilians on the left.

Vlamertinge British Cemetery (*above*), with its unusual gates, and (*right*) the grave of Captain F. Grenfell, VC.

A right turn in the centre of Brandhoek leads to the new highway and, across it, some of the cemeteries made when the hamlet was the centre of hospitals and casualty clearing stations. Cross the railway and the new road and immediately go right and bear left and, in a few metres, two cemeteries are reached. In that on the right, **Brandhoek New Military Cemetery**, lies Captain N. G. Chavasse, VC and Bar, MC, RAMC, who died from wounds on August 4, 1917 (Plot III, Grave B15). Medical Officer to the 1st Bn. Liverpool Scottish, he went to France with the battalion in November 1914. He was awarded the Military Cross in 1915 in recognition of his gallantry at Hooge, and for his devotion to duty and his self-sacrifice and extraordinary energy and inspiration at Guillemont in August 1916, the Victoria Cross. For similar services in July and August 1917 he was awarded posthumously the Bar to the VC. He died two days after his action in Brandhoek Military Hospital. His headstone is unique, for it bears two small representations of the VC in place of the usual large one.

Returning to the crossroads, the third cemetery of Brandhoek is seen on the right. Turn right on to the N308 again. About 1¼ km further along on the north side of the road stands a tall red-brick building, the **Hop Store**. Just beyond the trees behind it is the **Hop Store Cemetery** recalling the casualty clearing station there. Until they were rebuilt in the 1970s, against the wall of the abutting cottage was a water pump from which men and horses going to and from Ypres were refreshed.

Another kilometre and **Vlamertinge** is reached. Almost totally destroyed in artillery barrages, the village was held by the Germans between October 7-10, 1914. All around, the BEF built camps and stores and the inevitable hospitals and casualty clearing stations. By 1918, only the battered tower of the church remained. To the left of the church is **Vlamertinge Military Cemetery** which is entered by a pair of unusual gates. These are of special design in memory of Major, the Hon. C. B. O. Mitford who lies within this cemetery (Plot I, Grave E8). It is also the last resting place of Captain Francis Grenfell, VC (Plot II, Grave B14).

In the second Vlamertinge cemetery, the **New British Cemetery**, on the Ouderdom road to the south of the village (across the railway and the new road), there lies another VC — CSM John Skinner, VC, DCM, of the King's Own Scottish Borderers (Plot XIII, Grave H15). He won his award in 1917 for bravery in the Third Battle of Ypres when he put three blockhouses out of action in one continuous battle in August. He returned to England for the investiture by King George V and the customary 14 days leave. At the end of this time, when he reached Folkestone, he was sent to hospital and posted to the Reserve Battalion in Edinburgh. However, a few days later, he was seen with his company back in the Salient. He had refused to go to Edinburgh and, having his return leave warrant in his pocket, after two days in hospital he had risked a court-martial to return to his men. He also had a bet with a pal, CSM Ross. Both had been wounded eight times and the wager was: who would

get the ninth first. Skinner won the bet on March 17, 1918 when he was shot between the eyes trying to rescue a wounded man.

His funeral was remarkable. The South Wales Borderers' Padre, the Rev. Kenelm Swallow, officiated at the ceremony in the pouring rain when his body was brought to the cemetery in Vlamertinge on a gun carriage drawn by a magnificent team of horses and then carried to the grave by six brother VCs of the 29th Division. The ceremony took place on March 19, 1918 and is unique in military history.

Another 2 kms along the N308 and the spires of Ypres are in full view ahead as the straight road bends and is crossed by the railway. In the trees, before the crossing, once stood a solitary house. Set in a pleasant garden with ponds before the front door, this was **Rossières Château**, or better known as **'Goldfish Château'**. It was hardly damaged during the war, despite its occupation by many formations' headquarters including V Corps, the Canadians and other divisions, and the proximity of the railway and enormous stores dumps nearby. Then, in 1920, it was entirely destroyed when an ammunition dump blew up. It was said that the German General von Bissing, who occupied it briefly in October 1914, was enchanted by it and stated then that he wanted it as his 'prix de guerre' and therefore the German artillery carefully avoided it. Today, a bungalow occupies the site.

Another kilometre and **Ypres** (Ieper) is entered. On the left, a red brick wall encloses the famous **Asylum**. This Victorian-style building has been rebuilt in almost identical form as it was completely destroyed during the bombardments. In 1915, the Friends' Ambulance Unit, which had established itself there in December 1914, was driven to the cellars before it, and the nuns who assisted, evacuated it in May 1915. At a ceremony in 1965, three of these gallant ladies were present although all have now passed away, the last in 1979. Sister Marguerite became famous for her work with the wounded and wrote a book about her experiences. Now, new quarters for the patients have been erected in the gardens.

A few hundred metres further on, the road crosses the old canal and the level crossing known as **Bridge No. 10** or **'Devil's Bridge'**. Turn right towards the station and, in front of the latter, left into Stationsstraat. The one-way street leads into Boterstraat, Ypres' main shopping street. By turning right, the Grand Place is reached and the Cloth Hall comes into view.

The hop store near Vlamertinge — once a casualty clearing station.

The Castel Yvonne in Cassel was once occupied by General Plumer.

Maréchal Foch surveys the battlefields before the reconstructed Flanders mill.

The memorial to the Cassel battles with, behind it, the old Second Army HQ.

ROUTE II Via Cassel

Leave Calais by the N1 towards Gravelines and Dunkerque. This road leads through modern residential areas amid which the occasional large concrete bunker can be glimpsed, but most of these have now gone. The little single-storey dwellings in the rue de Phaisbourg are replacements for the wooden bungalow residences of the BEF encampments mentioned earlier.

The N1 is straight and very uninteresting. The rather drab ribbon development gives way to the flat agricultural region of beet and corn fields, market gardens and the occasional old sugar factory standing idle now the crops are taken direct to the modern refineries outside Dunkerque. In 22 kms, the outskirts of Gravelines are reached. Turn right onto the D11 from the ring-road signposted Bourbourg-Cassel. The road crosses the flat meadows and small fields with their attendant farms, and the new A16-E40 motorway, to the country town of **Bourbourg** astride a canal. Follow the signs for Cassel through the town, having crossed the canal and railway, and continue onwards over the **Canal de la Haute Colme** at Looberghe and thence through the Erkelsbrugge road junction to Arnèke.

After 21 kms, we reach **Arnèke**, a sleepy village belying the fact that it was a busy railway centre surrounded by training depots and reinforcement camps. Ahead, the solitary hill of Cassel rises above the gently undulating landscape. The road climbs up and around the wooded slopes of the steep hill and joins the D933 from St Omer after 7 kms at the entry to the town.

Cassel. As the narrow street rises, a square, until recently Place du General Plumer, now Place du Général Vandamme, opens on the left. Immediately thereafter, the main road, even narrower, proceeds downhill to the Grand Place. The town clings to the crest and slopes of the 156-metre-high **Mont Cassel** which, since Roman times, has been an important road junction as major highways converge from each cardinal point.

The scene of many sieges through the centuries, it had been burnt and devastated no less than nine times when, in 1914, once more it became an important military centre. Once more, the medieval streets, houses and cellars rang with the voices of soldiers and, not for the first time either, English accents were heard. An earlier occupation placed it forever in the nursery literature of British children, for here it was that the Grand Old Duke of York marched his 10,000 men up the hill only to march them down again. This was during the 1793-94 campaign in Flanders mounted by the Duke of Coburg when the Duke of York led the English contingent against the French revolutionary army and was soundly beaten in a battle fought nearby.

In October 1914, Sir John French set up a base in Cassel for the period of October 11-24, but it is as the headquarters of Maréchal Foch (from October 1914 to June 1915 and again in April 1918) and as that of General Plumer's Second Army (from 1916 to 1918) that Cassel will be remembered.

Although the town suffered considerable damage in the Second World War, in many aspects it still appears much the same as 80 years ago as the rebuilding has been in character.

On the summit of the Mont Cassel are the **Jardin Public**, once the Place de Castel Moulin now the Terrasse du Château, which can easily be reached from the square below, up the narrow winding street passing the tall red-brick house on the left, **Castel Yvonne** (No. 1 rue St Nicolas), where Lord Plumer lived. His rooms overlooked the great plateau with Ypres and the grey mass of the Messines Ridge in the distance.

The Jardin Public is dominated by a wooden windmill of the type which, until the early years of this century, were found throughout this part of Flanders. This mill, which is open to the public, is a reconstruction based on a mill salvaged from Arnèke.

Nearby is the equestrian **statue of Maréchal Foch** by Georges Malissard, a copy of which is in Grosvenor Gardens, close to Victoria Station, London. The statue, on a pedestal of Soignies and Breton granite, was unveiled by Raymond Poincaré in the presence of the Maréchal on July 7, 1928 and looks out over the battlefields of the Yser, Ypres and Messines. The square face of the pedestal represents the stubborn resistance of the Allied armies. An arc of trees frames the statue which is set on the spot from where Foch was given to watching the smoke of battle rise from the trenches in the distance.

Beneath the gardens are the **cellars of the old castle** which stood here and were used by the military in both wars. Second Army Headquarters also used the **large white building** (now a café), as well as other houses in the town. In front of the café, in the centre of the car park, is a **memorial to the three major battles of Cassel**, 1071, 1328 and 1677. An archway leads from the garden direct to the main square by an extremely steep path and road. Near the path leading to the gateway is a **concrete bunker** (now almost hidden by conifer trees and with an old farm cart on top) and an entrance to the cellars.

At various strategic points around the park, **orientation tables** are set into the tops of the balustrades. Distance and directions for towns all over the globe are etched in slate. From these viewpoints, the magnificent **panorama** unfolds. In bygone times, it was said that from the summit of the Mont Cassel could be viewed five kingdoms: those of France, England, Belgium, Holland, and of God. Certainly on a clear day, the view encompasses the hills of Kemmel and the Mont de Cats, Vimy Ridge and the lighthouse of Dunkerque. With the aid of binoculars, the spires of Ypres, or the pillars of the Vimy Ridge memorial, can be discerned.

Mont Cassel. A surviving bunker in the shade on the summit of the Jardin Public.

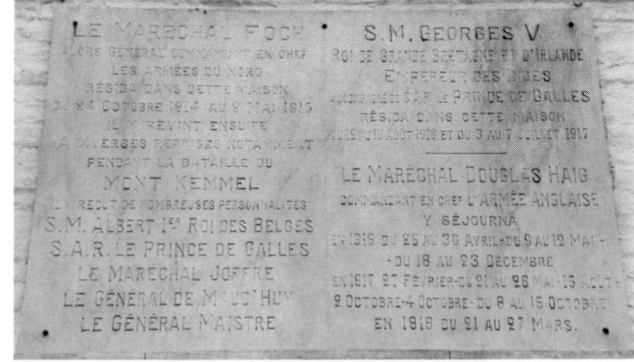

The Hôtel de Schoebeque (*left*) was used by King George V and other notable visitors — the wall plaque (*right*) records the dates.

Closer at hand, the old Roman roads and those built by Napoleon's engineers like spokes from a wheel can be determined. The roofs of the Renaissance-style buildings straggle immediately below the park, among them the Hôtel de Ville with its many dormer windows, each said to represent one of the cantons in the province of Flandres Maritime of which Cassel was the capital.

In the **Hôtel de Ville**, the erstwhile Hôtel de la Noble Cour set on the Grand Place, Maréchal Foch had his office. It used to be preserved as a museum, but everything — the Maréchal's furniture, uniform, documents, photographs and other treasures — has been transferred to the **Town Museum**, across the square, where more exhibits relating to the war effort of Cassel are displayed together with relics of other past glories. The museum is open every day except Tuesdays from mid-June to mid-September, 10 to 12 a.m and 2 to 6.30 p.m.

The rue d'Ypres, now renamed rue du Maréchal Foch, leads from the Grand Place eastwards. At No. 32, the **Hôtel de Schoebeque** was the residence of the Maréchal during his tour of duty and it was here he received notabilities and where King George V, the Prince of Wales, the King of the Belgians and Sir Douglas Haig stayed on different occasions. A **plaque** on the wall of the modern hotel commemorates these dates and visits.

The road bends past the white buildings at the end of the street as it begins its tortuous descent to the valley. At the corner is an old archway, the ancient Porte d'Ypres. The town cemetery is on the precipitous slopes in between two very dangerous hairpin bends.

At the foot of the hill, the road to Poperinge and Ypres crosses the D916 for Bailleul. Just off this road, some 2 kms away, is the hilltop village of **St Marie Cappel** below which are the fields where the **Royal Flying Corps aerodrome** was established. Today, little or no sign of the aerodrome can be traced.

After crossing the D916, the road (D948) enters the wooded slopes of the **Mont des Recollets** and some further dangerous corners have to be negotiated before the long straight road to Steenvoorde (6 kms).

Among the copses on the right of the road just before **Steenvoorde** is the hunting lodge so vividly described by R. H. Mottram in his *Spanish Farm* trilogy. Steenvoorde is a dusty market town with an unusual church spire. The D37 now bypasses the town but it is quite simple to bear left and drive through on the D948 and rejoin the main road before it crosses the Dunkerque-Lille autoroute.

For 4 kms, the D948 runs dead straight to the frontier station and customs post, now no longer operational, where the juggernaut lorries used to queue for clearance. One road on the right leads across the beet and wheat fields to the village of **Godewaersvelde** — this name defeated the Tommies who referred to it always as 'Gertie wore velvet'.

The road up from the frontier post is international, France lying on the right, Belgium to the left. A little way along, the new road is joined by the old one to **Abeele** on the left. It is also the way to gain access to the small **Abeele Aerodrome Military Cemetery** near the site of the **RFC aerodrome**. The Cross of Sacrifice can be seen above the shrubs along the road.

Today, the direct road to Poperinge, 4 kms from the frontier, avoids the tortuous narrow road through Abeele leaving it to tractors and local traffic. Using the new road, in 2½ kms take a small road on the right — Lijssenthoek (GR5a) — and then left and, in 1 km, the beautiful **Lijssenthoek British Cemetery**, with 10,786 graves the second largest in Flanders after Tyne Cot Cemetery (*see page 40*), is reached. Here, men of many nationalities lie amid beautiful gardens and trees. Begun in 1914 by the French (who had established a casualty clearing station at **Remi Farm**, visible behind the cemetery, to which a railway spur was laid from the Poperinge line), the cemetery bears the unusual dates 1914-1920. In these peaceful surroundings, Frenchmen are the earliest burials but close by lies the last officer to die in the Salient — Lieutenant-Colonel G. E. Beaty-Pownall (Plot XXX, Grave B14) — together with his comrades who lost their lives in September and October 1918. Men from the Commonwealth, the Chinese Labour Corps and the **only three Americans to be buried in the Salient** lie close to the French plots.

Remi Farm has changed little over the years. In the great barn, where men were sheltered during the war of 1914-18, the beams bear signs of earlier military occupations. Etched on them and on the walls are initials and dates of soldiers' visits of a previous century. Graffiti of Poilu and Tommy are intermingled.

To the south of the cemetery is a **CWGC nursery garden** where plants are propagated for use in the cemeteries of the region.

Poperinge is reached by continuing through the hopfields and then turning left at the crossroad and rejoining the main road, going right. **Ypres** is 12 kms away. (*For a description of this part of the route, see pages 10-12.*)

A casualty clearing station was established by the French Army at Remi Farm (*below*) beside which a burial ground was laid out which was to become the second largest cemetery in the Ypres Salient — Lijssenthoek British Military Cemetery (*above*).

St Omer. No. 50, rue Carnot, where Field-Marshal Roberts died.   No. 37, rue St Bertin — used by both French and Haig.

ROUTE III Via St Omer

Now that the autoroute A26-E15 has connected with the outskirts of Calais, it is possible to use it for a fast journey to St Omer, but the more attractive and interesting route is the N43. This road runs close to two major canals of the region, the Canal de Calais and the Canal de la Haute Colme. Both played important rôles in the Great War carrying supply barges up to the back areas and depots.

Pont d'Ardres (12 kms), on the **Canal de Calais**, was a bustling base bristling with soldiers working on the barges and in the dockside establishments. Today, it is little more than a village near the new bridges which span the canals on whose banks new industries are springing up.

Ardres (5 kms). A quaint little town through which the road climbs as it leaves the flat plain for the more undulating country before St Omer. In these fields, the training camps and ranges were built. The occasional rough mound and bramble-strewn ditch may be the remnants of practice trenches and the full-size replica of sectors of the front line which were made in 1916 and 1917.

St Omer (23 kms). A quiet and attractive town set on hills between the canals. From October 12, 1914 to April 31, 1916, the British General Headquarters was based here. In 1917, it became the Royal Flying Corps and Royal Air Force Headquarters until the end of the war. In 1917, it also began to become a regular target for enemy air raids and, with the opening of the German Spring Offensive in 1918, it came within easy artillery range. Evidence of the destruction can be noted now only in a few

isolated buildings, as much of the town has been repaired or rebuilt. In the Second World War, the town was a German Luftwaffe base and was raided by the Allied air forces more than 20 times, inflicting further damage now made good.

The arrival of the BEF in 1914 was far from being the first time that contact with England had been felt. This started in Saxon times, when Hereward the Wake stayed here and later during the sieges of the Middle Ages and the 18th Century wars of Marlborough. In the **Jardin Public** remnants of the Vauban ramparts are preserved below the eminence on which stands the Basilica of Notre Dame. This large 13th Century church is crowded with reminders of the town's historic past and still bears witness to the attacks of both wars.

Among the few remaining signs of the British presence in 1914-18 is a small, faded, bluish-green circular **plaque**, similar to those seen around London, on the crumbling walls of **No. 50 rue Carnot**, one block to the south-

west from the town square. It records the death in this house of Field-Marshal Lord Roberts on November 14, 1914. The grand old man had been visiting the Indian Corps when he returned to Sir John French's headquarters with a chill which turned to pneumonia. On November 17, his body was moved in military state to the Hôtel de Ville, the streets being lined by troops from every unit in France. A large number attended the short service held in the **Place Gambetta** (as the Place du Maréchal Foch was then known) before the cortège moved to the station through troop-lined streets.

Also in the rue Carnot is the **Hôtel Sandelin**, a beautiful 18th Century house which is an excellent provincial museum and art gallery. **No. 37 rue St Bertin,** one block further west from the rue Carnot, bears no marks to recall it being the residence of Sir John French and later Sir Douglas Haig. Further down this street, which leads to the ruins of the **Abbey of St Bertin**, are the old buildings of the **Hôpital Militaire** (at No. 49), previously a school solely for the education of Roman Catholic boys from Britain. Opened in 1592, it was moved firstly to Bruges and later, in the 18th Century, Liège, before going to Stoneyhurst in Lancashire in 1794 where it still flourishes.

St Omer was a very popular leave town as it provided many amenities for leisure not readily available closer to the front. In the unique marshes to the north and in the eastern outskirts, called the **Watergangs** (from the curious labyrinths of canals and drains of this reclaimed region), many estaminets were opened for the officers and men who enjoyed the fishing or boating. In the **Forest of Clairmarais** were huge camps and supply depots and special facilities for the men on

St Omer. *Left:* **Place du Maréchal Foch, scene of Lord Roberts' funeral in 1914.** *Right:* **No. 49, rue St Bertin; The Hôpital Militaire.**

Château de l'Eminence, used during royal tours of the front.

Hazebrouck's superb town hall overlooks the main square.

leave. Within the walls of the ancient farms, whole battalions could be accommodated and several of these are situated at the forest edge. Near one farm rises the ruined tower of the **Abbey of St Omer** — a refuge where Thomas à Becket sought shelter after his contretemps with Henry II.

To the west of St Omer, on the Boulogne road (N42) at the **Wisques** crossroad is the **Abbey of St Paul**, and, a short distance up the road to Wisques village, its sister convent. To these were brought the typhoid victims from Ypres in 1915 and here were established schools for the evacuated children. Some 3 kms south of here, at **Wizernes**, in the quarries along the D210 to Blendeques and Arques, was a complex for the V2 missiles of 1944.

To the south of St Omer is the residential suburb of **Blendeques** in whose pleasant valleys and woods are a number of elegant homes, many being classified as châteaux. Here HM King George and Queen Mary resided during their visits to the troops. Some of the châteaux still bear military placards on their walls proclaiming the offices which they once housed. The **Château de l'Eminence** (today stud-farm L'Ecusson, on the D77 from St Omer) proudly displays a fire point notice by its crumbling front door; another, the **Château Bellevue**, was the main office of an officer school.

Taking the N42 from St Omer eastward through the new suburbs and industrial complex growing up on the dried marshes, **Arques** is reached in 4 kms. The road crosses the major **Canal de la Haute Colme**, and at **Les Fontinettes** (first right turn after crossing the bridge), it was connected by a remarkable hydraulic barge lift to the Canal de Neuf Fosse. The lift transported the barges up and down the 45ft difference in levels. It was built in 1887 and was in use without a break until recently replaced by a slope, as in both wars there was an unwritten agreement between

belligerents not to bomb it. Beside the new facilities, the old Ascenseur des Fontinettes can still be seen with a barge in the lift.

Just beyond the crest of the rise outside Arques, a wide flat plateau is reached and the **site of the aerodrome** comes into view. The roads were lined with concrete shelters but these are now crumbling and gradually disappearing amid the beet fields.

After 2 kms, the road forks; take the N42 for Hazebrouck, passing through **Renescure**, a railway station well known to the BEF, and **Ebblinghem**, a village with associations with the training camps.

Hazebrouck (15 kms). A name known to every British soldier. Thousands passed through the station en route for Ypres or the Somme. From the outbreak of war, the name of this quiet market town and vital junction for road and rail communications was rarely out of the news, having become an Army headquarters in October 1914.

In the first German drive westwards, the town was surrendered peacefully by the Abbé Deputy, Lemire, to avoid destruction, but the British Cavalry Corps cleared the town and nearby **Forest of Nieppe** and the I British Corps set up its headquarters here. Once again a British Army, the First Army, was based in the town, for in 1815 Wellington used it as one of his major bases. In 1915, the Second Army took over. General French resided in one of the graceful houses in the then Grande Place but now, as the traveller enters from the rue Louis Warein, it will be noticed the name has changed to **Place Général de Gaulle**.

This huge rectangular market place, with its unusual classical Hôtel de Ville, was always bustling with troops and is still the hub of a thriving town. Here and there, uneven cobblestones survive from earlier times to shake the unwary driver. In another square round the corner — **Place de la Victoire** — is the town **War Memorial** and one of the few ancient buildings remaining — the church of St Eloi dating from the 16th Century. On the house behind the memorial is a **Monument to the Civilian Victims** of the enemy bombardment of December 13-14, 1917.

Hazebrouck was a major advance base, there being ordnance, signals, engineer, medical and transport depots crowded around this important railway junction. Army workshops, where all manner of equipment was produced from odds and ends, opened in the town. Administrative offices occupied the large halls and other requisitioned buildings. Training areas and reinforcement camps opened in the surrounding countryside; to the south-west were sited the hospitals and casualty clearing stations.

Towards the end of 1917, the town, which had previously suffered occasional bombardments, was seriously damaged by shellfire. One gun operating from near Lille was said to be a British high-velocity piece captured during the Battle of Cambrai. The Forest of Nieppe, the scene of the British cavalry

action in October 1914 which cleared the advancing German troops, was threatened again in the Spring Offensive from the south-east and heavy fighting ensued in April 1918. Hazebrouck was menaced and the civilian population was evacuated, but the stands of the 29th, 31st and Guards Divisions and the 1st Australian Division which stemmed the onslaught saved the town. Casualty clearing stations which had operated from 1916 to 1917 returned in the summer of 1918 as did No. 9 Field Hospital.

In the Second World War, the town was again very badly damaged but, in many aspects, it is still very recognisable as the soldiers' centre of rest and leisure and of the base works and junction for the front which it was for so long. Many of the billets and buildings the military used have been repaired in the old style.

Leave Hazebrouck by the rue de Bailleul (N42) out into the area of the 1918 battles for Hazebrouck, now once more a peaceful agricultural region which becomes slightly more undulating as the road approaches **Strazeele**, 7 kms away.

This village was the Germans' first objective in their attack on Hazebrouck from the east in April 1918, but the 33rd Division and the Australians stood in their way and held on. The nearby villages of **Méteren** (to the north-east) and **Merris** (to the south) were overrun but were recaptured by the 9th Scottish Division and 1st Australian Division respectively on July 9 and 19. In 1914, the German advance on Méteren was the scene of a bayonet charge by 2nd Bn. Seaforth Highlanders in III British Corps' (General Pulteney) checking and clearing action.

Four kilometres south of Méteren, the N42 crosses the Dunkerque-Lille motorway before entering **Bailleul** in 3 kms as the D944/D933. A picturesque market town, famed since ancient times for its lacemaking which, with linen, is still one of the major

This abbey chapel (now part of the town museum) was signals HQ.

Hazebrouck's memorial to the civilian victims of the German 1917 shelling.

Bailleul. The reconstructed Hôtel de Ville beside the Belfry.

The memorial to the 25th Division which recaptured the ruins on August 30, 1918.

The ruins of St Armand church form the backcloth for the town's war memorial.

industries, Bailleul was a military base for much of the war — a real front-line town. It fell briefly to the Germans but was recaptured by the British on October 14, 1914 and thereafter, for three-and-a-half years, it was to act as a forward base for the British and French before being almost totally destroyed in the savage fighting of the Battle of the Lys in the spring of 1918. Bailleul provided a welcome respite to the fighting forces and a haven for the wounded in the hospital facilities of its well-known asylum and clinic. Troops thronged its pleasant market square above which the **Belfry of the Hôtel de Ville** rose defiantly. Cafés and estaminets flourished and one in particular, 'Tina's', in the rue de Dunkerque, became a famous and popular officers' haunt.

The town had hardly suffered from artillery bombardment but, in July 1917, the relative peace was shattered by heavy shells which caused much damage. Then, the almost complete destruction of the town came when the Germans advanced to capture the ruins on April 15, 1918 after the heroic defence of the British 34th and 59th Divisions which were forced to retire exhausted. For four months, the town was in German hands and then, on August 30, the British 25th Division regained possession of the ruins.

Today, the old market square once more is the centre of a charming busy little town; the Hôtel de Ville and the Belfry have been rebuilt in warm red brick and the cafés and shops welcome both resident and visitor.

The road enters the centre of the town at a roundabout, in the centre of which is the obelisk of the **25th Division Memorial**, and, turning left, the square is reached. On the left, in the street behind the Hôtel de Ville, can be seen the ruins of the **Church of St Amand**, now forming an integral part of the town's **War Memorial**. Behind it now stands a **Demarcation Stone**.

The road to Belgium, the D23, leaves the square at the opposite end and, almost immediately, a green CWGC sign can be seen indicating the way, down a small street on the right, to the **Bailleul Communal Cemetery and Extension**. The entrance to these cemeteries is just beyond the main gates to the town cemetery. Whilst the Communal Cemetery is relatively small (some 610 graves), the Communal Cemetery Extension provides the last resting place of over 4,600 men of many nationalities. Alongside their British and Commonwealth comrades lie French, Belgian, Chinese, and many Germans. From the cemetery walls, a

'A good reputation endures for ever' . . . 'faithful unto death'. So are the Chinese Labour Corps casualties remembered in Bailleul British Cemetery Extension. (RC)

panoramic view of the Monts des Flandres provides a background to the **site of the old Royal Flying Corps base and aerodrome**. Among those buried here is Sergeant T. Mottershead, VC of No. 20 Squadron, RFC (Plot III, Grave A126).

Returning to the D23, turn right on to the Loker (Locre) road for about 1½ km, passing round the walls of the old **Asylum** and the hospital which was so vital to the troops. I understand the present-day aspect resembles very closely that of 80 years ago.

Ahead now rise the **Monts des Flandres**, the hills of Flanders — Mont Noir, Mont Rouge and Mont Kemmel with the Mont des Cats far over to the left. At the first road junction, take the left fork, the D223, for **Mont Noir**. As the road approaches the village, one of the 1939-45 concrete bunkers which surround the hill comes into view on the right, followed by another one, and almost immediately on the left is the entrance to a **small cemetery** where British

The Bailleul Asylum and hospital cared for great numbers of casualties.

The 34th Division Memorial, Mont Noir. Note the divisional chequerboard badge.

The French memorial at Loker commemorating three cavalry units and one infantry unit which saw action here in 1918.

and French soldiers who died in 1918 lie together. Between April and September 1918, there was heavy fighting in this area when, having secured Kemmel, the Germans were thrown back by the 34th British Division.

The wooded slopes of Scherpenberg today hide the dugouts built into its sides.

Sunset over the peaceful waters of Dickebush Lake.

At the junction further up the hill, turn left for about 300 metres. On the crest, next to and almost hidden by the Hôtel de Mont Noir, is the **34th Division Memorial**. For many years, this was known locally as Nurse Cavell for who else could be the Angel of Victory.

Return to the junction and the customs post just below the summit. Around it now are cafés, hotels and souvenir shops. Between Mont Noir and **Mont Rouge**, across the valley and the lower Mont Vidaigne, is a téléphérique. On the slopes of both hills are sports facilities, many with camp sites and caravan parks nestling amid the trees.

Descend 3 kms, rejoining the D23 (now named N375) and turn left into **Loker** (Locre). This village was almost entirely destroyed in the battles for Mont Kemmel. To the right of the church, is a stone with three **memorial plaques** commemorating French units which participated in the 1918 operations: the **2ème Brigade de Cavalerie Légère** (which reached the area after having ridden 200 kilometres in three days); the **4ème and 12ème Régiments de Dragons**; and the **23ème Régiment d'Infanterie**.

A little further on, down a side road on the left and past the convent from which it got its name, is **Locre Hospice Cemetery**. Outside its walls is the **lone grave** of Major W. H. K. Redmond of the 6th Bn. Royal Irish Regiment, mortally wounded at Wytschaete in June 1918 (*see page 60*).

The direct route to Ypres, the N375, passes beneath the **Scherpenberg** rising on the right of the road. As it is approached, the entrance to a series of **dugouts** can be seen above the tree-line. Scherpenberg was heavily defended by the French and the British 21st, 25th and 49th Divisions when it was attacked on April 29, 1918, but it was not captured. About 1½ km further along is the hamlet of La Clytte (De Klijte) where the Poperinge-Kemmel road crosses.

After 3 kms, **Dickebush** (Dikkebus) is reached, a familiar name to all who served in the Salient. The artificial lake was lined with trenches and hutments. Access to the lake (Dikkebusvijver) is gained from the first crossroad after the village when, taking the right-hand road, the old white **brewery** (which was a delousing station and bath centre) is passed. It is difficult today, as one sits on the terrace of the café overlooking the peaceful waters, to envisage the devastation and mud and the appalling conditions which prevailed in 1917 and 1918 along the banks, but, with the right light, traces of the revetments can be clearly discerned. After a further 3½ kms, **Ypres** is reached by way of the modern station, now flanked by the bypass.

Above left: '**In memory of St George's Day, 1918 when every moment had its deed and every deed its hero.**' So read the inscription on the original memorial at Zeebrugge unveiled in 1925. In 1942, German forces destroyed the monument — all that was saved were a few of the stones which were set in the pavement after the war in front of a new memorial *(above*

right). **In the background stands the old Palace Hotel, demolished after it was closed in 1978. With the reclamation of a large area of the former harbour for new dock facilities, the replacement memorial has been resited *(below)* with new stonework incorporating the plaque from the mole, the pavement stones and original fragments — dedicated in April 1983.**

Zeebrugge-Ypres

An interesting route to Ypres is via **Zeebrugge** — the port where the 3rd Cavalry Division disembarked in October 1914. They had been sent there to cover the Belgian retreat from Antwerp but, five days later, the Germans occupied the town. They set about converting the port into a front-line naval and seaplane base and by December it was operational.

The modern ferry terminal is part of a huge new dock complex catering for container ships, tankers, freighters and ferries. To the west of the **old mole**, great areas of once open seas have been reclaimed and a new sea wall has been erected enclosing an enormous area for future port facilities and expansion. The old mole is still discernible along the new road — Leopold II Dam — which leads to and beyond the North Sea Ferry Terminal. Doverlaan, the road from the Dover-Felixstowe terminal, filters into Leopold II Dam and the spacious roundabout before the major traffic junction of Kustlaan — the Ostend to Knokke-Heist road (N34) — and Baron de Maerelaan — the new road (N31) to Brugge (Bruges) joining the motorways.

To the west of the ferry port access road, there is a new pedestrian promenade from the eastern end of the Zeedijk. The new footway is called Sint George's Day Wandeling and is at present ½ km long.

The old mole, built in 1895-1907, was 2½ kms in length and protected the entrance to the harbour and the Brugge canal. For much of its length, it was some 150 feet wide with the esplanade being on the seaward side right up to the narrower extremity and the lighthouse. Near the place where HMS *Vindictive* with the tiny *Daffodil* and *Iris* came alongside on St George's Day, 1918, there was once a weather-beaten bronze plaque, but gone are the quay over which the Marines and sailors swarmed and fought and the bridge which connected the mole to the shore, penetrated by the old submarine *C3* under Lieutenant Sandford, VC. The site of the Lübeck Battery has disappeared in the new complex as has the place where in 1925 an elegant monument, some 46 feet high, was erected. It was surmounted by a bronze sculpture of St George and the Dragon and was the scene of an annual ceremony during the pilgrimage of the men of the Zeebrugge Association. In 1942, the Germans destroyed the memorial and melted down the bronze.

On April 23, 1983, an attractive **memorial** to the events of April 1918 was dedicated. It stands at the landward end of Sint George's Day Wandeling and incorporates the memorial which replaced the original column erected in 1925 and destroyed in 1942 by the German occupation forces, with fragments salvaged from the original column and the plaques from the old mole which marked the site where HMS *Vindictive* went alongside and the breach in the mole made by Lieutenant Sandford and his submarine.

Previously, in the basement of the **Palace Hotel**, demolished in the modernisation of the port and its access road, the **Zeebrugge Museum** was housed. The future of this museum is still uncertain. The exhibits are in store in Brugge and plans for a new museum appear unlikely to be realised in the foreseeable future. The hotel building had been the German headquarters and the museum included reproductions of the murals they had used to decorate the walls of various rooms. Relics of the men and ships (Captain Fryatt and the SS *Brussels* included), the uniforms and medals, badges and equipment, photographs and documents of the naval actions were displayed together with artifacts relating to civilians, the Second World War and the two occupations of the port. Actual portions of the ships, life-size dioramas and models depicting St George's Day 1918 and coastal defence were shown.

Leaving the terminal, turn left at the traffic lights onto N34 (Kustlaan), and in 1½ kms, having crossed the locks to the inner harbour, **Zeebrugge church** will be seen off to the right between the new bypass highway and the old main road, the Heiststraat (the left turn in the bend of Kustlaan). Here, in the **small cemetery**, originally a German burial ground (note the — now largely overgrown — inscription over the gateway), British seamen and Royal Marines are buried alongside 173 German dead. Here also is the smallest of the **Memorials to the Missing**, a small stone panel set in the wall commemorating three officers and one mechanic who had lost their lives on that memorable day and have no known grave, among them Lieutenant-Commander A. L. Harrison, VC, killed whilst leading one of the storming parties from HMS *Vindictive*. There is also a simple **memorial** erected in 1920 to a unit of the **British Salvage Corps**.

Return to the N34 for **Blankenberge** in about 5 kms. In the **Communal Cemetery** (follow the N34 well past the town centre, then turn left into K. Deswertlaan), Lieutenant-Commander G. N. Bradford, VC, of the *Iris* lies buried (Row A, Grave 5). The small WWI plot is to the left of the gate.

Another 21 kms and Ostend is reached. At a few places along the road, Atlantic Wall bunkers can still be seen, but none of the 1914-18 fortifications or gun sites remain.

German and British casualties were buried together in Zeebrugge churchyard overlooked by the Salvage Corps Memorial.

The smallest Memorial to the Missing of all — to four men lost during the attack. (RC)

Above left: **HMS** *Vindictive* **alongside Ostend mole, October 1918 (IWM), and** *right:* **the bow of the ship preserved today. (RC)**

Ostend (Oostende) is one of the main holiday resorts on this long sandy coastline as well as being a major port for ferries to the UK. A railway terminus for the long-distance continental trains and an airport add to its importance. The N34 enters Ostend over a series of bridges crossing the locks into the inner harbour and the canal to Brugge. As the road rises and turns to the left over the outer end of the lock leading into the dry dock (i.e. the third bridge), a small park will be noticed on the left, between the two lock bridges. (Stopping here is difficult. It is best to park a little further on and walk back to the park.) There, amid the flower beds, rests the **bow section of the** *Vindictive* **and the masts of the** *Intrepid* **and** *Thetis*. The upper sections of the mast of HMS *Thetis* (nearest the road) is fairly new as the original fell to pieces with wood-rot.

On August 27, 1914, a small force of Royal Marines landed in Ostend to protect the evacuation of thousands of refugees to England. On October 4, the Royal Naval Division disembarked for the ill-fated expedition to Antwerp and, two days later, the 7th Division landed to proceed to the front.

When the Belgian Government and King Albert had to evacuate Antwerp, they made their HQ in Ostend. However, on October 13, the Government left for Le Havre and the King went to lead his army on the Yser (IJzer). Ostend was occupied by the Germans on the 15th.

Here, as at Zeebrugge, the Germans constructed a naval base for their submarines but, because it was constantly under attack from both the air and sea, the repair shops and stores were moved to Brugge and Zeebrugge. Ostend then became a secondary port for small craft only and Zeebrugge took precedence both as a destroyer and submarine base.

On April 23, 1918, at the same time as the major attack on Zeebrugge, an attempt was made to block the canal and harbour entrances using two old cruisers, the *Brilliant* and *Sirius*. This was unsuccessful and, on May 9-10, another attempt was made, this time with HMS *Vindictive* which had been filled with concrete and was sunk between the piers in the harbour entrance sealing the large craft in the basins. After doing a great deal of demolition, the Germans left Ostend on October 17, 1918.

There is a choice of roads from Ostend to Nieuwpoort: the N34 runs close on the coast along the dunes past large modern blocks of flats through the busy streets of the resorts, whilst the N318 runs behind the built-up area passing the airfield and gives views over to the left of the **Yser battlefields**.

In 16 kms, the roads converge close by the huge circular **Memorial to King Albert** erected above the multiple sluices for the canals at the inland end of **Nieuwpoort**. The striking brick archways surround a mounted statue of the King; on one wall is a small bronze plaque to his wife, Queen Elisabeth, who died in 1968. A lift takes visitors to the balcony at the top of the arch, giving magnificent views of the Yser, the canals, Nieuwpoort and Lombardsijde. This was the western end of the front line which ran 600 miles to the Swiss border; the whole region was utterly devastated.

This end of the line was usually in the hands of the French and Belgians but, in June 1917, the British XV Corps took over the line with men of the 1st and 32nd Divisions and, later, the 66th Division. They held the line from St Georges-Ramskapelle to the sea at Nieuwpoort and withstood the onslaught of the major German attack of July 10, 1917. Although the battalions were cut off, they held on until the battle eased on

The Memorial to King Albert beside the lock gates at Nieuwpoort. These were the sluices opened by the lock-keeper in 1914 to flood the surrounding countryside. (RC)

July 17, when they were relieved by the 49th and 33rd Divisions after having suffered very heavy casualties. The 41st and 42nd Divisions came in September but the other divisions left the area which was now a stagnating front and, in November, these last two divisions were relieved by the French.

In a triangular plot beside the road, beneath the gaze of King Albert, three lions guard the cenotaph of the **British Memorial to the Missing**, Nieuwpoort. This memorial is to the 566 officers and men who died in the operations at Antwerp in 1914 and later actions on the Belgian coast, particularly those in 1917.

The **six sluices** over which runs the road to Ramskapelle, control the canals to Veurne and Dunkerque, the Canal de Passchendaele (to Brugge) and two regulate the Yser. These were opened by the lock-keeper during the Battle of the Yser in 1914, flooding the lower reaches of the Yser and stemming the German advance. The Nieuwpoort garrison was aided by British naval machine-gunners.

The Nieuwpoort Memorial to the Missing, remembering those who lost their lives at Antwerp in 1914 and along the coast between 1914-18 having no known grave. (RC)

Memorial of the French 81ème Division behind the lock gates at Nieuwpoort.

A Belgian Memorial to the Yser battles which was erected in 1930.

Nearby is the memorial to Belgian Lieutenant Leopold Calberg.

Across the water from the King Albert Memorial, between the second and third canal from the left, is the **Memorial to the French 81ème Division d'Infanterie Territoriale**. Between the fourth and the fifth canal is a another **Belgian Memorial to the Yser Battle**, erected in 1930. Next to it is the **lone grave** of a Belgian engineer officer, Lieutenant Leopold Calberg, who fell on this spot on October 16, 1917.

Take the N367 for a short distance and then the N356 to the right for Ramskapelle

with the **Ramskapelle British Cemetery** on the right. Here are buried over 800 men from scattered graves in the region. Shortly, the new A18-E40 autoroute crosses our road and, passing the **Belgian Cemetery** on the left, we reach the village in 3 kms.

Ramskapelle was a vital position on the railway to Diksmuide (Dixmude) in the Yser battles of 1914 and was on the edge of the flooded areas. On the churchyard wall in the centre of the village is the **Franco-Belgian Memorial**. Just before it, the road on the left

(Molenstraat) leads to the edge of the village. Just before joining the main road, on the right will be seen a **Demarcation Stone** with behind it across the lawn a model windmill, actually a transformer station. The Demarcation Stone was damaged in the fighting here in 1944 and has been moved from its original site in road improvements. A ceremony is held here each year on October 31 in memory of the battle of 1914.

Take the N355 to the left and travel 5 kms through the rich pasture of this fen and

Ramskapelle British Cemetery was used to collect many scattered graves.

The Franco-Belgian memorial situated in the centre of Ramskapelle village.

The Demarcation Stone once marked the extent of the front line in 1918. (RC)

A tower in Pervijze used as an OP or 'O-Pip' — soldiers' slang for observation post.

Oud-Stuivekenskerke. This is the Memorial Chapel of the Belgian Army built close to the ruins of the old one defended by the Belgians in 1914.

patrol in the drowned land anno 1914-18. Turn right at the café to reach, by a very narrow road, the **Belgian Army Memorial Chapel**. This is set in a remote point on the Belgian front line at **Oud-Stuivekenskerke** (it is shown on the map and signposted as O.L. Vrouwhoekje). The modern chapel is built close to the ruins of the old one which was fortified and defended by the Belgian Army during the Yser battles of 1914 and October 1918.

Around the chapel are tablets bearing the badges of many Belgian regiments and several memorials including a **Demarcation Stone** bearing the name Diksmuide. The chapel is worth visiting purely for the beautiful stained-glass windows — portraits of the King and Queen of the Belgians and Belgian soldiers. One window illustrates how the Virgin and Child which now stands on the altar was found in one of the nearby farms with an unexploded shell stuck underneath. Part of the old fortified chapel nearby remains with a **Memorial to Lieutenant Martial Lekeux**, the Belgian artillery officer (and Franciscan monk) who commanded the OP position. Steps lead to an **orientation tablet** on the roof.

Return to the road and continue to Stuivekenskerke, keeping to the right in the village, past **Vicogne Château**, another Belgian outpost position in the drowned land during the Yser battles, and then right, along the banks of the canalised Yser. Dotted about the area will be seen **concrete shelters**, mostly of French origin but some German and a few Belgian.

In 5 kms, we reach the **Boyau de la Mort** — the Trench of Death. This is a section of trench along the river bank which is preserved, somewhat artificially but based on genuine Belgian trenches. They were repaired by Belgian Army Engineers in 1974. The trenches are entered through a small **museum**, and nearby are the ruins of a blockhouse and the old mill which was here when the trenches were built. Within the trench area is another **Demarcation Stone**.

Diksmuide (Dixmude), 2 kms further on, is once again the sleepy market town it was when the war came in October 1914. It was defended to the death by the French troops of Général Jacques, the French Marines of Admiral Ronarc'h and the Belgian Army. Fighting against a much stronger opponent, who bombarded the town incessantly, it fell on November 10. Many artillery batteries were then emplaced in and around the town.

marshland to **Pervijze**. An observation post used during the 1914 actions was situated in **a tower** in the village, on the right-hand side of the N355.

Keep with the N355 for 3½ kms, then turn left onto a small road and, in about ½ km, left again. After 1 km, we reach a café with a peculiar exterior **mural** depicting a front-line

The gateway to Vicogne Château.

The huge Free Flemish AVV-VVK tower in Diksmuide.

This is the Boyau de la Mort — the Trench of Death. Situated near Stuivekenskerke, it is a section of Belgian trench which has been preserved, rather artificially, with concrete. There is a blockhouse and old mill nearby, all from the First War. (RC)

It was not recaptured until the end of September 1918 when it fell to the Belgians.

Our road actually arrives in Diksmuide close to the **IJzertoren**, the huge memorial tower of the Free Flemish — AVV-VVK (standing for 'All for Flanders — Flanders for Christ'). This memorial has been an object of much political strife and the original was blown up in 1946. The present tower stands a little behind the site of its predecessor which is in ruins near the entrance to the park. In the crypt are various memorials to the Flemish patriots. In the new tower is a **museum** which has some quite interesting and varied exhibits, including works of the Belgian artist, Joe English. There is a good explanation of the battles involving Diksmuide and collections of papers and other relics. A recent addition is an auditorium where a film is shown (in Flemish). The adjoining chapel has stained-glass windows depicting scenes of the war. There is a lift to the top where the windows look out over the surrounding countryside.

In the main square of Diksmuide is a **statue of Général Jacques** and in the local park, off the square to the east, a **Memorial to the French Marines and Admiral Ronarc'h**. The town hall is in the old Flemish style (as are the other houses in the square) and was rebuilt in the late 1920s. The exhibition of war relics, which used to be housed in the town hall and later in Esen Château on Woumenweg (N369), was closed in 1989 and is now defunct.

Not far north-east of Diksmuide is the large **German Cemetery of Vladslo** famous for the **Kollwitz sculptures**. These can be seen in the distance from the entrance (which houses an information room) and consist of two granite figures representing Mourning Parents. The famous German

The Kollwitz sculptures representing Mourning Parents watch over the 25,000 German soldiers who lie in Vladslo Cemetery. (RC)

artist and sculptress, Käthe Kollwitz, gave them in memory of her son, Peter Kollwitz, killed October 23, 1914, whose grave is in front of them. To reach the cemetery, take the N369 from Diksmuide for 3½ kms, then turn right at Beerst onto N363. Continue for 4½ kms, then turn left towards Leke. The cemetery is then found on the left.

Return to Diksmuide. Ypres is 23 kms distant. The road crosses much of the region that was flooded and the 1914 battlefield.

Now it is once more a rich agricultural plain with a large nature reserve at Blankaert. About halfway to Ypres, at **Hoekske** (near Merkem), on the right of the road, is a **private memorial**, a statue in memory of Armand van Eecke of the Belgian 3e Linie-Regiment, killed here in the attack of September 9, 1918. Just past the village, again on the right, is the **Memorial of the Belgian 3ème Division d'Infanterie** *(see also page 35)*. In 12 kms, **Ypres** is reached.

Battles of the Ypres Salient 1914-1918

A BRIEF OUTLINE SUMMARY

First Battle of Ypres, October-November 1914

October: The front line extended from Langemark — Zonnebeke — Gheluvelt — Zandvoorde — Messines to Armentières. British Army held the line in the eastern and southern sectors with the French on their left and the Belgian Army to the north.

7: German cavalry enter Ypres but remain only briefly.

13: Northumberland Hussars enter.

14: British and French troops enter and occupy Ypres entirely. The British force was IV Corps led by 7th Division. Their Divisional Headquarters was at the Château, later called Stirling Castle, on the Menin Road. IV Corps had their HQ in the convent in Poperinge, Advance HQ was set up in the Hôtel de Ville in Ypres with the overflow on the upper floor of the Cloth Hall. Below were the French Cuirassiers who used the ground floor level as stables. General Rawlinson was billeted at No. 10 rue de Lille (Rijselstraat). In the 7th Division were the first members of the Territorial Army to see action, the Northumberland Hussars, a Yeomanry regiment. They were in Bruges on October 6 and in action on the 12th. The London Scottish and the Oxford Hussars, another Yeomanry regiment, were first in action on October 31.

22: German concentrated bombardment and attack on Ypres commences and they advance westward.

29-30: The front had contracted onto Ypres despite many gallant charges and stands by the British cavalry and infantry who were well outnumbered. The line now ran from Langemark — Broodseinde — Kleine Zillebeke — Hollebeke — Messines.

31: Germans pushed back to Gheluvelt.

November 1: Messines-Wytschaete Ridge captured by Germans who reach Wulvergem and Neuve-Eglise.

2: French XIVème Corps d'Armée recapture the Ridge and British I Corps held furious attack on Gheluvelt.

10: German second bombardment of Ypres commences.

22: Cloth Hall, St Martin's Church and many other buildings destroyed or badly damaged.

1915
Front line stabilised from Bikschote — Langemark — St Julien — Broodseinde — Hooge — Zillebeke — St Eloi — Wytschaete — Ploegsteert. Line remained almost unchanged without much gain or loss although continuous activity.

March: Heavy fighting on the Lys front. St Eloi changed hands on two occasions. The civilian population who had fled Ypres during the bombardments trickled back to their ruined homes.

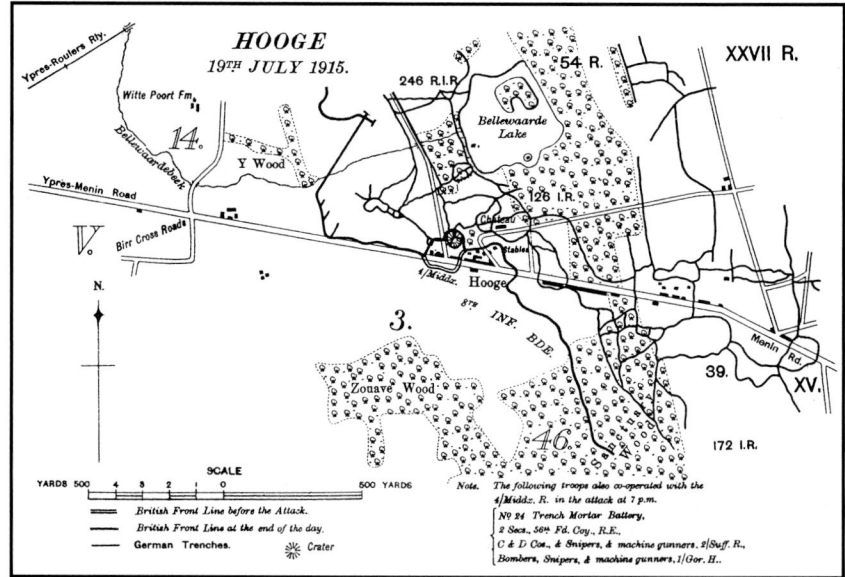

Just one battle in Second Ypres — the German liquid fire attack at Hooge. These maps show the situation around this dreadful area on July 19 *(above)* before the offensive, and the attack itself *(below)* as depicted in the Official History.

Second Battle of Ypres, April-June 1915

April 14: Battle opens. Germans commence bombardment of Ypres which continued for nearly a month, completely destroying the town.

17: British capture Hill 60.

22: First gas attack on French territorial and colonial troops holding the line near Bikschote. The Belgian Corps were on the French left and the Canadian 3rd Brigade on their right. The French were pushed back to Steenstraat but the Canadians held the line at St Julien.

25: Main thrust of the German attack on British line. By the end of the month, the front line ran south from Steenstraat to Zuidschoote — Boezinge — Hill 60 — Hollebeke — Wytschaete — Ploegsteert.

May: Heavy fighting with severe casualties to both sides continued.

5: Hill 60 attacked. British line pushed back on 3rd/4th from St Julien and Frezenberg and to Hooge later. Hooge Château fell but was recaptured on June 2.

July 22-26: British advance along Menin road near Hooge.

29-30: First use of liquid fire by Germans.

August 7: Gas attack on Hooge.

1915-1917
Front line remained almost static with artillery activity punctuated by infantry attacks on varying scales by both armies. Mining in certain areas constantly undertaken by both sides. St Eloi and Hill 60 were scenes of perpetual engagements.

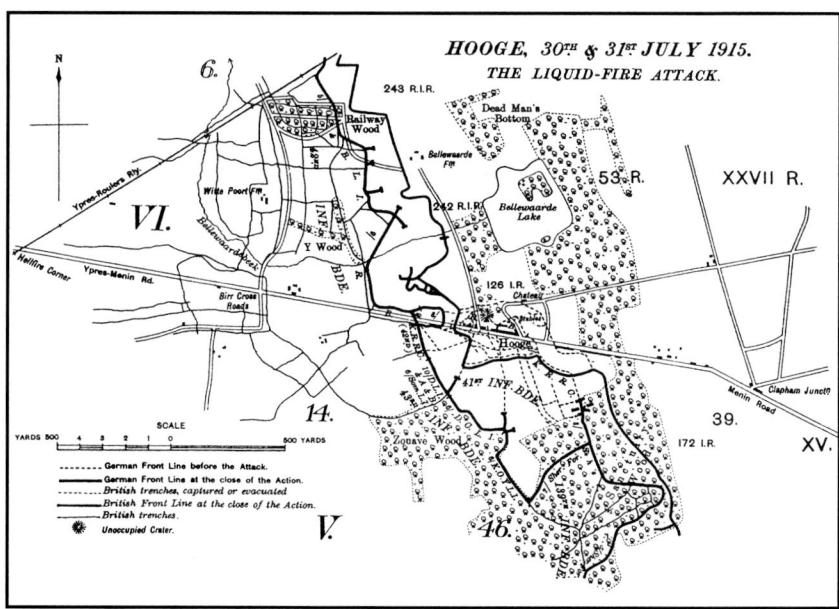

1916

Hill 62 captured by the Canadian Corps who also stemmed the German advance in the direction of Zillebeke and Hooge, fighting over Sanctuary Wood and across the open country beyond to within 1,000 yards of Hill 60. The front line extended from Steenstraat and Lizerne to Zuidschoote and Pilkem to Wieltje and Frezenberg, Zillebeke and Hill 60 and Hill 62, St Eloi and Hollebeke, Kemmel and Wytschaete, Wulvergem and Messines, Ploegsteert Wood and St Yvon. Gains and losses fluctuating on either side.

1917

Battle of Messines.

June: 1-7: British offensive heralded by unusually heavy and prolonged artillery bombardment obliterating Messines and Wytschaete.

7: In the early hours of the morning, 19 mines extending along the whole curve of the front line from Hill 60 and St Eloi to Messines were exploded. The New Zealand Division captured the highest point on the Ridge and advanced to beyond Messines village.

11: The advance along two miles of the front had continued and consolidated east and north of Messines. German counterattacks in the St Yvon—St Eloi regions were abandoned by June 14.

July: At the end of the month, the line ran from Diksmuide along the Yser Canal to Lizerne, Het Sas and Boezinge, then down the Ypres-Bruges railway (*now lifted*) to Quatre Chemins crossroads on to the Pilkem road. It continued west of Wieltje village to Verlorenhoek, then west of Hooge skirting Sanctuary Wood passing west of Hollebeke and to the east of Ploegsteert Wood.

Third Battle of Ypres, July-November 1917

July 31: The Allied offensive began in bad weather in the early morning. In the region of Bikschote, the enemy trenches were overcome to a depth of nearly two miles.

August 1: St Julien, Frezenberg, Pilkem, Westhoek were captured and Sanctuary Wood and Hooge fell after very severe fighting.

16: After a lull, the Allied offensive resumed all along the line. Despite desperate fighting, the advance continued until September 20.

September 20: Langemark and Zonnebeke attacked and many fortified farms and trenches captured. Polygon Wood was the scene of heavy fighting by the Australians and Tower Hamlets also under attack.

26: Polygon Wood fell to the Australians and Tower Hamlets to the British infantry.

October 4: The offensive was maintained along the front from Langemark to Tower Hamlets against increasingly-determined resistance, the Germans defending the Passchendaele Ridge by all means.

9: British front extended now some seven miles from Poelkapelle to Broodseinde with the right flank on the slope of the Ridge. Casualties continued to be extremely heavy on both sides.

30: Passchendaele Ridge finally cleared of the enemy after the bloodiest battle in history. Ypres relieved completely.

November 6: Passchendaele taken.

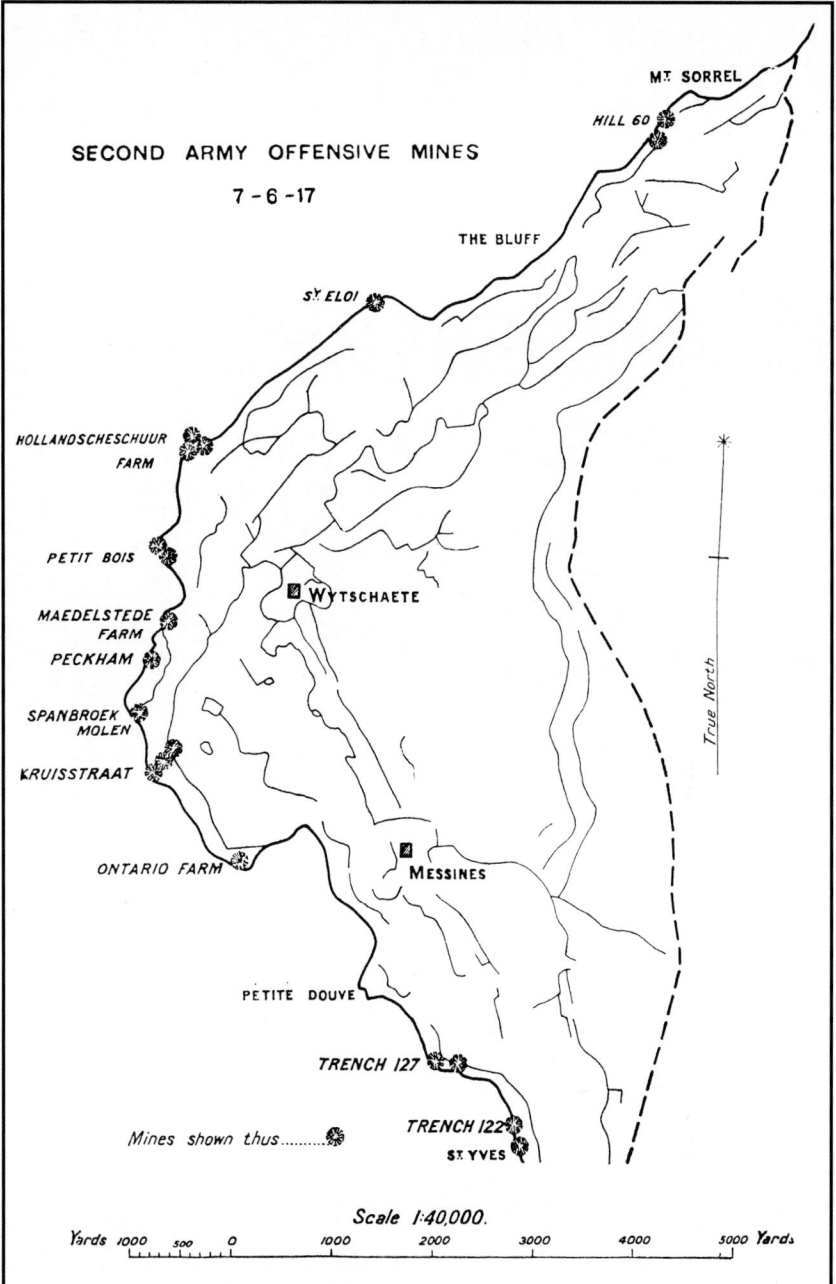

SECOND ARMY OFFENSIVE MINES
7 - 6 -17

Scale 1:40,000.

Mines shown thus.........

The mining programme of the Messines battle is one of the few success stories of World War I. The work had started on August 22, 1915 at Hill 60 — the last mine to be constructed started life at Ontario Farm on January 28, 1917. The result was the explosion of 19 mines using a total of 1,000,000 lbs of HE.

1918

German Spring Offensive

April 9-20: The Spring Offensive broke through the lines south of Ypres and the British and Portuguese forces withdrew on an arc from Neuve-Eglise, Bailleul, Méteren, Vieux-Berquin, Festubert and La Bassée.

22-24: Germans capture Mont Kemmel. Loker changed hands several times.

29: Severe German attacks between La Clytte and Zillebeke were repulsed and Mont Kemmel recaptured. Later, the British division was forced to withdraw to Kemmel village.

Fourth Battle of Ypres, July-October, 1918

July 19: Battle of the Lys begins. The British attack.

September 1: The Allied advance begun in August had by this date reached La Bassée, Laventie, Neuve-Eglise, Mont Kemmel, Wulvergem and Voormezele.

October: Ploegsteert, Messines, Warneton, Gheluvelt, Houthulst Forest, etc., had all been recaptured.

14: Last shell dropped on Ypres town, as the last German forces were chased out of the Ypres Salient.

16: Menin occupied by British Second Army.

At the end of the war, the honours of the British Military Cross and the French Croix de Guerre were conferred on the town of Ypres. These decorations can be seen together with the documents relating to them on permanent exhibition in the Salient Museum.

YPRES

This is the skeleton of Ypres as seen from the air in 1918. The ruins of St Peter's church are visible at the top centre of the picture. The ramparts in the foreground lie either side of the Lille Gate. (IWM)

Ypres — Ieper — Ypern — there are said to be at least 27 different ways in which the name has been spelled over the centuries — dates from about 962. Centuries earlier, there had been a settlement on the site, vestiges of which can still be seen beneath the Lille Gate.

By the Middle Ages, the town had become one of the strongest and wealthiest in all Flanders and was the centre of a flourishing textile trade. Only Bruges and Ghent rivalled it and the inter-city squabbles were frequent and warlike. In the 13th Century, Ypres reached its zenith with a population of 40,000 in the city and some 150,000 in the surrounding region. In 1260, its most famous building — the Cloth Hall — the largest of its type, was begun when the Belfry and east wing were built. By 1286, the west and side wings were completed and in 1304 the whole magnificent hall was finished. The building was a covered market and store where ships could moor alongside and load and discharge cargoes onto the covered quay along the banks of the Ieperlee. Forty-eight doors led from the street direct to the vaulted sale area, with store rooms on the upper floor. No great additions were made until 1619 when the Nieuwerck was constructed along the eastern walls.

In 1383, the town was besieged by the English under the Bishop of Norwich assisted by 20,000 troops from Ghent. Ypres withstood the siege but the flourishing trade was severely affected as the weavers in the neighbourhood left rather than starve, taking the livelihood of the town with them. The importance and influence of Ypres then continually diminished until two centuries later the population had been reduced to 5,000.

Commercially, the position of Ypres may have waned, but never so its strategic importance. Since the 14th Century, it has undergone many sieges and been vassal to several princes. The centre of resistance to Spanish

domination, it was sacked by the Duke of Parma in 1584 and throughout the next 90 years was constantly fought over by the French and Spaniards. Each left their mark on the fortifications and outlying defences. By the Peace of Nijmegen in 1678, Ypres became French and Vauban was entrusted with the defence works. Previously there had been six gates, a wall and moat beyond which the Spanish had formed defences of demilunes. On the eastern front, where the Antwerp gate had stood, they built a pentagonal-shaped citadel. This Vauban removed and replaced with a strong work — the Corne d'Anvers. Between it and the Corne de Thourot to the north, a passage led to the Menin Road. Crenellated stone walls were replaced by stone- and brick-finished ramparts and bastions. Casemates in the ramparts behind St Jacques church were constructed in 1690. Vauban also reduced the number of gates to the town to four, three of which had ornate façades. The Antwerp gate was the most beautiful and bore on its inner face a long Latin inscription to the glory of Ludovicus Magnus dated 1688. These defences withstood the wars of 1689-1712 when Ypres was not taken. However, in 1713 the Dutch took the city and held it until 1744 when King Louis XV forced the surrender.

In 1792, Ypres was taken and retaken several times during the war between France and Austria. In 1793, the Austrians entered the town again and rebuilt some of the earlier defences which had been dismantled by Emperor Joseph II. These were in their turn levelled in 1794 after the French regained the city.

In 1804, Napoleon visited Ypres and the main gate was named after him, having an imperial eagle carved into the stonework. Thus, in name at least, the Antwerp gate disappeared.

In 1815, prior to Waterloo, all the exterior works were hastily rebuilt under Colonel

Carmichael-Smyth of the Royal Engineers and were manned by British troops from Ostend and Nieuwpoort.

After Waterloo, when Belgium was united with Holland, Ypres was again strongly fortified against any possible French invasion and, at this time, the Napoleon Gate was renamed the Menin Gate. With the grant of independence to Belgium in 1838, Ypres became Belgian. The Belgian government in 1852 decided that Ypres no longer required to be a fortified town and levelled all the outer works and pulled down the Vauban walls on the north front. A year later, the western ramparts were removed to make room for the railway and the old gates demolished to give wider passage for the roads. Only the Lille Gate was retained.

In 1914, Ypres once again lay in the path of the warring nations and, during the advance of the cavalry of the German IV. Reiter-Korps, was entered by their 3. Reiter-Division on October 13. They requisitioned 75,000 BFr and held the Burgomaster to ransom. The BEF reached the town in force on the next day and occupied it entirely.

Then began the first agony of Ypres; the great artillery barrage started on November 22 wreaking great damage to the ancient buildings and setting the Cloth Hall on fire. The civilian population suffered considerable casualties and the names of the Abbé Delaere and Sister Marguerite are remembered to this day for the gallant work they did among the homeless and wounded. Not until May 9, 1915, during the month-long barrages of the Second Battle of Ypres, when the Cloth Hall together with the Collegiate Church of St Martin and many other important houses and buildings were destroyed, were the civilians finally and compulsorily evacuated and Ypres left to the military. This was the second agony of Ypres and lasted until after the Third Battle of Ypres in 1917. However, during the comparative quiet of 1916, many people briefly returned.

Almost an exact match from a slightly higher altitude. In the centre of the city, behind the church of St Peter, we see the Cloth Hall. Note Ramparts Cemetery just to the left of the Lille Gate — its fledgling original is also visible in the 1918 shot.

In the spring of 1918, Ypres came perilously near to falling to the Germans but, although they reached the outskirts on the eastern and south-eastern flanks, the British lines held and, in the final Allied advance, Ypres was relieved when the last German troops were ousted from the Salient on September 28.

The **Grote Markt** — the Grand Place, one of the most impressive in Flanders, is dominated by the reconstructed **Cloth Hall**. Under the guidance of architects J. Coomans and P. A. Pauwels, this great building was rebuilt in its original form externally between 1920 and 1962. Internally, the great halls on the first floor were constructed much as they had been but, for the most part, the other rooms — offices, council chambers, etc. — are of modern aspect. In 1967, King Baudouin unveiled a stone in the main foyer to commemorate the actual completion and reoccupation of the Nieuwerck as the offices of the Burgomaster and his staff. The main entrance is in the eastern arcade. Here is the

Tourist Office, where, in addition to the excellent leaflets issued by the town, a variety of guide-books can be purchased. The most important Council Chamber — the **Raadszaal** — is on the first floor. It is lit by a huge modern stained-glass window, the design tracing the history of Ypres, its traditions, legends and industries, in vivid colours. Here are held all major receptions and functions.

Another doorway leads to the **Salient 1914-1918 War Museum** (Entrance fee 30 BFr). Open from April 1 to November 15. Modernised in 1984, this excellent museum is concerned with every aspect of the Great War, its causes and aftermath in West Flanders. Elegantly displayed in sequence, dioramas and models, equipment, weapons, uniforms and badges, medals, documents, photographs, pictures, maps and posters tell the story as it concerns the Belgian, British, French, American and German forces and the civilians. Every item has been found either in the area or is similar to that used or worn here. Relics of some of the person-

alities connected with the war are included: Sir John French, later the Earl of Ypres, is represented by his banner and a pair of shining boots; Lord Plumer's hat rests nearby; the travelling tea service presented by Lady Haig in memory of her husband, and the sword of Prince Maurice of Battenburg presented by his sorrowing mother. Fragments of the old buildings are to be found, including the façade of the last example extant of a King Albert House, a type of temporary residence provided immediately after hostilities ceased; a door from the old Cloth Hall stands close by in a new section of the display. Specimens of grave markers of the British, Belgian, French and German cemeteries with photographs and pictures of the memorials and cemeteries can be seen beside examples of children's artwork of their view of the war and the graves. The dioramas include a representation of the battlefield in 1917, a typical airfield of 1917-18, the old Menin Gate and Lille Gate, and the town as it was in 1918. Near the entrance desk at the head of the stairs is a full-size trench section with some of the fine collection of trench signs. Examples of trench art are shown in cases

The magnificent Cloth Hall is the home of the Salient War Museum which has saved much memorabilia from the Salient. (RC)

The spire of St Martin's Collegiate Church . . . a pre-war dream fulfilled. (RC)

A typical CWGC British Memorial plaque; this one in St Martin's, Ypres. (RC)

The memorial commemorating the men of the Munster Regiments.

alongside the shell-cases from which they were made. Guide-books and a small selection of appropriate literature are on sale at the desk.

The **Belfry** is open to the public and access is obtained by application to the museum custodian. From the museum, the upper chambers are reached by a narrow winding stairway. Fine views of the town and country beyond are gained from the galleries. On a clear day, the coast can be seen across the flat plain. The bell chamber houses the famous carillon which plays each day at set hours and the chiming bells which toll the hours half-an-hour before their due time. It is not advised to visit this chamber when the hour of midday is tolled as the reverberations and vibrations can be injurious.

Of the original Cloth Hall of 1260, only the lower portals of the Belfry around the 'Donkerpoort' and a few pillars in the Tourist Office and halls beyond it remain. On the walls above the Donkerpoort are the municipal coat-of-arms and flanking the passage are the statues of Earl Baldwin IX and his Queen, Margaret of Champagne, King Albert and Queen Elisabeth. Above is the statue to Our Lady of Thuyne, the patroness of Ypres since the siege of 1383. A plaque commemorating the dedication of the town to the Sacred Heart (on the Jubilee feast of Our Lady of Thuyne in 1933) is to the left of the gateway, and on the right is the **Memorial to the French killed during 1914-18 in the Salient**.

The present-day aspect of the Grote Markt closely resembles that which it held in the 18th Century as most of the houses are, externally at least, copies of those destroyed. Among them is the old house of the canteen of the Cloth Hall, now the **In 't Klein Stadhuis restaurant** which dated from 1624. A near neighbour, now another café, **'Den Anker'**, was a copy of its 1611 counterpart. Further along, beyond the Diksmuidsestraat, is the old **Kasselrij** building which until 1967 officially housed the Burgomaster and served as Hôtel de Ville during the years of the reconstruction of the Cloth Hall. Opposite, between Meensestraat and Korte Torhoutstraat, is the **Court of Justice** which was formerly the Hospital of Our Lady. On the southern side, the hotels are close copies of earlier houses but, as the years go by, the modern shop fronts are detracting somewhat from the grace of the Renaissance façades.

Through the Donkerpoort — beneath which is a large shell and the entrance to an inner courtyard of the Cloth Hall (where remnants of the old buildings are stored) — access to **St Martin's Cathedral** (St Maartens-Kathedraal) is reached, across some of the few remaining old cobblestones of Ypres. High above the south door is the magnificent **Rose Window** which is the **British Army and RAF Memorial to King Albert**. During the design process for the window, it was discovered that there was no official crest for the British Army and one had to be created and approved by King George V. This is to be found in the upper segment of the window opposite those of the RAF and the 5th Dragoon Guards.

The church was completely destroyed during the war and, when it was rebuilt, the design included the present spire, which, although included in the pre-1914 plans, had never been built. The original cathedral was built in the 13th Century on the site of an earlier church founded in 1073 and was the seat of a bishop until it became the collegiate church under the administration of a dean in the 19th Century. The church is in Gothic style and is lofty and full of light from the many windows.

On the wall of the south transept is a **Memorial Plaque to the French soldiers killed in Belgium in 1914-18**. On the wall of the north transept is a **Memorial Plaque to the British Commonwealth War Dead in the Ypres Salient**. It is one of several placed in cathedrals all along the 1914-18 front line. In 1973, archaeological excavations in the north aisle resulted in the discovery of the grave of Robert of Béthune — the Lion of Flanders — one of the greatest of the Counts of Flanders who died at Ypres in 1322. Long and widespread research led to this discovery and one of the most vital documents used was a photograph taken in early 1915 by Professor Barbour, then attached to the Friends' Ambulance Unit, which he took the day after one of the bombardments. This photograph showed a mural on the wall of the north aisle and, from a copy of the photograph made by the Imperial War Museum in 1972, it was possible to read the inscription which identified the figure as being Robert of Béthune and referred to his tomb being close by. After the bombardments, nothing was left of the wall and no other photographs were known.

Behind the cathedral are the remains of the old cloisters, now a repository of fragments from the ruined church. In the garden to the south-east of the church is the **Munster Memorial** — a beautiful Celtic Cross commemorating the men of the Munster Regiments who died in the Great War.

Across the A. Vandepeereboomplein — once partly a waterway to the Cloth Hall — is **St George's Memorial Church**. The main door is in Elverdingestraat which carries the traffic to the west. The church was designed by Sir Reginald Blomfield and was built in 1928-29 as part of the British settlement. The idea came from Earl Haig who suggested that a church should be founded for use as the place of worship for the British colony (which was quite large immediately after the Great War) and for pilgrims to the Salient. The site also included the Eton Memorial School for the children of the gardeners and other officials working in the region and the community centre for them.

Today, the church, a memorial to all who died in the Salient, and the old school-room, now the Parish Hall, are all that remain of the settlement. The school closed after the Second World War and the community buildings were sold. The church foundation stone was laid by Field-Marshal Lord Plumer on July 24, 1927. Almost every item contained within the precincts is a memorial. The windows, the furnishings and the decorations all commemorate a unit or an individual. Recent additions include memorials to Sir Winston Churchill, Field-Marshal Montgomery and a number of officers and men. Services are held regularly each Sunday evening and the Chaplain is in attendance on certain other occasions. The vigorous Friends of St George's Memorial Church, Ypres, who are always glad to welcome new members, keep it in repair; their meetings are held usually in London under the auspices of the Bishop of Gibraltar in Europe.

Further along **Elverdingestraat**, on the right-hand side, is the **town prison** in the cellars of which many British soldiers found refuge, including the Guards and, I believe, on occasion the Town Major. Beyond it, at No. 82, are the **headquarters of the Commonwealth War Graves Commission**. This is the office of the Superintendent of the North-West Europe area.

By far the most important edifice in Ypres to the British visitor is the **Menin Gate** (Meense Poort). Built on the site of the original Hangoart Gate (later the Antwerp Gate), this magnificent archway was also designed by Sir Reginald Blomfield and was inaugurated by Field-Marshal Plumer on July 24, 1927 in the presence of King Albert. At the time of the Great War, there was no actual gate on the site. It was indicated by the presence of two lions, one on each side of the roadway which cut through the walls. These lions are now in Canberra, Australia. Through this cutting, many thousands of men wended their way to the Salient. A tag line at the time was: 'Tell the last man through to bolt the Menin Gate'.

Now, the archway forms the **British Memorial to the Missing** and bears the names of 54,896 of those who died between 1914 and August 15, 1917, and who have no known grave. Their names are engraved on panels which form the walls both inside the archway and on the walls on the terraces and stairways to them. Over the archway, a British lion broods above the inscription detailing the purpose of the memorial. On either side of the arch, the Commission maintains a quiet garden of green lawns and shrubs. Incorporated into the foundations of the memorial is one of the bastions of the old ramparts with one of the sallyports on the northern side.

Immediately after the conclusion of the inauguration ceremony in 1927, the buglers of the Somerset Light Infantry sounded the Last Post, and pipers of the Scots Guards played a lament. The simple ceremony of sounding the Last Post each and every night at 8 p.m. was conceived by Mr P. Vandenbraambussche, the then-Superintendent of the Ypres Police, soon after the unveiling. The buglers of the Ypres Fire Brigade co-operated with the police chief and early in the summer of 1928 the nightly ceremony began. In October of that year, it was discontinued until the following spring. The Last Post Committee was formed and soon afterwards the Brussels and Antwerp Branch of the British Legion announced their wish to present to Ypres four silver bugles. In 1935, the British Legion of the County of Surrey subscribed £400 to go towards a fund to fulfil the aims of the Committee:

' . . . to ensure the sounding of the Last Post each evening for all time at the British Memorial at the Menin Gate in honour of the soldiers of the British Empire who fell at Ypres or in the neighbourhood during the war of 1914-1918 and in addition to do everything . . . that could increase the significance of this tribute to the Armies of the British Empire.'

Although Vauban's original gate no longer stood, virtually every man who fell in the Salient would have known the twin lions which guarded the Menin Gate in 1914. (IWM)

It was only fitting therefore that this was the location chosen for the Memorial to the Missing, designed by Sir Reginald Blomfield, surmounted by a lion, now at rest, looking over the Salient.

Some of the 'Old Contemptibles' return to Ypres . . . and the memorial, in August 1982. All around them are the inscribed names of fellow soldiers . . . over 54,000 of them . . . who fought and died in the Salient and yet have no known grave. The missing who fell subsequent to August 15, 1917 are commemorated at Tyne Cot. (RC)

The **ramparts**, which to this day encircle the eastern and southern sectors of the town, can provide a most-pleasant promenade, from north of the Menin Gate to west of the Lille Gate. Refacing of the walls and rebuilding of the Lille Gate has finally removed the sections which for 50 years still bore signs of war damage. Beneath the massive fortifications was the best shelter the troops could wish for in the devastated town. For many years since, a number of the **casemates** have served a variety of useful purposes as workshops, stores and garages. Until relatively recently, those along Bollingstraat from the Menin Gate contained relics dating from their usage as a signals headquarters and alterations made by the German Army during their occupation from 1940-44. Further along, in one of the casemates in Houten Paard (the road that bends back from Bukkerstraat), the famous trench journal *Wipers Times* was once printed and published by the Sherwood Foresters. In 1989, this section of the inner façade of the ramparts was refurbished and the interiors renovated in the original Vauban style. This particular casemate is now preserved under the auspices of the Salient Museum. Requests for visiting it can be made at the Tourist Information.

The **Lille Gate** (Rijselse Poort), with its medieval round bastions was called the Messines Gate for centuries. In his defence works, Vauban retained the two main bastions of the old gate and these remain although refaced in the recent refurbishing. The balcony above the gate and the roadway over the moat of the Kasteelgracht have been modified. The Lille Gate was perhaps even more familiar to the BEF than the Menin Gate as, due to the extremely exposed position of the latter, the more-sheltered southern exit was used as the main route to the front by the troops leaving Ypres.

Within the gateway on the eastern bastion is a doorway from which entry is gained to the **vaulted chambers** within. For many years, this was a museum and called 'Plumer's Headquarters'. The inner room was very probably used as a signals office and was frequented by officers and men from Plumer's staff, but I have it on the authority of his secretary that never was it his headquarters. The outer bastion walls are pierced by loopholes from which machine guns were trained. The late Sergeant Back told me that, on the night before the attack on the Messines Ridge, there were staff officers here and that some of the orders for the attack were given from this site. This chamber can also be viewed by application to

Thus was born a tradition. For ever since November 11, 1929 — except for the break during the German occupation of Ypres (from May 20, 1940 to September 6, 1944) — it has continued. The day the Germans left Ypres, the Call sounded out that evening.

Two more silver bugles were presented by the Old Contemptibles' Association of Blackpool and Fleetwood and, in 1959, Colonel I. Whitaker presented two silver trumpets in memory of former Cavalry and Artillerymen and himself who served in the Salient. Each night, two of the firemen in civilian dress take up their positions in the centre of the road beneath the Salient face of the Memorial and the police halt the flow of traffic through the gateway. Then, in a simple ceremony, the pure tones of the silver bugles ring out and echo away, never to a completely-deserted scene. On major anniversaries and ceremonies, up to six firemen in full dress blow the Call and often Reveille. The Chaplain of St George's and perhaps the Dean will say prayers before a congregation of hundreds and wreaths will be laid on the stairways.

The shell-scarred Lille Gate was the main route for leaving Ypres . . .

The casemate on Houten Paard where *Wipers Times* was printed.

On the town side of the walls slope the esplanade gardens where various sports can be played. Standing in the corner of this area is the **old powder magazine** built in 1818 on the foundations of an even older magazine which had been built before Vauban's time. It is now the oldest building in Ypres. It was rumoured at the time to be bomb-proof and it seems this was true as it survived all the bombardments. The ramparts promenade ends in the square in front of the station — René Colaert-Plein.

In addition to the churches already mentioned, there are in Ypres three others: **St Peter** (St Pieterskerk), **St Jacques** (St Jacobskerk) and **St Nicholas** (St Niklaaskerk). The oldest of these is St Peter's in Rijselstraat (Rue de Lille). All three were almost totally destroyed but in St Peter's there are vestiges of the original 12th Century church and fragments of later embellishments.

In Rijselstraat there are several other interesting buildings, some not necessarily

Little Toc H stands in the rue de Lille alternatively named Rijselstraat.

the Tourist Office. Inside the western postern are traces of the old Roman-style walls and from here the Ieperlee rises.

The old **'Wooden House'**, just inside the gate, is a replica of a similar building destroyed in 1917; at that time, it was one of the oldest in the town.

Just across the Lille Gate is the British Military Cemetery, **Ramparts Cemetery**. This is the only one within the old walls of the town. From it is a very beautiful view over the moat. (The other cemetery in the town is the **Reservoir Cemetery** which lies on Plumerlaan, a road running parallel to Elverdingestraat, in the region of the Plaine d'Amour. Beyond the Menin Gate, alongside the town cemetery, are the **Ypres Town British Military Cemetery** and **Ypres Town Cemetery Extension**, the entrance to both being on Zonnebeekseweg (*see page 42*).)

Resuming our walk along the ramparts, just beyond Ramparts Cemetery, the paths meander over the corner bastion known as the **Lion Tower** which like the Lille Gate dates from 1383. From here, a view of the two half-moon (demi-lune) defences erected by Vauban in 1678 can be seen across the moat. Incidentally, the moat is fed by three rivers — the Zillebeek, the Bollaertbeek and the Vijverbeek (the latter from Dickebush Lake) — and this part of it is known as the Majoorgracht. Around the next corner within the walls, is the local deer park and further along under the trees, along the last part of the ramparts promenade, are two **machine gun cupolas** of 1914-18 vintage.

Below: **One of the British machine gun cupolas sited on the ramparts.**

Its wartime wounds were healed in a restoration programme in 1985. (RC)

connected with the Great War although largely destroyed in it. One of these is No. 38 — the **Belle Alms House**. The present building incorporates some of the original 16th and 17th Century portions of the chapel which served the Belle Institution founded in about 1276. On the wall in the side street is a plaque to the memory of Master Jan Yperman, the father of Flemish surgery, closely connected with this almshouse from 1304-29. The building now houses the OCMW (Public Assistance Organisations) Museum.

At No. 70 is the **Post Office**, a replica of one of the stone-built houses of 14th Century Ypres. It may have been owned by the Templars. A short distance further down the street, on the opposite side, is the building which once housed **Little Toc H** — the Ypres branch of the Poperinge club (*see page 10*).

On the corner of Rijselstraat and Merghelynckstraat is the **Merghelynck Museum**, which is a reconstructed town house of an 18th Century gentleman and it is well worth a visit as it depicts the pure French style of the period. From the gracious exterior in the Louis XV and Louis XVI style to the beautifully-proportioned interior and period furnishings, one gains a fair idea of the way people of the upper classes lived in this merchant town.

Over on the other side of Rijselstraat, in Ieperleestraat, is the old **St John's Alms House** which was founded by a rich local family, the Broederlaans, in 1277. Here now is the Municipal Art Gallery. In the Oude Vismarkt there are some other replicas of the old architecture of Ypres which give a good idea of the town's original appearance.

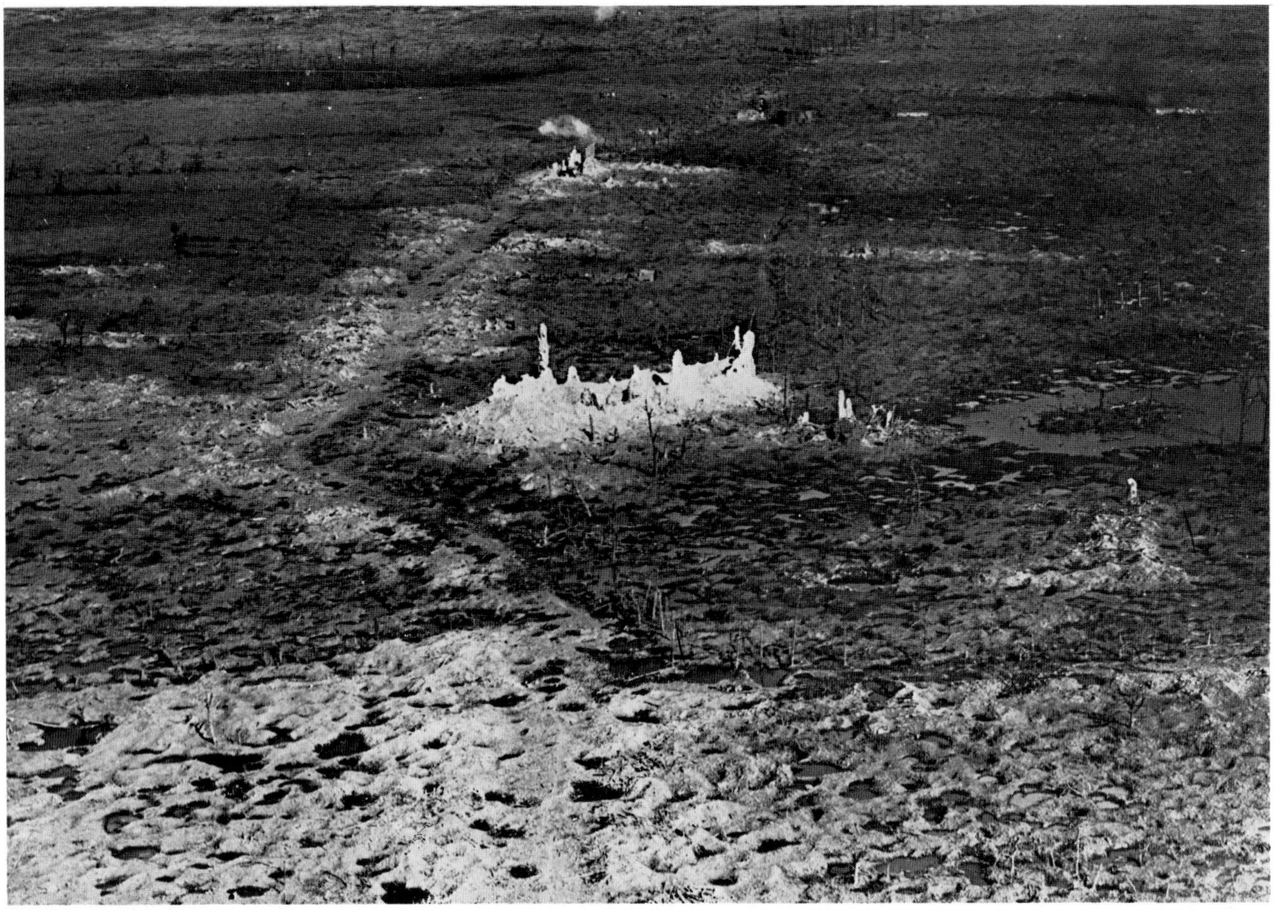

YPRES SALIENT BATTLEFIELD TOUR

Zonnebeke destroyed *(top)* — it changed hands several times — the road and church provide the reference points today *(above)*.

Essex Farm Cemetery with the 49th Division Memorial overlooking it. Close to the entrance stands a memorial to Lieutenant-Colonel John McCrae.

One of the youngest casualties in the Salient — Private Strudwick, aged 15. (RC)

ROUTE 1 The Northern Sector

Leave by the Diksmuidsestraat (N369) on the north side of the Grand Place shortly crossing the Wieltjegracht, a narrow weed-covered waterway at the site of the old **Diksmuide Gate** (Diksmuidse Poort). Carry on and turn left at the T-junction to reach the canal basin at the Kaaie, known to the BEF as **Tattenham Corner**. Turn left with the road and, after crossing the canal, bear right at the next major turning. This is **Salvation Corner**, so called from the hut which the Salvation Army ran here for troops going up the line.

The road runs parallel to the little Ieperlee and the canal. Amid the modern residential area on the right is **Duhallow A.D.S. Cemetery** which was used in 1917 during the Pilkem Ridge battles. About ½ km further along, after leaving the built-up area and passing beneath the new road bridge, the canal bank rises to the right and the obelisk of the **49th Division Memorial** comes into view. Access is through **Essex Farm Cemetery** before it. A new lay-by now enables visitors to park off the busy road. In November 1985, a memorial was erected by the cemetery entrance to Lieutenant-Colonel John M. McCrae, Royal Canadian Army Medical Corps, close to the track which leads down to the canal and the towpath. This lane crosses a small bridge on the far side of which is a **group of British dugouts** recently repaired and restored. The bridge was at the west end of Bridge No. 4, **Brielen Bridge**, and it was here, between the bridge and the memorial, that was the site of the dressing station above which Colonel McCrae in 1915 wrote his famous poem 'In Flanders fields the poppies grow. . . .' (*See also page 129*) Dugouts used by British divisions once stretched along both sides of the bridge in the canal bank.

In the cemetery are buried over 1,100 soldiers from the British and Commonwealth Forces and five Germans. Among the British graves are those of Private T. Barratt, VC, of the South Staffordshire Regiment (Plot I, Grave Z8), and Private V. J. Strudwick, who, at the age of 15 years, was one of the youngest casualties to be buried here (Plot I, Grave U8).

Continuing on towards Boezinge, remains of other canal bank dugouts can be seen to the right whilst on the left, a little further up, is **Bard Cottage Cemetery** and, 1 km further

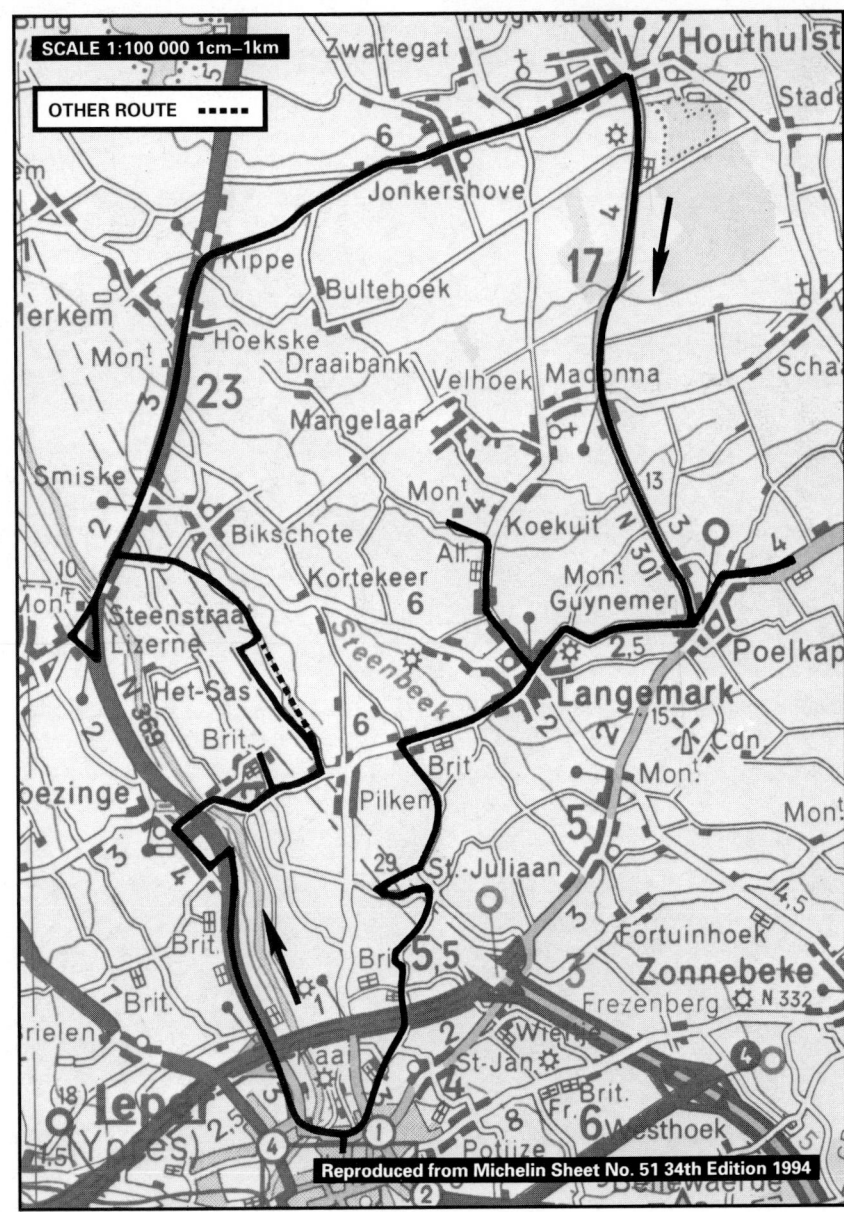

SCALE 1:100 000 1cm–1km

OTHER ROUTE

Reproduced from Michelin Sheet No. 51 34th Edition 1994

Tattenham Corner, to the Tommies, also called Dead End. (RC)   No Sally Army to be found now at Salvation Corner.

Waterlogged British dressing station bunkers at Brielen Bridge.

on, a footpath leads off to **Talana Farm Cemetery**.

After 2 kms, leave the modern highway to enter **Boezinge** by a new side road on the left. Burned by the Germans during their brief stay here in October 1914, it was for the next three years the most northerly boundary of the British sector. New housing development surrounds the area of the ditch which was the actual boundary close to a farm on the right which remains. Beyond this point, the French held the line joining with the Belgian Army near Diksmuide. Fierce battles were fought in the region in 1915 during the Second Battle of Ypres and again in the Third Battle in 1917, during which the French made a successful attack and crossed the canal to the eastern bank. In the centre of the village, on the left-hand side, is a **Demarcation Stone** and in a garden is a **concrete blockhouse** surmounted by a **German mortar** — a Minenwerfer known as 'Kleine Berta'.

To gain the eastern flank of the canal and to cross the **Pilkem Ridge,** turn right at the Demarcation Stone into Brugstraat, soon crossing the bypass and the canal, and take

the Langemark road. The canal has changed greatly as previously the only lock was at **Het Sas** further north. Since 1918, a southern lock has been added and the banks raised.

One kilometre later, the **Carrefour de la Rose** is reached. On the left is one of the most unusual and attractive memorials in the whole Salient. It is the **Memorial to the French 87ème Division d'Infanterie Territoriale and the 45ème Division d'Infanterie Algerienne** and is in the form of a Breton calvary and dolmen with a most useful orientation table and map. The map shows the stand made by the two divisions in the gas attack in April 1915. The calvary is a genuine one from Plouagat in Brittany and the dolmen was brought from Henanbiken.

A short way down the road on the left lies **Artillery Wood Cemetery**, named after the small copse which was here, and the road to the right leads to **Dragon Camp**, **Welsh (Caesar's Nose)** and **Colne Valley Cemeteries**, but continue straight on 1 km to reach **Pilkem** village. Turn left into Bikschootsestraat. Across the cycle path (which runs along the line of the old Ypres-Bruges

Behind Boezinge Demarcation Stone, a 'Kleine Berta' rests on a German bunker.

The Breton Memorial to the French 87ème and 45ème Divisions at the Carrefour de la Rose. The map nearby shows their stand in the April 1915 gas attack.

The largest German bunker remaining in the Salient near Pilkem Road.

railway), there is a road junction: the left turning (Slaaktestraat) takes you by the **largest German bunker** remaining (built as a signal station), while the right fork passes two **bunkers** on the right and one on the left. Both roads join the Bikschote road with two more **bunkers**. These are, like others in the area, part of the chain of defences built by the Germans in the winter of 1915-16. They form a huge arc across the northern and eastern sectors of the Salient. At the next fork, go left past **Bikschote Mill**, burnt down in 1977 but now rebuilt.

After ¾ km, turn left at the crossroads for Steenstraat. Two more **bunkers** can be seen along the road to the left. The road crosses over the path of the A19, the Veurne to Kortrijk autoroute, which now sweeps down to the south-east, cleaving its way across the Salient below St Julien and Zonnebeke, skirting Polygon Wood and Nonneboschen to Gheluvelt. In another ¾ km, turn left to join the N369 at **Steenstraat**. This village, lying amid the rich fields, was at the western end of the French line on April 22, 1915. Their line ran eastwards to a point south of Poelkapelle where it joined the sector held by the Canadian Corps, with the British 27th and 28th Divisions beyond them east of Zonnebeke and Polygon Wood.

April 22 had been a beautiful sunny day when, at about 5 p.m., a greenish-yellow cloud began to appear on either side of Langemark and slowly creep towards the French lines. Soon, the whole four-mile length of the front held by the Algerian soldiers of the 87ème and 45ème Divisions was shrouded in the noxious cloud of chlorine gas. Within an hour, the whole front had given way as the French and their colonial troops took the brunt of the unexpected horror which now hid their sector completely from view and they fell back to the canal. The Canadians on their right flank were, at the outset, beyond the field of the gas but, as they went to fill in the gap they were drawn into it, falling back to St Julien. The French recaptured Steenstraat on May 15 and some 2,000 Germans were found dead on the battlefield. On July 31, 1917, the French re-crossed the canal by night with the aid of many pontoon bridges.

Having crossed the canal, the tall, graceful aluminium **Cross of Reconciliation** will be seen up the slightly-rising ground on the right-hand side. This is a French memorial which replaced the original cross which had been erected to the memory of those who were gassed in April 1915. It was destroyed in 1942 by the occupation forces who objected to the reference in the inscription to the Germans as barbarians.

It was in this area that the French and Belgian lines joined during the 1915 battles and the short circuit from here through **Lizerne** (now part of the municipality of Zuidschote) — turning right at the next

Cross of Reconciliation near Steenstraat, commemorating the gas casualties of 1915.

The Belgian Grenadiers Regiment Memorial near Lizerne.

The memorial of the Belgian 3ème Division d'Infanterie at Hoekske.

junction and then taking the first right twice — will bring you back to the great Cross. At the village crossroads is a **Demarcation Stone** and along the third leg of the triangle stands the **Belgian Grenadiers Regiment Memorial** recalling the gas attack of April 22, 1915. At the Cross, turn left back onto the N369 and, on the left-hand side, next to the canal bridge, is the **Belgian 3e Linie-Regiment Memorial**.

Continue on the N369 for 5 kms to Kippe. **Bikschote**, which was one of the centres of the gas attack of April 1915, lies over to the right; in 2½ kms, just before **Hoekske** and on the left-hand side, stands the **Belgian 3ème Division Memorial** and, a little further on between the houses, a **private memorial** to Adjutant Armand van Eecke of the Belgian 3e Linie-Regiment, killed here in September 1918. To the left of the N369 lies the small town of **Merkem**.

The hamlet of **Kippe** is the northern extremity of the Ypres Salient. Turn right for Houthulst, passing **Jonkershove** in 3 kms. Another 3 kms and **Houthulst** is reached. Turn right onto N301 at the crossroad. The road soon comes to the edge of **Houthulst Forest** whose western side it skirts for 3 kms. This forest was described by Napoleon as the key to the Low Countries. After a bitter defence by the Belgian Army, with support by French cavalry and territorial troops, it fell to the Germans on October 21, 1914. In the Allied advance during the Third Battle of Ypres, the southern extremities were reached. The whole region was subjected to gas attacks and, although the defending Germans suffered very heavy casualties, all attempts to outflank the forest were defeated by their holding the Spriet Ridge. It was not until September 28, 1918, that the Belgians

Moving memorial to Adjutant van Eecke of 5e Kompagnie of 3e Linie-Regiment.

finally recaptured it. During their occupation, the Germans had converted the entire forest into a fortress. From here, their heavy artillery bombarded the Allied lines to the south. When the forest was captured, the Belgians took 150 guns and over 6,000 prisoners.

On the edge of the forest is the **Belgian Military Cemetery**. As the Belgian Army did not hold a sector in the Salient, this is their only cemetery in the immediate area. Besides the 1,704 Belgian dead, there are also 81 Italians and some French buried here.

Access to parts of the forest is restricted for in its depths is a **Belgian Army bomb disposal unit base**. Here are brought the large numbers of shells, bombs, grenades and other ammunition still found in the Salient (and elsewhere in this part of Belgium) to be detonated and destroyed. Farmers still find dangerous relics as they till the land; the spring and autumn ploughing particularly bring forth the 'iron harvest'. This local hazard — builders and developers are affected also — is faced with phlegmatic acceptance with the Belgian Army constantly on call making regular patrols, yet each year casualties, often fatal, still occur.

The Belgian Cemetery in Houthulst Forest with its distinctive headstones. (RC)

The Guynemer Memorial, Poelkapelle, to the 54-victory French ace.

Poelkapelle British Cemetery. *Left:* **Private Condon at 14 is believed to be the youngest to die in the Salient.** *Right:* **The special memorial to Hugh Langton.**

In 4 kms **Velhoek**, a hamlet on the furthest edge of the Allied advance in October 1917, **Poelkapelle** is another 3 kms. This small town was briefly in the British Cavalry area in October 1914 after which (until 1917) it was well inside the German line and became a fortress. It was ravaged by bombardment and reduced to ruins in the latter stages of the autumn 1917 attacks. The 53rd Brigade of 18th Division captured it on October 23. Among the other divisions involved were the 29th, 4th and 11th. One of the tanks which was in support of the 11th was knocked out and bogged down in the centre of the town and was still there when the **Memorial to Georges Guynemer** was unveiled in July 1923.

The great French air ace was killed on September 11, 1917 during a combat with an Aviatik. His flight companion, Lieutenant Benjamin Bozon-Verduraz, did not see his Spad fall as at the vital moment he was busy attending to another group of enemy machines. It was later reported that the German infantry in Poelkapelle had found the wrecked machine and the dead pilot (who had been shot through the head), and had moved his body to a dugout, but that an

artillery barrage had almost immediately destroyed the trench and the aircraft. I have been told that the flying stork — emblem of his squadron — flies in the direction of his crash.

About 1 km to the east of the town, on the Westrozebeke road (N313), lies **Poelkapelle British Cemetery**, the third largest in the region. It was created after the war from battlefield graves. Over 7,400 men lie here. Amongst them is Private J. Condon, Royal Irish Regiment (Plot LVI, Grave F8), at 14 perhaps the youngest to die here. Another is 2nd Lieutenant H. G. Langton, 4th Bn. London Regiment, whose headstone is unusual for its musical inscription — it can be seen by the far left-hand wall.

At the Guynemer crossroads, turn right for **Langemark**, 2½ kms. This town was attacked by the Germans on October 23, 1914, but the untried divisions were no match for either the 2nd British Division or the French, and the student troops suffered heavy casualties. In the wake of the gas attack of April 22, 1915, Langemark was occupied by the German 51. Reserve-Division and it remained in German hands until August 16, 1917, when 20th Light

Division recaptured the ruined town and 2,000 prisoners. In April 1918, the Allies withdrew in the face of the Spring Offensive and it was not until September 28 that the town was finally recaptured by X Corps supporting the Belgian Army. By this time, there was not a building left standing — all had been pulverised in the bombardments.

At the main crossroads, turn right, passing the square and the modern church on the left, and cross the line of the old railway (now a bike path). After a short distance, the houses give way to beet fields (on the right) whilst, on the left, is the sombre **German Military Cemetery, the Soldatenfriedhof**. A long, low, dark-red granite building houses the gateway and incorporates the student memorial. The left-hand room contains the Registers of those who are known to be buried between the tall oak trees and in the newer section to the north of the entrance. A visitors' book is also provided. Both chapels are entered through magnificent cast-iron doors of intricate design. The chapel walls are covered with the names of the students who died and on the wall of the second room is a map depicting the locations of the other German graveyards. The cemetery is in two almost distinct sections. The **Alter Friedhof**, the old cemetery, is under the shade of the great oak trees, which stand like enormous Imperial Guardsmen above the greensward, and has grey slatish stones with the names of the dead picked out in white-painted lettering. In this part lie 10,143, of whom 3,836 are unknown. Here and there, groups of small basalt crosses break the serried ranks of stones. Immediately through the entrance is the **Kameradengrab** — the mass grave of 24,917 men. Eighty-six bronze pillars bearing their names flank the grave, with memorials to the regiments of various parts of Germany. Away over the far side of the cemetery stand the brooding figures of mourning comrades.

The northern end of the cemetery, beyond the protection of the oak trees and behind the three concrete bunkers and their linking memorial stones, which are part of the fortifications of the Langemark Line, is the **Einbettungsfriedhof-Nord** where 9,475 men lie buried (making a total of over 44,000 for the whole cemetery). Divisional memorials are to be found on the slabs of stone between the bunkers. A quiet pool marks the boundary of the graveyard in which is reflected the Teutonic cross. This is a forbidding place with its subdued colours and gloomy atmosphere heightened by the very neatness and trimness of the lawns, hedges, walls and trees.

Continue past the cemetery, turning left immediately after crossing the Broenbeek bridge. A little way along this road is another large **bunker** of the same line as those in the cemetery. In front of it is the **Memorial to the Royal Artillery and Royal Engineers of the 34th Division**. After the bunker was captured in September 1918, it was used as an advanced dressing station under the command of Robert Lawrence, a brother of T. E. Lawrence. He described to me the frightful conditions in this region in 1917 and 1918. There were no trenches, just a sea of mud across which duck-boards led from shell-hole to shell-hole right back to Velhoek and Koekuit. The concrete pillboxes were the only stable buildings remaining. At certain times, more men were lost by drowning than by the bullet.

Return to Langemark and, at the traffic lights, go right on the Boezinge road. A short distance along the road, on the left and now flanked by modern villas, is the stark grey **Memorial to the 20th Light Division**. Over the Steenbeek (where stands a **memorial marker to the Final Offensive** started here on September 28, 1918), and in the yard of a large farm, is a square pillbox, **Cement House**, now so much overgrown by ivy as to be almost unrecognisable as a bunker. On its right, next door to the farm, is the large **British Cemetery** which bears this name. Until recently, all bodies found in the Salient and identified as British were buried here.

Blockhouses of the Einbettungsfriedhof-Nord in Langemark German Cemetery. (RC)

Goumier Farm blockhouse with British and German concrete reinforcement. (RC)

Some time ago, a tiny cemetery near Mons had to be closed due to road-works at Maisières and the eighteen or so officers and men (who had died in August 1914) were transferred here. Among them is Captain J. E. Knowles (Plot XVIII, Grave D1-16), one of the first British officers to lose his life (*see pages 112 and 113*).

At the next crossroads, known as **Iron Cross** — a heavily-bombarded spot as it was a main crossing of the transport routes to Langemark — turn left (Groenestraat) and in about ½ km turn right, thereby crossing the eastern side of the **Pilkem Ridge**. On the right, 2 kms further on, is a large and most-interesting concrete bunker. It is a fortified Belgian farmhouse, **Goumier Farm**. On some British maps it is called Gournier Farm. Although it has been in almost constant use by farmers as a cattle shelter or pigsty in the years since the war, it remains in fair condition. The Germans were the first to fortify it, enclosing the brick walls in concrete, and in places it is possible to discern the imprint of the shuttering. As a strong point with excellent visibility, it was under frequent attack and changed hands on many occasions until the end of July 1917 when the 38th Welsh Division captured Pilkem. The Royal Engineers added further strengthening and blast walls to Goumier and thus it is one place where the two differing styles of work can be studied closely. After again falling into enemy hands, it was finally recaptured by the Black Watch. Some years ago, a **plaque in memory of the 38th Welsh Division** was placed on the bunker and, with the farmer's permission, visitors can inspect it.

Keep to the left at the fork just beyond the farm and continue for about 2 kms along this road across the ridge, passing between small

farms often with a blockhouse or concrete observation post now incorporated in their buildings, until a five-way cross is reached. Take the first left (Moortelweg) and, after a couple of **bunkers** have been passed, a panorama unfolds. At the next crossroad, turn right (Briekestraat). Proceed along this, the old **Boundary Road**, for 1 km and over a small crossroad, once known as **Hammond's Corner**, and the large **New Irish Farm Cemetery** is on the right. Among over 4,600 British and Commonwealth graves are a number of Chinese Labour Corps casualties. In a short distance, the N38 (the Ypres bypass) is crossed and the descent into Ypres is made through the suburb of De Brieke. Take the right-hand fork, passing the small **La Brigue Cemetery No. 2** on the right, and enter Ypres at the site of the old **Diksmuide Gate**.

The 34th Division RA and RE Memorial stands in front of a German bunker.

The 20th Light Division's Memorial now surrounded by modern houses.

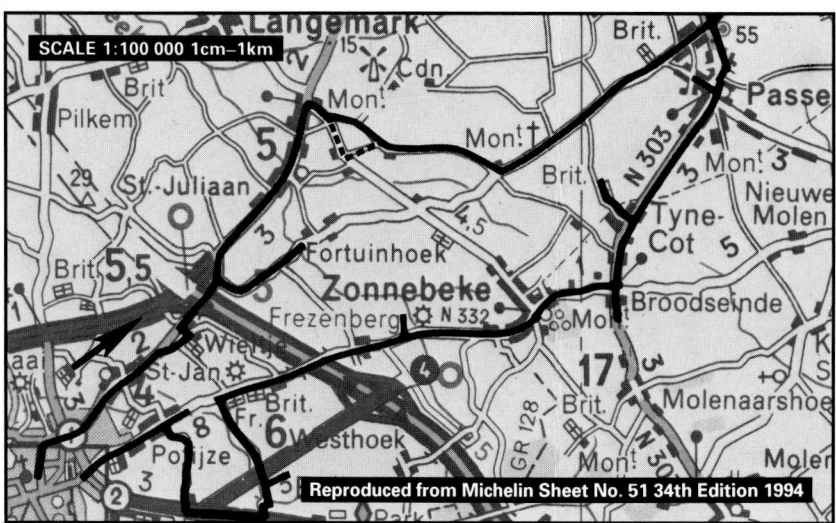

SCALE 1:100 000 1cm—1km

Reproduced from Michelin Sheet No. 51 34th Edition 1994

ROUTE II The North-eastern Sector

Leave Ypres by Brugseweg (N313), soon passing the large **White House Cemetery** on the rising ground above the little **Belle-waerdebeek** at **St Jan** (St Jean). The village was the site of forward dressing stations, all housed in cellars in 1915. By 1917, the village had been completely destroyed.

About 1 km on the left is the footpath to **Wieltje Farm Cemetery**. In the fields on the opposite side of the road stood **Prowse Farm**, named after Brigadier-General C. B. Prowse, DSO, but today only a portion of the cellars and a large water-filled shellhole are all that remain.

Take the right fork shortly after to drive on **Oxford Road**. The **cemetery** of this name is on the right and, further down the lane, is the **50th Northumbrian Division Memorial**. After the Second World War, an inscription relative to the division's effort in 1939-45 was added to the column. In the fields behind the memorial, two lines of bunkers and emplacements, now only barely visible above the ground, mark the line of the **Cambrai Redoubt** of 1917.

Returning to the main road, pass under the motorway and take the right-hand road (Roeselaarsestraat) for **Fortuinehoek**. It leads to Passchendaele and it was built shortly after the war. Soon after the turning (note the bunkers in the fields), on the right is the **grey limestone memorial** to the memory of Lieutenant H. A. Birrell-Anthony and the officers and men of the **1st Monmouthshire Regiment** who fell near this spot in the Second Battle of Ypres on May 8, 1915. The memorial, set in a small stone-walled enclosure, is cared for by the Commonwealth War Graves Commission.

Return to the N313, and turn right along the highway, greatly widened here as it joins the Ypres ring-road. Off to the far side of this highway, from Wieltje village still runs the straight road (Moortelweg) to **Pilkem Ridge** known as **Admiral's Road**. The name derives from 1915 when an unnamed captain of the 6th Division used to charge up and down it in an armoured car of the Royal Naval Division. Regrettably, when the motorway is completed, the road may be diverted.

A little way along the N313 now is the site of the notorious **Mousetrap Farm**. Originally known as Shelltrap Farm or Death Farm, the present house is nearer to the road. These names were considered too ominous and so the famous name was acquired. It was the headquarters of the 3rd Canadian Brigade during the gas attack and, in the ensuing battle of St Julien, came into the line.

Soon after joining the main road, the little cemetery on the left is **Seaforth Cemetery**. Here lie 101 men of the 2nd Bn. Seaforth Highlanders who were killed near here on April 25-26, 1915. Almost next door is a farm in which is incorporated a large bunker, **Chedder Villa**. As the cost of demolishing this typical German bunker would have been exorbitant, the farmer has designed his extension around it. It was captured in July 1917, and was utilised first as an aid post and then as a battalion headquarters by 1/4th Bn. Oxford and Buckinghamshire Light Infantry. The wide entrance of this bunker was the scene of a disastrous shelling on the night of August 7, 1917 when a platoon of the 1st Bn. Buckinghamshires was sheltering within it; direct hits killed many and all were wounded. It will be noted that the bunker, although set on the crest of a slope giving a wide field of vision, is also unsheltered.

The Canadian Memorial at Vancouver Corner. *Below:* **The new plaque was erected in 1986. (RC)**

THIS·COLUMN·MARKS·THE BATTLEFIELD·WHERE·18,000 CANADIANS·ON·THE·BRITISH LEFT·WITHSTOOD·THE·FIRST GERMAN·GAS·ATTACKS·THE 22-24 APRIL 1915·2,000·FELL AND·LIE·BURIED·NEARBY

In the distance to the north-east, another bunker comes into view. This formed part of the German second line in front of **Kitchener's Wood** — now an open field — around which there was very heavy fighting in 1915.

After 1 km, we come to **St Julien** (St Juliaan). This village was captured by the Germans on April 24, 1915, after the gas attack and the gallant defence by the Canadians. By July 1917, the Germans had completed their lines of concrete block-houses in the area. The heavy bombardments which preceded the Allied attack, and the thunderstorms of the last few days of the month, turned the area into a sea of stinking, yellowish, slimy mud. These strong points were the only firm places left and the battle was a series of actions from one strong point to another, and it was disastrous in the extremely-heavy casualties which it cost. St Julien was finally captured on August 3 by the 39th Division, whose casualties were 145 officers and 3,716 other ranks killed, wounded or missing.

Kerselaar — **Vancouver Corner** — is 1 km further on. This crossroads is dominated by the **Canadian Memorial**, a pillar surmounted by the head and shoulders of a soldier resting on his arms reversed, set amid green lawns, conifer trees and juniper bushes. Originally, the trees were clipped close to represent shell tops and the juniper to resemble shell-holes. New trees have replaced the old in recent years. Until 1988, the inscription on the pillar misleadingly stated that '2000 fell and here lie buried' when in fact they lie in many cemeteries across the area of the April 1915 gas attack and not within the confines of the memorial park. The memorial faces the notorious **Triangle** of which the old road junction formed part.

50th Northumbrian Div. Memorial. (RC)

The 1st Bn. Monmouths Memorial.

38

A modern mill stands on the site of the Totenmühle, a German OP. (RC)

's-Graventafel New Zealand Memorial on the road to Passchendaele. (RC)

Modern marker just outside Passchendaele New British Cemetery. (RC)

The Canadians crossed the valley — then a treacherous morass — to capture and hold Crest Farm on Passchendaele Ridge.

Turn right. Take either the first or second left turning. The first will lead past the mill built on the highest point in the sector. The Germans called it the **Totenmühle** — the mill of the dead — for it was one of their observation points constantly under attack. The present mill is a reproduction (completed in 1923) of the actual mill of 1915 and is often open to the public. From it can be gained a 360-degree view. After the mill, continue past the two farm lanes on the left and past the T-junction. The road coming up from the right (St Juliaanstraat) is a continuation of the second left turning from Vancouver Corner down the Zonnebeke road. The name of this second corner is **Winnipeg**, a vital position in 1915 and 1917.

Travel 2 kms across the now peaceful meadows with small farms scattered beside clumps of trees and the inevitable pond. In 1917, this was completely torn up by shelling and entrenching, becoming many feet deep in Flanders mud. Only duck-board tracks were safe to use from one trench to another as few roads remained. The artillery was bogged down by the sticky, glutinous mud and trenches were two feet or more deep in it. Crossing the region from east to west are the several small rivers or streams which, due to the continuous rain which followed the dry spell of July 1917, flooded the area.

The next crossroad, **'s-Graventafel**, is marked by the **New Zealand Memorial** to their dead in the Passchendaele battles. The hamlet was captured on October 4, 1917. Turn left past the memorial and cross the area where the New Zealand Expeditionary Force made their stand.

In 3 kms, **Passchendaele New British Cemetery** with the new marker recalling the end of the 1918 battles is on the left. At the main road (1 km), go right into **Passchendaele** (Passendale). The village sprawls across the ridge at this point and, even though there has been much building beyond the old boundary of the village, it can be seen just what a valuable position it commands. For over three years, the Germans held the ridge until, on November 6, 1917, in the culmination of Third Ypres, the rubble which had been the village was captured by the Canadian Corps. Behind them were the gentle slopes of the western side of the ridge, a terrible scene of mud and blood, whilst ahead lay the green fields of an almost peaceful country hardly touched by war. In April 1918, following the German Spring Offensive, the Allied Command withdrew from the ridge and the Germans took possession again. On October 14, the Belgian Army drove them from the ridge.

The 66th Division memorial window in Passchendaele church.

The 85th Canadian Infantry Bn. Memorial on the eastern slope of the Ridge.

The Western Front Association plaque on the walls of the town hall.

In the centre of the village is the church, whose north windows form the **Memorial to the 66th Division**. From the porch, it is possible to look down the slope and across the shallow valley to the rise of **Crest Farm** where the **Canadian Memorial** to the capture of Passchendaele Ridge stands. On the wall of the town hall (Stadhuis), across the road from the church, are several **memorial plaques**, including two to the Belgian regiments which took the village — the **4e Carabiniers Regiment** and the **Grenadiers** — and a **Western Front Association Plaque**, the latter unveiled in 1988.

Continue along the N303 on the crest of the ridge, now a modern highway, to Broodseinde. Just outside Passchendaele, on the left and some 200 yards out into the beet fields, will be seen a small obelisk. This is the **Memorial to the 85th Canadian Infantry Battalion**, the Nova Scotia Highlanders, who participated in the capture of the ridge in 1917.

After 2 kms along the ridge, take the right-hand road, signposted to **Tyne Cot British Military Cemetery and Memorial to the Missing**, noting bunkers behind the houses. Here, within a kilometre of the farthest point in Belgium reached by the British forces, lie the greatest number to be buried in any Commonwealth war cemetery anywhere in the world. There are 11,908 graves in this quiet place of beauty. The entrance is a flint-stone lich-gate and the view up the gentle slope to the Great Cross and the arc of the Memorial to the Missing, which curves between the two domed pavilions in the background, is a never-to-be-forgotten experience.

Tyne Cot was so named by the men of the 50th Northumbrian Division, who were among the many who fought to capture the complex of bunkers and pillboxes which surrounded the old barn which stood about 50 metres west of the level-crossing on the Passchendaele to Broodseinde road. It was captured by the 3rd Australian Division on October 4, 1917. The five bunkers which formed the redoubt were part of the German Flanders I Line. The largest of the bunkers was then used as a dressing station by the 33rd and 50th Divisions and two Canadian formations, burying their dead around it. The station and the cemetery were in use until the end of March 1918 when, after the Allied withdrawal, the area fell again into enemy hands.

After the war, over 11,500 dead were brought here from the surrounding battle-field; many of the missing listed on the panels of the memorial will be among them. The cemetery was designed by Sir Herbert Baker who wished to create the appearance of a huge English churchyard, and the flint walls and gate were laid out with the walls of the precincts of Winchester College in mind. In May 1922, King George V included a visit to this cemetery in his pilgrimage. It was then in course of construction and, at the King's suggestion, the Great Cross was built above the largest of the remaining blockhouses, leaving a small section exposed to show the concrete. Thus, this Cross of Sacrifice differs from all others with its pyramid of gleaming white Nimy stone 'pierre romaine de Lens', lifting it above the serried ranks of head-stones and the many varieties of flowers, shrubs and trees. A **plaque** on the block-house below the cross recalls its capture by

One of the original bunkers which have been retained within Tyne Cot Cemetery.

Behind the Cross of Sacrifice are the original graves, well over 300 of them, which remain as they were found after the Armistice. Beyond them is the Stone of Remembrance and the terrace, raised up a few steps. At this level, the graves are in fan-like sections in front of the flint and Portland stone panels of the **Memorial to the Missing**. At intervals, the wall is broken by groups of Tuscan pillars behind which open two circular cloisters on either side of a central apse which is the **New Zealand Memorial to their Missing**. From it, iron gates open into quiet greenswards shaded by cedars.

In all, there are 34,888 names on the panels which cover the period from August 16, 1917 to the end of the war. Six recipients of the Victoria Cross are either buried in the cemetery or listed on the panels. Two of these lie buried close to the site of their heroic action — the spot where they lost their lives. They are Sergeant L. McGee, 40th Bn., AIF (Plot XX, Grave D1), and Captain C. S. Jeffries, 34th Bn. AIF (Plot XL, Grave E1).

Return to the main road. Before taking the right turn at the **Broodseinde** crossroads for Zonnebeke, carry on a short distance in the Beselare direction to the **7th Division Memorial**. One of the earliest monuments to be erected in the Salient, it commemorates the actions of the division in the early days of 1914 and in 1917, and also other battles elsewhere. It stands on a field battery position with views over the ridge to the east and, down the slopes to the west, the tower of Zonnebeke church rises between the trees. Sergeant Nick Keating, then a spritely 90-year-old, described to me in August 1982 how his battery suffered its first casualty here in October 1914, when a cow objected to being milked inexpertly by the battery sergeant. He was laid out by a well-delivered kick! Return to the Broodseinde crossroads,

the **3rd Australian Division**. (For many years, the plaque credited the capture to the *2nd* Australian Division, but this was corrected in 1992.) From the base of the cross, all the Salient stretching away to the south-west can be seen — right to Kemmel and beyond. On a bright, clear, sunny day, the cross can be identified from the Dunkerque lighthouse. Tall trees guard the other two blockhouses retained within the cemetery.

Ex-Sergeant Nick Keating, RA, poses in August 1982 (then aged 90) beside the 7th Division Memorial on the site of his battery position in October 1914. (RC)

where a modern **Memorial to the French Soldiers** (erected in 1977) recalls their participation in the battles for **Broodseinde Ridge**.

Left: **A really remarkable sight at the Zonnebeke brickworks quarry where the excavations have sliced through a cross-section of the battlefield and exposed the former trenches 'end on'. This is the view from the dugout.** *Right*: **Below ground, the author steps back in time to where men once rested in what is now known to have been part of Bremen Redoubt. (RC)**

Turning down the hill (N332) known to the troops as **Devil's Hill** (one of many), **Zonnebeke** is entered. This large prosperous village was completely destroyed, being the focal point of many actions, and was reduced to an ocean of mud. In the First Battle of Ypres, it was successfully defended when Gheluvelt fell in October 1914, and then it was captured by the Germans in May 1915. It was recaptured by the 3rd British Division in September 1917. Once again, in April 1918, Zonnebeke was overwhelmed in the German advance westward, but in September, when the Second Army began its great push eastward, Zonnebeke was recaptured on the first day, September 28 *(see photographs on page 32)*. On the southern wall of the church is a

small bronze **plaque commemorating D21 Battery, Canadian Field Artillery**, which had a position amid the ruins in 1917. In 1989, a deep dugout system thought to be of Australian origin was excavated behind the church; too dangerous to be opened to the public, it has now been closed shut again.

Beside the church is the arched gateway to the present **Zonnebeke Château**, set in a pleasant park, the **Kasteeldomein**. The château houses the excellent **Streekmuseum** where the history of Zonnebeke, Beselare, Gheluvelt, Passchendaele and Zandvoorde is

displayed. Alongside artefacts from ancient times is a detailed display of the events of the war together with relics and the fine collection of maps, photographs, models and explanatory graphs produced for the 1987 exhibition at Passchendaele. The museum is open from April to November (Wednesdays and weekends only; daily in July-August).

Continue through the village on the N322 heading downhill for Frezenberg. A little way outside Zonnebeke, on the right, rises the flourishing Zonnebeke brickworks — **Vanbiervliet Steenbakkerij**. The clay is excavated from a huge quarry at the rear and it is interesting to note in the slope of the walls the layer of blue — London — clay clearly visible some 20 feet down and the variations in colour above caused by trenches and shell holes. In 1983, the diggers found a large **subterranean dugout**, just round the corner at the rear of the works, almost beneath the rail on which the trucks operate. It proved to be an L-shaped complex, possibly a forward post or a field dressing station and is thought to be of Australian origin from the style of work. There was provision for over 120 men with bunks in three tiers and an officer's quarter. It has since been established that this was the position known as **Bremen Redoubt** (on British maps) or **Brandenburg** (on German maps). The management of the brickworks has thoughtfully preserved it in its entirety, installing an access path, a concrete covering and electric lighting (with switches both at the upper and lower entrance doors), to enable visitors to taste the flavour of subterranean life. Much of the rusting wire of the bunks and the debris of occupation has been cleared but there still remains the damp atmosphere, the decaying corrugated iron, the original mud and cement steps, the makeshift wooden ladder and a few remnants of British gasmasks. When I saw it first shortly after discovery, all manner of bits and pieces were strewn around, including a few grenades and ammo (these artefacts are now at the Zonnebeke Streekmuseum), and from up above one of the lintels a petrified rat glared down. Visits are allowed without prior permission (follow the signs 'Bremen Redoubt'), but visitors are warned of the danger whilst the trucks and other vehicles are operating.

Return to the N332 and turn right for **Frezenberg**. The road runs down the northern edge of the ridge to which the village gave its name, and which was so vital in 1915 and 1917. The artillery, the 122nd Heavy and the 37th Howitzer Batteries being among those positioned here, stemmed the advance on April 24, 1915. On May 8, the 28th Division was holding the ridge but was forced to withdraw after very heavy bombardments. One battalion, the 1st

Suffolks, was almost destroyed, there being only seven men left alive at the end of the day. By July 1917, Frezenberg was a virtual fortress. It was attacked by the 15th Division through the mud and, with the aid of tanks, in particular one called 'Challenger', the village was taken.

Crossing the motorway, **Verlorenhoek**, involved in the 1915 and 1917 actions, is reached and in ½ km on the left, set back in the fields, is **Aeroplane British Cemetery**, so named from the wreck of such a machine close by. One field further on, also on the left, is the **French National Cemetery of St Charles de Potize** with its mass graves. Near the roadside is the **Crucifix and Mourning Women** erected in 1968 as a memorial.

The French National Cemetery at Potize. There are 3,748 graves and also the mass grave at St Charles de Potize.

Incidentally, the road to the right just before the cemetery is **Oxford Road**, leading to Wieltje, whilst the one on the left which we now take is **Cambridge Road**. In 1 km, at the junction of a farm lane on the left, is a **lone cross** — the memorial of Captain Henry L. Skrine, 6th Bn. Somerset Light Infantry, killed here and buried near the site on September 25, 1915. It is also the memorial of his battalion. A few yards up the lane is another **cross**; this is to the memory of Captain Geoffrey V. S. Bowlby of The Royal Horse Guards killed near here on May 13, 1915. Ahead on the left is **Railway Wood**. The old Ypres to Roeselaere railway, which ran in front of it, was lifted in the 1970s but, until very recently, vestiges of dugouts could still be seen in its embankment. However, in late 1993, this stretch was widened and surfaced into an access road for the A19 motorway and, with it, the dugouts have disappeared.

Cross the new road and turn right behind the wood. Up to the right on the ridge appears the lone cross of the **RE Grave**. This unusual memorial marks the grave of one officer and eleven NCOs and men of the 177th Tunnelling Company, RE, who were killed in the mining operations in this area 1915-17. It can be reached by a track further up the road (often too muddy for cars). Remains of craters made by the many mines exploded around here can be discerned along the ridge behind the cross. In the Second World War, the Germans attempted unsuccessfully to build a V1 site between two of the larger craters.

Return to the junction and turn left. Our road now dips down to cross the little Belle-waerdebeek, with away to the left the site of **Y Wood** and the trees of Hooge ('t Hoge). In ¾ km, we join the Menin Road (N8) at **Birr Crossroads**, so named by the Leinster Regiment in action here in April 1915. Turn right, and the **British Cemetery** of the same name is on the left. Another ½ km or so, we arrive at the most notorious spot in the entire

This is the lonely RE Grave, Railway Wood. Here lie one officer and 11 NCOs and men from the 177th Tunnelling Company, all killed in the area.

This was once called the hottest spot on earth — Hellfire Corner. Here the Menin Road, the Potize-Zillebeke Road and railway all met. With the railway lifted and the crossroad recently turned into a traffic circle, its appearance has now changed greatly. However, the Demarcation Stone recording the furthest advance of the Germans in 1918 is still there.

Salient — **Hellfire Corner** — the position on the Menin Road where both the Zillebeke-Potize road and the Ypres to Roeselaere railway crossed it. With the recent construction of the motorway access road along the line of the old railway, the historic crossroad has been changed into a traffic circle, which has considerably altered its appearance. The house on the north-east corner of the Potize road has gone and the **British Demarcation Stone** marking the limit of the German advance in 1918, which stood in front of it, has been moved a few yards to the left.

Turn right, reaching **Potize** (Potijze) in 1 km. At the entrance of the village on the right (behind No. 7) will be seen one of the best-preserved British observation posts remaining — **Hussar Farm**. The Royal

Monmouthshire Royal Engineers construct-ed the strong point inside the old farmhouse. Despite four years exposure to enemy bombardment, the OP survived to provide useful storage for the farmer. As a result of various hits, it is possible to see the manner in which the strengthening was carried out, with lengths of railway line reinforcing the brickwork and concrete; even some of the original corrugated iron is in situ still.

Potize village figured significantly in the British lines, being a divisional headquarters. **Potize Château**, also known as the White Château, was used as an advanced dressing station but it was almost destroyed by shell-fire. Around its site — reached, after a right turn at the crossroads onto N322 (Zonne-beekseweg), by a footpath on the left — now

there are three cemeteries: **Potize Château Grounds**, **Lawn** and **Wood Cemeteries**.

Back on the N322, return past the cross-roads to arrive in Ypres just above the Menin Gate at a very dangerous crossroads. Shortly before reaching them, on the left is the entrance to **Ypres Town Cemetery and Extension**. Here are buried men who died in October 1914, the early months of 1915 and 1918, and, today, gardeners of the Common-wealth War Graves Commission. The grave of Prince Maurice of Battenberg is here between the Town Cemetery and the Exten-sion, by the entrance to the latter. After the Armistice, the Cemetery Extension was enlarged to provide graves for the many iso-lated and small groups of burials in the area and now some 600 lie here.

Hussar Farm was a British observation post which was fortified by the Royal Monmouthshire Royal Engineers.

Just a few dozen yards apart, the memorials to Captain Skrine (in the foreground) and Captain Bowlby behind.

The grave of Prince Maurice of Batten-berg, killed on October 27, 1914, serving with the King's Royal Rifle Corps.

Château Biebuyck *(above left)*. **The modern house marks the site of General Haig's White Château HQ which stood here in 1914.** *Above right:* **Zillebeke was decimated but rebuilt in its original style. Some of the earliest British graves lie in its cemetery.**

ROUTE III The Eastern Sector

Proceed through the Menin Gate (Meensestraat is one-way, so leave the town via Bollingstraat) into Maarschalk Frenchlaan, bearing right at the crossroads into the Menin Road. Soon, **Menin Road South Cemetery** will be passed on the right, and, just before reaching Hellfire Corner (*see page 42*), on the left is the site of **White Château** (another of them). General Haig's headquarters during the First Battle of Ypres, Château Biebuyck was in constant use even though badly damaged as the cellars provided shelter. Now the site is occupied by a yellow-brick mansion set back amid the trees.

At the Hellfire Corner crossroads — now a roundabout — just 1 km from Ypres, turn right to visit **Zillebeke**. On the crest of the rise to the left is **Perth (China Wall) British Cemetery** where over 2,600 men of the Commonwealth lie, having died in this front-line area, particularly in 1915, 1917 and 1918. It is not difficult to appreciate the significance of the rise, slight as it may be, as it overlooks such a panorama. Another ½ km down in the valley nestles the village at the eastern end of the lake bearing its name. From October 31, 1914 until September 28, 1918, Zillebeke was either in the front line or very close to it and was completely destroyed. It has been rebuilt on the old foundations, the church almost to the same design. Some of the earliest British burials are in the churchyard, others are in **Tuileries Cemetery**, a little way before the church off to the right. Near the church is the track to **Hellblast Corner** (*see page 52*) on the eastern extremity of the lake. Return up the hill to take the first right turn to reach Birr Crossroads (*see page 42*) in 1 km.

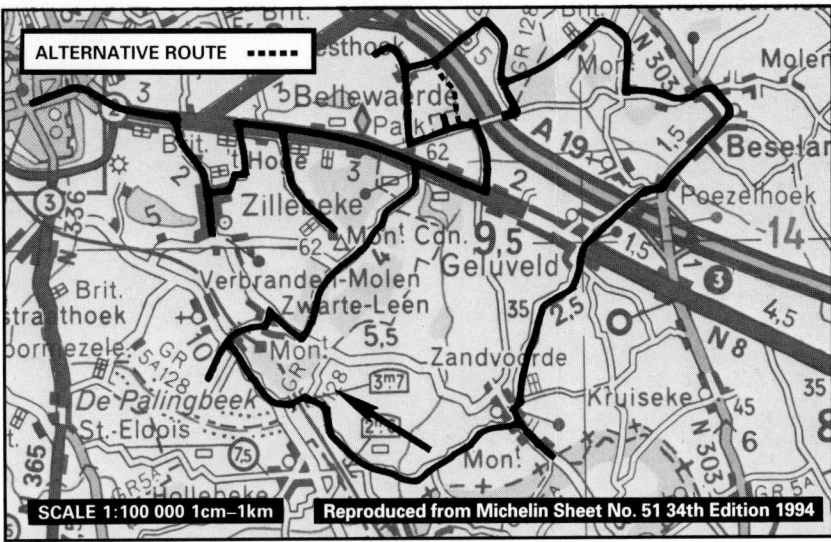

ALTERNATIVE ROUTE ·····

SCALE 1:100 000 1cm–1km   Reproduced from Michelin Sheet No. 51 34th Edition 1994

Turn right onto the Menin Road and in some 200 metres, at the end of the row of houses, turn right into **Canadalaan — Maple Avenue**. This road was built especially to make access easy to the Canadian Memorial on Hill 62 and Sanctuary Wood Cemetery. As it curves towards the woods and hill, a magnificent view of Hooge Crater Cemetery, away on the left, can be gained. The gentle rise of the ridge is also very clear. **Sanctuary Wood Cemetery** is on the right in about 1½ km. In this graveyard lies Lieutenant Gilbert Talbot, MC (Plot I, Grave G1), in whose memory Toc H was named (*see pages 10 & 11*). Here also, against the south wall of the cemetery, lies the German aviator Hans Roser, who was shot down by Major Lanoe G. Hawker, VC. Outside is the private **cross** in memory of a friend of Lieutenant Talbot, 2nd Lieutenant Keith Rae of the 8th Bn. The Rifle Brigade, killed near Hooge Crater on July 13, 1915. Originally erected in 1921 on the grounds of Hooge Château, it was moved here in 1966.

Sanctuary Wood Cemetery: this is Lieutenant Gilbert Talbot's grave. (RC)

The memorial to Lieutenant Keith Rae, a close friend of Talbot. (RC)

The grave of Hans Roser, shot down by Major Hawker, VC. (RC)

A few metres further up Maple Avenue is a café behind which is a **Musée des Tranchées**. The family Schier, who own the café, have preserved this small part of the wood as it was found at the end of the war and it is now the only really-authentic sector of trenches remaining in the Salient. The trenches belong to the **Vince Street-Jam Row** system of front and support lines of 1916. Battlefield debris of all kinds are strewn around the copse and the trench lines. In the little indoor museum, to which visitors are shown before walking through the trenches, are on display many items found in the Salient or nearby, including two sea mines from the Nieuwpoort area and some early German gravestones.

Sanctuary Wood was so named because in October 1914, when this was a relatively quiet sector, stragglers were gathered together in the wood where they came under the orders of General E. S. Bulfin of the 2nd Infantry Brigade. His instructions were that they were in sanctuary and not to be employed without his permission. By 1915, the wood began to lose its original usage and was soon in the front line or close to it. The 16th Lancers were in action in Shrewsbury Forest to the south-east in February 1915, as were the Leinsters. After the advance in May 1915, the Germans were in the eastern sectors of the wood and harrassed the British and French encamped on the western edges. June 1916 was the time of a violent German attack which lasted for four days, then came the Canadian counterattack and assault on Hills 61 and 62 (known collectively as 'Tor Top') and Mount Sorrel, ending with the Canadians regaining all the lost ground. The trees were shot to pieces and the ground was often a quagmire. Bunkers and strong points were built (of which a few remain in the sector of the wood opposite the café, today private grounds), and a few shallow subways, or rather covered trenches, were dug to replace those of 1914. Two short lengths of these can be seen in the museum but are only passable during dry weather.

Sanctuary Wood and its trench museum *(above)* **are today the most authentic and vivid portrayal of what it was like to live in the filth and mud of Flanders — the museum's trenches themselves are only completely traversable in the summer months! Many unique exhibits to be seen include these early German gravestones** *(left)* **erected during the war and discarded when the graves were centralised post-war. Note the original shell-blasted tree stumps behind.**

The summit of the slope — **Hill 62** — is crowned with the **Canadian Memorial** commemorating the battles of 1916. (The memorial's inscription is a bit confusing as Mount Sorrel is not identical with Hill 62, but lies in fact a short distance to the south of it.) Views of the immediate region can be enjoyed from the gardens which surround the memorial. The proximity of Ypres (5 kms to the north-west) and Hill 60 (2 kms to the south-west, with Shrewsbury Forest in front of it to the left) can be well appreciated and, on clear days, Mont Kemmel (12 kms to the south-west) appears very near indeed.

Return to the Menin Road and turn right for **Hooge** ('t Hoge), ½ km up the slope of the modern highway, once a mere muddy track, shell-torn and dangerous — or dusty and dangerous — but always busy. As we approach Hooge, the **Hooge Crater Museum**, in what was formerly the private chapel of the château, looms up on the left

The Canadian Memorial on Hill 62 *(left)* **commemorates the 1916 battles. Although the inscription names the position Mount Sorrel, that hill actually lies just to the south of Hill 62.**

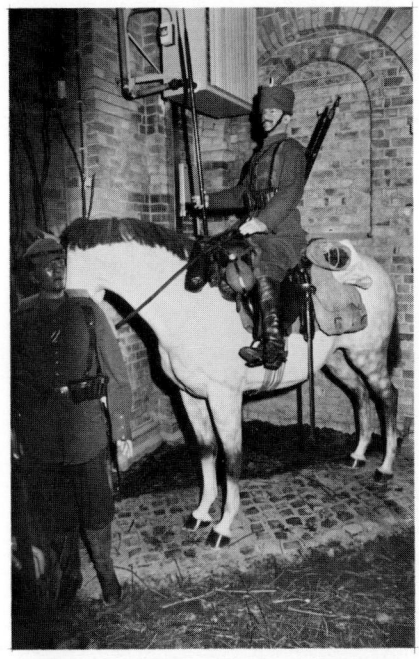

Exhibits in the Hooge Crater Museum are well presented in lifelike dioramas like this German cavalryman *(left)* and British infantry officer *(right)*.

The King's Royal Rifle Corps Memorial at Hooge, beside the Menin Road.

opposite **Hooge Crater Cemetery**. **Hooge Château** was a British headquarters in 1914 and from it Sir John French and Sir Douglas Haig watched the 1st Division rally and capture Gheluvelt. The château of the day was a red-brick building with a large conservatory set at the end of a straight drive some distance away from the present mansion, its parkland extending down to the lake and woodlands of Bellewaerde to the left of the Menin Road. Always under fire, it was captured in May 1915 by the Germans and it was the scene of fierce fighting in June and July and often changed hands. On July 30, the Germans used 'liquid fire' (burning petrol) for the first time and, not long before, the British fired a large mine, one of many to be used in the vicinity during the attacks. One was across the Menin Road and now a stylised crater forms the entrance to the cemetery. This slopes down the valley overlooking Sanctuary Wood. Nearly 6,000 men are buried or commemorated here.

The new **Hooge Crater Museum** (it opened in 1994) has an interesting collection of uniforms, arms and equipment, all neatly displayed in dioramas and showcases. Prime among them are two full-size dummies of mounted cavalrymen. Entrance is through the former classroom of the small school attached to the chapel, now renovated to house a cafeteria.

In the grounds of the château, to the right of the museum, are vestiges of two more **craters**. The late Baron de Vinck preserved and landscaped these into a beautiful garden. He told me that the site of the old château, of which nothing was left, was marked by two trees which survived and the stump of a third. After the baron's death, the modern château was sold and, after a spell as a hotel, it now stands empty and neglected.

East of Hooge, the Menin road was heavily fortified; the Germans built a subway beneath it which remains today an obstacle for the modern builders. Almost hidden at the edge of the road near the entrance to Bellewaerde Safari Park, is the **King's Royal Rifle Corps Memorial** close to the site of their action.

Hooge Château, used by the British in 1914 and the Germans in 1915, stood beyond the tree in the centre of the picture *(right)*. **Bellewaerde Lake is in the background. (RC)**

Hooge Crater Cemetery with its symbolic crater by the Cross of Sacrifice.

Clapham Junction with 18th Division and Gloucestershire Regiment Memorials.

Captain Brodie's private memorial in Glencorse Wood.

The Princess Patricia's Canadian Light Infantry Memorial at Westhoek.

Continue for 1 km up the Menin Road as it curves to the right and climbs upwards; it straddles the location of the **Tank Grave** where in 1917 fourteen tanks sank beneath the glutinous mud as they were disabled in the attack on Polygon Wood. At the crest is the famous **Clapham Junction**, another notorious position, with the woods of **Stirling Castle** on the right. Here also is the obelisk of the **18th Division Memorial**, whilst on the left is another, that of the **Gloucestershire Regiment**. Both obelisks mark positions of particular interest to the respective formations. The 18th Division was much involved here in 1917 operations; the 1st Bn. Gloucestershire Regiment participated in the 1914 battles for Gheluvelt and the 2nd Battalion was heavily engaged here in 1915. Stirling Castle (the château which served as HQ for the 7th Division in October 1914) was so named by the Argyll and Sutherland Highlanders in 1915 when they had a depot here. Further along the Menin Road, in the distance on the right, are the woods of **Dumbarton Lake**; in front of them, are those of **Château Herentage**, both hotly contested. For years, the memorial of the 2nd Bn. Worcestershire Regiment was on the façade of a small villa on the opposite side of the road, marking their deeds here and at Gheluvelt. Today, it is at the latter village (*see page 47*). Next, also on the left, is **Inverness Copse** with its **mine craters**, now pretty pools.

At the first crossroads at Veldhoek at the end of the woods, turn left (Waterstraat). In about 1 km, we reach **Black Watch Corner**, near a cluster of cottages close to the new motorway bridge. This was the site of the great fight of the Royal Highland Regiment and the Cameron Highlanders with the Prussian Guard in November 1914. **Polygon**

Wood is just on the other side of the motorway. However, do not cross the bridge, but turn left (Oude Kortrijkstraat). From here, two routes present themselves around Glencorse and Nonnebosschen Woods. Straight ahead, the roads climbs the eastern flank of the Bellewaerde Ridge, skirting the southern edges of **Glencorse Wood** on the right, and passing the **site of FitzClarence Farm** on the left. About ½ km beyond the wood, a sharp turn right (Frezenbergstraat) leads to Westhoek. As we pass beyond Glencorse Wood, Nonnebosschen Wood comes into view behind it.

Alternatively, the first right hand turning on Oude Kortrijkstraat (Nonnebossenstraat) skirts the eastern edges of **Nonnebosschen Wood**, now with Glencorse Wood beyond it. Much of this region is being developed into a residential area with service roads to the houses in the woods. Nonnebosschen and Glencorse Woods were the scene of heavy fighting in 1914 and 1917. Here on November 12, 1914, Brigadier Charles FitzClarence, VC, was killed leading the survivors of the 1st Guards Brigade in the counter-attack on the Prussian Guard. This gallant soldier, after whom FitzClarence Farm was named, was known to the troops as 'GOC Menin Road'; his name is on the Menin Gate Memorial right at the top of Panel 3.

Cart tracks and paths still pierce the woods but are not suitable for cars. From Oude Kortrijkstraat, a private road runs into Glencorse Wood. As it emerges at the wood's northern flank in about ½ km, the soft curves of the Bellewaerde Ridge come into view ahead; Nonnebosschen is on the right. (The same spot can be reached from the Nonnebosschen road by taking the first path into the wood after passing the last of the new

villas.) In this quiet, peaceful area, once the scene of hectic activity and devastation, is the lone **memorial to Captain Ewen J. Brodie** of the 1st Bn. Cameron Highlanders who was killed in Glencorse Wood on November 11, 1914.

Regain Nonnebossenstraat and, in 1 km (with the motorway running parallel on the right), turn left towards Westhoek, crossing the **Bellewaerde Ridge** and part of **Frezenberg Ridge**, scene of fierce fighting in 1915 and again in 1917. Here, the trenches were obliterated by withering artillery fire, leaving a shell-pocked desert. Among the regiments which stubbornly defended this region was the famous Canadian unit — the **Princess Patricia's Canadian Light Infantry**.

At the road junction in **Westhoek** (where the two routes around the woods reunite), turn right on to Frezenbergstraat and in ½ km left on to Princes Patriciastraat. Half a kilometre down this narrow lane on the left stands the unusual **Memorial to the PPCLI** — a maple tree encircled by a stone seat. It was dedicated and unveiled in 1958.

Return to Westhoek and turn left in the village to cross the motorway and, in about ½ km, turn right to approach **Polygon Wood**. At the first corner of the wood, turn left into a long, straight, narrow road (Langedreve) which clings to the edge of the famous wood. Before 1914, the Ypres Military Riding School — the Polygon — was situated here and also the Belgian Army's old firing range which ceased to be used in 1870. The old butts, a large mound on the north-east side of the wood, still remain.

In October 1914, the wood, as it lay in the front line, was the scene of very heavy fighting and was attacked by the Prussian Guard. On October 24, 1914, the Northumberland Hussars were in action here, the first Territorial unit to be engaged. Despite terrible casualties, the British held on and retained the area until May 3, 1915 when, in the wake of the gas attack, the Germans overran it. On September 27, 1917, the 5th Australian Division retook the wood.

In about ½ km along the edge of the wood, now a leisure park, will be seen the entrance to **Polygon Wood Cemetery** on the left and, on the right, the glade leading to the **Buttes New British Cemetery** and the **New Zealand Memorial to the Missing** and, crowning the mound of the old Butte, the **5th Australian Division Memorial**.

In the wood are the remains of several concrete shelters built by both sides during its occupation. The type of ground here made trenches difficult to dig and maintain and, by 1918, when the Australians evacuated it during the spring advance, only a few shattered tree trunks were left from the pulverising fire which had rained down on it. The bunkers were the only cover remaining.

Polygon Wood. The Australian Memorial and Buttes New Cemetery.

Continue round the corner of the wood, following the road into open country. Turn right (Kruisbierboomstraat) and bear right at the next junction. At **Reutel** (2 kms), take the left turn to **Beselare**, joining the N303. Beyond the village, **Polderhoek Ridge** (Poezelhoek) rises to the right off this road. The **château** was razed to the ground in 1917 having served both armies as headquarters. Now the whole region has been altered by the access roads for the autoroute. In 1¾ kms, at the Nieuwe Kruiseke junction, take the small road to the right signposted Gheluvelt to climb up to the village in 1 km along the edge of the château park. This road formed part of the route of 1st Division in 1914.

As **Gheluvelt** (Geluveld) is approached, the **old windmill** is on the left, now almost hidden by trees, but with a lane leading to it. A reproduction of the original, and itself in much need of repair, it shelters the **Memorial of the South Wales Borderers**. Here also is the **2nd Bn. Worcestershire Regiment Memorial** removed from its old position on the Menin Road (*see previous page*). The entrance to the château is just to the right, behind the church beyond the small village square. Here, during First Ypres, the 2nd Worcesters counter-attacked after the 2nd Bn. Welsh Regiment in front of the village (i.e. near the mill) and the 1st Bn. South Wales Borderers were driven out of their trenches and forced to withdraw into the château grounds on October 30, 1914. In the counter-attack, the Worcesters penetrated the captured village, driving the Bavarians before them and at the same time rescuing the South Wales Borderers in the park. The gallant actions of these men on October 31 stemmed the advance and barred the road to

Gheluvelt Château, the Worcesters' battleground in October 1914.

the west. Although the village was finally taken by the Germans, the stand of the 1st Division enabled the British line to be withdrawn without interference. The Worcesters' counter-attack from the château grounds was inspired by Brigadier-General FitzClarence, VC, of the 1st Guards Brigade. The château was hardly damaged during the war, even in the action recapturing the ruined village on September 28, 1918, and it is one of the few large mansions in the Salient which looks much as it did in 1914. It is now owned by the Belgian Nobility Foundation and on occasion is open to the public. The interior is very gracious and beautiful, providing an elegant background to official events.

Continue to the crossroads with the Menin Road (a dangerous place still) and go straight over to descend the ridge south to **Zandvoorde** (2½ kms). The importance of Gheluvelt, as it strides the main road at the highest point of the ridge, can be appreciated very well from here. Zandvoorde, on a hill, commanded a vital crossroads in 1914. The slope up from Zillebeke (to the right) was

the site of the charge by the Household Cavalry on October 26, 1914. During the next few days, other squadrons of the Household Brigade manned trenches in the village and the outskirts despite massive artillery fire which plastered the slopes. When the German XV. Armeekorps took the village, they found two complete British cavalry squadrons with their machine guns, dead or dying in one meadow. On the eastern edge of the village, at the back of a garden on the right of the Ten Brielen road (Komenstraat), is the tall column of the **Household Brigade Memorial** erected on the site of the place where Lord Worsley's body was found at the end of the war. (Today, he lies buried in Ypres Town Cemetery.) This marks the centre of the position held on October 31, 1914.

Some little way down the slope, nestling into the hillside on the right, is the **Ten Brielen German bunker**, for years the only example bearing still the original ground cover. It was built in 1916, and is engraved with the name of the unit and date.

The memorials by the replica mill.

The Worcestershire Memorial.

The Household Brigade Memorial.

The Ten Brielen bunker at Zandvoorde erected by the German 3. Kompanie, Arm.-Battailon 27. Built in 1916, and restored in 1988.

Return to Zandvoorde and take the first left-hand road (Houtemstraat) for Hollebeke. After descending the slope for about 1 km, turn right and immediately left again. After crossing the Bassevillebeek, a small stream, there is a **cluster of bunkers** on the left and, on the right, behind the farm at the T-junction (at the end of Klijtgatstraat) is a small mound in an orchard. This is the **site of Hollebeke Château**. The village of **Hollebeke**, on the Ypres—Comines railway line and canal, was another of the hotly-contested positions in 1914 and 1917.

At the junction, turn right and, just before the railway viaduct, right again. The road runs parallel to the railway and in the embankment are several **bunkers and concrete shelters**. After crossing the stream again, turn left under the railway. The modern village of Hollebeke is on the left on the Comines road. It was entirely destroyed but, unlike the château, it was rebuilt.

Turn left. Almost immediately on the right is the ruin of **Lock 6bis** of the old **Ypres–Comines Canal**. This is also the eastern entrance to the leisure area, **Palingbeek Park**. The woodland beyond the lock stretches away to the west, along the canal and the hills on either side, right through to the site

Hollebeke. This is the site of the château which was entirely destroyed by the war. (RC)

These German bunkers and concrete shelters can still be seen today set into the railway embankment at Hollebeke, on the opposite side to the village.

The old ruin of Lock 6bis on the Ypres–Comines Canal, Hollebeke.

of **The Bluff**. The trenches of the 14th Light Division on this narrow ridge were captured by the Germans in February 1916 and re-taken by the 3rd Division on March 2. In July 1917, the enemy blew a mine under it, but failed to capture the ground. It was given up in the spring of 1918, but regained by the 14th Division on September 28.

It is possible to walk from Lock 6bis the length of the canal to Spoilbank, along Kingsway (*see page 52*) and into Ypres near the station. Little remains to record the many operations which took place along this part of the canal but towards the western end at the Bluff there are several mine craters, now duck ponds, which recall the protracted mining operations of 1915 and 1916. To reach the main entrance and car park of Palingbeek Park, turn back north up the road to Ypres, with **Battle Wood** on the right, and take the first road on the left. This comparatively-new road, which follows an avenue of trees, terminates in a large car park in the middle of the park. A short distance from the car park is now a modern complex of an information and study centre for the nature

reserve and café where once were bunkers and trenches. Nothing remains of the bunker on which the iron railings from the White Château gates were used for reinforcement. In the ravine and along the crests there are some reminders of the war — old brickworks from the canal, mine craters which are now ponds, and broken hillsides. New paths take the visitor through this sanctuary today. Hidden beyond the woods on the southern flank, is the **White Château**, or **Bayershof** as the Germans called it, for a long time a German base. Although the track remains, there is no public access to the château today and the Dammstrasse — the German name for the drive up to the Chateau from Warneton, which they had turned into a fortified position (*see page 54*) — can no longer be reached from the canal. Among the many trenches which crossed and re-crossed the canal between the car park and the Bluff were the famous **International**, **Impudence** and **Imperial Trenches**.

Return to the main road and turn left. Take the next turn to the right. Signpost for Hill 60. On the right, in private grounds, is

the **Caterpillar position and crater**. Across the railway and on the right is **Hill 60**.

This hillock was created in the 19th century when the railway was built. The low mound formed from the spoil from the cutting, some 230 metres by 190 metres wide, was called 'Côte des amants' or 'Lovers' Knoll'. On top was rich, loamy clay; underneath came seven metres of firm, dry sand separated from the hard, underlying blue clay by a very wet two-metre layer of quicksand. This then was the problem which was to face the infantry, the artillery and, most important, the mining companies of the engineers of the French, British and German armies during four years of bitter fighting.

Early in November 1914, at the end of the battles of First Ypres, the cavalry under General Byng was dug in on the forward slopes, following the famous charge of the Household Cavalry at Zwarteleen on November 6. Then the French XVIème Corps d'Armée relieved the British and the French support troops on the hill until the German 39. Division captured it on December 10. It was then established as a strategic

CATERPILLAR CRATER

GERMAN BUNKER

HILL 60

14th LIGHT DIVISION MEMORIAL

1917 CRATER

AUSTRALIAN TUNNELLERS' MEMORIAL

QVR MEMORIAL

1915/16 CRATERS

The famous Hill 60 and the Caterpillar mine crater at Zwarteleen have been preserved more or less as they were left in 1918.

observation post, giving the Germans excellent views over the British lines to Ypres.

In the same month, preparations commenced to regain the summit and Lieutenant Bruyeat was ordered to undermine and blow up the enemy fortifications on the crest. The Royal Monmouthshire Royal Engineers were brought in to assist in the mining which was completed in the spring of 1915.

In February 1915, 28th Division, II Corps, took over the line from the French. The officer in charge, Major J. Norton-Griffiths, was one of the most colourful characters of the period, an eccentric but brilliant officer. One of his quirks was to use his own Rolls-Royce, adapted for military purposes, to travel around the battle area. Special mining companies were only then in the process of being formed and when, in April, the 5th Division relieved the 28th, the original mining parties were retained and reinforced by the new 171st Tunnelling Company, RE.

Five chambers were excavated and charged; the northern pair with 2,000lbs of powder each, the central pair with 2,700lbs

each, and the southern one with 500lbs of gun cotton. As this last mine was very close to the German workings, it was not fully completed in order to avoid detection by the enemy. The 13th Brigade, who relieved the 15th Brigade on the night of April 16-17, 1915 in the line directly opposite Hill 60, were to carry out the initial attack following the explosion of the mines.

At 7.05 p.m. on April 17, after a very quiet day, the mines were blown in two pairs followed by the single one at ten-second intervals. One hundred and fifty of the enemy and two REs were killed in the explosions. Immediately, the first artillery barrage began by the 15th and 27th Field Artillery Brigades and the 9th Heavy Artillery Brigade, with two French and three Belgian batteries supporting them. At the same moment, 'C' Company, 1st Bn. Royal West Kent Regiment, stormed the hill followed by the 1st/2nd Home Counties Field Company, RE, and, with complete surprise, gained the crest of the slope and took the craters. Casualties to the storming party were light as the German garrison was

overwhelmed. Another company of the West Kents and two from the 2nd Bn. King's Own Scottish Borderers came up and began to consolidate the position. At this time, the 2nd Bn. Duke of Wellington's Regiment was in support near Zillebeke and the 2nd Bn. King's Own Yorkshire Light Infantry was in reserve. The machine gun section of the Queen Victoria's Rifles followed the first storming parties onto the crest.

A little after midnight, the KOSB began to relieve the West Kents but, before this task was completed, the Germans launched three counter-attacks. Previously, there had been some wild artillery firing but, as these infantry attacks approached the craters in which the defenders were dug in, their fire became more accurate. Each counter-attack was repulsed by the extraordinary fine machine gun and rifle fire.

The Duke of Wellington's Regiment relieved the West Kents and KOSB at 8.30 a.m. to face heavy shelling and close fighting all day. The attacks by the Germans had won the right-hand sector by the railway cutting, but the tiny salient on the crest remained in

14th Light Division Memorial, moved in 1978 from Railway Wood to Hill 60.

The memorial to the 1st Australian Tunnelling Company.

Queen Victoria's Rifles Memorial, Hill 60, rebuilt after Second World War damage.

British hands. At 6 p.m., the Duke of Wellington's, supported by the KOYLI, counter-attacked and won back the whole hill. That night (18-19), the 15th Brigade relieved the 13th Brigade. The 15th Brigade (1st Bn. Norfolk Regiment, 1st Bn. Cheshire Regiment, 1st Bn. Bedfordshire Regiment and 1st Bn. Dorsetshire Regiment) with the 1st Bn. East Surrey Regiment (14th Brigade) was attacked and, with the Bedfordshires, were first in the front line.

On the evening of the 19th, the QVRs (13th Brigade) moved up in close support. It had been a fairly quiet day but, on the 20th, furious fighting broke out again and continued on the 21st. The 1st Bn. Devonshire Regiment (14th Brigade) relieved the two front-line battalions that day. By now, the hill was unrecognisable: the top gone in the mine explosion, the trenches had disappeared and the craters were a mass of debris and corpses.

On the 19th, the British accounts claim that the Germans used gas shells in the artillery bombardment although this is not confirmed in the German archives. The German 4. Armee records say it was on April 20 that 60 gas shells were fired at the hill. It is probable that the gas detected on the earlier date came from the cylinders dug into the hill ready for attack but, up to then, unused.

The hill remained in British hands until, on the evening of May 1, a gas attack was launched on the 1st Dorsets (15th Brigade), the 1st Devons (14th Brigade) and the 1st Bedfords (15th Brigade). This was the first occasion that a gas attack failed to achieve its object, for the British battalions, although suffering heavy casualties, held on.

On May 5, when the Duke of Wellington's (15th Brigade) were again holding the hill, another gas attack was launched. On this occasion, the gas was released on a favourable wind along the British lines. This attack affected a great length of the line and the advancing Germans were able to get a foothold on the lower slope. Before reinforcements could arrive, a second gas attack was mounted, this time on the 1st Bedfords and the 6th Bn. King's Liverpool Regiment. In the evening, after a further gas attack, the 13th Brigade were ordered in to counter-attack and regain the hill but, although some KOSB did reach the top, they were pushed back by fire from the Caterpillar.

Another attempt to regain the hill was made by the KOYLI on May 7 but it was a failure, all the men taking part being either killed or taken prisoner. The Germans were in full possession of the hill; they fortified it and retained it until June 1917. In the two

The remains of a Hill 60 bunker near the rim of the large crater.

This bunker on Hill 60 built during the First War also saw service in the Second.

periods of fighting, and the comparative lull between them, the 5th Division suffered casualties of over 100 officers and 3,000 other ranks.

In the months following the great May battles, the main struggle went on underground. Deep mining began in August 1915 by 175th Tunnelling Company from an entrance in the bank of the railway cutting some 220 yards behind the British front line. It was to pass 90 feet below the surface. In April 1916, the 3rd Canadian Tunnelling Company took over and mines were commenced on the Caterpillar as well. After

Hill 60 (Queen Victoria's Rifles) Museum.

a long underground struggle between the miners of both sides, the Hill 60 gallery was finished in July 1916 and charged with 53,500lbs of high explosive. In October, the gallery under the Caterpillar was also completed and 70,000lbs of explosive was placed there. In order to achieve this, the German main gallery had to be destroyed by a camouflet.

In November 1916, the 1st Australian Tunnelling Company took over the maintenance of these mines. This entailed fighting above and below ground to keep the enemy from discovering the galleries and charges.

The two mines were to be the most northerly in the long chain of 24 mines which were being prepared for the attack on the Messines Ridge. In the event, only 19 were blown. It was at 3.10 a.m. precisely on June 7, 1917 that these exploded with a tremendous shock, similar to that of an earthquake. It was felt even in London and other places in England.

Immediately after the mines had been fired, and almost before the earth ceased to heave, the entire artillery force of the Second Army opened a three-pronged barrage on the German lines. Fifteen minutes later, at Hill 60, the men of the 69th and 70th Brigades, Yorkshire Bns. attacked the hill and gained the feature with few casualties and no trouble.

The craters which were left after the eruption can still be seen today all along the line of the Messines-Wytschaete Ridge (the southern arc of the Salient) — most of these are small ponds now used by farmers. In 1917, the Hill 60 crater was 60 feet deep and 260 feet wide at the rim, and the Caterpillar position disappeared into a hole 90 feet deep and 334 feet wide at the brim. The German 204. Division, which held the two positions, lost 10 officers and 677 men killed by the explosions.

The following Victoria Crosses were among the many awards for gallantry in the Hill 60 operations: Lieutenant G. R. P. Roupell, 1st Bn. East Surrey Regiment, for his magnificent example of courage and devotion on April 20; Private E. Dwyer, 1st Bn. East Surrey Regiment, for gallantry in bombing and assistance under fire to wounded comrades; Second Lieutenant G. H. Woolley, 9th Bn. London Regiment (Queen Victoria's Rifles). He was the first Territorial officer to receive the VC which was awarded for defence on the night of April 20-21 when, for a time, he was the only officer on the hill; and Second Lieutenant B. H. Geary, 4th Bn., attached 1st Bn. East Surrey Regiment, for conspicuous bravery and determination on April 20-21.

Hill 60 can be visited today as it is in the care of the Commonwealth War Graves Commission. Immediately over the railway bridge, beside which a small **monument**

recalls the death of two members of the French Resistance here in World War Two, is a small car park. Overlooking this is the **14th Light Division Memorial**, which in September 1978 was moved here from Railway Wood where it had suffered from subsidence and as local needs required the land for development. Alongside is the shrapnel-pocked **1st Australian Tunnelling Company Memorial**.

The area immediately to the northwest of the railway bridge was called **The Dump** by the British soldiers. Supplies to The Dump were manhandled to the line from Ypres and 'Ypres Express' was the name given to the trucks on their return journey as the gradient was just sufficient to travel at a greater speed with less effort.

The entrance to the hill, which bears no resemblance to its original shape, is just beyond the Australian memorial. Here too is a simple **stone** carved with an eloquent account of the horrific happenings of this historic place.

Paths lead through the shell-pocked ground up to the **Queen Victoria's Rifles Memorial**. Although badly damaged in the Second World War, it has been re-created on its old site despite the loss of the original stone mounting. On the crest of the hill stands a concrete **bunker** showing British as well as the basic German work whilst the remains of other strong points are scattered over the hillside. There are vestiges of five of the small **craters** and, although the walls have crumbled and the base filled in, the high crater, usually dry, still dominates the scene. Vestiges of dugouts and trenches can be seen in the far bank of the railway, below the Caterpillar, and to the west of The Dump.

Trench museums, which existed until just after the Second World War, were situated on the left-hand side of the road opposite the

Queen Victoria Rifles Memorial. They no longer exist. Over the years their owners changed, as did the layout of the trenches! However, in 1985, the Menin Road War Museum moved to the café across the road from the hill. Now called the **Hill 60 (Queen Victoria's Rifles) Museum**, the rooms off the café and upstairs contain some most-interesting items, weapons, badges, equipment and battlefield debris; the larger examples are outside the café parking area — much came from the old museum at Sanctuary Wood.

Continuing straight on, in ¼ km we reach the road junction in **Zwarteleen**. Turn right towards **Kleine Zillebeke**. In ½ km, take a left turn through the woods (Pappotstraat). **Shrewsbury Forest**, to the right of this road, contains several bunkers reminiscent of actions fought here in 1917. It is possible the area will become another leisure park, enabling visitors to wander along the glades off which some trenches are visible. Emerging from the trees, the road crosses open ground sloping up to the Menin Road. **Mount Sorrel**, **Observatory Ridge** and **Hill 62** rise to the left. This is **Green Jacket Ride**.

In about 1 km, the road from Zillebeke joins from the left and, soon after, the woods of Mount Sorrel are seen beyond the fields on the same side. In the nearest copse is one of the mine craters. On the right is **Clonmel Copse**. This road was criss-crossed with trenches and was the scene of many actions, particularly those in June 1916, when the Canadian Corps captured Mount Sorrel and Hill 62. Again in the summer of 1917, this area was the focal point of much action. Since the removal of the circlet of tall maples around the Canadian Memorial on Hill 62, a fine view of it can be seen.

Some 4 kms from Kleine Zillebeke, the Menin Road is regained at Clapham Junction. Turn left to return to Ypres (6 kms).

Hill 60 railway cutting at The Dump.

German bunker in Shrewsbury Forest. (RC)

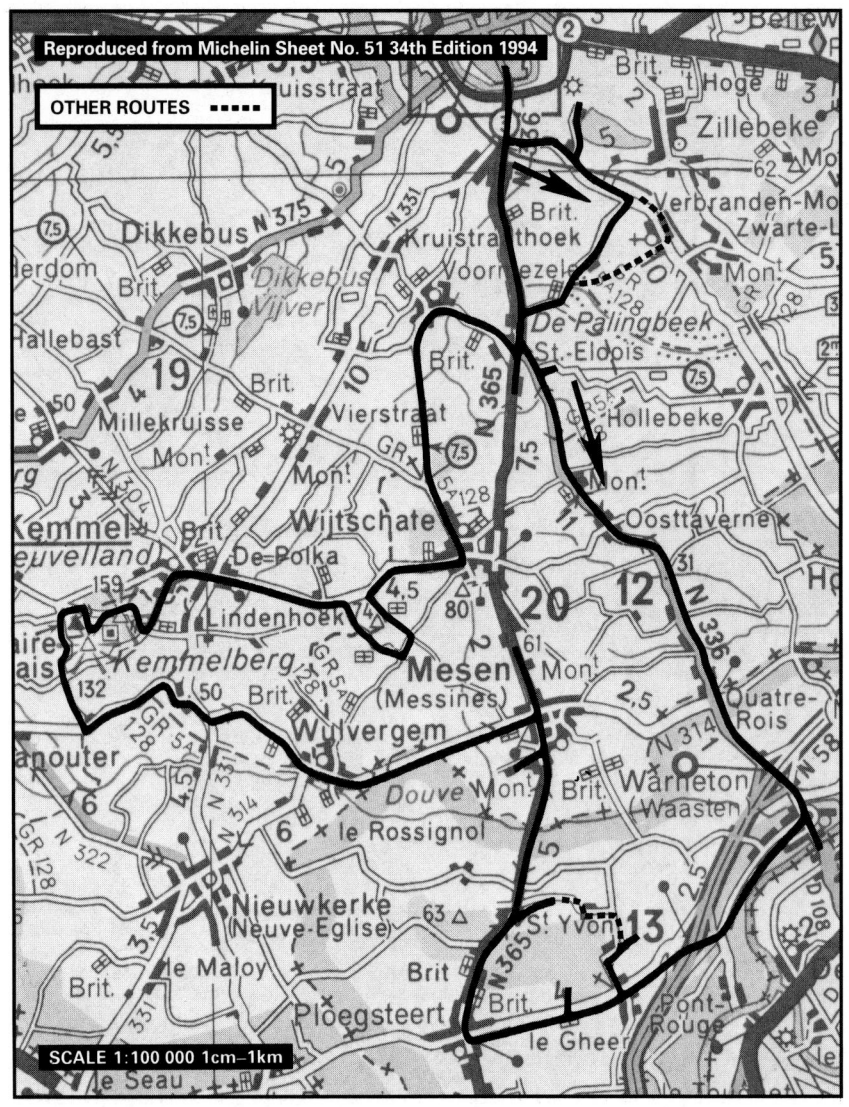

SCALE 1:100 000 1cm=1km

ROUTE IV The South-eastern Sector

Depart from Ypres by Rijselstraat and the Lille Gate (Rijselpoort), the N365, perhaps the most frequented route of the war. Due to the exposed position of the Menin Gate exit, most departures for the front were this way.

After ½ km **Shrapnel Corner**, a most unhealthy spot as it was constantly shelled by the German artillery and then by long-range guns in 1918. Before the railway crossing, turn to the left.

Then 1 km to **Transport Farm** and, next to it, **Railway Dugouts Cemetery**, both on the right. In the embankment behind the cemetery there are still vestiges of the shelters and

dugouts. On the left is the drive leading to **Zillebeke Lake** and restaurant. A promenade encircles this artificial lake so well known to the BEF as a prairie of mud and blasted trees. It is the older of the two great ponds (the other is Dikkebus) formed in medieval times to provide for Ypres. In 1295, there was already a fish pond in existence. From 1914 onwards, there were positions all along the banks and many an artillery unit was bogged down in the mud. It was often a target for the German guns and one English gunnery officer found a unique method to keep his men from being hit: take them out into the lake in an old punt he had found and sit there somewhat damp but in moderate

safety. Only a few remnants of the shelters which were in the vicinity of the lake now remain on the north banks.

The eastern end of the lake is almost in Zillebeke village and the woods and fields in that area were the scenes of many terrible battles. In October 1914, the Irish Guards fought a lengthy action in holding Zillebeke Wood. Then, in 1915, the Cavalry Corps were in action and, in July, the 18th Division held the sector whilst the artillery were always there. In April 1918, the British withdrew from Zillebeke, returning in September. **Hellblast Corner** (*see page 43*) is at the easternmost end of the lake.

Retrace the way to the road and turn left, crossing the railway. At the next road junction, note the **British Demarcation Stone** on

the left. In a short distance, the road on the right leads in 2 kms to **Chester Farm** and **Spoilbank Cemeteries** and the western entrance to **Palingbeek Park** (*see page 48*).

However, by continuing for ½ km or so, **Verbrandenmolen** is reached and a very narrow road between the houses on the right (Verbrandemolenstraat) leads down to a group of cemeteries on the fringe of **Ravine Wood**. These are **Woods Cemetery**, made originally by the 1st Bn. Dorsetshire Regiment and 1st Bn. East Surrey Regiment in April 1915; then, higher up amid the fields, **1st DCLI (The Bluff) Cemetery**, dating from the same period; and lastly, up a track on the edge of The Bluff, **Hedge Row Trench Cemetery**. Soon afterwards, the road swings round sharply to the right and rejoins the Spoilbank road.

Almost beside Spoilbank Cemetery is a section of the old Ypres–Comines Canal which was known as **Kingsway** to the BEF. Alongside it are two ruined locks and dugouts. Our road bends slightly round, roughly following the 1917 front line.

Shrapnel Corner road junction was a regular target for German artillery seeking easy targets of opportunity.

Zillebeke Lake was the scene of bitter fighting. This is Hellblast Corner at the eastern end. (RC)

BUS HOUSE CEMETERY   TO YPRES

TO MESSINES

MINE BLOWN 7.6.17

BRITISH DUGOUT

MINE BLOWN 27.3.16

MINE BLOWN 27.3.16

MINE BLOWN 27.3.16

WARNETON   TO HOLLEBEKE

The St Eloi Craters still straddle the old German lines of 1916-17. More than 30 British and German mines were fired in the area, six of the British, totalling 73,000 lbs, being fired together. The largest single mine of 95,600lbs was blown here on June 7, 1917. The German dugout on the Messines road has fallen to housing development since this aerial photograph was taken in 1976.

Another ¾ km and we join the N365, turning left for the **St Eloi** (St Eloois) crossroads. Many actions were fought in this neighbourhood but it is chiefly remembered for the protracted mine warfare which began when the Germans fired their first mine in March 1915. This was part of their counter-attack to earlier British attacks for this position. In the ensuing 12 months, the British fired 13 mines and 29 camouflets and the Germans 20 mines and 2 camouflets. Six of the British mines were fired on March 27, 1916 and consisted of a total of 73,000lbs of charges but, due to the artillery barrages, it was impossible for the troops to consolidate the position and it was retained by the Germans. During the mine explosions heralding the Messines Ridge attack of June 7, 1917, the largest single charge was 95,600lbs of ammonal blown at St Eloi (by the 1st Canadian Tunnelling Company) and this time the position was captured by the 41st Division.

Two of the largest of these **craters**, now ponds (both from mines blown on March 27, 1916), lie on the left of the Hollebeke road which forks left off the Warneton road; both are private and used for fishing or swimming. The one nearest the road is surrounded by reeds and the other by tall trees and hedges. In the apex of the Messines and Warneton roads is the third crater, but it is not easily visible from the road. On the higher ground behind it is an excellent example of a **British shelter**. Its roof still retains the elephant iron (large corrugated iron) lining. The bunker is easily visible from the Messines road, on the left-hand side behind No. 17, one of several new villas built along this stretch. Prior to the new houses being built, there also remained a German concrete dugout in front of the British one, but this went in 1991 when the site was developed.

The 1st DCLI Cemetery with Woods Cemetery on the horizon.

A British concrete shelter, still retaining the iron lining, built near the large crater formed on June 7, 1917. Its nearby German counterpart has now gone.

The Dammstrasse — the drive to the Bayershof German HQ on the horizon — with a British dugout in the foreground.

The Oosttaverne crossroads — scene of two 19th Division actions. The 19th Division's sobriquet derives from its divisional emblem — a butterfly.

Take the N336, the Warneton road. The country now undulates along gentle ridges and the road passes through pleasant meadows. A short distance, about 1 km along on the left, the ridge of the **Dammstrasse** can be discerned. The Dammstrasse is the old drive to the **White Château** occupied by the Germans and known to them as the **Bayershof**. The ridge was also a strong fortified position. In the field before it is another good **British dugout**.

In 1 km, **Oosttaverne crossroads** with the **19th 'Butterfly' Division Memorial** on the left. This marks the site of the division's attack during the Messines battles of July 7, 1917 and later their great fight during the Battle of the Lys in April 1918. **Oosttaverne Wood Cemetery** is on the right, with two **bunkers** in the fields behind it. The road runs through rolling country, then descends into the Lys valley in 3 kms.

After 4 kms, pass under the new Lys ring-road before entering **Warneton** (Waasten), dominated by its huge church, the cathedral of the Lys. The opening thrusts of the First Battle of Ypres were made here when the 1st and 2nd Cavalry Divisions were driven back towards Messines, attempting to gain the Lys on October 20, 1914. Warneton remained in German hands until September 1918 and was one of their most important forward bases. The Belgian frontier station (now closed) is on the north end of the bridge. Turn right in the centre of the town for Ploegsteert and in about 2 kms, at Basseville, bear right and pass under the ring-road again.

In 1½ km, we reach **Le Gheer**, a hamlet on the eastern edge of Ploegsteert Wood. It was

the scene of much activity in 1914 when the 4th Division carried out a brilliant counter-attack before withdrawing.

Before visiting Ploegsteert Wood, an interesting deviation presents itself from Le Gheer. About 1 km up the road leading off to the right from the hamlet (and bearing right at the Y-junction of Le Pelegrin), in the beet field on the left, is the **site of the mine explosion of July 17, 1955**. Here, 38 years after the event, one of the mines laid in 1917 for the Messines attack exploded when a willow tree was hit by lightning during a severe thunderstorm. Fortunately, there were no casualties. The crater has since been filled in and no trace of it remains.

Return to Le Gheer and turn right. **Ploeg-steert Wood — Plugstreet Wood** to the British Army — Ploegsteertbos in Flemish, and now Bois de la Hutte et du Gheer, is on the right.

For the greater part of the war, the wood was a relatively quiet area which every now and then burst into violence. In October 1914, the British 1st Cavalry Division captured it, but later it was again retaken by the Germans who were not finally dislodged until mid-1917. Although the lines had been fortified on April 10-11, 1918, in the big advance the Germans captured it completely. The British recaptured it in their advance in September. For four years, it provided comparative shelter to some one million men in its labyrinth of glades and connecting trenches. Among those who squelched in the mud here was Bruce Bairnsfather, drawer of the famous 'Old Bill' caricatures, who at one time had a billet in a cottage in St Yvon.

Today, the wood is again a pleasant forest and game reserve to which access can be had in a number of locations denoted by large notice boards bearing a map of the woods and the tracks to which access is permitted. The main entry in the north is from Prowse Point Farm Cemetery; that in the south used to be Hunters Avenue, about ½ km from Le Gheer. Here is the verderer's house but the avenue is no longer a right of way or marked on the map. The nearest official entry is from a new road about ½ km further west. As the wood is a game reserve there are times when

access is forbidden, particularly in the spring when the birds are nesting; and in the autumn, when the guns are out. It would be highly dangerous to venture into the woods without the gamekeeper's knowledge.

Hunters Avenue was one of the main arteries and almost at the edge of the woods there, hidden in the undergrowth on the left, is the first of a line of eight **concrete machine gun shelters** which are visible through the trees. Nowadays, they provide excellent cover for the breeding birds. The most famous bunker in the wood, **Blighty Hall**, or Hole, is not easily reached, being in a muddy area some 15 metres to the left off the glade some 150 metres along it. A first aid post shelter, it retains the bench for stretchers but is nearly always flooded or very damp and muddy. Although it is possible to reach the cemeteries which lie deeper inside the wood from Hunters Avenue, they are much more easily visited via the northern entry.

Continuing westward from Hunters Avenue towards Ploegsteert village along the southern flank of the wood, clusters of farm buildings can be seen amid the fields to the left. One of these is **Lawrence Farm**, painted by Winston Churchill when serving with the 6th Bn. Royal Scots Fusiliers. **Lancashire Cottage Cemetery** is on the left, next to the site of **East Lancashire Cottage**, one of 29th Division's positions when they cleared Ploegsteert of the Germans in September 1918. (The present-day cottage is a new one.) **Hampshire Farm** is opposite, in the fields to the right of the road, before the ever-growing outskirts of the village are reached and the road to the new entry and parking area for the wood.

Ploegsteert was badly damaged during the war, being so close to the front line for so long. Behind the church in the village grave-yard are a few early graves, several being Hampshire Regiment casualties of 1914. Turn right at the crossroads and travel along the long straight road to Hyde Park Corner. In ¾ km, on the right is **Strand Cemetery**, named after a glade which emerges from the wood beside it. A little further on, behind a house on the same side, three **British bunkers** can be found in good repair.

The site of the mine explosion near Le Pelegrin. Laid in 1917, it exploded in 1955!

Left: **Hunters Avenue as it was in 1917. (IWM)** *Above:* **Over 75 years of growth have transformed the scene entirely — this is Hunters Avenue as it appears today.**

Ploegsteert Wood, which was quickly dubbed 'Plugstreet Wood' by the Tommies, still displays the relics of both sides.

Above left and *right:* **Two of the eight German machine gun posts mouldering in Plugstreet Wood today.**

Blighty Hall (some say Blighty Hole) — a British first aid post in Plugstreet Wood — still retains the bench for the stretchers.

Deep in the wood is Rifle House Cemetery which took its name from a small building, the ruins of which still stand nearby.

A trio of British dugouts on the edge of Ploegsteert Wood near Hyde Park Corner.

British Lions guard the Ploegsteert Memorial to the Missing and Berks Corner Cemetery Extension at Hyde Park Corner.

Peaceful reflections at Prowse Point Cemetery, with Ploegsteert Wood behind. (RC)

Vestiges of the Château de la Hutte on Hill 63.

In another ½ km, **Hyde Park Corner** is reached. On the left stands the **Ploegsteert Memorial to the Missing** and **Berks Corner Cemetery Extension**. On the right is the original **Berks Corner Cemetery**. The memorial, unique in the Salient, is a circular temple with pillars guarded by two lions, one snarling in defiance whilst the other gazes serenely into the distance. The memorial was designed by H. Charlton-Bradshaw, and the sculptor was Sir Gilbert Ledward. The missing from the battles of Armentières, Aubers Ridge 1914, Loos, Fromelles 1915, Estaires 1916, Hazebrouck, Scherpenberg, and Outtersteene Ridge 1918, in all 11,447 men, are listed on the panels within the colonnade. Seventy feet in diameter and 38½ feet high, it was unveiled on June 7, 1931 by the Duke of Brabant. Over 380 men lie in the cemetery beneath the flowering cherries.

The N365 begins to climb up towards **Château de la Hutte** and the high point, **Hill 63**, on which was a vital 'O-Pip' defended by the 25th Division in April 1918. The château, now only a few crumbling ruins which lessen as the years pass, is in the fields on the left. Often the road surface is subject to subsidence due to the presence below of crumbling subways running into the hillside.

On the crest of the hill, the right turn at the crossroads leads to St Yvon and **Prowse Point Cemetery**. This is some 400 metres from the road junction and is the only one in the area to be named after an individual, and marks the site of a gallant stand by the Hampshire Regiment and the Somerset Light Infantry in the actions for St Yvon in October 1914 at which Major, later Brigadier-General, C. B. Prowse, DSO, was the hero. Later, in the Wieltje sector near St Jean, his brigade was in violent action again and the farm there was called Prowse Farm (*see page 38*).

In November 1914, the northern edge of the wood was in the sector of the 2nd Bn. Dublin Fusiliers and the 1st Bn. Warwickshire Regiment, many of whose casualties lie in the cemetery. Beside the Cross of Sacrifice, the hollow, often a pool, is part of the old front line. Within the cemetery walls, the roof of a **concrete shelter** can be seen in the grass.

The official access to the Ploegsteert Wood group of cemeteries is down the often very muddy lane beside the cemetery. The first is **Mud Corner Cemetery**, then in the wood lies **Toronto Farm Cemetery**, which, despite the name, contains only Australians, whilst the former is mostly of New Zealanders. **Ploegsteert Wood Cemetery** and **Rifle House Cemetery** are found by following the main track through the wood for some 500 metres or more. They are two of the most beautiful in the Salient (strictly speaking, they are beyond the southern limit of it). The latter takes its name from the small fortified building whose remains are nearby. Some of the trees here are those which survived the holocaust.

By continuing along the road, past **St Yvon** and turning right at the T-junction in 1 km, a circuit of the wood can be made. This is one

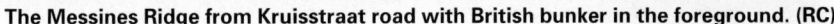

The Messines Ridge from Kruisstraat road with British bunker in the foreground. (RC)

of the sectors involved in the 'Christmas Truce' of 1914. Just past the junction and 200 metres up the small road to the left, two clumps of trees, one on either side of the road, mark the site of two craters from the 19 mines blown for the Messines attack of June 7, 1917. They are, left, **Factory Farm Crater** and, right, **Trench 122 Crater**, both fired by the 3rd Canadian Tunnelling Company.

Return to the N365 and continue northward, with the panorama of the **Messines Ridge** ahead. The road descends into the valley of the River Douve before climbing up the ridge.

Messines (Mesen) was taken by the Württembergers from the exhausted Cavalry Corps on November 1, 1914, the latter having held them at bay for over 48 hours after weeks of continuous fighting. The London Scottish made a gallant but fruitless charge in their support only a matter of hours after arriving in the Salient, being the first Territorial infantry unit to go into action. From the town's ruins, the Germans dominated the British lines until the Battle of Messines, the successful British attack of June 1917 so well remembered because of the series of simultaneous mine detonations with which it opened.

As early as August 1915, the first plans for the mining of the Messines-Wytschaete Ridge were made, and for 18 months work was under way in the tunnelling and laying of charges in a number of sites on an arc from Hill 60 to east of Ploegsteert Wood. During this time, the enemy blew a number of mines and camouflets, thereby interrupting the work of the British companies, but all the difficulties were overcome and finally all was ready for the big 'blow'. This was to precede the artillery barrage by a fraction and then the main attack by General Plumer's II Corps was to follow. The Inspector of Mines watched the explosion from a dugout at

Kemmel and he described the scene in his diary as the 19 mines, containing nearly 1,000,000lbs of high explosive, erupted on June 7, 1917:

'3.10 a.m. A violent earth tremor, then a gorgeous sheet of flame from Spanbroekmolen, and at the same moment every gun opened fire. At short intervals of seconds, the mines continued to explode; period which elapsed between first and last mine, about 30 seconds. I found it difficult to concentrate on looking for the mines, there was so much going on, and the scene, which baffles description, developed so quickly that my attention was distracted. . . . The earth shake was remarkable, and was felt as far as Cassel.'

The New Zealand Division captured Messines and the 16th Irish and 36th Ulster Divisions captured Wytschaete. By June 10, the German salient west of Messines and Wytschaete had been straightened from east of Hill 60 all the way down to east of Ploegsteert Wood. It was the first outright British victory since the war began.

In 1918, Messines changed hands several times before it was finally captured on September 29 by the 30th, 31st and 34th Divisions clearing the entire ridge.

Messines Church can be seen from far and wide and, from it, there is an expansive panorama to the south. The only church in the area with a crypt, this was all that was left of the building and in it today can be seen vestiges of the battle. The church was also the subject of a number of water-colour drawings by a German infantryman, one Adolf Hitler.

As our road runs into the village, there is a sharp left-hand turning, along which is the

Messines church, showing the windows of the crypt which was at one time a billet for Gefreiter Adolf Hitler.

New Zealand Memorial Park. In the park a white **monument** (similar in design to that at 's-Graventafel — *see page 39*) rises between the evergreen trees and shrubs. At the edge of the park, overlooking the Douve valley and the hills of Flanders, are **two German pillboxes** — part of the Messines line of defence. One of them can be entered, but the entrance to the other has now been filled in.

The Messines **Hôtel de Ville** is in a red-brick house overlooking the wide square with its English-looking bandstand on the right of the main road to Ypres. Inside is a small but excellent **War Museum** which commemorates the actions of the New Zealanders in particular, but also those of the Australians and London Scottish. It was the work of the then-Mayor, the late Dr

Left: **The New Zealand Battle Memorial for 1917 on the Messines Ridge which was captured on September 29, 1918,** by the 30th, 31st and 34th Divisions. *Right:* **One of a pair of German bunkers in the New Zealand Memorial Park.**

Above left: **The London Scottish Memorial and,** *above right,* **Four Huns Dugout, both on 'Whitesheet' Road outside Messines.**

Roger Lambelin, OBE, the Town Clerk and the local schoolmaster, M. Constandt. It is usually open during office hours in the summer. A short distance north on the Ypres road, on the right-hand side, is the **Memorial to the London Scottish**, the first TA infantry unit to be engaged in the war; about 1 km further on, and by the left-hand side of the road, stands **Four Huns Dugout** bunker, now partly ivy-grown.

Return to Messines and take the Wulvergem road to the right. Just before the road drops down into the valley, the **Messines Ridge British Cemetery** and the **New Zealand Memorial to the Missing** are on the left. The New Zealand memorial is a Cross of Sacrifice and around the base the panels bear the names of all those with no known grave from every regiment and corps of the New Zealand Expeditionary Force. In the cemetery is a pavilion similar to the New Zealand memorial at Polygon Wood.

After sweeping down the valley and over the **Kraaienberg** and then down again, **Wulvergem** is reached in 3 kms. The village was close to the front line in 1914 and was on the receiving end of a gas attack in 1916. In 1918, it was taken in the German spring advance but recaptured in September.

The Dranouter road rises out of the Douve valley and along the undulating slopes of the **Monts des Flandres**, crossing the direct road to Kemmel (N331) 2 kms from Wulvergem. After another 2 kms, turn right on to a smaller road (Smijterstraat) to begin the climb up to the western slope of **Mount Kemmel**.

In ¾ km crossroad; continue straight ahead when in 1 km the road forks. Take the right fork and then, almost immediately at the crossroad, take the right-hand turn to climb steeply up to the summit of Kemmel, passing the **French Ossuary** on the right just prior to the final, steep 50 metres. The mass grave, with the Gallic cock crowing above, is the last resting place of 5,294 unknown French soldiers.

At the summit of Mount Kemmel is the **French Memorial**. This site, 159 metres high, was chosen for the monument to the Frenchmen who died in Belgium, particularly on the Mount in 1918.

The column is 18 metres high and was originally capped with a stone representation of a poilu's helmet crowned with laurel. In the front of the column is a Winged Victory. The memorial was unveiled in September 1932 by Général Petin. During a thunderstorm a few years ago, the pillar was hit by

The New Zealand Memorial to the Missing and the Messines Ridge British Cemetery.

The French Ossuary on the slopes of Mount Kemmel.

The French Memorial unveiled by Général Petin on the crest of the Mount.

lightning and damaged. When it was re-erected, the helmet was not replaced. The memorial stands in a clearing on the thickly-wooded summit. As we drive on, we pass the entrance to the **Belvédère Hôtel**, the Hostel-

lerie Mont Kemmel, from where there is a magnificent view across to Neuve-Eglise and the Douve valley.

Emerging from the trees into the open, the **Café Belvédère** is found on the right. This

Belvédère Café, Mount Kemmel, is on the site of the original building used as an OP and destroyed in 1918.

Kemmel village green was the location of many British Army band concerts enjoyed by the troops in quiet periods.

has been rebuilt on the site of the original one which was destroyed in the battles of 1918. On April 25, the French division then holding the line was dislodged by a strong German force using air support. From the **look-out tower**, one can see the same view as was had by Sir John French and other senior officers of the British Army during their long occupation. The hill remained in German hands, a constant and dire threat to Allied communications, until the end of August and the advance of the American 27th Division; on August 31, the British 34th Division finally drove the Germans from it. On the walls of the café are some interesting before and after illustrations of the battles.

The road descends steeply for another 500 metres when it comes to a junction where we turn left. The descent is less steep but goes on for 1 km into the village of **Kemmel**, passing the entrance to **Warande Château** on the right. On the village green will be seen another **bandstand**. Here, the military bands of the British Army, including the Brigade of Guards, played to the troops during lulls in the fighting in this area.

The **Kemmel information office** is on the right just before the road junction where we turn right and continue straight over the next crossroads (a dangerous one).

In 2 kms, pass through the hamlet of **Vroilanhoek** (municipality of Wytschaete). Take the second road on the right to reach the largest of the Messines 1917 mine craters, **Spanbroekmolen**, now the **Pool of Peace**, the property of Toc H. In 1930, Lord Wakefield purchased this, the **Lone Tree Crater**, at the suggestion of Tubby Clayton who thought that one of the huge craters should be preserved (*see page 11*). The pool has a rim some 4 metres deep; it is 27 metres in depth, with a diameter of 129 metres. The charge used (fired by the 171st Tunnelling Company) was 91,000lbs of ammonal which had been laid through a tunnel 513 metres long. On the northern side of the lip is the remains of one of the German pillboxes and

from here one can get a good idea of its importance and wide field of fire. At the entrance to the pool grounds stand two mountain ash trees, planted here by HRH Princess Alexandra and the Hon. Angus Ogilvy on April 22, 1985 to commemorate the 70th anniversary of Toc H.

Continue along by the farm on the right behind which is **Lone Tree Cemetery** where the men of the Royal Irish Rifles killed in the mine explosion lie, having left their trench too early. At **Kruisstraat** crossroad, groups of willow trees mark three more of the 1917 **mine craters**. Turn left at the crossroad and

Kruisstraat's craters provide excellent fishing today.

Comparison between original and current CWGC signposts at Lone Tree Crater.

Spanbroekmolen, the Pool of Peace. This was the Lone Tree Crater formed on June 7, 1917 and purchased in 1930 for preservation by Toc H.

Peckham Crater, Wytschaete Ridge *(above)* — **from here King George V viewed the battlefront in July 1917. (IWM) As near as can be ascertained, this is the same spot today** *(right)*.

left again to pass the lane to **Spanbroek-molen Cemetery**. Just out of view as the road regains the main road for Wytschaete, the smaller pool of the **Peckham mine crater** is on the right. This is the one visited by King George V in July 1917.

Turn right for Wytschaete and after ¼ km, on the left, is the site of **Maedelstede Farm** and the large **crater** named after it. About ½ km north of this are the two **Petit Bois mine craters**, another two of the series of 19 formed on June 7, 1917.

Wytschaete (Wijtschate) is entered 1 km further on with the **16th Irish Division Memorial Cross** on the left just before the **Wytschaete Cemetery**. 'Whitesheet' to the Tommies is on a high ridge, even higher than that of Messines in places. In 1914, the village changed hands at least three times before the Germans captured it and began to convert it into a formidable fortress. In the II Corps attack of June 1917, the 16th and 36th Divisions captured the ruins. Among the casualties was Major William Redmond, the Irish Nationalist MP, who was mortally wounded and taken to the divisional dressing station at Dranouter and then to the 36th Division Dressing Station nearby, where he died. His body was then taken to Locre hospice, which was the base of 16th Irish Division, and he was buried in the garden. Now, his grave is beyond the walls of the convent, just outside Locre Hospice Cemetery *(see page 18)*. Wytschaete was lost again in the spring advance of 1918, being recaptured on September 28.

Turn left in the centre of the village, leaving the church on the right and in 1 km across the ridge, at the fork in the road, take the right-hand route to pass beside **Grand Bois** and then on the right is **Bois 40** or **Cronaert Wood** to the Germans. Once, behind the café at the far end of the wood, there was a trench museum which included two of the **German bunkers** of this vital position, renovated trenches and narrow-gauge railway. Since the death of the proprietor, it has become derelict and overgrown, but the bunkers are still there. Adolf Hitler reportedly served here in 1917 and revisited it on his tour of Flanders in 1940.

Passing **Cronaert Chapel Cemetery** on the left and crossing the Bollartbeek at the bottom of the slope, and keeping to the right at the next fork, in about 2 kms **Voormezele** is reached. This village was just behind the British line at St Eloi and was captured after very heavy fighting in April 1918. The ruins were recaptured by the American 30th Division on August 31.

At the road junction, turn right and, after 1 km, **Bus House Cemetery** is passed on the right. It was named after an estaminet, originally on the same side of the road, but

The edge of one of the Maedelstede Farm craters.

The 16th Irish Division Memorial above Wytschaete village — 'Whitesheet' to the Tommies.

The grave of Major William Redmond just outside Locre Hospice Cemetery. He died in the convent nearby.

WYTSCHAETE

ROAD TO KEMMEL

PETIT BOIS

PETIT BOIS CRATERS

which was later moved to the north side. The café had got its name from an old London omnibus of the 'B' type which had broken down in no man's land after bringing troops to the front in 1914. Legend has it that it was one of those used by the London Scottish.

In 250 metres, we are back at **St Eloi** (*see page 53*). Turn left and after 1 km cross the old **Ypres-Comines Canal** at the western end

of **Kingsway**. A **Demarcation Stone**, with a British tin hat capstone will be seen on the left of the road.

A few metres further up on the right is **Langhof Farm** with its fine cluster of **seven British dugouts** on the island site of the old château. Access to these dugouts is only with the farmer's permission as they are used for his cattle.

About ½ km further on is **Bedford House Cemetery**. It is one of the largest in the Salient and has plots of 1939-45 graves as well as 1914-18. The ruins of the old **Rosendal Château** and its moats remain as integral parts of the cemetery. The drive is, in fact, in the same place.

Ypres is another 3 kms; we enter the town by the Lille Gate.

A group of seven British concrete shelters on the site of Langhof Château.

The ruins of Rosendal Château in the grounds of Bedford House Cemetery.

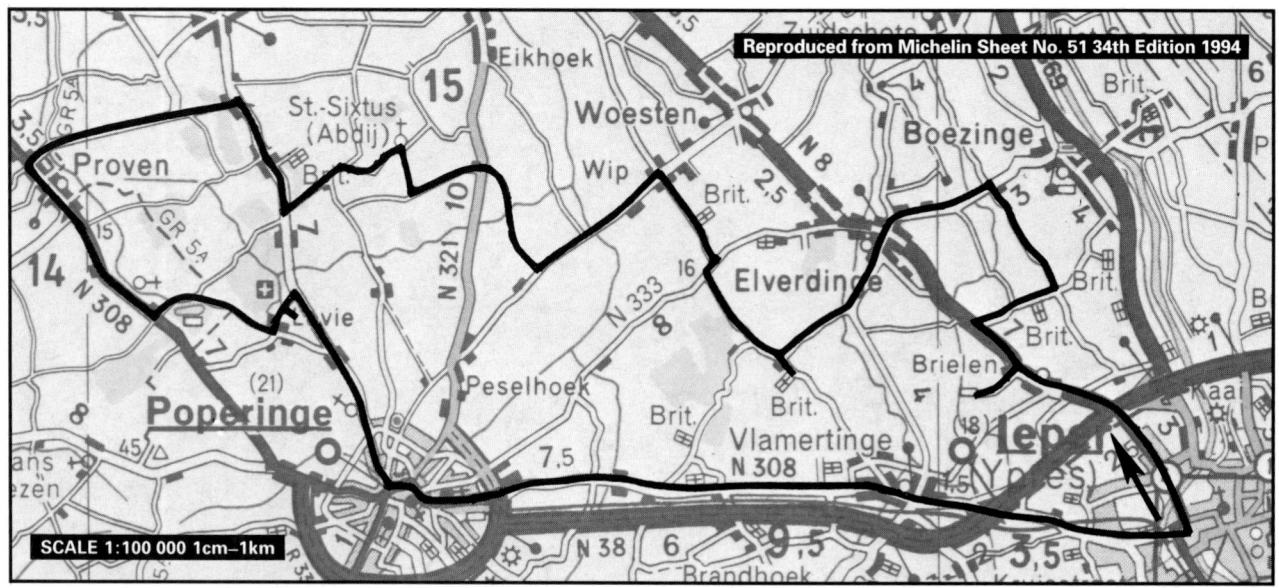

SCALE 1:100 000 1cm–1km

ROUTE V   The Rear Areas

Leave Ypres by the Maarschalk Haiglaan, the N8. After 1½ km, on the right, is the gate of the **Reigersburg Château**. This Victorian mansion was used as a base right from the early days of the war. The Royal Field Artillery were in occupation in October 1914 and there are still notices on the walls relating to their presence.

Brielen is 1 km further on. A small village, it was totally destroyed in the war, mainly by artillery fire, as it was a forward base for the troops in action around the Yser Canal. Just outside the village, the long straight drive to **Château de Trois Tours** bears off to the left. This château was utilised as an HQ by the 1st Canadian Division in 1915 and thereafter many divisions and brigades occupied it. By some amazing chance, although the village was destroyed, this house bore a charmed life

and was hardly damaged. After the war, it became an hotel the proprietors of which specialised in Salient tours. The Ypres League and the Anglo-Belgian Union had their headquarters here. Today, it is privately owned. A **concrete shelter** survives in the grounds, close to the gate.

After 1 km, **Dawson's Corner** — the name given to the camp here by the Canadian Corps in 1915. Turn right and, after 1 km, we reach **Solferino Cemetery** on the right. The French had a dressing station and camp here, later taken over by the BEF. In ½ km crossroads, turn left, then after another 1½ km crossroad, turn left again. **Bleuet Farm Cemetery** is ¾ km further on the right. Bleuet Farm was a dressing station during the 1917 battles.

In 1½ km, we reach **Elverdinge**. This large village was the centre of many camps, training areas, stores, hospitals and facilities for

leisure. It was almost entirely destroyed by artillery fire being a known British base and road junction. A light railway ran to it from Poperinge carrying casualties and supplies. The **château**, constantly used as an HQ, was also damaged and was accidentally burnt on one occasion when a cook let some fat catch fire. Later, it was rebuilt. The château is in a private park behind the church, but it is not easily visible from there. However, a good view will be had when leaving the village. Near the church is a **Belgian Krupp 95mm gun**, recently reinstated after conservation.

Leave the village by the Vlamertinge road, keeping the church to the right, and drive past the château grounds. An entrance on the right gives a good view of the house set far back. In 1 km, take the right fork crossing the stream and through the meadows and beet fields which once echoed to the noise of camp life.

The Reigersburg Château was an early billet of the BEF, and inscriptions are in evidence today on the walls relating to its occupation by the Royal Field Artillery.

One such inscription can still be seen at the side of the door to the stables.

Above: **The fairy-tale Château de Trois Tours — haven to many divisions.** *Right:* **A bunker crumbles in the grounds.**

Another 1¼ km to a road junction, take the right-hand road. The farm at the junction, **Hospital Farm**, was a dressing station — the **cemetery** of the same name lies behind the farm. The entrance is a little way to the left. The light railway from Poperinge ran right beside it.

The next ½ km goes through the site of **Dirty Bucket Camp**, so named after a farm which was near the small road on the left. After 1 km crossroads, go straight over. **Canada Farm Cemetery** is about 1 km along on the right. There was a dressing station here between June and October 1917.

In ¼ km **Wip crossroads**. Turn left. Then 1¾ kms across the Poperingevaart and take the right-hand road (Bosstraat) in the direction of Eikhoek. In 1½ kms, we reach **International Corner**, a junction of the British and Belgian lines. The name is to be found on the walls of a barn in the farm here. Go straight over. At the next road junction — about 1 km — turn right to **Abdij St Sixtus**. This monastery, with its modern brewery producing the famous Trappist beer and its own very special mead, cultivates much of the area around here which was a very large camp. A dressing station and local headquarters were situated in the abbey buildings. The Cistercian monks aided the care of casualties brought here in 1915. It was said that a deserter from the Lancashire Fusiliers was brought here and tried after the gas attack of April 1915 and shot. The bullet marks survive on a wall of the inner courtyard which, however, is a part of the monastery closed to the public. During the Second World War, General Montgomery paused here briefly with his 3rd Division Headquarters prior to Dunkerque, leaving some personal belongings with the Abbot until his return in 1944.

Turn left before the abbey and, in ¾ km, bear left at the junction, then right at the factory. In 1 km, turn right, passing **Dozinghem Cemetery** (a name coined by British troops to sound like the local Flemish ones, similar to Mendinghem and Bandaghem Cemeteries — *see page 10*) on the right. After 1¾ km, still in this very flat, low-lying country of meadows, arable land and small woods, turn left and in 1 km join the main road, bearing left to enter **Proven** in 2 kms. This was a large village which was damaged by bombing and long-range artillery fire. It was the centre of many British activities and camps. There was an aerodrome here and a large supply depot which had light railway connections with Dunkerque and Poperinge.

In the centre of the village, turn left onto the N308 and, in 3¾ kms, turn left for **La Lovie**. Here, in a beautiful park, is the large **château** which from May 1915 was a British HQ of importance. As it was the centre of the training and stores region, the house was well placed. VI Corps were here until February 1916, followed by XIV and VIII Corps. Then, in June 1917, the Fifth Army arrived and had their HQ in the house until November 1917. In July 1917, King George V used the house as one of his bases during his visit to the front that month. During 1918, various divisions and corps used its facilities, among them the 41st, 49th and 34th Divisions. August 30 saw II Corps in possession until the end of the operations to clear the Salient commenced when they moved up. The château was hardly damaged. Today, the house and its surrounding buildings are used as a school and training centre for mentally handicapped. In the vicinity is the site of **Lovie aerodrome**, used by the scout squadrons in 1918. Return from the park to the right and the back road into Poperinge. In 3 kms **Poperinge**, and thence 12 kms to Ypres. (*For a description of Poperinge and the route from there to Ypres, see pages 10-12.*)

Above: **Elverdinge Château used as a headquarters building.** *Right:* **The 95mm Krupp gun now on display.**

Although over 75 years old, this famous painted sign still remains to be seen.

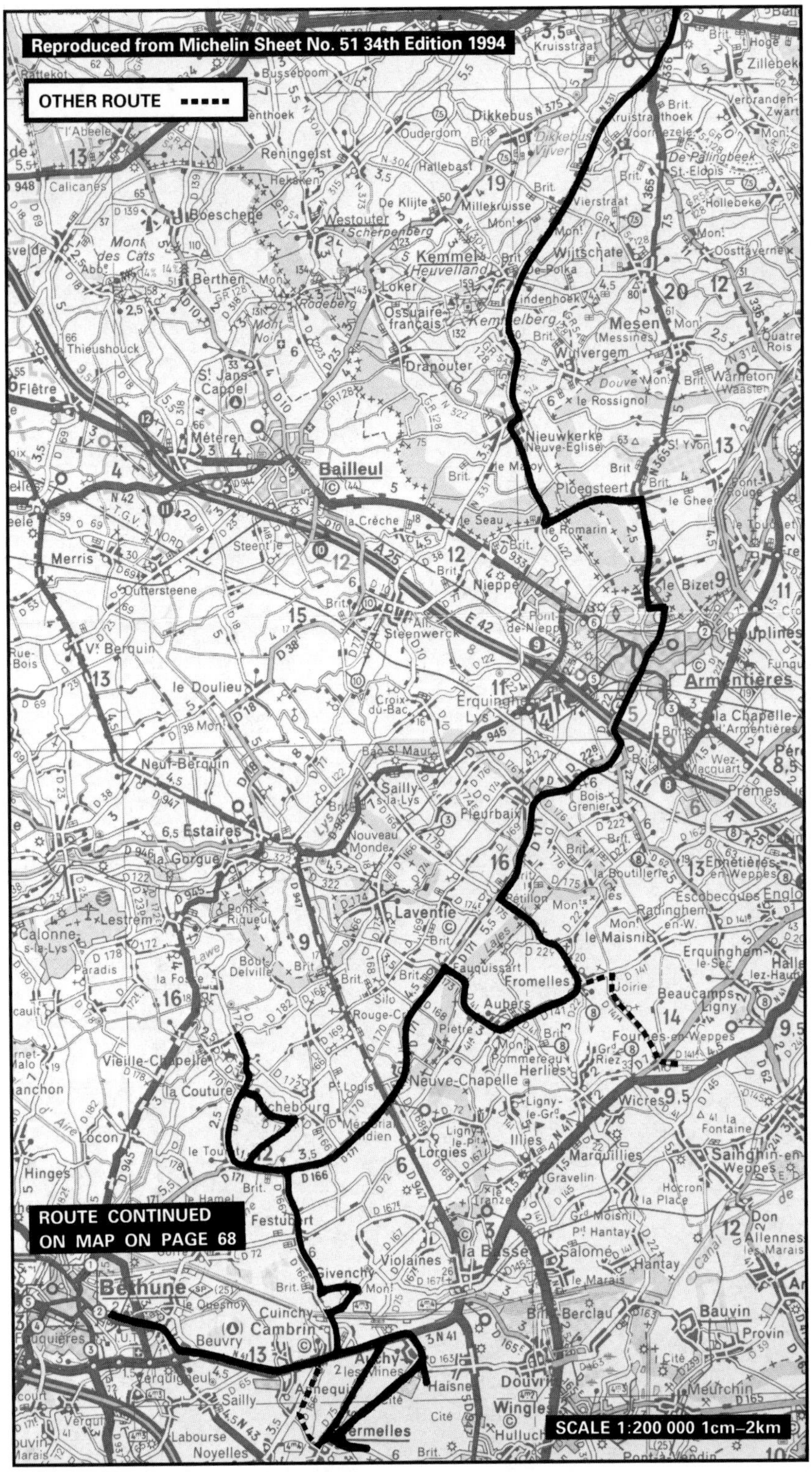

ROUTE CONTINUED
ON MAP ON PAGE 68

SCALE 1:200 000 1cm=2km

The road south

From Ypres to the French frontier at Le Bizet, the direct route is via the N365 and Messines, a distance of 19 kms. Via Neuve-Eglise it is 21 kms.

Depart Ypres via Lille Gate; at **Shrapnel Corner**, take the right fork immediately before the level crossing. Another level crossing is found directly after turning. **Ypres military barracks** are on the left — note the artillery pieces in the grounds. Cross the dry canal in the banks of which are remnants of trenchworks. The road travels through pretty country, at first quite flat but gradually, as Kemmel is approached, the landscape becomes more hilly as the **Monts des Flandres** are traversed.

Elzenwalle Château, an HQ in both wars.

After the crossroads of Kruistraathoek (4 kms), on the right **Elzenwalle Château**, an unusual construction of reinforced concrete with an open-ribbed dome. The **lodge house** is in the form of a concrete bunker, not unlike that of the Kronprinz in the Argonne area (*see page 144*). Behind the château is **Scottish Wood** and beyond that lies **Dickebush Lake** (Dikkebus). As the road rises to **Vierstraat** crossroads, another well-known copse comes into view, again on the right — **Ridge Wood**.

Shortly, on the left, is the **American Memorial to the 27th and 30th Divisions** who fought with the British Army in this region from August 18 to September 4, 1918. The memorial was erected in 1930. There are fine views of the Wytschaete Ridge and the wooded slopes. This section of the road was known as **York Road** and was much used for bringing up supplies. Another 6 kms further on, the edge of Kemmel village is reached; we continue straight on up to reach the next crossroad, **Lindenhoek**.

Wytschaete church crowns the ridge as seen from the American Memorial.

The Memorial to the US 27th and 30th Divisions near Vierstraat.

Armentières Grand Place and belfry.

VC Corner, Fromelles. Individuality is a cornerstone of British and Commonwealth principles in honouring war dead and this mass grave situated in the Australian Memorial Cemetery is very unusual. The names of each are inscribed in stone.

The Australian bronze relief map near VC Corner, one of several such memorials unveiled on the Western Front in 1993.

Neuve-Eglise from the Kemmel Road.

In 4 kms, we reach **Neuve-Eglise** (Nieuw-kerke). This village, a junction of many roads, was the scene of fierce fighting in April 1918 when it changed hands several times being defended by an exhausted 25th Division who were finally driven out on April 14. The British recaptured it on September 1.

Turn right into the village and, in the centre, left by the church and small **British cemetery**. The road soon begins to drop down into the Armentières-Bailleul plain with views of the **Rodeberg**, **Mont Noir** and **Mont de Cats** over to the right. Straight over the next crossroad. At the road junction 3 kms further on, turn left for **Ploegsteert** (*see page 54*) which is 2 kms down the road. At the main crossroad in Ploegsteert, turn right.

The frontier station at **Le Bizet** is 2½ kms away.

Proceed into **Armentières** by the new road, D22a, sweeping behind the old road and through new residential areas. At the junction with D33, turn left into **Place Général de Gaulle** with the gothic-style town hall and **war memorial** on the left.

Armentières was, and is now again, a flourishing industrial town whose industries are centered around both brewing and linen manufacture. In 1914, the town was briefly occupied by the Germans before being recaptured by General Pulteney's III Corps on October 17. For the next three and a half years, being just behind the lines, it became closely connected with the British Army for whom it was a forward base and recreation centre. Although it was intermittently bombed and shelled during these years, it was barely damaged. In the Battle of the Lys in April 1918, the German 4. Armée attacked and seized the town on the 10th after severe fighting. General Plumer's Second Army liberated the town on October 2. By then, it was a heap of ruins, for the Germans had mined or destroyed all the main buildings and wrecked the factories before leaving. During the British occupation, the main square was called **Eleven O'clock Square**, as the hands of the Hôtel de Ville clock had stopped at this time during an early bombardment.

Leave Armentières via the rue de Lille and then the rue de Béthune, the D22, crossing the railway by the level crossing west of the station. Shortly afterwards, the motorway is crossed by a bridge. Continue on the D22b, passing under the new line of the TGV superexpress train, 5 kms to **Fleurbaix**. The road leads through rather nondescript country — the scene of bitter fighting in 1916 and 1918. Continue on the D171 for 3 kms to **Petillon** crossroads passing **Rue de Bois Cemetery**. Here, a diversion along the road to the left (D175/D22c) leads in 1 km to **VC Corner Australian Memorial and Cemetery, Fromelles**. This is a very unusual graveyard as it has no headstones. The dead were brought here after the Armistice from the surrounding battle zone. On July 19, 1916, the 5th Australian Division with the 61st South Midland Division attacked the Fromelles positions. Over 400 lie buried with the names of 1,298 Australians recorded on the **Memorial to the Missing** on the panels between the shelters. This is one of the very few **British mass burial plots**.

Some 200 metres further along the narrow road, on the left, are the remains of **four German bunkers** and, between them, is an **Australian Memorial Plaque** explaining their actions in this area. This is one of a series of identical bronze relief maps with explanatory texts unveiled in 1993 at places where the Australian divisions fought important actions. Similar memorials are now at Pozières, Bullecourt, Mont-St Quentin and Villers-Bretonneux, all further to the south. All are part of a larger project initiated by Dr Ross J. Bastiaan of Melbourne in 1987 and which also includes Australian battles from the Second World War.

Continue along the road, bearing left at the fork, to reach **Fromelles** across the flat low-lying fields. Join the D141 and turn right.

'Hitler's blockhouse' along the Fromelles–Aubers road.

Immediately on the right is the Mairie (Town Hall). In its attic is housed a small, but very interesting **war museum**, dedicated mainly to the actions of the Australians. For visits, apply at the Mairie office.

Take the next fork right, continuing on the D141, and in ¾ km, on the right, is a **German concrete shelter** where it is reputed Adolf Hitler spent part of his front-line service with the Bavarian Infanterie-Regiment List.

For those interested in Hitler's 1914-18 career, his rear-line billets were in a house in the nearby village of **Fournes-en-Weppes**, 5 kms down the D141a from Fromelles. During the Second World War, this house, at **No. 1345 rue Froidherbe**, was adorned with a large marble plaque in April 1942 identifying it as the Führer's billet of 1916. The plaque was taken down in 1944 by the owner of the house (and retained by him), but the fittings can still be seen above the door.

From the bunker on the D141, in 2½ kms, **Aubers** is passed through with its **ridge** away to the left. Go right on D41 for **Fauquissart**;

the **Bois de Biez** is on the right. Thus the southern boundary of the battle area of 1915 is crossed. Rejoin D171 and turn left. South of Petillon, the road follows closely the 1914-15 front line and nearby some of the incidents of the 1914 'Christmas Truce' took place. The area was strongly contested but there is little remaining today to indicate the destruction and devastation which the countryside suffered other than the scattered fragments of bunkers. **Mauquissart**, yet another front-line village, is to the east of the road as we approach **Neuve-Chapelle** in 3 kms. This was the scene of the first major operation involving the Indian Corps when on October 27, 1914, this formation was responsible for retaking the village which had been captured earlier in the German advance. Later, the Allies withdrew and, on March 10, 1915, the Battle of Neuve-Chapelle commenced with the Indian Meerut Division taking a major rôle in the attack and capture of the village by the 8th Division. Due to the inadequate preliminary

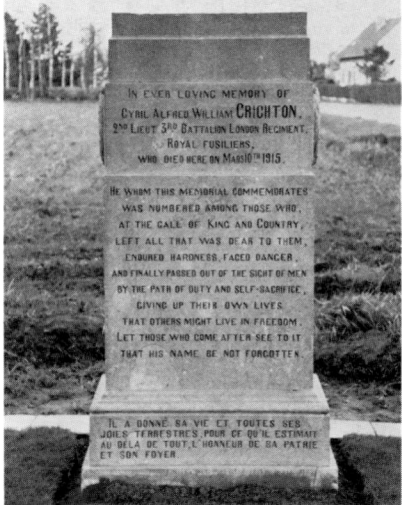

The graceful Indian Memorial at La Bombe crossroads, Neuve-Chapelle *above*, with the memorial to 2nd Lieutenant Cyril Crichton just outside it, *left*.

Portugal in France. *Left:* The beautiful entrance to the Portuguese Cemetery near La Bombe and the interior, *above*.

bombardment, much of the barbed-wire entanglements in front of the German positions remained uncut and caused heavy casualties, especially to the Middlesex Regiment and the Cameronians. By March 14, the front had moved forward just over 2 kms before it stabilised. In the Lys battles of 1918, the Portuguese Division held the ruins of the village.

Another 1 km and we reach the crossroads of **La Bombe**, the **site of the Port Arthur Salient** of the Indian Corps in 1915, commemorated in the **café sign** on the right. On the opposite corner is the fine **Indian Memorial to the Missing**. Designed by Sir Herbert Baker in completely-oriental style, 4,843 names are inscribed on the walls. A few yards down the D947 is the **Portuguese Military Cemetery** with its fine Manueline gateway. In the south-western corner of the cemetery is a small **museum room**. The **memorial chapel** across the road was added in 1975.

Above left: **The unusual Portuguese monument in La Couture.** *Above right:* **Le Touret British Cemetery and Memorial to the Missing.**

The almost-forgotten cavalry memorial at Vieille-Chapelle cemetery.

At Festubert, this British blockhouse, once a ration point and officers' shelter, was a comfortable home for a local resident from 1919 until her death in the late 1970s.

This road is the direct approach to **La Bassée**, 6 kms away. Completely destroyed in the Allied bombardments, it had been taken by the Germans in 1914 and, heavily fortified, it formed an extremely-strong bastion in their lines for over four years. It was taken by the Fifth Army under Lord Birdwood on October 2, 1918. The town is once again a thriving industrial area and it sprawls far outside its old boundaries. New roads have replaced the narrow busy ones of yore and recently a new ring-road has been instituted.

From Neuve-Chapelle, we remain on the D171 towards Béthune. As the Indian Memorial is passed, a **private memorial** will be seen outside the wall. This is to the memory of 2nd Lieutenant Cyril A. W. Crichton who died on these crossroads in March 1915 and now lies buried in **Le Touret British Cemetery**, reached after 3½ kms of rather uninteresting angular road. It was just behind the front of the Indian Corps in May 1915 in the battles of Festubert and Aubers Ridge. The cemetery dates from 1914 and the **Memorial to the Missing** is for those who fell in the battles of La Bassée, Neuve-Chapelle, Aubers Ridge and Festubert in 1914-15. The memorial was dedicated at the same time and day as those at Cambrai, Pozières and Vis-en-Artois in August 1930.

Just beyond the cemetery, a small road to the right leads to **Richebourg**, but before we reach the actual village, a left turn at the junction with the D170 brings one to **La Couture**. In front of the church is the **Portuguese Memorial** which commemorates their action here of April 9, 1918.

Turn left at the church, onto D169, then left onto D172. In the cemetery of the next village, **Vieille-Chapelle**, near the D182-

D172 crossroad, is a **memorial** for which I searched for many hours. It is that of the **1st King Edward's Horse** (The King's Overseas Dominions Regiment), a cavalry unit of the Special Reserve whose squadrons were used as divisional cavalry from early 1915 until in June 1916 they became a corps cavalry regiment. They served throughout the war in France and Flanders and were, I have always heard, a wild, hard-riding bunch. Their memorial was erected in the village after the war but with the changes in the road network and the widening that has occurred, it was moved for safety into the village cemetery . . . and almost forgotten.

Retrace the route past La Couture church, returning to **Le Touret** via the D169, noting the **house on the corner** at the junction. The sculpture surmounting it is one of a previous resident's works. Bas reliefs of French and Belgian leaders decorate the walls.

Turn left and, at **l'Epinette**, take the D166 on the right for **Festubert** 2 kms away. Festubert figured conspicuously in the October 1914 battles, in which the Indian Corps participated with Smith-Dorrien's II Corps, and later in the attacks on the Aubers Ridge on May 9-26, 1915. In 1918, the magnificent defence of Festubert and Givenchy in April checked the German advance in the Battle of the Lys, leaving the two villages and all their neighbours merely heaps of rubble. On the left of the D166, about ¼ km past Festubert church, is a **British bunker**. It has two chambers and an outside shelter and was a ration point and officers' dugout at the end of a light railway spur. From January 1919 until her death in the early seventies, it was the home of a Frenchwoman.

The 2 kms to **Givenchy** were among the most stalwartly defended positions by 55th

Division in the German attacks of April 9-10, 1918, and, despite all the enemy could do, the Lancashire units held out. The crossroads before the village is the famous **Windy Corner** with the **Guards Cemetery** just west of it. A left turn leads to the village centre on D167 and on a corner beyond the church stands the **55th Division Memorial**. On the

cross is the division's formation sign bearing their motto: 'They win or die who wear the Rose of Lancashire'. Here they did both.

Return to the D166 and cross the **La Bassée Canal** for **Cuinchy**, another front-line village devastated in 1915 and 1918. Heavy fighting here in January 1915 centred around the brickstacks, to the east of the village, where there is a **Guards Memorial**. Here and there, craters can still be discerned in the now peaceful area.

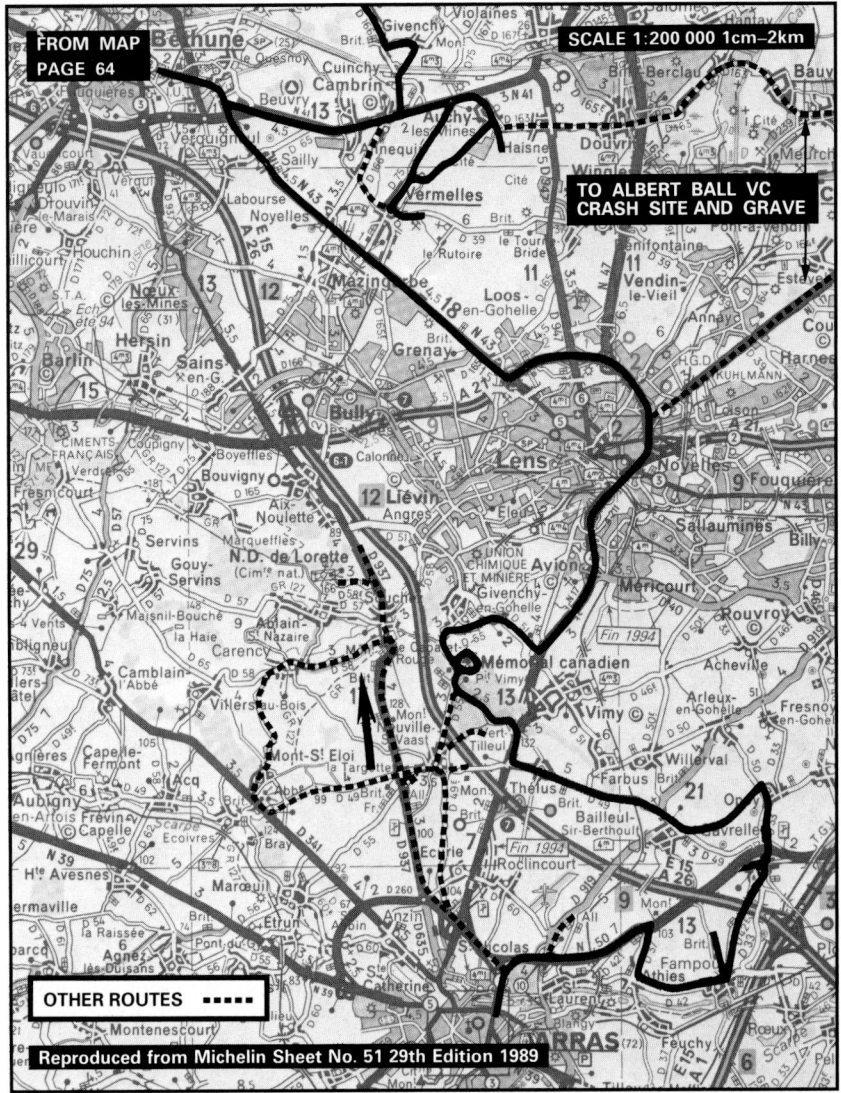

FROM MAP PAGE 64

SCALE 1:200 000 1cm–2km

TO ALBERT BALL VC
CRASH SITE AND GRAVE

OTHER ROUTES - - - - -

Reproduced from Michelin Sheet No. 51 29th Edition 1989

Further on is **Cambrin** (1 km), a straggling industrial village. At the junction with the main road, N41, a right turn takes you direct to Béthune, 8 kms distant. However, to visit the delightful Quarry Cemetery, from the vicinity of which an excellent view of the **northern half of the Loos 1915 battlefield** and the region of the Hohenzollern Redoubt can be had, turn left on N41 and head for **Auchy**, 1½ km away. In Auchy, turn right into the town centre and after about 1 km of straight, busy street, which is fairly narrow, it widens slightly near the Mairie. Turn right and then take the left fork and drive out of the built-up area along a straight, narrow road with small houses on the left and scrappy fields on the right for 1 km. At a road junction on the left, **Quarry Cemetery** is signposted along a muddy cart track. I strongly advise walking then along the ½ km to the cemetery, for the slippery clay track is a real car trap. The cemetery gate is on the local land level and steps lead down to the graves. Looking out from the gate, the area of the **Hohenzollern Redoubt** and **Fosse 8** (mine pithead) — both German strong points in the 1915 Battle of Loos, taken by the 9th Division on the first day, but lost again by the follow-up troops — lies before you: a flat plain criss-crossed now with electric pylons and in the distance the slag heap (**The Dump**). Sometimes, it is possible to discern the trenches in the beetfields around here, where such bitter fighting took place in 1915-16. Many of the graves in the cemetery are those of the dismounted cavalry who were engaged.

A more distant view of the redoubt is possible on the small road from Auchy to Vermelles (C6, not numbered on the map), from which the scene is laid out with just the gate and the roof of the cemetery pavilion visible over the fields. Turning left at **Vermelles** church on to the Hulluch road (D39), on the right just on the edge of the village, is the **46th Division Memorial Cross**.

The Hohenzollern Redoubt today from the fields between Vermelles and Haisnes.

Turning back into Vermelles, it is possible to join the N41 for Béthune at either Auchy by the D75, or via the D166 to Annequin.

Béthune. The ancient seat of the Counts of Flanders was fortified by Vauban in the 17th Century. The graceful Belfry, now standing in the centre of the Grand Place, was built in 1346. Most of the houses around the square have been rebuilt in the style of Flanders but those which originally clustered around three sides of the Belfry have not been replaced. As the centre of the mining villages and market gardens which abound in the locality, Béthune was a thriving town in 1914. For the next four years, it was an important British headquarters town subjected to intermittent bombardment between 1915 and 1918.

Quarry Cemetery, in a hollow of the Loos battlefield.

The Loos battlefield photographed from Dud Corner. British troops first used poison gas here on September 25, 1915.

From 1914 to 1915, the Indian Corps held the town which became an important railhead and billeting area for the rear lines, and a corps and divisional headquarters. In the German offensive of April 1918, a particularly-heavy bombardment almost destroyed the town. The great church of **St Waast** was a mere pile of ruins but the **Belfry** bore a

The houses surrounding the Belfry in Béthune were all destroyed.

charmed existence as only the top was dislodged, even the well-known gargoyles surviving intact. The top has been replaced in almost identical form but the great doors on the ground floor have been replaced with glass. In 1918, the 3rd, 51st and 55th Divisions successfully held the town which only partially fell to the Germans. The town was damaged again in 1939-45. The Town Museum, near the Gendarmerie, which had plans to open a section relating to 1914-18, has unfortunately been closed.

Leave via N41 which joins the N43 in 3 kms. The road crosses the plain dotted with mines and slag heaps, traversing the **southern sector of the Loos battlefield** which lies between the N43 and D947 (the old main road from La Bassée) and the new N47. The D947 can be reached from Loos by the D165 just on the north of **Hill 70**, the German strong point taken by the 15th Scottish Division on the first day and then lost again. Now there is a civil airfield and an enormous hypermarket on this part of the old battlefield whilst vestiges of the mine craters and trenches can still be discerned to the west of the hill.

In 10 kms, we reach **Dud Corner Cemetery** and **Loos Memorial to the Missing** who fell in the Battle of Loos in September-October 1915, and on the Lys, Estaires and Béthune fronts in April 1918. The names are recorded of 20,589 officers and men who fell.

The Battle of Loos, September 25 to October 19, 1915, was fought by the British I and IV Corps in support of Joffre's offensive

in Champagne. It is remembered today as the battle in which very heavy casualties were suffered by only partially trained troops and for the first use of poison gas by the British.

From the roofs of the two pavilions of the memorial entrance, a good view of the battlefield can be gained. It is also possible on a fine day to glimpse in the distance, north of Hulluch (on the D947), the site of the Hohenzollern Redoubt.

Continue for 4½ kms to **Lens**. This was the chief coal-mining town in France before the war almost entirely destroyed it. Now once more it is a thriving town and industrial area. However, most of the mines are now closed and the famous pit-head winding towers, so well known to the Tommy, are fast disappearing.

The Germans occupied Lens in October 1914 and, thereafter, set about fortifying it very strongly. It became the centre of a war fought from the warren of tunnels at many levels beneath the shell-torn ground. In August 1917, an Allied attack was launched from the north-west suburbs and Hill 70. The Canadian Corps forced their way through on a 2,000 yard front but the central part of the town held out. In spite of further attacks in September 1917 and January 1918, it was not until October 2 that the ruins were captured.

Lens is a very busy industrial town with complicated road systems so it is easier to join the C26 autoroute and proceed to the south-east following the signs for Arras and so bypass the traffic-choked streets.

The Loos Memorial to the Missing at the Dud Corner Cemetery, commemorating over 20,000 British officers and men.

The story and legend of **Captain Albert Ball, VC, DSO****, **MC**, is probably so well known that it is unnecessary to go into details here but it may be of interest to visit the **scene of his fatal crash** and **final resting place** whilst in this part of France. They are at Carnin and Annoeullin, villages which are perhaps most easily reached at this point in our route, by turning left on the N17 towards Carvin (10 kms) off the Lens bypass. Other possibilities are from Auchy (*see page 68*) by taking the D163/D39 via Douvrin and Bauvin (15 kms). Another choice is to use the A1 autoroute between Arras and Lille, leaving it at the Carvin-Nord–Libercourt turn-off (D954e), and proceed westward on to the D954 to Carvin.

In the centre of this busy town, go north-east on D925 for a short distance and then left on the D163/D41b reaching Annoeullin in 3½ kms.

Turn right to join the D41 on the edge of **Carnin**, crossing the flat farmland on which the Germans had a small airfield. Turn left on D41c driving for about 1 km. There is a solitary house on the left-hand side of the road and, some 30 metres beyond it, a grass track is seen in the field. It is not suitable for cars and it is only a short walk to the place where the grey **stone marker** stands some 15 metres in front of a small copse. This appears to be a composite of the original erected by his father made from two of the original stones which indicated the place where the aircraft fell — the third has disappeared. Today, this simple memorial is watched over by those who have inherited the traditions he and his fellows built so many years ago in No. 60 Squadron — still alive and well in the modern RAF.

Although Annoeullin and the other towns and villages hereabouts have grown, the immediate area around here can have changed little over the years. Maybe the lanes have deteriorated into paths and tracks but there has been hardly any development between these small fields and copse and the German Cemetery which can be seen on the far side of the field to the left of the copse. When the German airmen carried his body from the broken plane to lay him to rest, they traversed tracks which still cross the dull land to arrive at the cemetery entrance from the opposite end of the road used by cars.

From the crash-site follow the D41c into Allennes-les-Marais (1 km), and turn left for **Annoeullin**. After 1 km at the crossroad (traffic lights), turn left and in ½ km left again at the T-junction and follow the signs for the **German Cemetery**, where he lies among over 1,600 German (and some Russian) dead, and the Communal Cemetery, bearing left off D41 onto a cul-de-sac. This is the road which 200 metres beyond the cemeteries peters out into the track. Return to Lens, turning south on the C26 for Arras.

The Spirit of Canada weeps for her fallen countrymen. From Vimy Ridge, the view extends over the Douai plain towards Messines. The twin pillars of the Memorial itself stand on the summit of Hill 145.

After 6 kms, at **Noyelles**, the Arras road becomes the N17 but for the first 3 kms it is of motorway style. Soon after the complex of the Union Chimique et Minière at **Avion**, the road swings in a curve before the old road converges with it again below **Vimy Ridge**, thus providing a panoramic view of the twin pillars of the **Canadian Memorial** rising high above the wooded slopes of **Hill 145**.

In 7 kms, at the Vimy–Givenchy-en-Gohelle traffic circle, turn right onto D51 to the latter village. This straight road crosses the cornfields beneath the escarpment giving more fine vistas. Follow the signs to the memorial. The road now climbs up through **Givenchy** passing a **concrete dugout** — a German tunnel entrance to the subways tunnelled out by the men of both armies and by others in more ancient times. The largest of all, the **Vimy Cavern** was, in fact, mined out by Huguenots and chalk-burners many centuries ago. It was used for defensive purposes in the 18th and 19th Centuries and by refugees from various factions fighting to gain the supremacy of Arras.

Mining operations had begun in 1915 by the French, being continued by the Germans and later the British. There are still relics of their work and many craters are to be seen in the 240-acre park owned by Canada. This was a gift from the French Government and is under the management of the Canadian Ministry of Veterans Affairs (for whom the CWGC undertake the maintenance and gardening work).

In October 1916, the Royal Engineers commenced the construction of the tunnels which were sufficient to house large concentrations of troops on the Allied slopes of the ridge. Twelve infantry subways, each averaging half-a-mile with several more than a mile in length, were constructed by the 172nd, 176th, 182nd and 185th Tunnelling Companies, RE, under the command of Lieutenant-Colonel G. C. Williams, Controller of Mines, First Army. Later, Australian tunnelling companies continued the work. In the period October 1916 to

March 1917, over six miles of tunnels were dug, 6ft 6ins high and 3ft wide, lit throughout by electric light. Small lighting plants were installed in each subway and operated by the Australian Electrical and Mechanical Mining and Boring Company. Canadian tunnelling companies continued operations in the spring of 1917. The underground complex finally amounted to more than 22 miles of subways on four distinct levels. The top level is some 20 to 25 feet underground, the next 75 feet, and the other two at various levels beneath that. On the lowest floor is a narrow-gauge railway still, it is believed, carrying the small trucks used for moving ammunition. Fairly steep gradients bring the line up to higher levels in a few places. The Germans on their side were equally busy.

The shell-pocked Memorial Park photographed in March 1976 — a battlefield preserved and owned in perpetuity by Canada.

In the labyrinth were constructed assembly chambers, brigade and battalion headquarters, dressing stations, accommodation for men, trench mortar and bomb stores, signal offices, etc. Water supplies were laid on, signal cables connected up throughout and narrow-gauge railways laid. Numerous entrances and exits were provided, some for the railways (which linked up with the exterior tramways) for bringing up supplies and for evacuating wounded. Ventilation shafts provided excellent air conditioning, the only difficulty being the risk of gas attacks when this good air flow increased the danger.

The tunnel system proved most useful and almost bomb-proof. Here and there, large shells did penetrate to the first level, and one remains in situ today. Only the entrances required continuous attention and a repair gang was kept in each main subway for this purpose by the tunnelling companies.

Long before the great memorial was unveiled by King Edward VIII on July 26, 1936, work began on the preservation of the battlefield under the eye of Colonel A. F. Duguid, DSO, RCA. The front-line trenches were preserved with concrete sandbags and duck-boards which today look very artificial because of their very neatness. However, the sectors do follow the right lines and do provide the visitor with an inkling of the horrors which they held. At the rear of the German part of the line is a **pillbox** and entrance. A large German trench mortar, found within the park, has been set up and other weapons are scattered around. On the Canadian side, a short length of supporting trench has been left in its natural state. The closeness between the two front lines is clearly indicated across the mine craters.

From the concrete trenches, it is only a short distance to the entrance of the tunnel which is open for public inspection from April 1 to November 15. The guides are usually Canadian students. This tunnel is **Grange Tunnel** and was re-opened for visitors in 1926 by Captain Unwin Simson, Royal Canadian Engineers. Originally, it was nearly 800 yards in length, with many off-shoots and three exits near the 'jumping off' trenches. Grange Tunnel was completed and occupied by the 7th Canadian Infantry Brigade. The visitor can see the guard rooms, the cook house, the hospital and ammunition dumps, and the commander's quarters, with many items of equipment lying about, including the disintegrating bed used by Lieutenant-Colonel Agar Adamson, CO of the Princess Patricia's Canadian Light Infantry (7th Canadian Brigade). The lower levels are indicated but only two of the upper levels are visited during the tour. Some of the damage done by the occupying forces in the Second World War can be seen and more recent (1989) construction to reinforce the

The Memorial of the French-Moroccan Division on Vimy Ridge.

The old German front line, surrounded by mine craters.

original work of the tunnellers. At present, no part of the German complex is open as much of it has flooded.

As one arrives from Givenchy, the **Memorial to the French Division Marocaine** is seen on the right at the roundabout. It commemorates the colonial troops who fought in this sector with distinction in May 1915 when they broke through the German lines for the first time and reached Hill 140, to the west of Vimy. Swing round to the left, the road being a one-way system as it cleaves across the shell-pocked park. A large car park is provided on the right. Here, on the wall flanking the toilets, is a **bronze map** of the battlefield. Access to the memorial is via the footpaths commencing beneath the two tall flagpoles from which the Canadian and French national flags fly. Take a look at the enchanting beavers at the bases of the poles. Beyond the car park is the Superintendent's house and office.

The view from the **Canadian Memorial** is extensive — the Scarpe valley in the foreground, the Lens minefields to the north, and Notre Dame de Lorette (with the tower of the French National Memorial clearly visible) and Souchez to the west. On a clear day, the Messines Ridge can be discerned over the slag heaps.

The CO's quarters, with what is left of his bed.

The circuit of the hill provides more excellent views over the **Douai Plain**. There are more car parks at the lower level to which we make our way, passing the memorial and back to the roundabout having passed a **German bunker** on the right. Proceed southward to take the second road to the left (a detour along the narrow road to the right will take you to two of the cemeteries in the park — **Givenchy Road Cemetery** and **Canadian Cemetery No. 2** — through acres of shellholes and wooded enclosure) to visit the trenches and Grange Tunnel. The approach road runs below part of the line of

A first aid post gallery with relics, and an underground junction.

The old German front line preserved in concrete.

Canadian trenches lead to Grange Tunnel subway.

mine craters, many blown in 1915-16, and it too is set off with trees. Driving or walking through the park, the visitor will see many wired-off enclosures with small notices attached to the wires. Almost all are planted with fir trees and are definitely *not* for exploration; the signs make it obvious that danger lurks amid the pines and often rusting shells and grenades come to light as the land has not been cleared. The areas of the park which can be explored are clearly defined and indicated by other notices and well-worn paths. Frequently, a flock of sheep can be observed in the beautiful close-clipped cratered areas, doing their bit to aid the Commission gardeners.

Beside the entrance to Grange Tunnel and the preserved trench system is a small building housing the Guides' office (and toilets), where free pamphlets are available on this and other Canadian memorials. The visitor should be wary of walking in the trenches as the concrete duck-boards are lethal to anyone wearing high heels.

The narrowness of no man's land at this point is clearly demonstrated as on either side of **Winnipeg Crater** stands a sign indicating the respective front line. The long swerve of the craters can be observed from this point in both directions. To the left, they arc up towards Hill 145, to the right they swing down to **Folie Farm**. The site of the farm is marked by a cross. Visitors are asked to remember that the whole park is a memorial; picnics are not allowed among the shell-holes and neither are games.

One way to leave the park is by the road above the trench sector; this skirts the southern limits of the park and joins the N17 1 km north of Thélus crossroads.

Alternatively, and in order to make a detour circuit to the west to include the French battlefields of 1915, the other road away from the park is the D55 to Neuville-St Vaast. In recent years, the aspect of the countryside around Vimy Memorial Park has changed considerably due to the advent of the Calais autoroute which cuts across north of Arras. This is now crossed before entering **Neuville-St Vaast**. Here, the second side road to the left leads to **Lichfield Crater**, one of two cemeteries where there are no separate graves as all fell together in the explosions. The men, mostly Canadians, were all killed on April 9 or 10, 1917. The other cemetery is **Zivy Crater**, which is 1½ km from Neuville, turning left in the village onto D49. Just below the new bridge across the A26, a spur on the left leads to it. The names of 48 Canadian soldiers who perished here with 5 unknown comrades are engraved below the Cross of Sacrifice.

Return to Neuville-St Vaast. The village was totally destroyed in 1915-16. In the centre of the village, carry on up the D49, bearing right at the fork with the giant concrete cross to reach the D937 in 1 km at

Right: **Trenches and craters surround the 'battlefield' cemeteries of Canadian No. 2 (top), and Givenchy Road (lower left) on Vimy Ridge.**

From the air, the opposing front lines — Canadian on the left and German on the right — are seen to be separated only by line of mine craters.

Lichfield Crater Cemetery near Neuville-St Vaast and Zivy Crater Cemetery — dedicated to those who died in the mine explosions.

The memorial at La Targette to commemorate the destruction of the village in 1915-16.

La Targette. A large memorial of unusual design and dimensions stands in a small park at the crossroads. The huge hand bearing aloft a torch is seen through a gateway bearing the inscription **Cité des Mutilés.** Known as the **Monument du Flambeau,** it commemorates the destruction of the village in the mining operations by the French on May 9, 1916. Beneath the whole region are caverns and subways and, for many years until they became unsafe, there was a famous complex which formed part of the **Maison Blanche sector** which was reached from an entrance at the crossroad. Entombed in these caverns are many fine carvings made by the Canadians and others who were billeted in them from 1916 onwards.

Across the street from the memorial is a war museum, the **Musée de la Targette 1914-18 et 1939-45,** with a very good collection of uniforms, arms and equipment from both wars. The museum is open every day from 9 a.m. to 8 p.m.

The war museum at La Targette.

The entrance to an underground shelter in La Targette.

The German Cemetery of Neuville-St Vaast near La Targette.

The Czech Memorial and Cemetery on Hill 140.

The Polish Memorial on Hill 140, the height to the west of Vimy Ridge attacked by the French in May 1915.

A left turn on to the D937, brings us to the next crossroads where, to the right, lie **La Targette British Cemetery** and the vast **French Cemetery,** while across the junction on the left, is **Souterrain 1914-18,** an entrance to one of the chalk caves. About 1 km further up D937, on the left, is the huge **German Cemetery of Neuville-St Vaast** containing 44,833 graves.

Return to La Targette and continue north on the D937. In 1½ km, on the right, is the **Polish Memorial** with the **Czech Memorial and Cemetery** (which also contains graves from 1939-45) opposite. The memorials commemorate the fight by the Polish and Czech volunteers here on **Hill 140** on May 9, 1915, the first day of the French 10ème Armée attack towards Vimy Ridge in conjunction with First Army's attack on Aubers Ridge further north.

A neat patchwork of graves in the huge French Cemetery at Neuville-St Vaast with the British Cemetery at the top left-hand corner.

Another 1½ km on is **Souchez**. The French fought a fierce action here in June 1915. On the left, before descending the hill, lies **Cabaret Rouge Cemetery** with its Indian-style portal. Further down the hill, also on the left, is the **Memorial to the French 77ème Division d'Infanterie** incorporating a statue of its commander, Général Barbot, who fell here on May 10, 1915.

Continue up the hill and take the left turn, the D58e, to **Notre Dame de Lorette** 3 kms further on. An old legend declares the victor in any war in Flanders and Picardy will be the conqueror of the range of hills which culminate in the crest of Notre Dame de Lorette. A chapel stood on the eastern spur of the ridge which was won by the French after heavy fighting in May 1915. Today, the **French National Memorial and Cemetery** crown the ridge, the site of the old chapel being marked by a simple stone. The cemetery covers 26 acres. A lighthouse tower, 52 metres high, and a chapel are the dominant features. In the top of the tower is a searchlight which shines all night rotating 360 degrees. From the tower, magnificent views

Cabaret Rouge British Cemetery and its Indian-style gateway.

Memorial to the French 77ème Division and its GOC Général Barbot at Souchez.

The Notre Dame de Lorette French National Memorial and Cemetery. Apart from 20,000 individual graves, another 20,000 unknown lie in the Ossuary.

The still-ruined towers of the abbey at Mont-St Eloi overlook the site of the old Royal Flying Corps aerodrome.

of all the surrounding countryside can be had. Between the tower and the chapel is a perpetual flame. The chapel is famous for its stained-glass windows, some of which were presented by the British Commonwealth. In the crypt below are the remains of tens of thousands of dead. Across the street from the cemetery gate stands an **orientation table** and, further to the left, a **statue of Général Maistre**, the commander of the French 21ème Corps d'Armée. The road leads around the cemetery to the **Musée de Notre Dame de Lorette**, which records mainly the French operations of May 1915. It has a fine collection, including some very realistic dioramas with sound in French and English. The museum is open every day from March to November, 9 a.m to 8 p.m.

Return to Souchez and turn left on to D937 towards **Aix-Noulette**. In about 1 km, at the roadside on the right, are two French memorials, one a **Memorial to the French 158ème Régiment d'Infanterie**, the other a **private memorial** in memory of Sous-Lieutenant Jean Leon of the 28ème Régiment d'Infanterie, who fell near here on May 28, 1915. Down the lane beside them, under the shadow of the motorway, another **private memorial** stands on a **blockhouse**.

The direct route back along D937 to Arras is 13 kms. However, a detour (7 kms) to include a visit to **Mont-St Eloi** can be made by taking the D58 right from Souchy to **Carency** and then, just before the last houses of this village, taking the left fork onto an unclassified road.

Mont-St Eloi was the site of an Augustinian abbey in the 7th Century but the ruined towers are from the 17th Century. They were all but destroyed by German artillery fire in 1914 and used by Foch's army in 1915 as an observation post. It is possible, but not advised, to climb the ancient stairs to see the view. In the valley below the village was the **RFC aerodrome of St Eloi**.

Continue via the D49 to La Targette (4 kms), and thence via the D937 to Arras (8 kms). A quieter road than this highway can be taken from Neuville-St Vaast. It is the D49e and goes down the slopes of the back of Vimy ridge to **Ecurie**, once a Canadian base. All roads into Arras have changed radically lately and converge into a ring road around the northern approaches.

'To the glory of the Regiment of Lorette' — the 158ème Régiment d'Infanterie. The memorial on the right was erected by the comrades of those soldiers of France who still lie buried in various places on the battlefield. On the left is one such grave: that of Sous-Lieutenant Jean Leon killed in May 1915.

The Canadian Artillery Memorial at Thélus crossroads to the men who fell in the Vimy operations of April 1917.

At Christmas in 1917, men of the 1st Canadian Division erected this memorial to their comrades.

The alternative route from Vimy Ridge to Arras takes us to the north-eastern sector of the Arras and Scarpe battlefields of 1917-18. Leaving Vimy via the N17, going south to Thélus, turn left when you reach the crossroads onto the D49. The **Canadian Artillery Memorial** here was built and unveiled a year to the day after the capture of Vimy Ridge. General Byng performed the ceremony on April 9, 1918. The South African Heavy Artillery Battery, who also participated, are remembered on the plaque. The memorial stands directly over a dugout, the entrance for which was under the steps in front. **Thélus** village is about ½ km from here. It was of course involved in the 1917-18 operations being captured by the 1st Canadian Division on April 9, 1917. A little to the east along our road, is the **Bois Carré Cemetery** and vestiges of trenches can still be seen in the nearby copse from which the cemetery got its name. In the fields beyond stands a lone cross on a stone cairn — the **1st Canadian Division Memorial** — which they erected at Christmas in 1917 in memory of their several engagements between March and July 1917. Later, there was further fighting over and under these fields as the Germans tried to force Arras in March 1918, but the sector held.

After 3 kms, we reach **Bailleul-Sir-Berthoult** — a German front-line position stormed and captured by the 51st Highland and 34th Divisions on April 13, 1917, after much heavy fighting. Stay on the D49, bearing left at the junction and, at the far side of the village, take an unnumbered road to the left for **Oppy**, 3 kms.

The notorious **Oppy Wood** is on the right as the village is neared. In the years the German Army were in occupation of this village, they transformed it into one of the strongest forts on the Western Front and defied any attack to dislodge them. It was eventually captured by 8th Division with heavy losses on both sides as they evicted the enemy, trench by trench, in September 1918. Fighting in the vicinity had gone on for months and months. It was a sea of mud and destruction from bombardments, and many British battalions had endured periods in the line here — men of the Royal Fusiliers, several Home Counties regiments and the East Yorkshires to mention just a few. Often, the trenches changed hands for brief periods and soon there was little of the old wood left. It is approached by various tracks but all are private. On the right is rather an unusual **memorial** with the wood as backdrop. Here, the men of **Kingston upon Hull** are remembered with their comrades from the local area, including the son of the donor of the land who died on the Somme in August 1918.

The Kingston upon Hull Memorial at Oppy Wood.

Continue across the 1917 battlefield on the D33 to **Gavrelle**. Here was the scene of the attack by the 63rd Royal Naval Division on April 23, 1917 and their magnificent defence for many days thereafter through innumerable counter-attacks. It was held until the 56th London Division, which stubbornly defended it in March 1918, were overwhelmed on the 28th. The 51st Highland Division recaptured it on August 27 and it was occupied by the 8th Division.

Under the bypass turn right, noting the **Memorial to the French 34ème Division d'Infanterie and the 23ème Régiment de Dragons** on the village green. Continue past the church up the road (a one-way street, as it is the exit road from the busy N50, but one is allowed to drive up as far as the memorial) to the **63rd Naval Division Memorial**. This is a fairly-recent, nicely-designed memorial consisting of a ship's anchor positioned in a stylised ruin of a house, on the walls of which are the badges of the division's units.

Beware of continuing past the memorial, but instead turn back to Gavrelle, taking the right turn onto D33, then right again onto D42e. Traversing the 1917 battlefields and the motorway, descend into **Fampoux** in the Scarpe valley in 3 kms. This is yet another place of evil memory to both cavalry and infantry, as was its neighbour **Roeux**, being the scene of extensive fighting both above and below the ground.

The Memorial to the French 34ème Division and the 23ème Régiment de Dragons at Gavrelle.

The unusual 63rd Naval Division Memorial at Gavrelle.

All is quiet now at Fampoux where so many men from the Seaforth Highlanders Battalion were cut down in the battles of 1917 and 1918. Their memorial stands to record their sacrifice.

The deep subways were to play a similar rôle in 1940.

As the road drops into the village, it joins another on the immediate right. It is a very tight turn but it leads up what was known to the British soldier of 1917 as **York Road** towards the **Seaforth Highlanders' Celtic Cross** and 4th Division's **Sunken Road Cemetery** on the crest of the ridge. The Scottish battalion was almost annihilated on these open plains in April 1917 in the operations between Roclincourt and Monchy, on which the Vimy Ridge attack depended upon for being a success. It is still possible to join the N50 by our little road, but it deteriorates considerably as it approaches the dual carriageway, and one is much better advised to return to Fampoux and turn right to **Athies** (2½ kms) and then right up the D37 which reaches the N50 just east of **Point du Jour British Cemetery**. Just along the main road is the **9th Scottish Division Memorial** on the Point du Jour. The site is now beautifully landscaped in an oasis between the dual carriageways. The only casualty has been the crumbling dugout used as part of the Divisional Headquarters in 1917. The memorial, still set amid a border of rough-hewn granite boulders, each bearing the name of a unit in the division, provides an excellent place to view the terrain. The boundary markers carry the thistle badge of the division and newly-planted trees edge the ample car parking.

Arras is a mere 7 kms away, but a detour can be made up the first road to the right as the descent into the city suburbs begins. This passes the **Bailleul Road West British Cemetery** in the fields to the left and, after ½ km, reaches the larger **Bailleul Road East British Cemetery** with many Scottish graves. A little way up the lane beside it is the large **German Cemetery of St Laurent-Blangy** where over 31,000 men are commemorated on the grassy slopes and under sombre trees, many in a mass grave.

Return to the N50 to go right and enter Arras through **St Laurent-Blangy**.

'Remember with honour the 9th Scottish Division who on the fields of France and Flanders 1915-1918 served well.'

ARRAS

North-west of Arras beside the N39, a trench runs like a phantom image across the fields after nearly 60 years of ploughing, when this photograph was taken in 1976.

The focal point of many wars in this region, the various occupying powers have each left their mark on this ancient city. Long before the Romans came and established a Legion here, there was a thriving Atrebates community here. By 863, it was part of Flanders, then the Normans came and sacked it. In the centuries thereafter, the English, the French, the Austrians and the Spanish held sway for varying periods. In 1430, it was the era of Joan of Arc and she was imprisoned here for a while. Then, in 1541, the English and the Spaniards fought the French for the city. Between 1633 and 1707, the great Citadel was built on designs by Vauban. Marlborough was here in 1708, and Arras was also Robespierre's birthplace; his house can still be seen.

From September 18, 1914, Arras was occupied by the Germans but they were forced to retire by Général Maud'huy and many fierce battles were fought with the French army holding on to the town against von Bülow. In the years which followed, the 'boves', or **underground caves**, became an underground city. Above them, the town was badly damaged and in ruins after the attacks of 1915. Arras suffered also from aerial bombardment, the heaviest raid being possibly that of November 10, 1916 when 40 German machines raided the town — six enemy machines were shot down.

Despite all, the French and British garrisons held on to the somewhat small salient which the city formed. The Battle of Arras began on April 9, 1917 with a British attack on a 12-mile front from Givenchy-en-Gohelle in the north to Croissilles in the south. Four Canadian divisions advanced against the Vimy Ridge with notable success and many prisoners and guns were captured in the first few days of the offensive as the Germans retreated towards Lens. Then followed a period of indecisive engagements, very costly to both sides with few gains or losses with a return to static warfare, until the German advance of March 1918. Von Bülow's army attacked toward Vimy but the British Third Army, after falling back to Feuchy and Neuville-St Vaast, held the line.

In 1940, the city was once more under siege when the British Army was involved in a rearguard action.

The 'Boves' of Arras beneath the streets as they are today *(above and below left)*.

The 56th London Division plaque on the rue du Saumon.

Arras. Place des Héros and Hôtel de Ville. Seen here before the Great War, immediately after, and today.

Today, the city has been completely rebuilt. Among the notable buildings are the **Palais Saint Vaast**, a former Benedictine abbey, rebuilt in the 18th Century and again after its destruction in the war; **the cathedral**, a 17th Century edifice which was almost destroyed in the 1915 artillery bombardment; and the **Hôtel de Ville** on the Place des Héros. This beautiful building was entirely demolished by fire and bombardment but has been rebuilt in the original style of the 15th and 16th Centuries with more modern 19th Century wings. The Belfry, which was first completed in 1553 and which collapsed in October 1914, is now one of the most beautiful. There are various **memorial plaques** and pictures of war-damaged Arras in the foyer and, on the exterior near the main entrance, is the modern **1939-44 Resistance Memorial**. The **Tourist Office** is housed inside the building, its entrance being through a side door on the left.

From the basement of the Hôtel de Ville, in which is a **museum** of the history of Arras, guided tours take visitors through some of the 'boves' beneath the Place des Héros. These subways, many of great antiquity, were occupied by harassed citizens and defenders throughout the centuries. At other times, they provided excellent cellars. Tens of thousands of British soldiers lived and worked in the complicated maze of tunnels. Visits to the Belfry and the magnificent salons on the first floor of the Hôtel de Ville can commence here as well.

An unusual sight in Arras Cemetery: the grave of Major N. B. Sinclair-Travis, Royal Garrison Artillery, who died on March 3, 1918. The original grave cross has been placed behind the official headstone (Plot 6, Grave D1).

A short walk from the Place des Héros, on a side wall of the former St Augustine Convent on the corner of rue du Saumon and rue Pasteur, is a **Memorial Plaque to the 56th London Division** who fought in the April-May 1917 Battles of the Scarpe.

On the Faubourg d'Amiens (Boulevard du Général de Gaulle), in the **British Military Cemetery** and the **Arras Memorial to the Missing**, is a beautiful colonnade with the **RFC, RNAS and Royal Air Force Memorial** as a central monument. The memorial records the 35,942 missing in the battles of Arras, Vimy Ridge, the Scarfe, and those of Arleux, Bullecourt and Hill 70 of 1917. The Air Services Memorial records all those missing on the Western Front. High up at the head of the panels are the names of Major Lanoe Hawker, VC, and Major E. Mannock, VC. The globe which surmounts the pillar is decorated with a flight of doves on the exact path of the sun on November 11, 1918. In the cemetery are over 2,600 graves.

By the side of the memorial is a narrow road which leads to the moat of the Citadel and the extremely sombre **Mur des Fusillés** with its 200 plaques forming the memorial to the French patriots who were shot in this dismal place between July 1941 and July 1944 by the Germans. A solitary stone post stands where the execution post was sited. Remembrance services held here are extremely moving and simple. Other sections of the massive ramparts are incorporated into public parks.

The combined Memorial to the Missing to those of the Royal Flying Corps, Royal Naval Air Service and Royal Air Force forms the centrepiece to the British Cemetery at Arras.

The grimmest place in Arras — the Mur des Fusillés with its execution post and memorial plaques for those who died there during the Second World War.

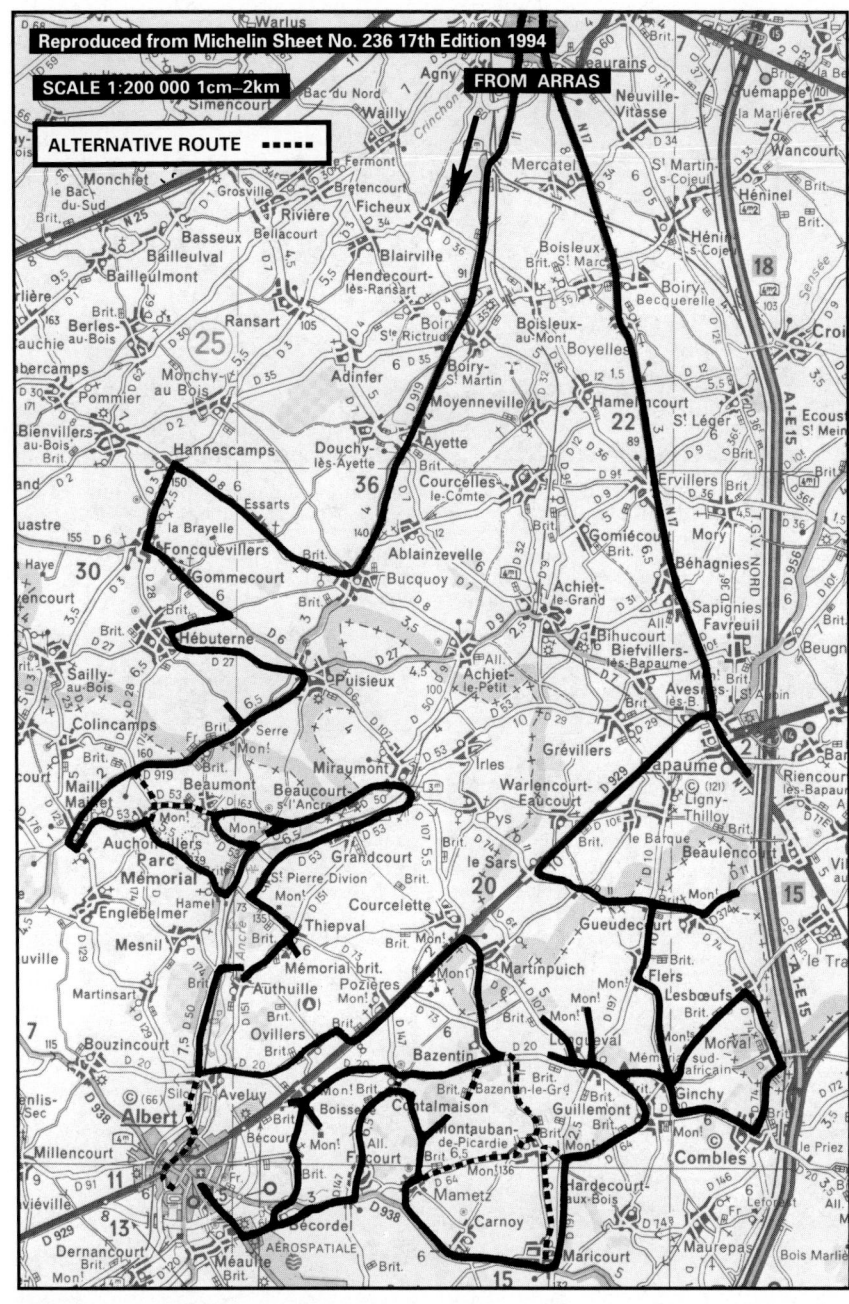

FROM ARRAS

The Battles of the Somme

Leave Arras by the D919. It is 11 kms to **Boiry** and another 4 kms to **Ayette**, scene of fierce fighting by 31st and 32nd Divisions in March and April 1918. It has a rather unusual **Indian and Chinese Cemetery**. We then reach **Bucquoy** 4 kms. This village was behind the German lines, providing a base and billeting area until it came within the range of British artillery. The village was captured in March 1917 and for a year was well known to the BEF. In the German spring advance, it was desperately defended by the 62nd Division after the first battle on March 26 by British Whippet light tanks.

Turn right in the centre of the village onto the D8 for **Hannescamps** (6 kms) — always behind the lines but heavily bombarded. Then turn left onto the D3 for 2¼ kms to **Foncquevillers**, in the lines from 1915-16 and badly damaged by artillery. The village war memorial incorporates a **Memorial Plaque to the North Staffordshire Regiment**.

We then take the D6 road past **Gommecourt Wood**, 1 km to **Gommecourt** which was the Third Army front of July 1, 1916. The 46th North Midland Division attacked the wood and reached the outskirts of the village which did not completely come within the British line until February 27, 1917. Not far from the village is the triangular-shaped **Bois de Riez** — a landmark frequently used by the RFC on patrol.

About 2 kms further on, taking the small road on the right beyond **Gommecourt Cemetery No. 2**, in 1½ km we reach **Hébuterne**, a British fortress village immediately behind the front line from which the 56th London Division attacked Gommecourt on July 1, 1916.

Now take the D27, the left-hand road (note the damaged **Demarcation Stone** in the left-hand verge) to **Puisieux** (4½ kms). This is an example of the many villages in this undulating country which were completely destroyed by artillery fire. It did not fall to the Allies until the spring of 1917 when it was merely a ruin.

Rejoin the D919 turning right for **Serre**, 2 kms. On the far edge of the village is the **Memorial to the 12th Bn. York and Lancaster Regiment** on the right hand. The road drops down through a group of British and French cemeteries marking this area of very severe fighting on July 1, 1916. Here, the 31st Division fought their way across the hilly country in a vain attempt to reach their objectives. They were mown down by hidden and well-placed machine gun nests or impaled on the barbed wire entanglements, supposedly cut up by the tremendous artillery bombardment preceding the attack. Beside the farm on the right at the bottom of the hill, a track leads up to a scattered group of small cemeteries, **Serre Road No. 3**,

The graceful entrance to the Indian and Chinese Cemetery at Ayette, 16 kilometres south of Arras. Ayette was the scene of fierce battles in 1918.

The North Staffordshires' plaque on the village war memorial at Foncquevillers.

81

Queens, **Railway Hollow** and **Luke Copse**. This last was one of several hotly-contested positions of which four were named after the Evangelists. **Sheffield Memorial Park** is a small enclosure on the reverse slope up which the British had to fight. A length of the front-line trench and shell-cratered rear line is preserved around the shelter of the **Sheffield Memorial**. A recent addition (1991) is the **'Accrington Pals' Memorial** to the 11th Bn. East Lancashire Regiment. The **wooden cross** is in memory of Private A. E. Bull of the 12th Bn. Yorks and Lancs, who was killed on this spot on July 1, 1916 but whose remains were not found until April 13, 1928. Fixed to trees in the park are several small **plaques**, including one for the **Barnsley Pals** and one for the **men of Chorley ('Y' Company of the 11th East Lancs)**. Away to the back of the crest of the hill, **La Signy Farm** can just be seen. In between, a clump of trees marks the site of **Basin Wood**, the casualty clearing station.

Back on the D919, **Serre Road No. 1 Cemetery** is just beyond the farm with the **French Cemetery** beside it and, further along on the left, the largest of the group — **Serre Road No. 2 Cemetery** with over 7,100 graves.

From the Sheffield Memorial, the view is down across the undulating ground of the former battlefield to Railway Hollow Cemetery, the Accrington Pals' Valhalla.

On the roadside, a **private memorial** to Lieutenant V. Braithwaite of the 1st Bn. P.A. Somerset Light Infantry is set on a grassy mound — the original wooden cross of the same design is preserved in the crypt of Winchester Cathedral.

The Accrington Pals' Memorial, erected in the memorial park in 1991. Small plaques remember the pals of Barnsley and Chorley.

Serre, scene of the 12th Bn. York and Lancaster Regiment's attack on July 1.

Sad memorial to Private A. E. Bull of the 12th Yorks and Lancs. Killed on this spot on July 1, 1916, his remains were not found until April 13, 1928, when they were buried in Serre No. 2 Cemetery.

Private memorial to Lieutenant Val Braithwaite, Somerset Light Infantry.

The price in human lives on one sector of the Somme — Serre No. 1 British Cemetery, *left,* **and Serre No. 2 British Cemetery,** *right.*

In 1½ kms, the crossroads at the top of the hill was once the site of the **sucrerie**, an important position in the British lines. Turn left for the direct route to Auchonvillers, but it is worth continuing on 2½ kms to **Mailly-Maillet**, observing the fine views of the **Thiepval Ridge** to the east across the Ancre valley, to visit the **village church** to see the unexpected sight of a medieval west doorway

8th Bn. Argylls and Sutherland Highlanders Memorial below Hawthorn Ridge.

The small but dignified Beaumont-Hamel Cemetery.

The battlefield of the Somme — at peace. The attack on July 1, 1916 began at this spot at 7.20 a.m. when the 252nd Company of the Royal Engineers blew up the German trenches held by the 119. Infanterie-Regiment. The explosion of the mine formed what came to be known as Hawthorn Ridge Crater. *Above:* **The view from the lip of the crater down towards Beaumont-Hamel Cemetery (centre) and the 8th Bn. Argylls and Sutherland Highlanders Memorial (left).** *Below:* **Looking from Beaumont village across Redan Ridge. The crater, now tree-filled, is in the centre.**

preserved through the forethought of the curé who had it protected during the war. This village, as with all the others just behind the British lines, was a very busy place before July 1 and also, like its neighbours, had many underground tunnels in the quarries below it from which the material for building the houses was taken. These subways provided vital cover for the troops and, although no longer open to view, still retain carvings and graffiti on their walls.

Take the D73 for **Auchonvillers**, 1¾ km beyond which is the **Newfoundland Memorial Park** entrance. Just before the park, a lane is signposted for **Hawthorn Ridge No. 1 Cemetery** near the clump of trees marking the site of the **Hawthorn Ridge crater**.

An alternative, perhaps better way to get to the crater is via the D174/D163 from Auchonvillers to Beaumont-Hamel village which passes through the valley behind the ridge. After 1½ km, on the left, a lane runs up onto **Redan Ridge** and back to Serre. At one side is the **Memorial of the 8th Bn. Argyll and Sutherland Highlanders** tucked under the slope and in the fields; on the other the small **Beaumont-Hamel Cemetery**. Up the steep field on the right of the D163, a pathway has been made up to the rim of **Hawthorn Ridge crater**, indicated by a multi-language signpost at the roadside. Although the crater is now filled with trees and bushes, the farmers having over the years tried to fill it in, a swathe has been cut down its precipitous side to show the depth. The crater was 150 yards in length, 100 yards wide and 80ft deep, 40,000lbs of ammonal being used to create it. The eruption was caught on film as it was prematurely exploded and is one of the best-known and frequently-screened examples of the 1914-18 cameraman's art.

Newfoundland Memorial Park covers more than 80 acres of which some 40 are in the sector held on July 1 by the Royal Newfoundland Regiment of the 29th Division. The regiment was annihilated in the initial attack following the explosion which, being ten minutes too early, enabled the ground to be occupied by the enemy.

At the entrance to the park is the **29th Division Memorial** and all around are the grass-covered trenches of the battlefield. All have been preserved as they were left in 1918 and, due to the fact that later battles did not alter them very much, it is possible to study and appreciate the actions fought here. Even on a fine, sunny summer's day, the park seems to have a definitely foreboding atmosphere and, after a thunderstorm, I have smelt the awful stench of battle in the still, deep trenches. Nowhere else in my travels on the Western Front has the horror of war come nearer to me than here on one very hot evening following a clear day. It was late July and, as I wandered across the shell-torn slopes towards the German lines, the sound of thunder was heard in the distance, getting gradually nearer as might an artillery barrage. The light grew dim and black clouds gathered overhead. Lightning streaked across the sky — a veritable reincarnation of what a barrage must have been like.

As the rain drops began to fall, I dived into one of the trenches for cover and tripped and

The 29th Division's simple monument in the Newfoundland Memorial Park.

stumbled along until I found better shelter close to the great **Caribou monument** which stands guard over the park from a raised mound above a dugout. All the light I had was a tiny torch and this gave little help in avoiding the occasional shell-case or jagged pieces of iron which litter the trenches. After

the hot day, the usual smell of rainsoaked grass began to permeate my nostrils . . . but with a difference . . . I realised that this was the smell of battle. It was a never-to-be-forgotten experience, and one which I have found on return visits when the conditions have been similar.

The Newfoundland Memorial Park is one of the best preserved of the trench memorials on the Western Front to be seen today.

St John's Road *(left)* and the Caribou Memorial and Memorial to the Missing *(right)* above a dugout at Beaumont-Hamel.

A 1916 relic — the petrified Danger Tree in no man's land. Y Ravine is behind.

Y Ravine Cemetery contains the headstones of men known or believed to be buried there, their graves being lost in later battles.

The Kilted Scotsman of the 51st Highland Division overlooks Y Ravine.The Celtic cross once stood in nearby High Wood, commemorating the Division's losses there.

A smaller memorial of the 51st Highland Division stands at the foot of Redan Ridge in Beaumont village itself.

Before the visitor to the park reaches the Caribou, along the gravel path between the trenches a **memorial plaque** bearing a verse by John Oxenham bids the beholder to tread softly over the hallowed ground. At the base of the Caribou is the **Memorial to the Newfoundland Missing** on land and sea and the names of over 800 men from this small country are listed on the bronze panels. Around the foot of the plinth of stone on which the monument stands is an **orientation table**. From this level, a good view can be had of all the park and beyond to Beaumont and Thiepval. Across the expanse of the park, the various lines are indicated by signboards, the British and German front lines being clearly marked amid the rough shell holes.

The modern house of the Superintendent can be seen across towards Thiepval and, over the small ridge where the skeleton of the **Danger Tree** rises in front of the German trenches, is the ridge where the kilted Scotsman of the **51st Highland Division Memorial** gazes out across the countryside. Tall fir trees, planted many years ago when this area became the Newfoundland National Memorial, grow around the statue. The sweep of these trees is interrupted down in the hollow by the **Y Ravine Cemetery**. Hidden over to the left is **Hawthorn Ridge Cemetery No. 2**. Between it and the 51st Highland Division Memorial is the smallest of the cemeteries in the park, **Hunter's Cemetery**. A small wall encircles the Cross of Sacrifice around the base of which are the headstones of 46 men,

mostly of the Black Watch of the 51st Highland Division, who died here when the area was captured by the division in the autumn of 1916. The division memorial overlooks the infamous **Y Ravine** which was a German position and from which their machine guns wreaked a devastating fire. Entrances to dugouts were cut in the sides of the ravine, but these are now peacefully grass covered.

As the visitor crosses the battle area, it is noticeable that some of the shell holes contain battlefield debris: rusting helmets, broken shells, barbed wire and the iron pickets on which the wire was hung. In the old days, these collections were much larger but, over the years, a lot has disappeared. What remains is not there for the taking and it is requested that it should be looked at and not pilfered. Even today, many shells and often hand-grenades can be found emerging from the greensward. Should the visitor find a dangerous item, leave it alone and advise the Superintendent or one of the gardeners working in the park.

In 1959, the Canadian Battlefield Monuments Commission took over the park and the CWGC provide the work force to keep it in beautiful condition. To aid them, a flock of sheep grazes peacefully. Before the CWGC took over, long lines of pickets and barbed wire were to be seen across the park, since removed to the shell-holes. The **Newfoundland Roll of Honour** is kept in the Superintendent's house together with other interesting references to the history of the regiment and park.

Leave the park and continue eastward, dropping suddenly down into the Ancre valley at **Hamel**. We then follow a short but interesting circular detour by taking the left fork in the village and joining the D50. Then, after 1½ km, take the left fork on the D163e for Beaumont, leaving the railway which runs between the D50 and the Ancre. In **Beaumont**, take the right-hand road, the D163, for Beaucourt. Just to the left of the T-junction stands a steel pillar which is the **51st Highland Division Memorial** presented by the division to Beaumont-Hamel to commemorate the recapture of the village on November 13, 1916. The D163 passes several **British cemeteries** along the way and there are some very fine views to be had over the 1916 battlefield.

In **Beaucourt**, rejoin the D50. A right turn into the village leads in 300 metres to the **Memorial of the 63rd Royal Naval Division** on the left-hand side of the road; the left turn leads to **Miraumont** (3 kms) where the Germans had a supply base and a reserve ammunition store near the **old water-mill**, close to the railway line. This was blown up by the British artillery on August 5, 1916, destroying much of the village.

Overleaf: **A trench map in reality; Beaumont-Hamel Memorial Park, seen from the air in April 1976.**

The tiny Hunter's Cemetery of Highland graves arranged around the Cross of Sacrifice with the 51st Division Memorial in the background.

The 63rd Royal Naval Division Memorial at Beaucourt.

HAWTHORN RIDGE

HAWTHORN RIDGE CEMETERY No. 2

BRITISH FRONT LINE

ST JOHN'S ROAD

ROYAL NEWFOUNDLAND REGIMENT MEMORIAL

NEWFOUNDLAND MEMORIAL
TO THE MISSING

29th DIVISION MEMORIAL

MAN MAIN POSITIONS

Y-RAVINE

51st HIGHLAND DIVISION MEMORIAL

NTER'S
METERY

GERMAN FRONT LINE

Y-RAVINE CEMETERY

DANGER TREE

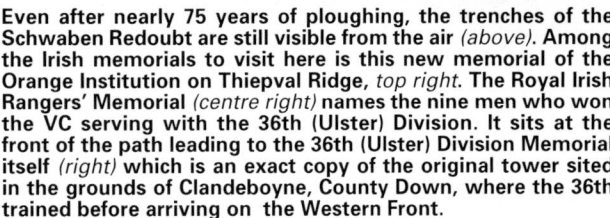

Even after nearly 75 years of ploughing, the trenches of the Schwaben Redoubt are still visible from the air *(above)*. Among the Irish memorials to visit here is this new memorial of the Orange Institution on Thiepval Ridge, *top right*. The Royal Irish Rangers' Memorial *(centre right)* names the nine men who won the VC serving with the 36th (Ulster) Division. It sits at the front of the path leading to the 36th (Ulster) Division Memorial itself *(right)* which is an exact copy of the original tower sited in the grounds of Clandeboyne, County Down, where the 36th trained before arriving on the Western Front.

In Miraumont, take the D107 and pass under the railway and then take the D151 to the right for **Grandcourt** (3 kms), which was part of the German entrenchment on the River Ancre. Go straight through the village, taking the D163e through **St Pierre Divion**, travelling along the region where the Germans were securely dug in. At the junction with the D73 will be seen the **ruins of the mill**. Turn left and climb up the steep slopes to Thiepval. At the top of the hill, the **Memorial to the 36th Ulster Division** is reached.

Set in a small park on the left of the road, on a site venerated as being the place where the 36th Division won glory on July 1, 1916 in their gallant attempt to reach Thiepval and take the Schwaben Redoubt, is a tall grey memorial. It is a copy of the memorial to Helen, the greatly-loved mother of the Marquis of Dufferin, in the family park at Clandeboyne, County Down, where the division had its training grounds before coming to France. Within the tower are a chapel and an apartment normally occupied by a caretaker/guide of the Somme Association. The tower is open every day except Mondays. Behind the tower is a new visitors' centre.

Outside the park, to the left of the entrance, stands the **Orange Institution Memorial Obelisk** (inaugurated on November 11, 1993) 'to the Irish men and women who gave up their own lives that others

might live in freedom.' As one enters the park, on the left, is the **Royal Irish Rangers Memorial**, naming the nine VC winners in the 36th Division. It was unveiled by the Duke of Kent on July 1, 1991, the 75th anniversary of the battle. Opposite stands a **flag-pole** from which the flag first flew on Armistice Day 1921 when it was hoisted by the Duchess of Abercorn at the unveiling of the memorial.

In the spring and autumn, after the ploughing has been done, the fields behind the memorial are criss-crossed with chalk slicks which follow the course of the German trenches leading to the **Schwaben Redoubt** which lies in the fields under Mill Road Cemetery, and Thiepval hamlet. In 1966, 1976, 1986 and again in 1991, gatherings of survivors of 1916 met to celebrate the 50th, 60th, 70th and 75th anniversaries of their heroism. The 36th Division held special ceremonies at the Ulster Tower recalling their 5,500 casualties.

A little higher up the road is the cemetery where many of them are buried, **Connaught Road Cemetery**, with part of **Thiepval Wood** as a backdrop. Others lie in **Mill Road Cemetery**, away in the fields on the left. Here, due to the continual subsidence caused by the movement underground as the many subways and caverns of the Schwaben Redoubt crumble, the headstones in the path of one of the tunnels are laid flat. The cemetery marks one of the main entrances to

the underground fortress. It was one of several in the area, the others being Stuff, Zollern and Leipzig. It was from these underground strongholds that the German forces emerged to cause such devastation among the attacking forces.

Mill Road British Cemetery.

Thiepval Memorial to over 73,000 men who have no known graves. It was built on the site of the old château — scene of commemorations in 1966, 1976, 1986 and 1991. The German strong point at Moquet Farm stood at the top left of the picture.

Continue 1 km to **Thiepval**. This hamlet, once a flourishing village, was totally destroyed by the end of 1916. It was a German fortress, both above and below ground, and was a vital position to be taken by the British. Terrible injuries were suffered on both sides in the attacks which were made on that dreadful first day of the Somme, and it did not fall until September 28, 1916, when the 51st Highland Division captured the ridge.

The great **Thiepval Memorial to the Missing** of the Somme battles is along the road behind the church on the right. This colossal arched memorial was designed by Sir Edwin Lutyens and is built of brick with stone facing. The immense central archway is flanked by smaller arches resting on 16 main pillars. On the panels of stone are recorded the names of 73,367 men who died in 1916-17 and have no known graves. Behind the memorial is a **cemetery** where equal numbers of British and French unknown soldiers lie buried.

The inscription above the arches of the memorial, which stands on the site of the grounds of **Thiepval Château** and on part of the **Leipzig Redoubt**, records that the monument is dedicated to both the British and French. The memorial was unveiled by the Prince of Wales on July 31, 1932, and can be seen from every direction for considerable distances. Beneath is the labyrinth of trenches which formed the vital arteries of this impregnable fortress. **Moquet Farm**, over the valley towards Courcelette, was the forward advance HQ of the defending German army. The majority of the casualties recorded here were lost in the attempts to capture this fortress. The siege dragged on for nearly two months but the most-disastrous day was July 1 when the British lost nearly 60,000 men. In September, the 11th and 18th Divisions, following in the footsteps of the 36th, 8th and 25th Divisions, finally took the village. The ridge was retaken by the Germans in their 1918 offensive when it was only lightly defended but on August 24 it was recaptured with ease by V Corps.

Across a wide green lawn from the great edifice is the **18th Division Memorial** (of identical design to that at Clapham Junction on the Menin Road — *see page 46*). This is passed as the D151 is joined for **Authuille**, 1½ kms away. The road descends to this village which clings to the east bank of the Ancre. A sharp left turn before the church (C5) leads down to and across the river, across the railway and, left, onto the road to Albert via **Aveluy Wood**. This wood is still cut by the remains of the trenches of the British lines; 36th Division's HQ was here, and **Lancashire Dump** was on the site of **Aveluy Wood Cemetery**. This road is the D50 and it rolls up and down to Albert, some 6 kms away.

However, before we enter this historic place, take the D20 left from Aveluy to visit Ovillers and La Boisselle via Pozières. Shortly after the junction with the D151 (1 km), there is a rise in the road and, on the left, a small road leads to **Ovillers**, passing its large **British cemetery** and overlooking the valley called **Mash Valley** by the BEF. Along the ridge of this valley up which the D929 rises, there were many mine craters in years gone by. They were part of the almost-continuous series blown in the mine warfare of 1915-16. Ovillers was stormed on July 1, 1916, but did not fall until the 16th.

18th Division Memorial at Thiepval village, with the Thiepval Memorial behind.

Aveluy Wood Cemetery, where men sleep amid crumbling trenches, was laid out on the site of what British troops knew as the Lancashire Dump.

Passing through the village, take the right-hand road to join the D929. Turn left up the slope to **Pozières**. This village, astride the main Albert—Bapaume road, was the focus of much heavy fighting and, by August 1916, had ceased to exist. It was taken on July 24 by the 1st Australian Division and the 48th British Division of General Gough's Fifth Army, lost again on March 24/25, 1918, and retaken by the 17th Division on August 24. Beside the long straight road before the village is reached, the **Pozières Military Cemetery** and the **Memorial to the Missing of the Fifth Army in 1918** are passed. This memorial records the names of 14,690 men of the Fifth Army who died in the battles of the Somme up to April 5, 1918, and all other casualties up to August 7 with no known graves.

At the entrance to Pozières, on the right, stands the **King's Royal Rifle Corps Memorial** (identical to that at Hooge — *see page 45*) and, opposite to it, the **1st Australian Division Memorial Obelisk** with, to the left of the entrance, a bronze **relief map** unveiled in August 1993. Across the

The memorial gateway to the Fifth Army Missing at Pozières Cemetery on which 14,690 names are recorded of men who died on the Somme.

side road leading up to the memorial is a **German concrete dugout** which has recently been excavated. This was the enemy strong point known to the Australians as **'Gibraltar'**.

Continue through the village and up the gradient, which increases until the crest is reached, beside the **Tank Corps Memorial** opposite the site of **Pozières Mill**. The obelisk of the Tank Memorial is set off by four fine scale models of tanks of the 1916-18 period, one of which bears bullet marks from the Second World War. It was from this area that the first tanks went into action towards Flers on September 15, 1916. Pozières Mill is now a grassy mound behind a trim lawn with simple stone markers of the **Australian Memorial** recalling the action of the Australians who stood here in July and August 1916, attempting to capture this feature, **Hill 160**. Here in this small sector, they suffered their most severe casualties in the battle. Here, too, now stands a bronze **relief map**, one of those unveiled by the Australians in 1993 (*see page 66*). The Pozières mill was fortified by a German bunker of which there is little left today. By looking around, it is possible to appreciate what a fine 'O-Pip' this was. Over to the westward, the Thiepval Memorial can be seen. The sites of other prominent actions can also be discerned, even the **sugar refinery** on the ridge.

South of the village is the King's Royal Rifle Corps Memorial.

The 1st Australian Division Memorial at the southern end of Pozières.

The other Australian Memorial at Pozières is located on the site of the mill.

The Tank Corps Memorial lies on the opposite side of the road.

Another 1½ km further north and the **Canadian Memorial** of **Courcelette** is reached which commemorates their great actions in November 1916 when they took, among other positions, the longest trench built by the Germans on the Western Front, which ran across this ridge — **Regina Trench**.

Turn right on to the D6 for **Martinpuich** (1 km). Martinpuich was battered to pulp long before it actually fell to the 15th Scottish Division on September 15, 1916, after the attack on Flers. Some of the tanks first used that day were in action here. After it was recaptured by the Germans in March 1918, they remained here until V Corps troops retook the position in August.

We now take the small unclassified road to the right for Bazentin, another village with a similar history. Just outside Martinpuich, on the right, is a **concrete shelter** in remarkably good condition. As one enters **Bazentin-le Petit**, at the junction with the D73, on the left is the small **Memorial to the 82nd Field Company, RE**.

The 82nd Field Company Memorial at Bazentin-le-Petit refurbished in 1989 by the Junior Leaders Regiment, RE.

Go straight across to turn right for **Contalmaison** on the D20 and proceed to **La Boisselle**. Above the village, a path beside the water tower on the right leads to the **34th Division Memorial** and, on the green before the church, is the **19th Division Memorial** (identical in design to that at Oosttaverne in Belgium — *see page 54*).

Taking the small road on the left and the immediate left fork (C102), in a few metres arrive at **Lochnagar Crater**. The purchase of it in 1979 by Richard Dunning of London has made its preservation more secure and the erosion of the site by encroaching agriculture halted. The crater, the largest on the Western Front, was one of a group blown on July 1, 1916, the explosion being felt for hundreds of miles. This mine alone comprised 60,000lbs of explosives, all carefully dragged underground along saps emanating from the direction of the **Tara-Usna Line** near the main road to Albert, and the crater today is some 300ft across and 90ft deep. From the rim, there are extensive

The 34th Division Memorial above La Boisselle.

The 19th Division Memorial on the village green at La Boisselle.

In April 1976, when the photo *(centre)* was taken, what was left of the battlefield surrounding Lochnagar Crater at La Boisselle was gradually being reclaimed. Although this, the largest crater on the Western Front, created on July 1, 1916 by the explosion of 60,000 lbs of guncotton, still remained amid the ruins of the old German front line, other smaller craters near the village were being filled in. The latest to go now has a house built over it. In 1979, Richard Dunning decided that this gradual encroachment of a unique piece of First World War history, and the Somme battles in particular, must be reversed and he purchased Lochnagar Crater personally that it might be saved as a permanent memorial, The picture *(above)* of the area in 1982 shows how much closer the surrounding fields had crept in those six years. In 1980, a memorial was erected; in 1986, a wooden cross.

The Memorial of the Tyneside Scottish and Tyneside Irish Brigades at the southern end of La Boiselle. These brigades of 34th Division were particularly hard hit on the first day of the attack, losing an appalling 80 percent of their men.

Artillery lines have left their mark behind Norfolk Cemetery just outside Albert — their trace just visible beyond the hedge.

views over Chapes Spur — **Sausage Valley** — so called by the British for the German observation balloon which hung over it. In the slopes of the shallow valley can be discerned the positions of some of the machine gun posts which poured forth their deadly fire to cause such devastation among the troops advancing from Tara and Usna — Bécourt Wood and Albert — the ridge towards Fricourt and upwards to Pozières and back to Ovillers. Nearer to hand are the small craters of the **Glory Hole** blown in 1915, easily visible behind the houses of La Boisselle and along the road (D20) which connects with D929 beside the **Tyneside Scottish and Tyneside Irish Memorial** close

to the positions where these two brigades of the 34th Division fought to win this sector in that infamous July. All around, there is still evidence in the shell holes of the many months of fighting in this valley. **Y Sap**, another of the large mines, lay on the western side of D929. Filled in some years ago, it is discernable today by a white circular patch in the field behind the bungalows.

Albert is 3 kms down the D929 or, taking the small road (C9) below Lochnagar Crater to **Bécourt** and **Bécordel**, more of the battle area is traversed. The two hamlets were in the British rear lines and were bases from which units moved into action. Little now marks the landscape except the chalk slicks

in newly-ploughed ground or the occasional artillery position in the embankments. Such a position is very clearly seen behind **Norfolk Cemetery** which lies between the two hamlets. **Dartmoor Cemetery**, on the edge of Bécordel, is mainly a Devonshire cemetery (8th and 9th Battalions, 7th Division). Here lie Lieutenant Henry ('Harry') Webber, at 68 the oldest man killed in action on the Somme (Plot I, Grave E54); Private J. Miller, VC, of the 7th Bn. King's Own (Royal Lancaster) Regiment (Plot I, Grave C64); and two members of one family, father G. and son R. F. Lee (Plot I, Graves A35-36). At Bécordel, turn left and then right (D64) joining the D938 to reach Albert in 3 kms.

The grave of Lieutenant 'Harry' Webber in Dartmoor Cemetery, at 68 the oldest man to die on the Somme. Webber had made strenuous efforts to enlist since 1914 and, as the 7th South Lancs transport officer, he was killed by a single stray shell on July 21, 1916.

Today, there are over 420,000 marked graves from the Great War in France but of every four men that died, one was unidentified. In the horrific Flanders battlefields in Belgium, the proportion is even higher with a third of the graves being those of unknown casualties. Every grave, be it identified or not, tells its own story of tragedy and bereavement; none more so than that of the Lee family whose father (aged 44) and son (aged 19) lie side by side in Dartmoor Cemetery on the edge of Bécordel, both killed serving in the same unit on the same day, September 5, 1916.

Albert, once called Ancre, is an industrial town which was very much in the front line in the various battles of the Somme and the Ancre. At the end of September 1914, it was almost occupied by the advancing German 2. Armee but the French 10ème Armée stood in its way and, with the support of the British cavalry, pushed them back. For the next two years, Albert was only a few kilometres from the front line and was frequently bombarded. On January 15, 1915, the **golden virgin and child** on the tower of the Basilica was toppled from her plinth when a shell hit the dome on which she stood. The statue did not fall but hung, precariously, head down out over the tower. The sight of the statue hanging almost at right angles was one of the most talked of incidents of Albert and led to the legend that when the 'Leaning Virgin' fell, the war would be over. In due course, the base of the statue was secured, first by French and later British engineers.

Being close to the front, Albert was always filled with the military, at first mostly by French forces but in March 1916 the British took over. Until October 1916, the town was well within the range of the German guns and was very badly damaged. On March 26, 1918, the German offensive swept through Albert after bitter fighting, and the town remained in German hands until the British advance in August when, on the 22nd, it was recaptured. As the Basilica tower was being utilised by the Germans as an observation post, orders were issued for its destruction. At 3.30 p.m. on April 16, the 35th British Divisional Artillery shelled the tower extremely accurately and, with the third shot, the tower fell, with, of course, the Virgin. So much for the legend!

None of the buildings in Albert are old, all having been rebuilt, although the Basilica and the imposing Hôtel de Ville were rebuilt in the 1920s very much in their old style. On the front wall of the **Hôtel de Ville** is a memorial plaque to the **Machine Gun Corps**.

In 1992, a new war museum, the **Musée des Abris**, opened in the underground galleries which run under the Place d'Armes. Excavated in the 16th Century, they were refurbished as air raid shelters in the Second World War. The entrance is to the right of the Basilica. The museum incorporates the collection which used to be in the now-defunct trench museum at Longueval and comprises a series of realistic trench and tunnel dioramas. A video is shown and there is a good relief map of the Somme battlefield commissioned by the Western Front Association and originally meant to be set up on the Butte de Warlencourt (*see page 101*).

Left: **The Leaning Virgin on the tower of the Basilica was dislodged in a bombardment in January 1915 and finally toppled on April 16, 1918.** *Right:* **Once again, the Golden Virgin and her child look out over modern Albert and further afield.**

The Machine Gun Corps Memorial on the façade of Albert's Hôtel de Ville.

The Musée des Abris at Albert has some very fine dioramas.

To resume the tour of the battlefields, leave Albert via the D329, turning left onto D64 at the aircraft factory at Méaulte for **Fricourt** (5 kms). At the beginning of the village, the **Fricourt British Cemetery** and the **7th Bn. Green Howards Memorial** is on the left. This was another of the villages turned into fortresses by the Germans during their long occupation. Mine warfare was fought for many months around the village which was, in time, utterly ruined. On the left of the D147, on the crest of the rising ground, the cratered ground of the **Tambour Mine** is visible. Above it is **Fricourt New Military Cemetery** out in the fields. Fricourt fell to the 17th Division on July 2, 1916 and this cemetery was one of their burial grounds. On the north-east side of the village is **Fricourt Wood**, again captured by 17th Division.

Three kilometres up the D147, past **Fricourt German Cemetery** (17,027 dead) and **Peake Wood British Cemetery**, is **Contalmaison**, captured by the 17th and 38th Divisions on July 9, 1916, after being attacked by the 7th, 17th and 23rd Divisions since the 3rd.

East of the village, **Mametz Wood** stretches southward for 1½ kms with **Mametz** itself another ½ km beyond the southern tip. To get there, take the first right-hand road on entering Contalmaison (C4). About 2 kms along this road, there is a narrow lane on the left. This leads to the **38th Welsh Division Memorial** hidden in the folds of the hills. The lane follows the contours of the site of the famous **Queen's Nullah** before there is a fork; the left track peters out as it crosses the fields to the **Willow Stream** over **Cliff Trench**, so continue straight on. Even though the surface deteriorates, it remains quite passable as it, too, drops downwards towards the cliffs. Suddenly, on a spur overlooking the **Hammerhead** of Mametz Wood, the fantastic **Red Dragon** glowers defiance. It was from here that the 38th Division fought through the wood to Bazentin Ridge suffering heavy casualties. Below the memorial is a small car park and turning circle. The lane beyond this point becomes a muddy rutted track (unfit for cars) as it winds its way to **Flat Iron Copse Cemetery**.

This striking 38th Division Welsh dragon *(right)* **overlooks Mametz Wood.**

Beside the Bray road on the outskirts of Fricourt lies the British Cemetery and the 7th Bn. Green Howards Memorial.

The 14th Bn. Royal Welch Fusiliers' Memorial in Danzig Alley Cemetery, where there is also a plaque to the whole regiment.

The memorial of the French 69ème Régiment d'Infanterie outside Montauban.

For an alternative circuit road around the wood from Contalmaison, take the right fork of the D20. The road leads towards **Bazentin-le-Petit** and **Bazentin-le-Grand** with their woods on the left skirting the northern edge of Mametz Wood with **Sabot Copse** and **Flat Iron Copse** and its **British Cemetery** down a narrow lane to the right. These features were in German lines, a labyrinth of trenches and deep dugouts. For several days, the British divisions fought every inch of the way, enduring bitter fighting in the battles for **Bazentin Ridge**, clearing the villages and woods by July 14, as they slowly but steadily pushed on during that dreadful summer. An unclassified road from Bazentin-le-Petit leads to **Montauban-de-Picardie** and the D64 thence to Mametz. Along the way, on the right, stands a **Memorial of the French 69ème Régiment d'Infanterie** who fought here in September

The memorial to the battalions of the Manchester Regiment in Mametz village.

In Mansell Copse is the Devonshire Cemetery where men of the regiment lie in their original wartime graves.

The grave of Captain D. L. Martin of the 9th Devons, who warned against the German machine gun which he suspected hid in the Mametz cemetery, only to die from its fire in the attack of July 1.

William Noel Hodgson was Bombing Officer of the 9th Devons, and a Cambridge contemporary of Rupert Brooke.

1914. In the vicinity are several British cemeteries including **Danzig Alley** on the D64 at the edge of Mametz. This overlooks what was known as **Death Valley** with Mametz Wood behind it. Near the entrance is a small **Memorial Plaque for the Royal Welch Fusiliers** and behind the Cross of Sacrifice there is stone bench which is the **Memorial to the 14th (S) Bn. Royal Welch Fusiliers** (38th Division).

At Mametz, the 7th Division Memorial has disappeared, but to the right of the village war memorial stands the small, fairly-recent **Memorial of the 20th, 21st, 22nd and 24th Bns. The Manchester Regiment** of that division who captured the village on July 1.

From Mametz, take the D64 west to join the D938 and then turn left. About 1¼ km along the recently widened and straightened road, a track proceeds up the slope to the right. The little wood here is **Mansell Copse** in the shelter of which is **Devonshire Cemetery**. It stands on the old British front line. Here lie 163 men of the 8th and 9th Devons as they were buried by their Padre after they had gone over the top on July 1. A small memorial erected in 1986 records that they held this position then and they hold it still. Among their number are Captain D. L. Martin of the 9th Devons (Grave A1) and the poet W. N. Hodgson, MC (Grave A3). Many of the casualties were victims of a German machine gun mounted by the crucifix in Mametz Cemetery which can be seen across the valley.

A little to the east of Mansell Copse is the small **Gordon Cemetery** created by 2nd Bn. Gordon Highlanders in one of the British support trenches which ran along here. Like the Devons and Manchesters, the Gordons were units of the 7th Division.

The next two roads on the left lead to **Carnoy** but continue on to **Maricourt** (4 kms), passing the road to Bronfay and Bray on the right. It was at Maricourt that the British and French lines merged in 1916. At the edge of the village, on the left facing **Happy Valley**, is the large **Peronne Road Cemetery** made by the concentration of battlefield graves. Turn left either via the unclassified road to the centre of **Montauban-de-Picardie** or the D197 which joins the D64 at the crossroads east of the village near the site of the **brickworks** which were completely destroyed in the battle when captured by the Liverpool Regiment when the 18th and 30th Divisions captured Montauban. During the Allied advance in August 1918, Montauban was once more captured by the 18th Division. These divisions, having withstood various counter-attacks, advanced

This is the tiny cemetery at Mametz created by the 2nd Bn. Gordon Highlanders. Trenches still remain below the hedges in the middle distance.

eastward towards **Bernafay Wood** and **Trones Wood** which will be passed soon after turning right on the D64. The 30th Division occupied Bernafay Wood between July 1 and 3, but the attacks on Trones Wood — the **Bois des Troncs** — did not begin until July 8. Between the woods is an open stretch of ground from which there is an excellent vista over **Caterpillar Valley** with **High Wood** on the further crest to the west and **Delville Wood** to the east. From July 8 to 13, the 30th Division made several attacks capturing Trones Wood but then being forced to retire by enemy counter-attacks, both sides suffering heavy casualties. On July 13, the 18th Division took over the assault with the 7th, 3rd and 9th Divisions on their left. After further difficult fighting, with German snipers hidden in the undergrowth and up in the trees, the wood was cleared finally on July 14. At the bend in the road stands the **18th Division Memorial Obelisk** at the edge of the wood. Today, the woods are healthy young forests and bear little resemblance to the muddy shattered areas the troops knew.

Guillemont is 2 kms, but just prior to reaching the village we pass on the left **Guillemont Road Cemetery** where Lieutenant Raymond Asquith, the son of the

The 18th Division Memorial at the edge of Trones Wood.

The 16th Irish Division Memorial at Guillemont. The 47th Brigade of the division helped to capture the village.

Memorial Cross to 'Bristol's Own' at Longueval with High Wood in the background.

The New Zealand Division Memorial lies between High Wood and Delville Wood on the site of Crest Farm.

then-Prime Minister is buried (Plot I, Grave B3). He was killed at Ginchy on September 15, 1916. Over 2,200 others lie with him on the site of a once formidable German entrenchment. Here again, the views are panoramic; across the fields can be discerned the route of the old railway and, on the right along the D20, the **site of Guillemont station**, now an agricultural complex, with Longueval and Delville Woods in the far right distance still dominating the landscape. The sucrerie which marked the **site of Waterlot Farm**, immediately in front of Longueval, has now been pulled down. Just to the left of the agricultural complex, in the fields and enclosed by a low wall, is a **lone memorial** to

2nd Lieutenant George Futvoye Marsden-Smedley, 3rd Bn. The Rifle Brigade, killed in action in the attack of August 18, 1916. (It can be reached by a rough track which leads into the field from behind the grain elevators.)

Guillemont fell to the 20th Light Division and a brigade of the 16th Irish Division on August 23, 1916, after bitter fighting which had involved many units since the end of July. Turning down into the village, the **16th Irish Division Memorial** stands by the church. Go straight ahead up the D20 to Longueval. Along the way, we pass the site of Guillemont station, with the track to the Marsden-Smedley memorial on the left; the site of Waterlot Farm is also on the left, in front of the first houses of Longueval. First attacked by the 5th Bn. Cameron High-landers of 9th Division, the farm was not taken until the 17th.

Caterpillar Valley Cemetery and New Zealand Memorial to the Missing of the Somme.

Before visiting Deville Wood continue into **Longueval** village. The village was the scene of furious fighting from July 15 to 29 when it was cleared by 5th Division and became the apex of a salient held by British troops. The trench museum which used to be behind the Café Calypso in the centre of the village has now closed, having moved its collection to Albert (*see page 93*).

In the centre of the village, first take the D197 right. In 300 metres, a road on the left leads up to the **New Zealand Division Memorial** on the **site of Crest Farm**, midway between High Wood and Delville Wood. Behind the memorial is a small cratered area.

Return to the village and turn right onto D20 for about ½ km. Here, on the corner, is the **wooden cross** of the **12th (Bristol) Bn. Gloucestershire Regiment**, recently erected on the site of the original lost some time ago. A little further along the D20 from the Gloucester Cross is **Caterpillar Valley Cemetery**, one of the largest in the Somme. Nearly 5,600 are buried here and by the eastern wall is the pavilion of the **New Zealand Memorial to the Missing** on the Somme.

Return to the Gloucester Cross and take the D107 left. Away on the rise to the right, the New Zealand Division Memorial can be seen. About 1½ km along is **Bois des Fourcaux** or, as it is better known, **High Wood**. On the roadside is the slightly-sagging

Memorial to the 47th London Division which fought here and finally cleared the wood of its German defenders on September 15, 1916 after fierce fighting. One of their trenches ran along the edge of the wood about where

the right-hand ditch is now. The British cavalry penetrated the wood on July 14 but the Germans were well dug in with concrete dugouts and positions, one of which can be seen from the road among the trees. On the eastern flank of the wood — reached by a muddy track at the edge of the field — is the **Memorial to the 1st Bn. Cameron Highlanders and 1st Bn. Black Watch** who fought here on September 3, the day when the large mine was blown. The **crater**, now filled with water, can be seen behind the memorial to the right.

Further along the D107 is **London Cemetery**, with over 3,800 graves the third largest in the Somme, where the fallen from 1916

The Cameron Highlanders and Black Watch Memorial at the edge of High Wood.

One of the most poignant of memorials: 192 stones from Scotland erected to remember a similar number of Highlanders who fell in High Wood.

were joined in 1946 by men of the 51st Highland Division and others killed in 1940. About 100 metres before it, set back in the edge of the wood, is a small cairn. This was unveiled in 1972 by Madame Mathon whose family own the wood; it is the **Memorial to the 9th Bn. Highland Light Infantry — The Glasgow Highlanders**, 192 of whom fell in the trench here on July 15, 1916, fighting shoulder to shoulder. They are now commemorated by 192 stones brought from Scotland by the Scottish historian Mr Alex Aitken and his wife, and carefully constructed on a slate plinth to a height of 5 feet 7

inches, the minimum height of men of the battalion.

The wood is privately owned and should not be entered without the permission of the owner who lives in the large house near the road. The trenches and some of the strong points remain amid the trees, but the area has not been completely cleared of battle debris and it could be dangerous to trespass. From the edge of the wood overlooking Delville Wood is the area fought over by the London Battalions after taking the wood. It was a pocket of resistance which the capture of Flers had outflanked.

The third largest of the British Cemeteries on the Somme — London Cemetery. Over 3,800 British troops of both wars lie here.

Left: **The South African Memorial in Delville Wood, unveiled in 1926, with the new museum opened in 1986** *(above)* **in the background.**

The new museum has been sited to encompass the Voortrekker Cross — the cross upon a cross — *(above left)* **which formerly stood isolated as the Cross of Consecration. Now, etched plate-glass windows which surround it tell the story of South Africa's participation in words and pictures.** *Above centre and right:* **Around the walls, massive bronze panels depict the various aspects of the conflict.**

Relics of the battle, discovered during construction of the museum building.

Return through Longueval to visit **Delville Wood** and the **South African National Memorial** and **Museum** on the road to Ginchy. As the wood is approached, one reaches the large car and coach park, the shop and toilets. The entrance to the memorial and museum is opposite **Delville Wood Cemetery**, a little further along the road. This cemetery contains the graves of men of the divisions who contested this sector — the 9th Scottish Division and the 2nd, 14th Light and 17th Divisions.

The **Bois d'Elville**, approximately half-a-mile square in an irregular shape, skirts the eastern flank of Longueval and reaches almost into Ginchy on the east. The battle for the wood, often called **Devil's Wood** by the troops, was the scene of the baptisms of fire of the South African Brigade of the 9th Scottish Division from July 14-20, 1916. Commanded by General H. T. Lukin, the South African Brigade had a strength of 121 officers and 3,032 NCOs and men. On July 14, they had been in reserve at Montauban. Less one battalion (which went to assist in the clearing of Longueval), the brigade went into action on the morning of the 15th. Under heavy bombardment by the defending force, the battalions fought their desperate way into the wood and, despite heavy losses, had taken all the wood except the north-west corner by July 17. The 3rd Battalion was cut off and had to surrender — three officers and 150 men. The colonel of the 2nd Battalion, Lieutenant-Colonel E. F. Thackeray, gathered together 140 of all ranks from the four battalions and fought his way through to rejoin the brigade. At 6 p.m. on the 20th, the brigade was withdrawn — 29 officers and 751 other ranks were all that were left.

The graceful memorial is approached across a broad lawn between two double lines of oak trees grown from acorns brought from French Hook, Cape Colony. Hundreds of young trees were planted in the 1920s to form a frame for the memorial which was designed by Sir Herbert Baker, ARA. A triumphal archway, surmounted by a bronze group, is flanked by a curved wall of flint and stone with a pavilion at either end. The bronze group of two figures either side of a great horse by Alfred Turner represents Castor and Pollux clasping hands in friendship, and was originally entitled 'Union'. The memorial itself was unveiled by General Louis Botha's widow in the presence of General Herzog, Field-Marshal Haig and other dignitaries on October 10, 1926. The altar Stone of Remembrance, placed in front of the arch, was added after the Second World War to commemorate South Africa's 1939-45 war dead. This was unveiled by Mrs O. M. Swales, mother of Captain E. Swales, VC, on June 5, 1952.

On November 11, 1986, the Hon. P. W. Botha, President of the Republic of South Africa, inaugurated the **Commemorative Museum** which is situated behind the

The sole remaining tree to survive the 1916 battles, *left*, despite its shrapnel-filled trunk, is carefully tended by the CWGC. Close by this memorial, *right*, are the trenches leading to the South African Brigade HQ dugout.

memorial crescent. In the shape of the Castle of the Cape of Good Hope which is depicted in the South African Defence Force insignia and the Cape of Good Hope Star, the five bastions enclose the beautiful **Cross of Consecration** (the **Voortrekker Cross**) in a central patio. The story of South Africa's participation in both World Wars and in Korea is told on massive bronze panels, delicately-engraved windows, and in photographs, paintings, documents and relics. One interesting display shows items found on the spot when the museum was being built. Pride of place in the gallery is taken by the **Memorial Books of Honour**. The central entrance is flanked by artillery pieces.

To the west of the museum is the **sole surviving original tree** — a hornbeam — carefully tended by the Commonwealth War Graves Commission and, despite being full of shrapnel, it is remarkably healthy.

In the rehabilitation of the wood, the original glades, which were named after streets in London, Edinburgh and Capetown, have been maintained and make a walk through the wood a very pleasant experience. It is difficult to realise the terrible past until a trench is noticed in the undergrowth where rusty pieces of shellcase, water bottles and odd rounds of small arms ammunition are frequently found. All the glades have stone signposts at their junctions so it is quite easy to follow the course of the battles which raged in all for 16 days before the 2nd Division finally cleared the wood on July 28, 1916. In 1918, heavy fighting again took place during the Allied advance when the 17th and 38th Divisions were engaged. In the south-west corner of the wood, on **Buchanan Street**, just north of the cross with **Rotten Row**, is a monument marking the site of the **South African Brigade HQ dugout**. Behind it, on the edge of the wood towards Longueval, stands an identical stone marking the **point of entrance** of the South Africans into the trees on July 15. Nearby, several trenches can be followed away into the wood.

Right: **The memorial marking the spot where the South Africans entered the wood on the morning of July 15, 1916.**

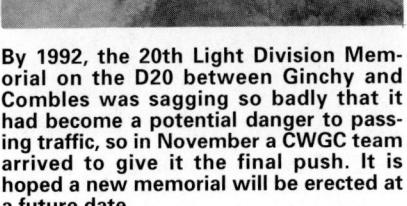

By 1992, the 20th Light Division Memorial on the D20 between Ginchy and Combles was sagging so badly that it had become a potential danger to passing traffic, so in November a CWGC team arrived to give it the final push. It is hoped a new memorial will be erected at a future date.

From Delville Wood continue eastwards to **Ginchy** — a forward position in the German defence line standing high on the plain above Combles. It was first captured by the 7th Division on July 3, but lost in a counter-attack only to be recaptured on July 9 by the 16th Irish Division. Turn right in the centre of the village to join the D20 in ½ km at the spot where until recently stood the **20th Light Division Memorial**. The memorial had begun to sag so badly that it threatened to tumble down on the road below; on November 10, 1992, a CWGC team arrived to push over and remove it. Now, only the steps remain, but plans exist for the memorial to be reinstated, funds permitting.

A simple wooden cross commemorates the death of Major Cedric Charles Dickens, a grandson of Charles Dickens. Although the trees of Bouleaux Wood in which it stood have now all been felled, the cross still stands, its preservation guaranteed by the municipality of Ginchy.

Turn left for Combles. In 1 km, **Leuze (Lousy) Wood** appears on the right. Through land reclamation its twin, **Bouleaux Wood**, on the left, is now completely gone. The last surviving fragment of it was cut down in 1994. These woods were the scene of heavy fighting by the 56th London Division in September 1916. About 300 metres up the muddy track into the fields that were Bouleaux Wood, and some 50 metres to the left of it, stands a **lone wooden cross** erected to commemorate the death on September 9, 1916 in Leuze Wood of a grandson of the novelist Charles Dickens. Major Cedric Charles Dickens served with the 1/13th Bn. (Kensington) London Regiment. Across the fields to the north-west lies the site of the formidable **Quadrilateral**, a fortified position captured by 6th Division on September 18, 1916.

In 1 km **Combles**, a small town built on a hill, was the last German redoubt to fall in September 1916. Just opposite was the junction between the BEF and the French lines. Protected by its surrounding hills, Combles did not suffer to the same degree as neighbouring villages. During their occupation of it, the German Army strongly fortified the town, which eventually fell to a joint Anglo-French attack on September 26. In the rock beneath **Lamotte Château**, tunnels and shelters had been cut before the war which the Germans extended, making a complete subterranean headquarters. The town has two British cemeteries: **Combles Cemetery Extension**, in the north-eastern part of town, and **Guards Cemetery**, tucked away on the western slopes.

Two kms along the D74/D11e is **Morval** which was captured on September 25, 1916. It was re-entered again by the advancing Germans in March 1918 as it lay in the gap between the Third and Fifth Armies.

A kilometre further on is **Lesboeufs** captured by the 6th and Guards Divisions on September 25. In March 1918, the 63rd Royal Naval Division was in action here, delaying the German advance. Machine-gunners fired 250,000 rounds whilst covering the division, creating havoc among the oncoming German forces.

Keep to the left and return to Ginchy by the road which crosses the heights. Some 300 metres beyond **Guards Cemetery** on the right, is a **private memorial** to Captain H. P. Meakin, attached to the Guards Machine Gun Company and killed here on September 25, 1916. Another ¾ km on, a stop at the **Guards Division Memorial** provides excellent views of the area of the September 1916 conflict and the March 1918 advance.

Continue to Ginchy and take the right turn for Flers, passing a **Memorial of the French 18ème Régiment Teritorial d'Infanterie** to the men who fell here on September 26, 1914. The road crosses the wide open country over which the tanks rolled for the first time on September 15, 1916. To our left can be seen Delville and High woods with Crest Farm in between.

As we reach **Flers** 2 kms further on, on the left corner of the junction with the D197 is the **Memorial of the French 82ème Division d'Infanterie Territoriale** who saw action here on September 26, 1914. At the end of the main street is the **41st Division Memorial**

The Guards' Cemetery is laid out on the slopes beyond Combles. This town, just opposite the junction of the British and French lines, was heavily fortified by the Germans. It was captured on September 26, 1916.

The memorial to Captain H. P. Meakin, killed here fighting with the Guards near Lesboeufs on September 25, 1916.

The Guards Division Memorial on the Lesboeufs-Ginchy road — a windswept viewpoint of the field of battle.

In these same fields, the French fought a defensive battle on September 26, 1914, as witnessed by the memorial of the 82ème Division d'Infanterie Territoriale at Flers *(left)* and that of the 18ème Régiment Territorial d'Infanterie outside Ginchy *(right)*.

(see front cover), a 'New Army' division with units from many parts of England. Their badges decorate the enclosing pillars. The rifle of the infantryman points in the direction that the tanks came from Pozières. Flers was the target of three corps of the Fourth Army on September 15, 1916 when, in the early morning, the tanks first took to the fields.

Proceed northward on D197 and, at the next crossroads, turn right on D74, passing **A.I.F. Burial Ground Cemetery** away to the right and reach **Gueudecourt** in 2 kms. The hub of many actions in September 1916, little remained of the village when it was captured. About 1 km on D74e, the Beaulencourt road, is the **Newfoundland Memorial** in a small fir-lined enclosure amid the expanse of cornfields (see back cover). The memorial is a Caribou similar to the one at Beaumont-Hamel. This one stands above a strong point within a curve of trenches and a machine gun post which were the site of a regimental position in September 1916.

Return to Gueudecourt and leave by the D74 for Le Sars crossing the **Warlencourt Ridge**. The hamlet of **Le Sars** is astride the D929 on the crest of one of the rises of the hills overlooking Bapaume, and marks the limit of the British advance on this sector in the 1916 Somme battles.

Turn right on to the D929. As we descend the hill, over to the right ahead, in the fold of one of the slopes of the hills, is a wooded mound. In 1916, this was the chalk-covered eminence known as the **Butte de Warlencourt**. At that time, it was higher than it is today and it stood out above the rest of the battlefield. The Butte was an artificial mound which had played a prominent part in the war of 1871, and was honeycombed with many tunnels even before the Germans took it and fortified it so strongly that it was almost impossible to capture. Several times, it was overrun by units of the 47th, 9th and 50th Divisions but the defenders from below counter-attacked, driving off the attacking forces until, on February 25, 1917, success was achieved and the Butte fell into British hands. During the following year, five of the attacking units erected memorials on the shell-torn crest including the Durham Light Infantry, the South Africans and other territorial units. None of these survive here today. In March 1918, the Germans retook the mound and they erected a cross on the summit. It was not until August 1918 that the Butte was again overrun, this time by 21st Division.

The remains of some of the fortified entrances can be traced in the undergrowth beneath the trees and the **base of the German memorial** can be found on the crest. In 1944, the German infantry battalion in the region erected a replacement cross on the old base but this has now gone too. The

Impressive Flers 41st Division Memorial.

Western Front Association purchased the site in 1990 and erected a **WFA Memorial** on the crest in its place.

The D929 continues across the undulating country to Bapaume, 5 kms away. Vestiges of the old trench lines remain here and there with the occasional **concrete shelter** and, nearer to Bapaume, the ridges and hedges show evidence of usage as artillery positions. To visit the town, turn right at the road junction.

Bapaume is a quiet market town with a long history dating back to Roman times. Situated at a strategic crossroads, it was frequently the scene of conflict and in the 16th Century was a fortified town. Beneath the quiet streets, many of the cellars are in fact relics of this period.

The town was in the battle-line in late August 1914 and, after the German push to the west, remained in their hands until March 17, 1917 when the Australian 2nd Division captured it. All the old buildings had by then been destroyed. Only one building remains today and that is a **barn** on the very outskirts of the town on the Péronne road (N17). Parts of the old ramparts, stripped of their brick cladding, can be seen on the western side of the town in a park. The **town museum** is housed in the **Lawrence School** in rue J. B. Lequette, on the other side of the main street, and includes relics from 1914-18. The school was the gift of a manufacturer from Sheffield.

During the German occupations of the town in both wars, they made use of one of the underground bastions, which dates from 1551, and on occasions this can be viewed.

The galleries of the **Bastion de la Reyne** lie beneath the houses north of Place Faidherbe and are in remarkable condition. The entrance is through the house at No. 9 rue de la République, three blocks away. The main gallery is some eight metres below the level of the pavement and consists of two large halls connected by narrow vaulted passages.

In many of the old gun ports there are piles of debris from the German occupations, including hundreds of bottles, proclaiming it as the site of an old mess. On the walls are earlier relics; on one brick is inscribed the palindrome '1551' which legend has it was scratched by Charles V. On another is a representation of the arms of Austria, Spain and Burgundy, the three major contestants for the town in the 16th Century. The wiring for telephone and electricity dates from 1916. Enquiries for further details should be made to the Société Archéologique de Bapaume which resides in the Lawrence School.

When the Germans evacuated Bapaume in March 1917, they left many of the buildings booby-trapped or mined. The Hôtel de Ville was one of these and it blew up some days after the Australians had entered the town. The Germans re-entered the ruins of Bapaume on March 24, 1918 but were dislodged by the New Zealand Division on August 29. After the war, the town was awarded the Croix de Guerre and the Légion d'Honneur.

Leave Bapaume for Arras by the N17, a distance of 22 kms. This road swings up and down through several small villages and hamlets well known to the BEF. In its day, this agricultural plain was a scene of utter devastation and sometimes, usually in the evening light, the tracks of a tortuous trench line can be discerned. Along the route, one passes the **memorial** which marks the site of the **Battle of Bapaume** (January 5, 1871) of the Franco-German War of 1870-71.

Some 4 kms from Bapaume, **Sapignies** and, a little further, **Béhagnies** were both in the front line in March 1918 when they fell in the face of the German advance. Both were recaptured in August by the 2nd Division.

We then pass through **Ervillers** in 2 kms, a German garrison village until March 1917 and then in March 1918 the scene of heavy fighting with the 42nd Division trying to delay the advance. It was recaptured on August 23. **Gomiécourt**, a short way to the south-west, was where the 3rd Division had a fierce fight in August 1918 when they took the village with many prisoners.

It is 6 kms to **Boiry-Becquerelle** (the modern road bypasses the village by a bridge) and 3 kms to **Mercatel**. This village was the junction of the **Hindenburg Line** with the old German line of 1914. We then reach **Beaurains**, a suburb of Arras through which the front line ran in 1917 and where the CWGC now have their offices.

The Butte de Warlencourt (above) which was purchased by the Western Front Association early in 1990 is surmounted by a new memorial, left. The old German memorial on the Butte, a wooden cross, disappeared several years ago.

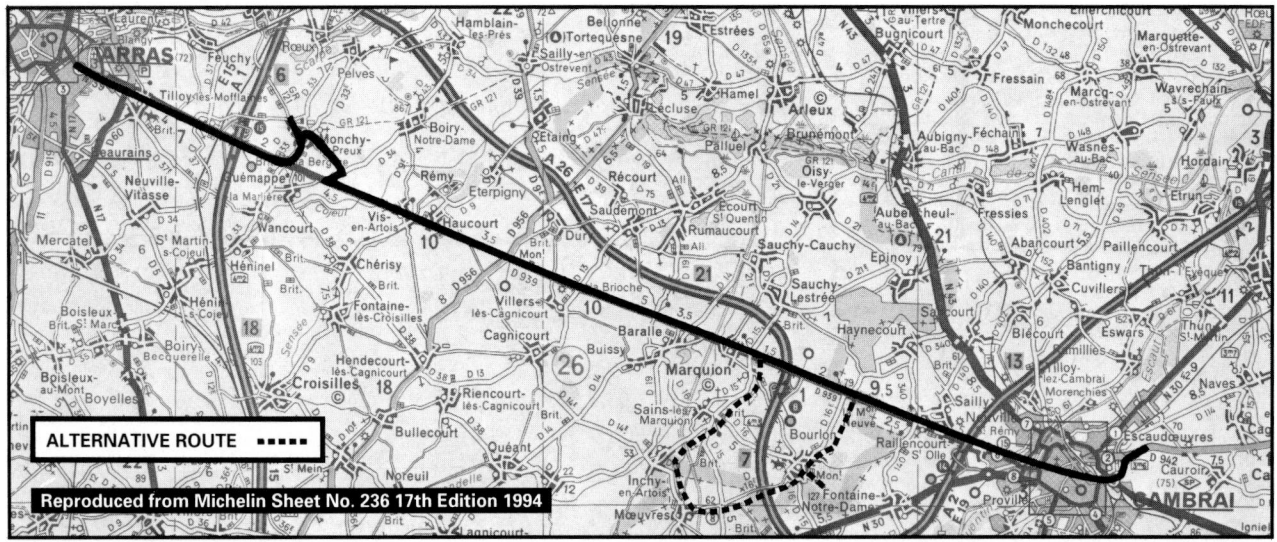

Arras to Cambrai

ROUTE I via Monchy-le-Preux

The direct route to Cambrai via the D939 is 30 kms, an absolutely straight road of Roman origin.

Tilloy-lès-Mofflaines (4 kms). North of this Arras suburb is the famous **Observatory Ridge** with the **Harp position** from which the Hindenburg Line swung southwards to Croisilles and Quéant. There were many actions fought around here in 1917 during the battle for Arras but few signs remain evident today. The construction of autoroutes A1 and A26 has removed most of the prominent ones but, here and there, a steep-sided ditch or a long earthwork may be a remnant of the old trench lines.

La Chapelle de Feuchy (2 kms). Access point for the A1-E15 Lille-Paris motorway. This was the furthest extent of the first day's advance in the April 1917 battle and the village where the 15th Scottish Division stood in the defence of Arras in 1918. Here, too, on April 9, 1917, the **12th Eastern Division** fought an action and their **memorial** stands on the south side of the road near the spot. This cross is one of two memorials, the other being at Malassie Farm near Epehy, south of Cambrai, a position held by the division in the capture of that town in September 1918. Both crosses are copies of a cross in York Minster. Opposite is a **Demarcation Stone**.

Leave the D939 by turning to the left on the D33 for **Monchy-le-Preux** (1 km). This village, built on high ground, provided the Germans with a commanding view of the Allied lines. It was captured by the 37th Division, on April 11, 1917 during a blizzard. It was protected by wide bands of barbed wire, such as those which covered the Hindenburg Line, making an attack a very costly affair. However, Monchy, despite many counter-attacks, was retained until the March 1918 advance. East from Monchy rises **Infantry Hill** which was in the 29th Division line held by the Royal Newfoundland Regiment. On a bunker in the village, in the front garden of a house, stands the Caribou of the **Newfoundland Regiment Memorial**. A little further up this same road, behind the château, stands the **37th Division Memorial**. Monchy was recaptured on August 26, 1918 by the Canadian Corps. Return to the D939 via rue de Vis and D34.

Vis-en-Artois (4 kms) is reached after crossing the River Cojeul. About ½ km past the village, on the upward slope, is the **Vis-en-Artois Cemetery and Memorial to the Missing** who fell in the 1918 advance in Picardy and Artois where 9,832 names are remembered. In the cemetery lie over 1,700 British and 582 Canadians who died in the capture of this sector on August 27, 1918.

In 3 kms, **Dury Crossroad** — now, like almost all the crossroads along this road, changed into a roundabout. Almost directly after it, on the left, is the **Canadian Memorial**, commemorating that here the Canadian Corps broke and turned the main German position on September 2, 1918.

Dury Crossroads Canadian Memorial.

The Memorial to the 12th Division on the HQ dugout site at La Chapelle de Feuchy.

The 37th Division's soldier trio which stands at Monchy-le-Preux.

Vis-en-Artois Cemetery and the Memorial to the Missing.

At Moeuvres, a German mass grave lies alongside the Allied war graves. Here Lieutenant Pope, an Australian VC, is buried *(right)*.

About 6½ kms of undulating road stretch across the expansive plain before the **Canal du Nord** and **Marquion** are reached. To assist the 4th, 63rd and 1st Canadian Divisions to take this small town in September 1918, the Royal Engineers built several bridges over the canal during the nights beforehand.

An interesting detour can be made by turning right onto the D15 at the end of the village and in 2½ kms reaching the edge of **Sains-les-Marquoin** with the **cemetery** — containing mainly Canadian graves — at the crossroads with the D16. Go straight ahead to the fork and take the D22 right for **Inchy-en-Artois** and then the D19/D34a left in the village for **Moeuvres** (2 kms). Both villages were German strongholds which did not fall in the 1917 battles despite all attempts, but in 1918 the former was captured by the 63rd Royal Naval Division on September 3, and the latter by the 52nd Lowland Division on the 19th. The **Canal du Nord**, recrossed back to the west as Inchy is entered, was still under construction and formed a deep and vital barrier for both attacker and defender.

As Moeuvres is reached, on the right is **Moeuvres Communal Cemetery Extension**. Near the entrance is a German mass grave of 94 officers and men named on the surrounding plinth. Lieutenant C. Pope of 11th Australian Battalion, a posthumous VC recipient, is also buried here (Plot V, Grave D22). He died on April 15, 1917 at Louverval in the action for which he won the decoration.

In November 1917, the 56th London Division were heavily engaged between the two villages.

In Moeuvres, take the second left of the church (D16e), recrossing the Canal du Nord and taking the second left at the five-road junction with the D15 for **Bourlon** 4 kms further on. **Bourlon Wood**, captured by the Canadians on September 27, 1918, is to the east of the village on rising ground. The **Canadian Memorial** is on the edge of the

wood on the hillside and is reached up a stepped path between ancient chestnut trees planted in Napoleon's honour. In the undergrowth of the wood are remains of a **bunker**. A path leads into the wood from the entrance to the memorial (up to the right as

you face the village). There is also a **memorial to the Free French** of the Second World War here.

From Bourlon, take the D16e to gain the D939 in 3½ kms. Turn right and Cambrai is 8 kms further on.

Cambrai, an historic town, is once more a bustling, prosperous industrial and market city. In 1815, Wellington took the surrender of the city after the fall of Napoleon. In 1870, the Germans took it and in August 1914 von Kluck recaptured it. The Germans held the town as a large garrison base until October 8, 1918. In 1916, Prince Rupprecht of Bavaria had his headquarters here. In the autumn of 1917, the city came within the range of the Allied artillery and damage was effected on the ancient buildings. However, most of the destruction was caused in 1918 when the retreating Germans mined and fired it as 3rd Canadian Division and the 57th Division converged on the city, from the north and the south respectively, to complete the operation on October 9.

After passing through the suburb of Raillencourt, we enter Cambrai via the rue d'Arras and, after crossing the St Quentin Canal, the rue des Feutriers leads up to the roundabout of the Place du 9 Octobre. On its grass stand two black-marble tablets: one the **Royal Canadian Regiment Memorial**, unveiled at the regiment's centenary in 1983, and, to its left, the **Liberation Memorial**, dedicated on October 9, 1978, the 60th anniversary of the town's deliverance.

Two memorials adorn Place du 9 Octobre at Cambrai: one to honour the Royal Canadian Regiment *(above left)* and one to commemorate the town's liberation by the 3rd Canadian and 57th British Divisions on October 9, 1918 *(above right)*.

Close to the war memorial *(above)* **in Cambrai's town park, a plaque** *(right)* **commemorates the Allied offensive of November 1917, the first time that tanks were used en masse.**

A little further on is the great Place Aristide Briand, once the Place d'Armes. The impressive **Hôtel de Ville** was severely damaged but has been rebuilt in its former design of the 19th Century. In the Belfry, above the central façade, are the oldest inhabitants of Cambrai: 'Martin' and 'Martine', the two mechanical figures of blackamoors which date from 1510 and which appear as the clock strikes the hour. Opposite, in the Mail St Martin, is the rebuilt **Belfry**, all that remains of the church of St Martin which dates from the 15th Century. Two of the city gates have survived, the **Porte Notre Dame** in the north-east and the **Porte de Paris** in the south. The **cathedral**, in

the Avenue de la Victoire leading south from the main square, is a Gothic church built in 1859 which was badly damaged. There is a **Municipal Museum** (at present being renovated) in the rue de l'Epée.

At the edge of the Jardin Public (reached by taking the street leading east from the square) is the **City War Memorial** and, a short distance along the street to its right (Rang St Jean), are the park steps with a **Memorial Plaque to the Third Army's Attack** of November 20, 1917, unveiled in 1977 by the British Ambassador and recording the participation of 381 tanks. The Jardin Public covers remnants of the ramparts designed by Charles Quint and Vauban. The

crumbling ruins of the old fortress and barracks of Château de Selles lie at the north end of Boulevard Faidherbe.

On the D942, the Solesmes road, about 1½ km out of town, is the **Cambrai East Military Cemetery**. This was originally a German graveyard, the British section of which was later taken over by the CWGC. (It lies in the south-east corner of the cemetery.) As with almost all the German burial grounds, the German section has green lawns about which are scattered lines of graves and very Teutonic monuments with the central huge black cross within a small walled area. In the cemetery are a mass grave containing 2,746 dead and a number of French graves.

Originally German, Cambrai East Military Cemetery is now looked after jointly by the CWGC and the Volksbund Deutsche Kriegsgräberfürsorge. The photograph, *above left,* **shows the original German memorial and that,** *right,* **the British section.**

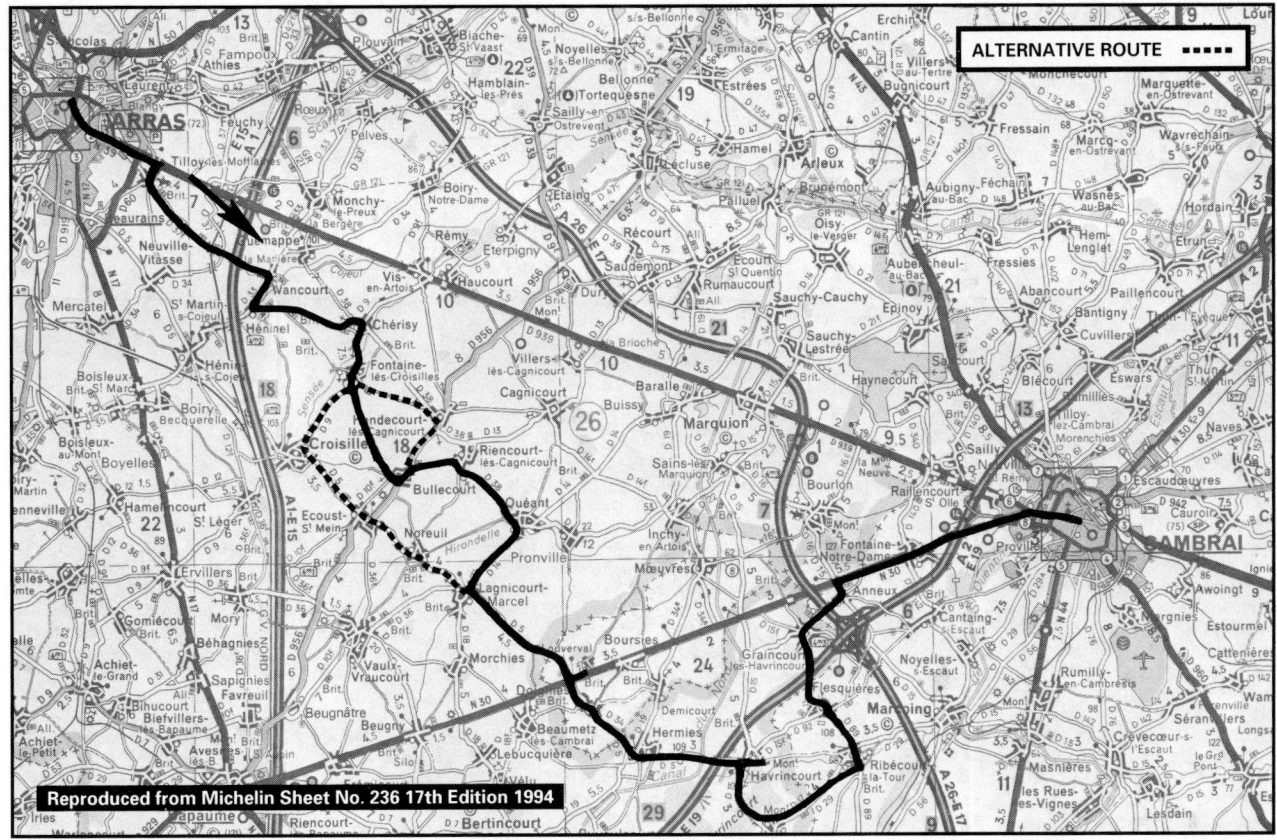

Reproduced from Michelin Sheet No. 236 17th Edition 1994

Arras to Cambrai

ROUTE II via Bullecourt

Leave Arras by the D939 and, after 3 kms, turn right onto D60 and immediately left onto D37a/D34 through the centre of **Tilloy** and then out into the country, crossing the area of the April 1917 attacks during the Arras battles.

In 5 kms, after going under the autoroute, enter **Wancourt** and, at the church, turn right on the D33 for **Héninel**, 1¼ km away. Both these villages played important rôles in the attacks by General Allenby's Third Army in 1917 and General Currie's Canadians in August 1918.

Turn left for **Chérisy** (4 kms), bearing left at the fork onto a pleasant if narrow road across the rolling countryside which was very cut about in 1917 and 1918. At Chérisy, turn right onto D9 for **Fontaine-lès-Croisilles** (2 kms) which lies on the east bank of the River Sensée. On the outskirts of the village (about 100 metres up the track on the right immediately before the river bridge) is a very well preserved **German concrete dugout**.

The D9/D5 leads to **Croisilles** and **Ecoust-St Mein**, while the first small road after the church leads to **Hendecourt** and the second one — our first choice here — to **Bullecourt** (3½ kms). This is all the area fought over by Australians and several British divisions during the Arras battles, and the breaching of the **Hindenburg Line**, which ran over the open country with wide belts of barbed-wire entanglements. Bullecourt was the scene of many gallant deeds by the 62nd West Riding Division and has retained long associations with units which took part. Before the church is a **memorial to the British and Australians** erected in 1980, and, taking the right-hand fork north out of the village (D38), leads to the new **Australian Memorial**. Unveiled on Anzac Day, April 25, 1992, on the 75th anniversary of the battle, the bronze statue of the Australian 'digger' commemorates the 10,000 Australians killed or wounded in the

Memorial at Bullecourt to the British and Australian dead of April and May 1917.

The Australian Digger Memorial outside Bullecourt, which was dedicated on Anzac Day, 1992.

Another memorial nearby commemorates the 2,423 Australians who went missing on the Bullecourt battlefield.

two Bullecourt battles of April-May 1917. A bronze **relief map**, added in 1993, explains the actions which took place here.

Some 400 metres along this same road, high up on the bank on the left, is the older **Australian Memorial Cross** to the 2,423 Australians who disappeared without a trace on these plains.

Continue north to Riencourt, bearing right to join the D38 to **Quéant** (3½ kms) and thence by the D14 to Lagnicourt-Marcel, to go over the sites of the **Hindenburg Line** or the **Quéant Switch** which stretched to Drocourt in the north. This region was eventually captured by the 63rd Royal Naval Division. (Alternatively, to get to Lagnicourt from Ecoust, take the D5 via **Noreuil**.)

On entering **Lagnicourt-Marcel**, take the first left, the D5/D34 to the crossroads on the N30 (4 kms). To the left of it, below the hamlet of **Louverval**, are the **Louverval Military Cemetery** and the **Cambrai Memorial to the Missing** of the 1917 Battle of Cambrai. On the walls of the memorial are some fine bas reliefs by C. S. Jagger relating to the Cambrai battles.

Return to the crossroads and turn left onto D34 for **Doignies** and, 3 kms further on, **Hermies**. This is a pleasant village of which the green was once a large mine crater in 1917 when the I Anzac Corps were here.

After 3 kms, the D5 crosses the Canal du Nord and the autoroute to enter **Havrincourt**. The **château**, which dominates this

village, was for a long time in German hands as an HQ and here, on occasion, the Kaiser stayed. Before the end of the 1917 campaign, the village and château were in ruins, either through constant artillery bombardment or demolition. In 1917, British divisions could not dislodge the enemy from the village or the wood which was fortified with concrete bunkers when the main attack on the Hindenburg Line began. Havrincourt was also on the edge of the Battle of Cambrai in November to December 1917. The 62nd West Riding Division fought here in 1917 and they captured the village in 1918. The New Zealand Corps took **Havrincourt Wood** on the edge of which is the **62nd Division Memorial** (It is found by following the street which, as you face the château gates, goes left through the village).

As with other villages in the area, Havrincourt has retained close relationships with its liberators and, each year, the Bradford Pals Pilgrimage used to pause here to meet the Maire and other personalities to drink a 'Vin d'Honneur' before visiting the château. This large, red-brick house has been destroyed three times by fire or battle this century and, after each tragedy, has been rebuilt exactly as it was. In the meadows behind the château, and in the wood beyond, are remains of concrete shelters and bunkers.

Return past the château for a pleasant detour through the woods, and **Trescault** (4 kms) — with the **42nd Division Memorial** at the far end of the village on the left-hand side of the road — via the D15 and then the D17/D29 to **Ribécourt-la-Tour**. Then take the D89 from Ribécourt to Flesquières and the area of the Cambrai battle.

Flesquières was strongly defended by the Germans when, on November 20, 1917, the Battle of Cambrai began with the advance of some 400 tanks from Havrincourt Wood to attack across the open fields on a 15-kilometre front. From artillery emplacements in and around the village, the Germans hit hard at the Allied tanks. Although several divisions of General Byng's Third Army carried their targets, Flesquières proved to be a difficult proposition and a fierce battle ensued before the 51st Highland Division successfully captured the village. Marcoing, 3 kms to the east, was captured by the 29th Division. The 62nd Division then went forward to take Graincourt and Anneux with many prisoners. The 6th Division took Ribécourt, whilst the 36th Division took Moeuvres in the north, and the 12th Division Bonavis Ridge and Lateau Wood. Meanwhile, the 20th Light Division had taken, and then after a heavy counter-attack lost, Les Rues-des-Vignes in the south. The 51st Division went forward to capture Fontaine-Notre-Dame and, as the 40th Division were attacking Bourlon Wood, the German 2. Armee counter-attacked. The 40th Division took the

Bas relief *(above)*, one of several carved by C. S. Jagger on the Cambrai Memorial at Louverval *(above left)*. This remembers those who fell in the Battle of Cambrai and have no known graves.

wood following a period of severe fighting with gas attacks but, by the end of November, the British divisions had taken nearly 11,000 prisoners and 140 guns. However, by the end of the first week in December, the reinforced German army had driven back the Allies to the Flesquières Ridge.

During the Allied advance in September 1918, the area was captured by the 2nd, 3rd, 5th, 42nd and Guards Divisions with the Canadians taking Bourlon Wood *(see page 103)*. The 57th and 63rd Divisions took Anneux and Graincourt and then Marcoing before reaching Cambrai.

From Flesquières, go across D92 and over the autoroute to **Graincourt-lès-Havrincourt** (2 kms) and turn right in the village for **Anneux** and there turn left on the D15 to reach the N30. Near the crossroads, where we turn right (and the D16 continues ahead to follow the south-western slopes of Bourlon Wood), is **Anneux British Cemetery** where many of those killed in November 1917 and in September 1918 are buried. In 2 kms, **Fontaine-Notre-Dame**, captured on November 21, 1917 by the 51st Highland Division, is passed through and in 4 kms **Cambrai** *(see page 103)* is entered.

The 62nd West Riding Division, whose memorial *(above)* is to be found on the edge of Havrincourt, captured the ruins of the village in 1918.

From Havrincourt, a detour can be made to take in the 42nd Division Memorial in the village of Trescault. The division fought in this area in September 1918.

Five routes to Mons

ROUTE I

The easiest and most direct route involved in this stage of our tour is via the A2-E19 autoroute. In this mode, Cambrai is 65 kms from Mons.

ROUTE II

Alternatively, we can use the N30 to Valenciennes (30 kms) through some varied countryside, increasingly industrial, as the coalfields are reached between Bouchain and Douchy-les-Mines into **Valenciennes**. This former lace-making city was occupied by the Germans in August 1914 and suffered considerably during the next four years. Factories and other establishments were taken over for use by the invading army, converting the area into a large base. By the time the Germans were driven out of the city in November 1918, by the Canadian Corps and the 4th, 49th and 61st Divisions, much had been destroyed. Damage was also caused by artillery fire during the Allied advance.

Some 12 kms out of Valenciennes on the N30 is the frontier post at **Quiévrechain**, from where the long straight road (N51) continues 22 kms to Mons. In its latter stages, the road passes through the region, south of the **Condé Canal**, which figured greatly in the 1914 BEF defence of Mons. General Allenby's Cavalry Corps were defending the bridges along the canal with the 19th Brigade in support from Valenciennes. The 5th Division was in action along the canal and, after the retreat had been ordered, the four bridges were blown. Today, however, there is nothing left to recall the brave acts of 1914.

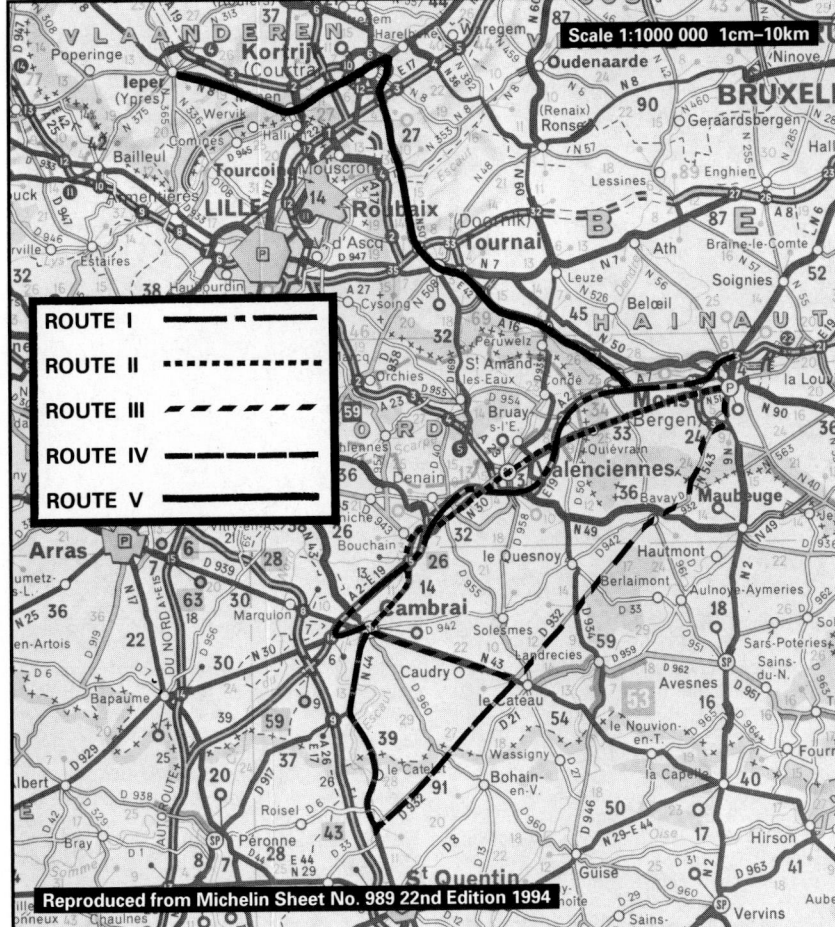

Scale 1:1000 000   1cm=10km

ROUTE I
ROUTE II
ROUTE III
ROUTE IV
ROUTE V

Reproduced from Michelin Sheet No. 989 22nd Edition 1994

Bottom left: **A modern bridge now spans the canal at Masnières, replacing the original one** *(left)* **sited a few yards to the side of it, which collapsed under the weight of a British tank, causing a hold-up in the Allied advance in 1917. (IWM)**

ROUTE III

The D932 route to Mons can be joined from Cambrai either at Le Cateau or south-west of Le Catelet. Using the N43, Le Cateau is 24 kms.

The town war memorial at Caudry has bas reliefs representing 17th Division's battle for the town in 1918.

The Masnières Caribou marks the Newfoundlanders' part in the Battle of Cambrai.

Masnières' own memorial by the bridge.

After leaving Cambrai, there is not a bend in this old Roman road over its total length. It sweeps up and down through open country and few towns or villages lie directly in its path. In recent years, it has been greatly widened and is now a very fast road indeed, with narrow stretches only through the outlying parts of Beauvois, Caudry and Inchy. In **Caudry** (16 kms) is rather a unique **town war memorial**. On the plinth are commemorated four incidents in the war: the defence of the town in 1914; the trials of the occupation; the battle of 1918; and the final liberation on October 10, 1918, in which the figures carved in bas relief actually represent the personalities concerned — the officers and NCOs of the 17th Division.

From Caudry, it is 8 kms to Le Cateau; Mons is another 52 kms north on the D932/N543. *(For a description of Le Cateau, see page 119; for the route from Le Cateau to Mons (in reverse direction), see pages 116-118.)*

ROUTE IV

For the more circular route via Le Catelet, leave Cambrai through the Porte de Paris on the N44, 7½ kms to **Masnières**. On the crest of the hill going down into the town, on the right, is the **Newfoundland Regiment's Caribou Memorial**; the 29th Division, of which it was a part, fought here in November 1917 during the Battle of Cambrai.

In the town, the **St Quentin Canal** is crossed not far from the **site of the bridge** which, after being mined by the Germans but not completely blown, was used by the British in their attacks in the Cambrai battle. However, when a tank attempted to drive across it, the much-weakened structure gave way and the accident was to cause a considerable hold up to the advancing forces.

Another 4 kms is **Bonavis**, the southern end of the line for the battle. Take the left-hand fork, the N44 for Le Catelet, travelling up and down across the plain (10 kms). Join the D932 about 7 kms south of the town, turning left. Le Cateau is 27 kms away, and Mons another 52. *(For a description (in reverse direction) of the route from Le Catelet via Le Cateau to Mons, see pages 116-120.)*

ROUTE V

For those wanting to travel direct from Ypres (Ieper), our route follows the most picturesque and historic roads. However, soon it will be possible to make the journey entirely by autoroute.

Take the N8 from Ypres to **Menin** (Menen), 18 kms. This industrial town (with its twin Halluin on the southern French bank of the Lys), was the major German base and supply depot for the battles of Ypres. In 1914, it was overrun before Sir John French could seize it and, for the next four years, the Germans retained it. On October 16, 1918, the 34th Division took the town in the great Allied advance.

Some 3 kms east of the town along the N8, just before entering Wevelgem, a road to the left leads to the **Menin German Cemetery** where 47,864 are buried.

Another 10 kms further along the N8 is **Courtrai** (Kortrijk), also used by the German Army as a large base. It fell to the 9th Division on October 17, 1918. The town was damaged during the Second World War by a number of air raids. One of its older fortifications, the **Broelen Toren**, survived. This is a bridge over the Lys with two huge towers, in one of which is a **small museum**.

Some 2¼ kms out of the town on the Ghent road (the N43), on the left-hand side just before **Harelbeke**, is the **Royal Newfoundland Regiment Memorial**, the Caribou marking their exploits here in 1918. Turn right at the Caribou crossroad and follow the ring-road south as far as the 323a/N50 exit for Tournai (Doornik), which is then 29 kms away. A pleasant road through varying country which for the last 10 kms follows closely the course of the Scheldt. At **Esquelmes**, 7 kms from Courtrai and 1 km to the left of the N50, in the little churchyard on the river bank, is a group of **British war graves** from late 1918. Away in the fields, a kilometre or so along the narrow road running parallel with the canal, is a **1939-45 cemetery**, where lie men killed in May 1940. Among the many Guardsmen buried here is the 9th Duke of Northumberland.

The ancient city of **Tournai** (Doornik) is entered through a long avenue of magnificent trees. The centre of the city is dominated by the enormous cathedral with its five towers. At the eastern end of the **Grand Place** is the **Belfroi**, the oldest in Belgium, and a magnificent view is gained from the gallery near the top.

Until the foundation of the modern Belgium in 1830, Tournai held allegiance to France. Many sieges have been withstood, including that by Edward III in 1340, and from 1513 to 1519 the city was in the hands of Henry VIII. He improved the old fortifications of the city and today one of these

Save for a month, Menin remained in German hands throughout the war. This is their war cemetery where over 47,000 are buried.

After Beaumont-Hamel (July 1916), Gueudecourt (September 1916), Monchy-le-Preux (April 1917) and Masnières (November 1917), we find the fifth Caribou Memorial at Courtrai commemorating the Newfoundland Regiment's action here of October 1918.

Tour Henri VIII provides a medieval setting for the Musée des Armes at Tournai. A relic of Bluff King Hal's fortifications of the 1513-19 era.

remains, the **Tour Henri VIII**. It stands across the river from the centre, in a park on the rue du Château near the station. A solid two-storey building, it now houses the small but most-interesting **Musée des Armes** including ancient and modern weapons. At the entrance is a 'Tallboy' and other, smaller bombs from the Second World War.

To the German Army, Tournai was a very important centre with routes connecting with their forward bases. They finally retreated in the face of the Fifth Army in the last Allied advance. The British Army entered the city on November 8, 1918, to find many wrecked buildings and all the bridges destroyed.

Our RFC heroes: George Bayly and Vincent Waterfall, the first to fall on August 22, 1914.

In **Tournai South Communal Cemetery**, ½ km up a left fork off the Avenue Montgomery (N508) and next to the church on the right, in the Allied Extension, lie two officers of the Royal Flying Corps who are presumed to be the first killed in action in 1914. They are 2nd Lieutenant Vincent Waterfall and Lieutenant Charles George Gordon Bayly of No. 5 Squadron. On August 22, 1914, they set out at 10.16 a.m. in an Avro from their base at Maubeuge on a reconnaissance flight and flew over Mons and Soignies and were brought down by enemy action near Enghien. It was from this success that the Germans received their first confirmation that British forces had arrived in Belgium. A fragment of the observer's report was picked up by Belgian peasants near the wreckage of their plane and eventually was sent to London. A photo of this tattered document is in the first volume of the official history *The War in the Air*. The two men were buried originally in the communal cemetery of Labliau-Marcq, before their bodies were later transferred to the Tournai cemetery, where they lie in Plot III, Grave G3 (Bayly) and G4 (Waterfall). For many years, there has been a pair of rusting iron plaques beside the Villers-St Ghislain–Harmignies road (*see page 113*) which intimated they marked the position of the crash, but investigations by Mr André Englebert have proved this false. I wonder how the error came about. Lieutenant Bayly was an officer in the 56th Field Company, RE, and 2nd Lieutenant Waterfall was in the East Yorkshire Regiment. Both were attached to the RFC and were 23 years of age.

The Tournai South Communal Cemetery was used extensively by the Germans during the occupation as it was close to a major hospital, the **Hôpital Notre Dame**, where British and Allied casualties were cared for. German casualties were sent to another hospital not far distant. The German graves were later moved and those of the British and Allied, mainly Russian and French, were concentrated into national plots. There are over 700 British Commonwealth graves and very many Russian.

Leave Tournai by N7 and at Warchin join the A16-E42 autoroute. In 30 kms, join the Paris–Bruxelles autoroute (A7-E19). It is constructed partly on the old **Condé Canal** and some of the buildings between which it passes were originally factories and warehouses with quays. The first exit (25) after the merging of the autoroutes is for St

Ghislain and Tertre. Some of the earliest fighting took place in this area and indeed in **St Ghislain** is a **memorial** to the casualties of an artillery battery which occupied a factory site near the canal. On one of the pillars of the ancient **Hôtel de Ville** in the main square is a **bronze plaque** to the memory of Major C. Holland, 120th Battery, 27th Brigade,

RA,,who was killed in action on August 23, 1914. At first, he was buried beneath the factory wall but later his body was moved to **Hautrage Military Cemetery** (on the southern side of the Tertre–Hautrage road) where British and German dead lie side by side. Major Holland is in Plot I, Grave B2. It is believed that the St Ghislain plaque may be the earliest memorial to be erected in the Mons region; it was dedicated on November 9, 1919.

Leave the autoroute at either junction 24a or 24 to enter **Mons** (Bergen). From St Ghislain, take the N51 through the busy industrial areas of Quaregnon and Jemappes with their sudden and unexpected areas of wild country. Exit 23 of the autoroute is for SHAPE and Nimy and joins the old Mons to Brussels road at Maisières.

109

MONS

Mons, as the run in will have shown, is a modern industrial town with a coalfield on two sides. Along the modernised Condé Canal, factories stand with their loading bays on the banks, ready to receive and deliver goods. In the distance, on either side, rise the hills, Mons itself being built on one.

Of the famous Battle of Mons of August 1914, or that of November 1918, no sign remains, for neither action lasted long enough to leave any lasting physical marks. There are, however, a number of memorials set at points which recall the actions of the corps to which they belong and, in spite of the German bombing of 1940 and fighting of 1944 (when the US VII Corps captured the town), the ancient municipal buildings and private houses look today very much as they did to the Old Contemptibles on August 21, 1914. In recent years, however, there have been many changes on the outskirts with the presence of Supreme Headquarters Allied Powers Europe (SHAPE) and as autoroutes and their link roads have been carved through the region. Encircling the town are wide boulevards which mark the lines of the old ramparts. The large modern railway station overlooks one of these boulevards.

The **Hôtel de Ville** which dates from the 15th and 17th Centuries is on the Grand Place. The **Musées du Centenaire**, in particular the **Musée de Guerre**, through the large gate to the municipal heart of the town and the garden behind it, is one of the main reasons for visiting Mons. Housed in an old pawnshop built in 1625 is one of the finest collections of relics from the First and Second Wars in Belgium. It represents the work of two men, Georges Licope and Léon Pepin. The late M. Licope was the recognised authority on all matters concerning the four battles of Mons: August 1914, November 1918, May 1940 and September 1944. On the ground floor of the building is the Great War collection, and on the third floor exhibits from the Second. In between are fine ceramic, numismatic and archaeological displays.

The Mons **Tourist Office** has produced a very useful battlefield guide, written by Yves Bourdin, to the 11 salient points in the region. Each point is clearly labelled.

At the gateway of the Hôtel de Ville there are several **bronze plaques**, including one for the **5th Royal Irish Lancers**. This regiment took part in both First World War battles, and an Irish Lancer was the last British soldier to be killed on Armistice Day, November 11, 1918. Another plaque is the **Canadian Memorial** commemorating the liberation by the Canadian 3rd Division. In the collegiate **church of Sainte Waudru**, on the wall of the south transept, will be seen a **British Memorial Plaque** similar to the one in Ypres. Unlike those erected in France, the inscriptions are in English and Latin.

The highest part of the old city is the site of the Citadel and the old château. Rising here today is the baroque **Belfry**, the only one of its type in Belgium, built in 1662. A carillon of 47 bells is housed within and a lift goes to the upper chamber. Until the current restoration began, visitors could enter the onion dome above via some rickety, precariously-balanced ladders to view the panoramic explanation of the battles of Mons seen through the windows. Subsidence forced the closure of the **Parc** and Belfry, the restoration of which will at least take another ten years. From October 1952 until 1986, a memorial unveiled by Field-Marshal Earl Alexander stood on the high point of the park, commemorating the two Battles of Mons of 1914 and 1918. In 1986, it was moved to the La Bascule crossroads on the outskirts of town (*see page 115*).

In 1935, the Belgians presented a silver model of the Belfry of Mons to HM King George V to mark his Silver Jubilee, and at the same ceremony was buried, on the left-hand side of the entrance to the Belfry, the **Special Symbol of the Battle of Mons** in another casket. This contains earth from the grave of every British soldier killed at Mons. Strangely enough, there is no plaque marking the site.

In the Mons Hôtel de Ville, the Musée de Guerre includes a comprehensive collection of weapons and uniforms. This display of drums covers every regiment which fought at the Battle of Mons in 1914. (RC)

The 5th Royal Irish Lancers fought in both the August 1914 and November 1918 battles of Mons.

The plaque of the Canadian 3rd Division which liberated Mons on the morning of Armistice Day, 1918.

Commemorative CWGC British memorial plaque in the Collegiate Church of Sainte Waudru.

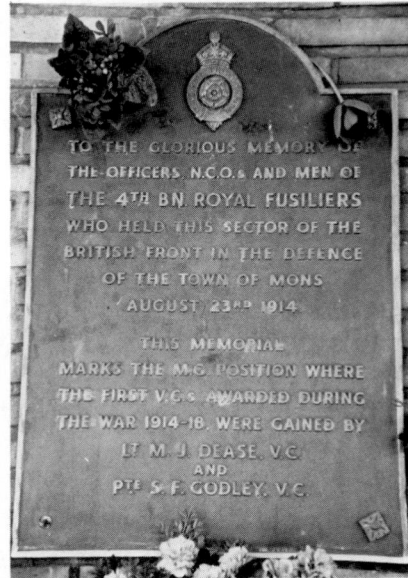

A railway bridge still spans the canal *(above left)* where Lieutenant Dease and Private Godley of the 4th Battalion, Royal Fusiliers, won their VCs. On the far 'German' side stands Nimy station. This is Stand 2 of the official Mons Battlefield Tour. The 4th Bn. Royal Fusiliers plaque below the bridge *(above right)* commemorates their gallant deeds here.

Mons Battlefield Tour

In the last ten years, the outskirts of Mons have been drastically altered with new road systems and many new buildings changing the landscape. The advent of SHAPE (Supreme Headquarters Allied Powers Europe) at Casteau is a major cause but the change of emphasis in the industrial life of the city, modern factories replacing the old smaller establishments, and the revival in the canal traffic, have all played their part.

Leaving Mons by the Chaussée de Bruxelles (N6), in 1½ km reach **Nimy**, an old industrial suburb through which the main railway passes. Soon, the first of the **battlefield tour signboards** will be seen as the road swings past the town square to the foot of the new road bridge on which it is placed. Take the small road on the right to go under the bridge and along the narrow road by the canal bank. The modern bridge spans the canal over the **site of the old swing bridge** which was so gallantly defended by 4th Bn. Royal Fusiliers (9th Brigade, 3rd Division). Further along the canal is the **modern railway bridge** which replaced that defended so well by another company of 4th Bn. Royal Fusiliers. **Nimy station** is on the far side of the canal. A **plaque** on the wall supporting the bridge commemorates the actions of Lieutenant M. J. Dease and Private S. F. Godley of the machine gun section. Every man in the section was either killed or wounded as they held up the German advance, permitting the battalions of their division to retire to new positions. Lieutenant Dease continued to keep the last gun firing until so badly wounded that he was unable to carry on. Private Godley then volunteered to man it until his wounds also forbade further action. He destroyed the gun and flung it into the canal before being taken prisoner. It is said that he was the inspiration for Bruce Bairnsfather's 'Old Bill'. The artist, away over in the Plugstreet Wood area, saw a photo of British prisoners from Mons entraining; in the foreground was the stocky, bushy-moustached Godley. Dease died from his wounds (he is buried at St Symphorien Cemetery — *see pages 114 and 115*); both he and Godley were awarded the Victoria Cross — the first of the Great War.

The bridge can be approached via the narrow road running along the canal bank to the artificial lake and marina, either by turn-

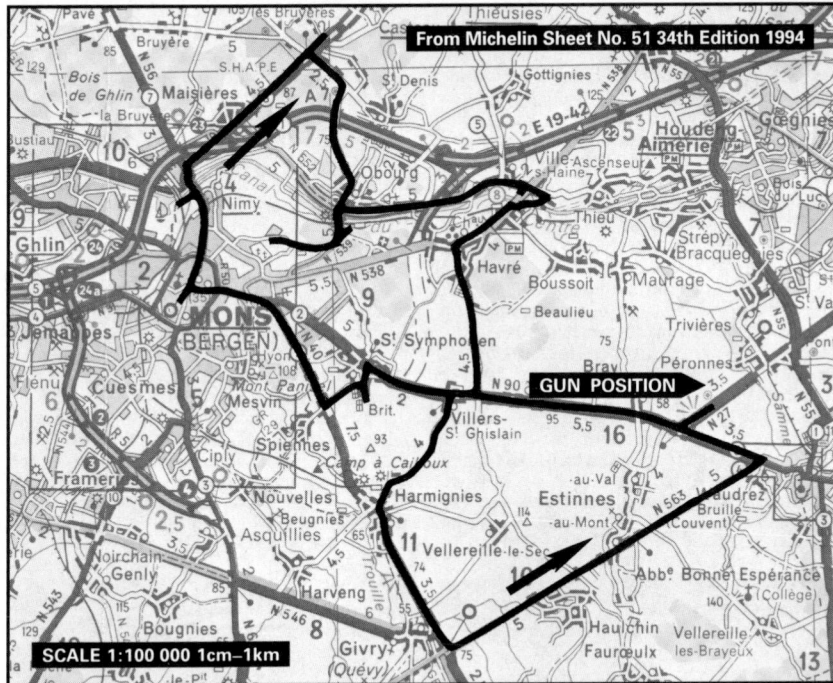

SCALE 1:100 000 1cm–1km

From Michelin Sheet No. 51 34th Edition 1994

GUN POSITION

ing left at the traffic lights in Nimy and then taking the small entry between the houses or by using the slip road on the right at the foot of the new bridge and turning left beneath it. A fine panorama of Mons opens out beyond the railway bridge. Return to Nimy and turn left over the bridge, bearing right to the next traffic lights and go straight on under the autoroute. This is **Maisières**, a front-line position on that August day in 1914. The village straggles on either side of the modern highway to the capital and forms one of the dormitories of the huge SHAPE complex but still retains many of its older buildings. To the right of the traffic lights in the centre of the village is the church where a **plaque** commemorates the British soldiers killed and the units of the BEF who were in the line in the Maisières region. Further up the hill, as the houses peter out, a slip road to the right signposted 'Cimetière' gives access across the highway to the communal cemetery on the left. At its entrance stands the village **war memorial** surrounded by evergreens. This is unusual for on its panels are the names not

The first shots of the First World War rang out near this monument *(left)* on the Casteau road at 7 a.m. on August 22, 1914. Almost directly opposite, a hotel now stands on the site of the 116th Canadian Infantry Battalion advance outpost at the cease-fire on November 11, 1918 — commemorated by a plaque on the wall.

only of the village dead but also those of Captain J. E. Knowles of the 4th Bn. Middlesex Regiment and other British casualties who died here in 1914. They were buried in a small cemetery nearby but, when the autoroute was built, they were moved and now lie in the peace of Cement House Cemetery *(see page 37)*.

Supreme Headquarters Allied Powers Europe now dominates the whole countryside to the left, the woods and copses which lined most of the road now replaced on the left-hand side by military blocks. One impact on Mons of the presence of the organisation has been the substantial growth of residential building and another is the difficulty one has of finding hotel accommodation in the district.

At 5 kms from Mons, having passed the main gates of SHAPE and the crossroads above, lies the village of **Casteau**. Almost on the crest of the rise, on the left, is a stone **memorial to the first contact between the BEF and the German 1. Armee** at 7 a.m. on August 22, 1914. 'C' Squadron of the 4th

Royal Irish Dragoon Guards, commanded by Major Tom Bridges, were on patrol on the road and in the woods following reports of German cavalry between Casteau and Soignies. Captain C. D. Hornby, the second in command, was in the van of the first two troops when a group of the German 4. Kürassier-Regiment were sighted. Corporal E. Thomas fired the first shots of a British Expeditionary Force on the Continent for nearly 100 years and Captain Hornby, sword raised, led the first charge. Across the road, on the wall of the Hôtel Le Medicis, is a **bronze plaque**. This memorial records that outposts of the **116th Canadian Infantry Battalion** were on this spot on November 11, 1918 when the cease-fire rang out at 11 a.m. 'Here beginneth and endeth the lesson . . .'

Return to the main crossroad and take the left-hand road to St Denis for 1 km and then turn right over the autoroute to reach **Obourg**, taking the road and bridge over the canal signed for Mons. At the south end of the bridge, a hairpin turning leads to **Obourg station**. A foot-bridge takes one over the rail-

way line and, on the canal bank where once stood the station building, now stands a **red-brick memorial**. This was fashioned in 1981 from bricks of the old station then being demolished. It was on the exterior wall of the old waiting room that the stand by the **4th Bn. Middlesex Regiment** (8th Brigade, 3rd Division) was remembered. They held the most easterly, and exposed, sector of the Salient around the north-east of Mons and had opened up on the oncoming Germans from every vantage point with fantastic rifle fire, ably displaying their skill with the Lee Enfield, typical of the regular British infantryman. All the units involved in Mons were capable of firing 16 aimed rounds per minute, some even more, thus giving the enemy the notion that every battalion was equipped with many machine guns instead of the pitiful few they actually had. Some of the company were sited on the roof of the station and the **plaque**, now on the memorial, records the events at about 8 a.m. on August 23. Each year a ceremony is held here on that day.

Obourg is a name synonymous with the first demonstration in action of the skills of the British rifleman equipped with the Rifle No. 1, Short, Magazine, Lee Enfield Mk III — the SMLE which had been adopted in January 1907. *Above right:* This was where the station stood until it was demolished in 1981. The plaque recording the events of August 23 *(above left)* has since been remounted on a memorial built from bricks salvaged from the old building.

Another position of the 4th Bn. Middlesex Regiment — that of 'A' Company (Major W. H. Abell) — was above the canal and railway, beyond the woods, around a farm now on the fringe of the modern residential estate. To get there, leave the station and drive up the hill towards Mons, taking the second turning on the right, passing through a wooded area. In 1 km, the road, now in more open country, bears to the left with a smaller, older road straight ahead. This is, in fact, the original road, the Vieux Chemin de Binche. Take it and drive past several of the old houses on the right, set much as they were on that morning so long ago. In about 300 metres, one of the new estate roads comes in on the left. It is **Avenue du 4th Middlesex** (so named since 1965) and, as our road becomes a lane, over to the right ahead the **L'Hermite Farm** comes into view. The Middlesex men had set up their outpost line in the farm and its field and orchard behind it on August 21-22.

The 23rd dawned misty and wet but blossomed out into a hot, dry, summer's day. Early in the morning, as the enemy began shelling, the men took up their positions and soon grey-clad figures began to emerge from the trees bordering the fields. Major Abell's bugler said he recognised them as Germans — he'd seen their like in the Legation Guard at Shanghai years previously. Now, the peaceful fields resounded to the heated exchange of rifle fire as the enemy advanced. Major Abell was shot through the head, the **first British officer to be killed** in action in the Great War and soon his second in command, Captain J. E. Knowles, was mortally wounded, as was the subaltern, 2nd Lieutenant Hancock. During the day, the 4th Middlesex suffered heavy casualties as they strategically retreated south-west, but they had inflicted considerable devastation on the overwhelming numbers of the enemy.

Major Abell and some 40 of his men were originally buried in the orchard but, 26 months later, were moved to St Symphorien Cemetery. Today, they lie there surrounding the memorial erected by the German Army in 1916 by the order of Prince Rupprecht of Bavaria in honour of their gallant foe. Captain Knowles and a few others were buried near Maisières in a little cemetery there, but when the complex road system and the autoroute were built they, too, had to be moved and are now in Cement House Cemetery near Ypres. After being badly burned, the farm was rebuilt but I understand from survivors that I have met there that the fields look much as they did — even the stone trough which gave support to the wounded is still there.

The farm at Obourg, visible in the distance *above*, occupied by 'A' Company of the 4th Middlesex. The road is now 'Avenue du 4th Middlesex' *(inset)* in memory of their stand and the first officer killed in the Great War in a nearby orchard.

Return to Obourg and cross the bridge, turning left under it, and drive along by the canal to **Ville-sur-Haine** for 4 kms. The road is for the most part a new wide highway running parallel to the now enlarged canal with its modern locks at intervals but, soon after the access road to the motorway joins it on the left, it narrows radically to enter the village. Now it turns and twists to become the rue du Coron up to the crossroads with the old Roeulx—Mons road. Turn right and descend towards the canal. The old road bridge has been replaced by a footbridge, but there beside the ramp is the **plaque to the last Canadian to be killed** in the Great War, Private George Price. Erected by his surviving comrades in 1968, it was originally on the wall of the house he was in when he was killed by a sniper, No. 71 rue de Mons, which stood on this spot. When the house was demolished in the modernisation of the canal, the plaque was moved to the wall of the nearby Hôtel de Ville, but now it is back on its old site, a special brick memorial having been erected for it. Private Price lies buried at St Symphorien Cemetery.

Return to the crossroads and turn right and then right again, across the bridge into **Havre**, a mining and industrial town. Beyond the church, a road between the houses on the left leads to **Villers-St Ghislain**. In 4½ kms, at the N90 junction, turn right and then first left up through the village. After a sharp left-hand corner, the road comes out onto the plateau, offering a magnificent panoramic view of the whole battle area. For many years, two rusty plaques could be found near the crest of the road. It was thought these commemorated the site where Lieutenant Bayly and 2nd Lieutenant Waterfall of No. 5 Squadron, RFC, crashed on August 22, 1914 (*see page 109*). Now it has been established that this was not the case — they were erected in the memory of horsemen who died nearby! The road now drops into **Harmignies** through the quarries which played a vital part in the battle. The hill to the right sheltered the Royal Horse Artillery who were based at Harmignies and, with other battalions, fought around it and the railway.

At the major crossroads, turn left onto N40 and drive 3½ kms through pleasant undulating country to **Givry**. Here it was that I Corps held the line immediately prior to the retreat. The commander, Sir Douglas Haig, had his headquarters on the road to Bavay. Their line was along Givry–Harmignies–Nouvelles, and General Allenby's cavalry were in support behind them in the Waudrez–Binche region.

Turn left onto N563 at the next crossroad, follow the very straight road and the 10 kms to **Waudrez** are soon accomplished. Turn left on to the N90 and take first right on to N27 which rises over the ridge prior to dropping down into **Péronnes**. About 200 metres along on the left is a water tower opposite a factory. This is an excellent vantage point to view the countryside littered with slag heaps and belching factory chimneys. In the near foreground is one large slag heap with a cluster of houses nearby. In the fields here, 'E' Battery, RHA, fired the **first artillery round of the war** on August 22. On the right-

The plaque at Ville-sur-Haine marking the death of the last Canadian soldier at 10.58 a.m. on November 11, 1918.

From the field beside the slag heap, the guns of 'E' Battery fired the first artillery round of the war on August 23, 1914. (RC)

hand side of the road, in the grounds of a large factory that was built close by, is a **small stone** which commemorates this event. From these positions on August 22, 1964, the same gun fired again in the presence of many of those who had participated 50 years previously. The artillery piece can be seen today in the Imperial War Museum.

General Allenby had his quarters in this red-brick house belonging to the school mistress at Villers-St Ghislain.

If one had to choose to visit just one cemetery from the First World War, that at St Symphorien would be high on the list where both British and German casualties lie side by side together with some of the most notable of the Allied dead.

Return to the N90 and turn right for **Villers-St Ghislain** (5½ kms). Here, General Allenby was billeted in the **house of the school mistress**. This house, at No. 334 on the left, nowadays in use as an infant school, has changed little over the years.

Continue another 2 kms to **St Symphorien**. Turn left (signpost) to visit the **British War Cemetery**. The road runs through a new estate and then deteriorates somewhat as it follows a brick wall and worsens as the lane comes to a junction at the cemetery gates.

This is possibly the most beautiful of all the British cemeteries in the Western Front area. It is also very different in layout, typifying a traditional English garden. There are shady paths and glades and many varieties of trees and shrubs in addition to the flowers on the actual graves and borders. The land was originally given to the Germans for use as a cemetery by a local landowner and here they buried both their own and the British casualties of August 1914, erecting a number of **special memorials**. One of these, set in a small circular glade surrounded by the graves, is in memory of the **'Royal' Middlesex Regiment** — the German personnel

could not believe that any regiment which had discipline and courage of the kind displayed by the Middlesex was not a 'Royal' regiment. This part of the cemetery is reached by taking the path to the right as you enter and is on the left, a little way up.

Nearby is buried L/14196 Private J. Parr, Middlesex Regiment (Plot I, Grave A10). It is very probable that he was the **first man to be killed in the BEF** in the Great War. His death on August 21, in the evening when he did not return from a scout mission with his bicycle, has now been confirmed and the

date on the headstone has been corrected. Opposite is the headstone of the **last man to die** on November 11, 1918 — Private G. E. Ellison of the 5th Royal Irish Lancers (Plot I, Grave B23). Beyond is the **German plot** where the original headstones have been retained. In contrast to the plain white

Left: Memorial erected by the German Army to the Royal Fusiliers and the Royal Irish Regiment. *Right:* The German obelisk to the dead of both armies.

British stones, these grey granite markers differ with officers often having more-flamboyant styles than those of the NCO or private soldier.

Up to the left, a group of British graves can be seen. Here lies Lieutenant M. J. Dease, VC, who died on August 23, 1914

(Plot V, Grave B2). In the row behind him is the grave of the **last Canadian to die**, Private G. L. Price of the 28th North West Bn. Canadian Infantry, who was killed at Ville-sur-Haine at 10.58 a.m. on November 11, 1918 (Plot V, Grave C4).

On the same level as the Cross of Sacrifice, which is placed at the highest part of the garden on the other side of the path, is a small rectangular lawn with a curved stone seat at the far end. In front is **another of the German memorials** to their British foes, this time to 53 members of the **Royal Fusiliers and the Royal Irish Regiment**. All about are a varied selection of shrubs and trees providing colour throughout the year.

A few hours after the first cavalry patrols entered Mons on August 21, 1914, this photograph was taken of Private Carter of the 4th Middlesex on sentry duty at La Bascule. The picture of the smiling 'young Contemptible' epitomised the spirit of the time. (IWM)

Leaving the cemetery, the path goes through a fringe of fir trees in the centre of which is the **German memorial to the men of both armies who died on August 23-24, 1914**. From this memorial, a flight of steps leads back to the entrance.

Return to the road junction and turn left. In 1¼ km, turn right onto the N40. On the left rises **Mont Panisel**, through the woods and fields of which run paths making very pleasant walking areas. Many fierce actions were fought in the orchards and fields on the lower slopes; this was the scene of the stand of the 3rd Infantry Division.

In 3 kms, our road arrives on the northern slope of the hill and converges at the wide crossroads with the Beaumont and Obourg roads. This is **La Bascule** where on August 21-22 the 3rd Division's 8th Brigade was centred. This was the formation to which the 4th Bn. Middlesex belonged, together with the 2nd Bn. Royal Scots, 2nd Bn. Royal Irish Regiment and 1st Bn. Gordon Highlanders. Here was taken one of the best-known photographs of the Mons period, a cheerful young sentry of the 4th Middlesex in the late afternoon sunshine *(see bottom left)*.

On August 23, 1986, the **BEF Memorial,** which originally stood in the Château Park under the Belfry, was unveiled on the spur of ground between the two major roads. On the far side of the Charleroi road, on the corner of the smaller road from Obourg, the Celtic cross of the **Memorial of the 2nd Bn. Royal Irish Regiment** has stood for 75 years to record their gallant stand here for many hours that August day, delaying the enemy's advance and suffering very heavy casualties. The brigade's Scottish battalions were in between the Beaumont and Charleroi roads, and their positions can be viewed along the

Beaumont road not far south from La Bascule. From around here, the brigade fell back on Mont Hyon and Mont Erebus on the road south towards Ciply.

The centre of Mons is now only 1 km away down the hill, passing the place where the **stables** of the **Château Gendebien** once stood. These were used as a Field Dressing Station in August 1914 and were set on fire by the advancing Germans' artillery fire. The château has in more recent times been the official residence of the Supreme Commander Allied Powers Europe. We enter the town of Mons itself along the attractive Avenue Reine Astrid.

The Royal Irish Regiment Memorial on the corner of La Bascule crossroads.

The BEF Memorial at Mons was moved in 1986 to La Bascule, and now stands appropriately near the spot where Private Carter had his picture taken in 1914.

Mons to Le Cateau

The route south from Mons is basically that of the retreat but the final advance followed much the same route.

Leave Mons by the N6 and in 2½ kms, at **Ciply,** take right fork N543. Pass straight through **Noirchain** (3½ kms), and reach **Blaregnies** 9 kms further on.

The area just passed was in the II Corps lines, the commander of which, General Sir Horace Smith-Dorrien, had his headquarters in a small château at **Sars-la-Bruyère**. The village and the château can be reached by taking the right-hand road at the crossroads in the centre of Blaregnies. In about 2½ kms, near the church of Sars-le-Bruyère, turn right and in a short distance along the road here, the drive up to the château is to be found on the right hand side.

Château de la Haie (also called Château de la Roche), a quiet red-brick house set in delightful surroundings, was the scene of a momentous meeting at 5 a.m. on August 23, 1914. Present were Field-Marshal French and his three corps commanders, Lieutenant-General Sir Douglas Haig, I Corps; Major-General Edmund Allenby, Cavalry Corps; and of course Sir Horace. Also present were Major-General Sir W. R. Robertson, the Quartermaster-General, and Major-General

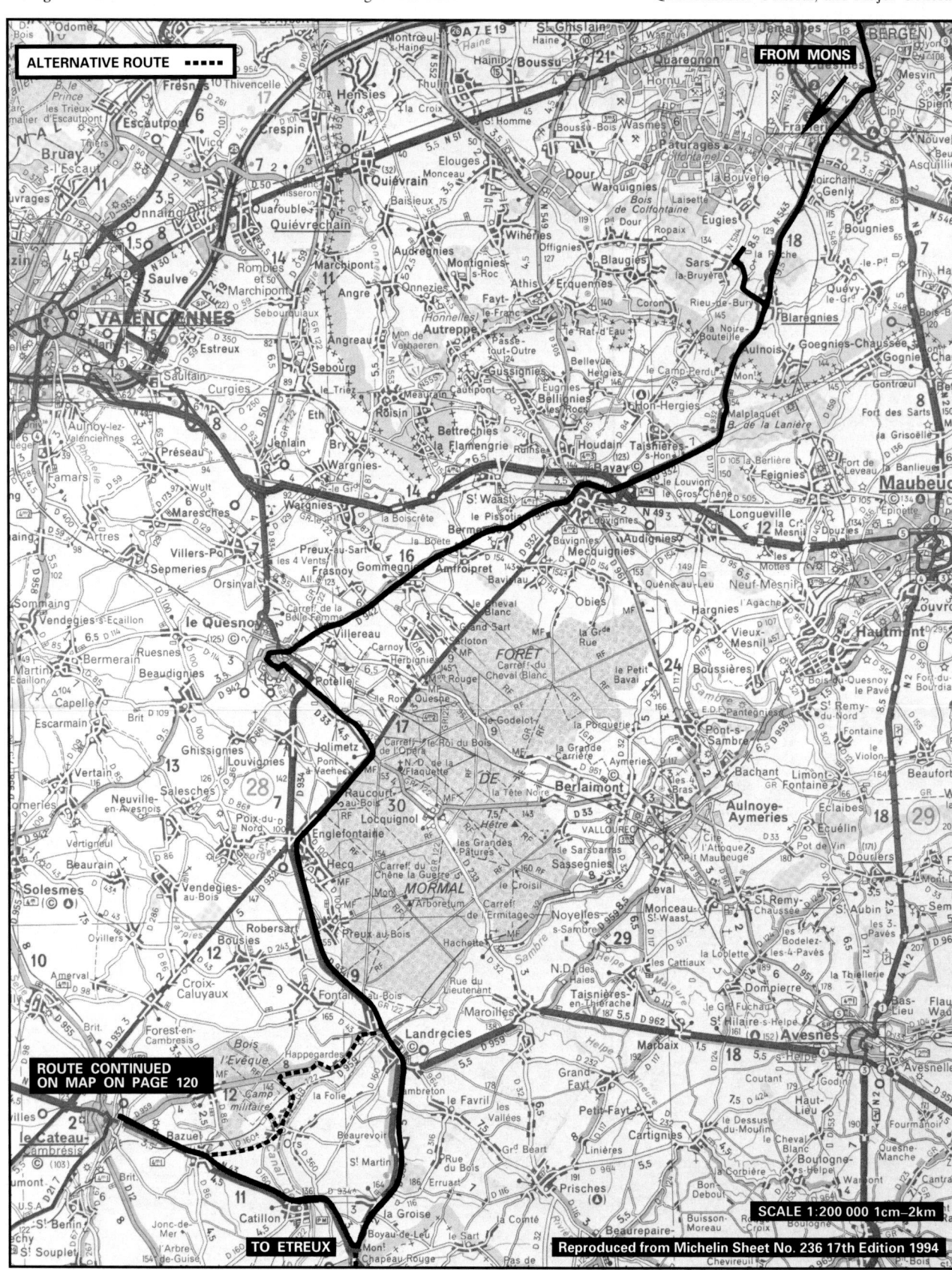

Château de la Haie, the scene of the momentous meeting on August 23, 1914, which decided the retreat from Mons.

A plaque in the hall reminds visitors of the historic meeting between Field-Marshal French and his corps commanders.

Sir A. J. Murray, Chief-of-Staff. The conference covered all eventualities including that of retreat. A **plaque in the hall** commemorates this momentous meeting which took place in the large room to the left of the front doors. On the morning of August 24, the headquarters was moved back some 10 kilometres to Hon.

The château was owned by the Comte d'Hendécourt, who was later killed in action. His son now lives in the house which remained unoccupied for many years. In 1940, the invading Germans attempted to remove the **artillery pieces** flanking the front doors but left them on discovering they were mounted in concrete. Today, they stand at the entrance gate.

Return to Blaregnies and turn right onto the N543 and within 2½ kms arrive at the frontier. Between the two stations is the **battlefield of Malplaquet** and a **monument**

on the left commemorates Marlborough's victory on September 11, 1709. On November 8, 1918, there was a sharp action here as the Allies advanced. Here, the N543 becomes D932.

Another 8 kms and we reach **Bavay**. This little town is situated on a hill close to which are **Riez de l'Erelle** and **Hon** where Haig and Smith-Dorrien had their respective corps headquarters at the beginning of the retreat. French had his advance headquarters in the **Mairie of Bavay** during the Battle of Mons, General Headquarters being then at Le Cateau. By August 25, all the British corps in the vicinity were making their way south on either side of the Forest of Mormal. The Guards Division recaptured the town on November 7, 1918.

Take the D942 for **Le Quesnoy** (14 kms). Le Quesnoy is a charming old town still enclosed with its 17th Century ramparts, another of Vauban's fortresses. On August 25, 1914, the town echoed to the noises of the retreating BEF and the refugees who hindered the army in their routes south. Thereafter, for four years, it was a German garrison town. On November 5, 1918, the town was attacked by men of the **New Zealand Division** who scaled the high walls of the outer ramparts and seized the German commander and his garrison of over 1,000 men. On the face of the walls climbed by the New Zealanders is a **memorial** to their effort which details, in bas relief, the use of medieval methods which proved so successful. The memorial is on the western side of the town, just south of the Porte St Martin gate, and can be reached through a tunnel underneath the ramparts from Boulevard Jeanne d'Arc.

The D33 leads in 4½ kms through **Jolimetz** to the D932 at the western edge of the **Forêt de Mormal**. The D932 was the road taken by II Corps, I Corps being on the eastern flank of the forest. The advancing German army made its way through the forest. This huge woodland of some 22,000 acres, which covers the slopes and high ground between Bavay and Landrecies, gave good cover and the

wide glades provided routes for the German transport. In November 1918, the forest again lay in the path of advancing troops, this time the Third and Fourth British Armies who drove all before them having cleared the area by November 5.

Turn right on the D932 to **Englefontaine** (5 kms), turning left on the D934 to travel 8 kms to the outskirts of **Landrecies**. On August 25, 1914, the Germans were said to have entered the town with some men dressed in French uniforms whilst the Guards slept, but once roused, the 4th Guards Brigade, 2nd Division, fought briskly in the streets as the rest of I Corps proceeded to retreat. In November 1918, the 25th Division captured the town and forced their way across the River Sambre, which is canalised here. On the bridge into the town is a

Memorial to General Sir Ronald Charles, the GOC, who, with 600 men, was killed in liberating the town on November 4.

The ramparts at Le Quesnoy. Beside the site of the assault, the New Zealand Memorial depicts soldiers climbing these walls just a week before the Armistice was signed.

Continue on the D934 for 8½ kms. The straight road undulates through attractive country and through **La Groise** to the crossroads of **Chapeau-Rouge**. Here, on August 26-27, 1914, the 1st Division stood and defied the German advance and, on November 4, 1918, the crossroads were in the centre of the line held by the same division as it advanced. A rather elegant **1st Division Memorial** on the left of the road recalls these facts.

Just 7 kms ahead on D934/D946 is **Etreux**, the scene of the heroic stand of the **2nd Bn. Royal Munster Fusiliers**. The **memorial and graveyard** mark the site with the headstones ranged in alphabetical order around the walls, the men being buried in three plots. The fields behind the cemetery and the farms close by are little changed from the dreaded day of August 27, 1914, when they were overwhelmed by nine German battalions. In **Etreux Communal Cemetery**, found by turning left across the bridge and proceeding past the church, other British soldiers lie buried. They were casualties of the August 1914 fighting in the village, but also include one man who was concealed for months in the village but, when discovered by the enemy, was shot in April 1915.

Return to Chapeau-Rouge and turn left onto the D934 for **Catillon**. Then, in 3 kms, cross over the Sambre and join the N43 for Le Cateau.

ALTERNATIVE ROUTE

An alternative route from Landrecies is via D959 through **Bois l'Eveque**, scene of

The 1st Division Memorial at the Chapeau-Rouge crossroads. Here, the Division held the German advance on August 26, 1914; in November 1918, it passed back through the same road junction.

'To the Glory of God and in proud and lasting memory . . . the Royal Munster Fusiliers who laid down their lives . . . in the cause of freedom and justice . . . their name liveth for evermore.' Fine words on a fine memorial at Etreux.

battles in 1914 and October 1918. In 4 kms, turn left for **Ors**. In the small plot of the **British Communal Cemetery** (signpost — not Ors British Cemetery) lie the poet Wilfred Owen, Lieutenant-Colonel J. N. Marshall, VC, MC, and 2nd Lieutenant J. Kirk, VC, all killed on November 4, 1918. At Bazuel, join the N43 via the D160a for Le Cateau.

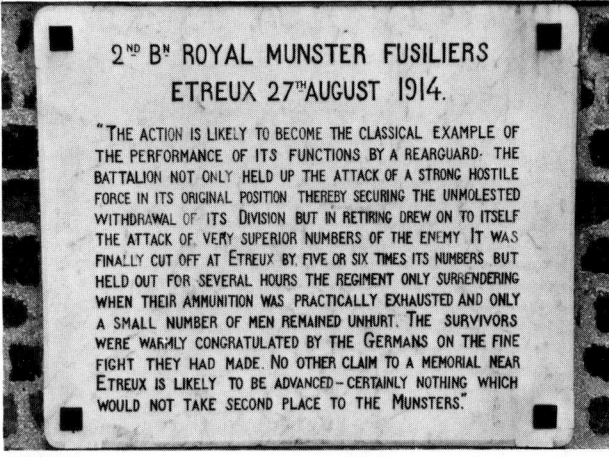

A small plaque in the cemetery wall at Etreux explains the heroic stand of the 2nd Battalion, Royal Munster Fusiliers.

In Ors Cemetery *(above)* rest 2nd Lieutenant Kirk, VC, Lieutenant-Colonel Marshall, VC, and Lieutenant Owen *(below)*.

Bravery recalled on a French hillside.

The 66th Division's practical memorial, a horse drinking trough.

LE CATEAU

Le Cateau is a name engraved in the memory of all Old Contemptibles, if not as the first location of British General Headquarters, then as the battle honour on so many of their Colours. Here, on August 26, 1914, was fought a desperate battle by the 3rd, 4th and 5th Divisions of II Corps against seven of von Kluck's 1. Armee's divisions. The Germans held the advantage, not only in infantry but also in artillery. The battle began to the west of the town, just south of the Cambrai road, and on through Caudry (*see page 108*) where the country is reminiscent of Salisbury Plain.

The site of the battle can be visited from tracks leading off the D932 or the D21. About 1 km south of the town, amid a grove of trees is a **simple cenotaph** on which the actions by the **2nd Battalions of the Suffolk Regiment**, the **Manchester Regiment**, the **Argyll and Sutherland Highlanders**, and by the **Royal Artillery** in their support, are remembered. To get there from the town, follow the signs to the Collège J. Rostand but, just before reaching the school, go straight ahead ¾ km along the sunken track into the fields, bearing right at the fork.

As one enters Le Cateau from Landrecies, look right at the crossroads with the Hostellerie du Marché on the corner. In front of the hotel (on the rue de la Fontaine à Gros Bouillons), is a horse trough now used very charmingly as a flower garden. This is the **Memorial of the British 66th Division** who fought here in October 1918 and who liberated the town on the 10th. Resistance in the station area lasted a week longer and was finally eliminated by the South African Brigade. After that, Le Cateau was shelled heavily by the Germans until their guns were forced out of range by the Allied advance.

Many of the narrow streets which climb the hills are still cobbled. In the main street is the **Hôtel de Ville**, where for many years just inside the entrance under the tower stood a **British 3.7 howitzer** flanked by pictures by one of the town's most illustrious sons, Henri Matisse. The latter are now displayed in the **Palais Fenelon Musée Matisse** further down the main street on the right. The gun was presented to the town by the 93rd Battery, Royal Field Artillery, to cement the friendship between the unit and the town for which it fought. Most years, gunners return to the town using the Hôtel du Midi (now renamed café Le Campagnard) in rue du Maréchal Mortier as their headquarters. Today, the howitzer — of 1932 vintage — is proudly displayed in the **town library** in the rue du

Marché aux Chevaux in a fine building, once a bank, rebuilt with reparations money. Beside the gun is a wooden **memorial bench** — a most useful comfort to the old soldiers who have walked up the street from their hotel. Festivities and receptions are held in

the upper rooms. Both gun and seat are to be seen by going through the entrance foyer to the corridor, off which is the library itself.

The **British Military Cemetery** is just north of the N43 and D932 crossroads and it gives a good overall view of the battlefield. The cemetery was opened originally by the Germans and there are several large **memorials** erected by them midst the many British and German graves. In one cluster are a group of Russian graves. Recently, the German war graves authority have made considerable renovations to the **German section** and many old crumbling memorials have been removed and the graves reset with new markers. There are now separate entrances to the British and German sections. In the British plot, men lie together who died in the battle of 1914, as prisoners of war, and in the 1918 actions. Among these is Lance-Corporal John W. Sayer who won the VC on March 21, 1918 at Le Verquier and who died of wounds in April 1918 (Plot I, Grave B59).

There is another British cemetery in Le Cateau, the **Communal Cemetery** in the town cemetery. Here, some 150 casualties of the battle are buried. There also is a **German memorial** to them and their German and French comrades.

Men from Germany, Russia and Great Britain lie together at Le Cateau. This, *above left,* **is the British section. The cemetery**

was originally opened by the Germans, thus it contains several German memorials — and a mass grave, *above right.*

Le Cateau to Amiens

Proceed from Le Cateau south along the D932. This long straight highway cleaves its way across the plains of Picardy to the St Quentin canal at Riqueval, but we leave it in 18½ kms at **Ponchaux**, taking the D28 (on the right) for **Beaurevoir** and Le Catelet (5½ kms). This wide country was the terrain of the Australians under Sir John Monash in their advance in October 1918.

Le Catelet is a straggling village across the N44 Cambrai-St Quentin road, and is the northern entrance of the **tunnel** of the **St Quentin Canal**. About 2 kms along the D444 to **Vendhuile**, under a group of chestnut trees on the right of the road opposite a red-brick house, footpaths lead down on either side of the early 19th Century canal to the tunnel entrance. This tunnel, over 7 kms in length, was built in the time of Napoleon in 1802-10. During the German occupation of the area, they incorporated this tunnel, and the shorter one between Le Haucourt and Le Tronquoy further south, into the defences forming the **Hindenburg Line**.

On an average, the tunnels are 16 metres below the surface and therefore almost impregnable. They were connected to the main works of the Hindenburg Line by shafts and were fully equipped with offices, stores, stables and hospitals. Barges were used as billets, the whole system being electrically lit.

At this northern end of the tunnel, all is now peaceful and few marks recall its use as a fortress. Neither do the banks of the sleepy canal carry many reminders that they were once part of an intricate trench system. The northern end of the tunnel figured in the heavy fighting in September and October 1918, when the American 27th and 30th Divisions and the British 50th Division fought successfully to breach the Line.

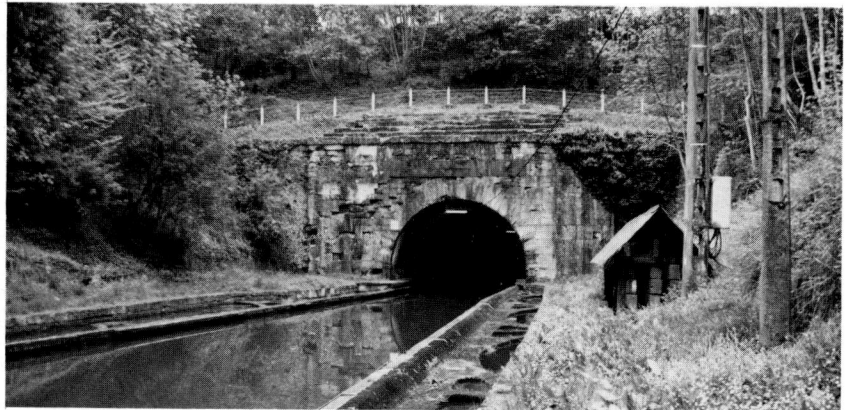

Above: **The northern entrance of an unassailable fortress — the St Quentin Canal Tunnel at Le Catelet. This was an integral part of the Hindenburg Line.**

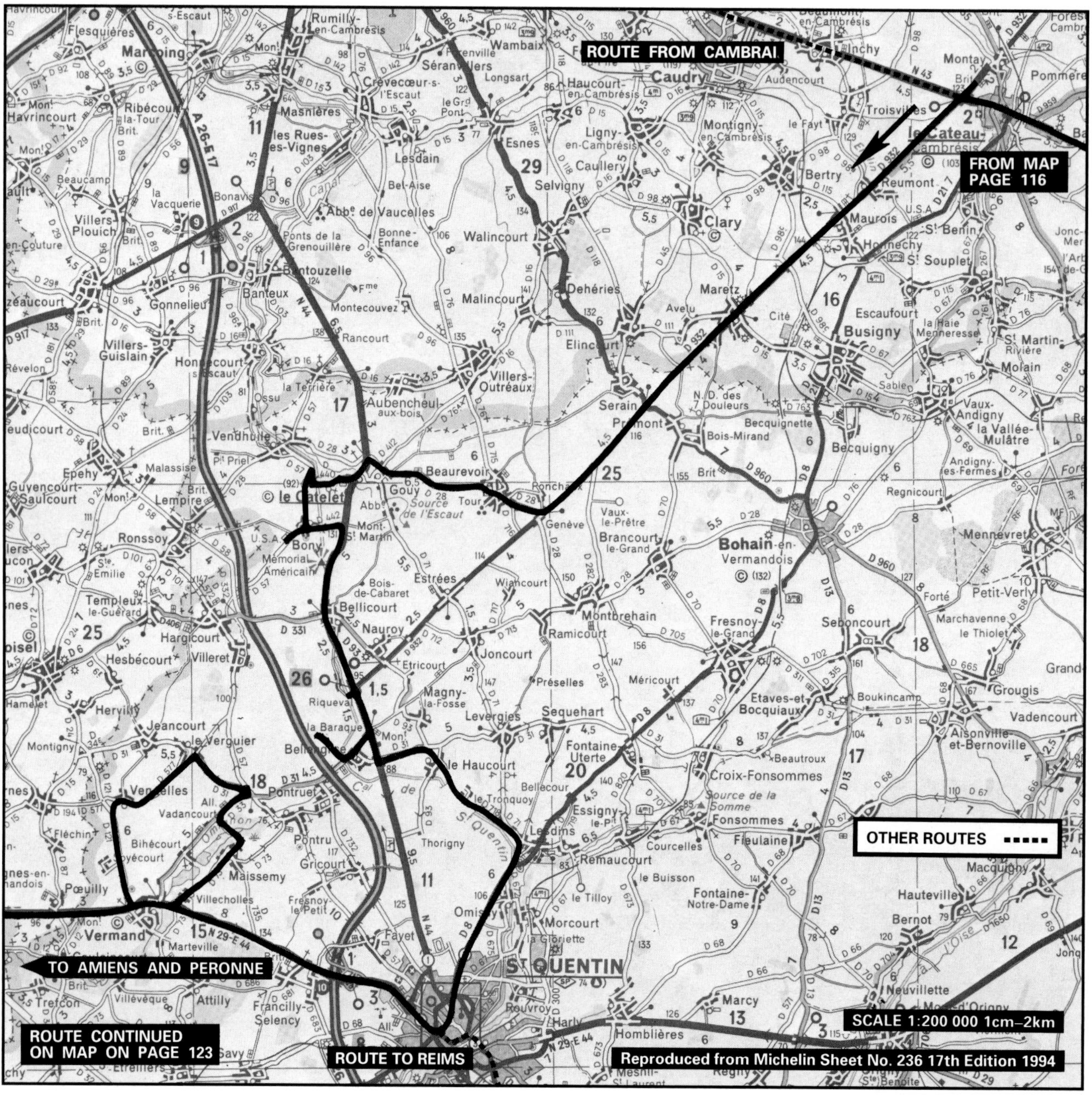

ROUTE FROM CAMBRAI
FROM MAP PAGE 116
OTHER ROUTES
TO AMIENS AND PERONNE
ROUTE CONTINUED ON MAP ON PAGE 123
ROUTE TO REIMS
SCALE 1:200 000 1cm–2km
Reproduced from Michelin Sheet No. 236 17th Edition 1994
Le Cateau-Cambrésis
Caudry
Clary
Busigny
Bohain-en-Vermandois
Le Catelet
Beaurevoir
Bony
Mémorial Américain
Bellicourt
Riqueval
Vendhuile
Vermand
St QUENTIN

About 300 metres beyond the tunnel, turn sharply left onto D57 for **Bony** (2 kms). Here, sloping up the hillside, is the **Somme American Cemetery** where 1,844 are buried and 333 missing are commemorated. Buried here are three Medal of Honor winners: Corporal Thomas E. O'Shea (Plot B, Row 6, Grave 14) and First Lieutenant William B. Turner (Plot B, Row 13, Grave 1), both of the 27th Division and killed in September 1918, and Private Robert L. Blackwell (Plot D, Row 20, Grave 2) of the 30th Division, killed in October 1918.

From Bony, return to the N44 (3 kms) and turn right. The St Quentin Canal re-emerges into daylight south of **Bellicourt** village,

South-west of Le Catelet lies the Somme American Cemetery at Bony *(above)*. **Three Medal of Honor winners lie in the cemetery** *(below)*: **Corporal Thomas E. O'Shea, First Lieutenant William B. Turner and Private Robert L. Blackwell.**

which is 5 kms from Le Catelet. On the heights before the village, and directly above the tunnel, is the impressive **American Memorial**, the Bellicourt Monument of the American Battle Monuments Commission. On the west face of the monument is an interesting map of the operations of the two US divisions which served with the British in the battles in the region. On the terrace overlooking the battlefield is an orientation table.

About 1½ km south (via N44) of Bellicourt village at **Riqueval**, on the right-hand side of the road, stands the **US 30th Division Memorial** to the soldiers from Tennessee who fought in the canal battle on September 29, 1918. Behind it, a path through the trees leads down to the actual **southern entrance of the canal tunnel**.

Right: **High above the canal tunnel, the American Memorial near Bellicourt overlooks the remnants of the old Hindenburg Line.**

Left: **The southern entrance to the St Quentin Canal tunnel at Riqueval.** *Right:* **The US 30th Division Memorial to the soldiers** of the State of Tennessee, killed in the battles for the canal, stands above the entrance.

Brigadier Campbell, VC, addresses men of the 137th British Brigade on the slopes of the St Quentin Canal from the ruined bridge at Riqueval. (IWM)

More than 75 years have passed. This is the comparison photograph taken from the same spot . . . the bridge is virtually unchanged.

About 1¼ km further along N44, a small road on the right leads directly over the gorge at this end of the canal via **Riqueval bridge**. This bridge appears in one of the most impressive photographs in the Imperial War Museum collection. Brigadier-General J. V. Campbell, VC, is shown on the ruined arch addressing his troops of 137th Brigade, 46th Division, who cover the steep banks of the gorge after they had captured this sector of the Hindenburg Line on September 29, 1918 by wading across the canal and scaling the walls here. Today, a new **Western Front**

Association Memorial records how the 6th Bn. North Staffordshire Regiment and engineers captured this vital bridge, the last one intact across the canal.

Back on N44, in 1½ kms **La Baraque** crossroads are reached. On the left is a small **British Cemetery** and, until a few years ago, the crumbling remains of part of the German defences were still hidden in the undergrowth nearby. To the right is **Bellenglise** village (1 km), from where signs lead back across the canal and right 1¾ km up a track to the crest of the hill where stands the

4th Australian Division Memorial. They fought here in September-October 1918.

Return to the N44 and turn right. Within 200 metres, the obelisk of the **46th Division Memorial** can be seen up on the left. This division captured Bellenglise in the attack of September 29, 1918. For a number of years after the road improvements in this region, the memorial fell into disrepair, but now it has been renovated.

To visit the other, **shorter tunnel of the St Quentin Canal**, take the D31 on the left and, in 1¾ km, turn right on D93 to **Le Haucourt**. In the centre of the village, turn left, then right onto the D718 to Lesdins. The northern entrance is then on the right, 1 km out of the village. Another kilometre further on, beyond **Le Tronquoy**, is the other entrance. The D71 follows the canal to **Lesdins** where, by joining the D8 and crossing the canal, St Quentin is then entered in 6 kms.

St Quentin is a large industrial town on the River Somme. The British General Headquarters was here on August 25-26, 1914,

The Australian 4th Division Memorial high on the hill north of Bellenglise. For a long time, it stood forgotten at its lone spot, but now a new road has been signposted to it.

before moving to Noyon and Compiègne. Units of II Corps arrived from Le Cateau exhausted and demoralised by the continuous march. The knowledge that the advance troops of the German Army were hard on their heels ceased to have any urgency for them and they fell where they stood, tired out, when the order to halt was given. Soon after, some squadrons of the 4th Dragoon Guards led by Major Tom Bridges (the same man who was involved in the very first contact with the Germans near Mons — *see page 112*) came on the scene. Bridges was horrified by the sight which met his eyes and was determined to move the men out of St Quentin. He realised that the most effective adjunct for making men march was missing — he had no band. Seeing a toy shop, he went in and bought a toy whistle and a drum. With his bugler on the whistle and himself on the drum, he succeeded in rousing the men and led them out of the town after the infectious music had induced others to join in with mouth organs.

The 46th Division Memorial at La Baraque near Bellenglise.

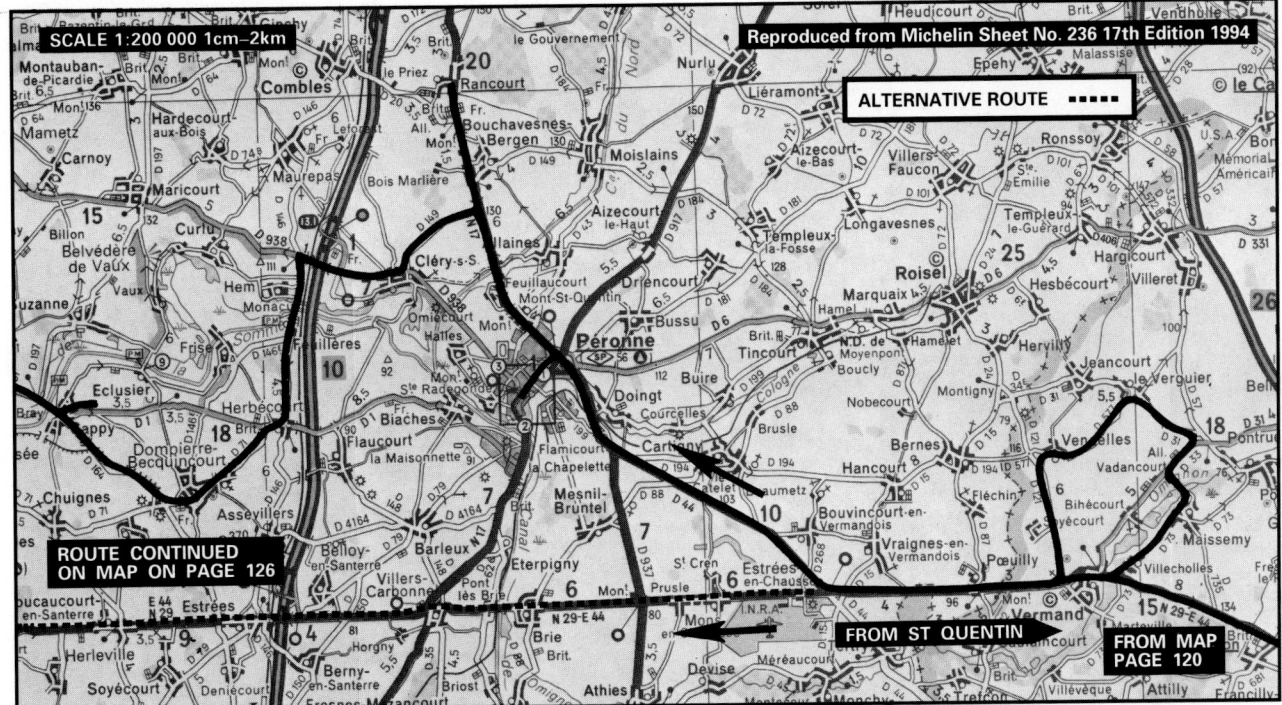

Reproduced from Michelin Sheet No. 236 17th Edition 1994

ALTERNATIVE ROUTE ∙∙∙∙∙

ROUTE CONTINUED ON MAP ON PAGE 126

FROM ST QUENTIN

FROM MAP PAGE 120

The Germans held the town from the end of August 1914 until October 1, 1918. In March 1918, they had set forth from St Quentin on their Spring Offensive driving back the British Third and Fifth Armies, taking many prisoners. In the Allied advance, the town was outflanked by the British and was entered by the French 1ère Armée of Général Débeney. By then, the town was in ruins, the **cathedral** had been burnt and, as the French army arrived, the Germans were completing the laying of charges in the bases of the great pillars in the church to complete its demolition. The swift intervention of the Frenchmen saved the building, but one pillar (the one to the right of the side entrance) still shows the square hole that had been drilled.

The impressive French Memorial at St Quentin with its interesting bas relief.

Down near the station is an impressive **French Memorial** depicting many different aspects of the army. The British and French lines joined opposite St Quentin and, after 1914, the British Army did not return again until 1918.

(Note: Before leaving St Quentin, readers are reminded that the south-eastern extension of our itinerary, to Reims and the Verdun battlefields and back to Compiègne, starts from here — see pages 132-167.)

To return to the western sector, take the N29 from St Quentin to **Francilly-Selency**. Today, the route of the **Hindenburg Line** here is crossed by the A26-E17 autoroute. Then we reach **Vermand** (5 kms), a small town totally destroyed in the German retreat in March 1917 and again in the front line in 1918 during March and the autumn of that year.

A pleasant detour can be made from here by taking the D73 on the right at the entrance to the town and driving along the valley of the River Omignon through the hamlet of Villecholles and close to the Etang de Bihecourt to **Maissemy** (3 kms), a village entirely ruined in 1918 during the stout defence put up by the 24th and 61st Divisions on March 21, 1918.

Turn left past the church and cross the river. At the next junction, turn right onto the D33. In 1 km on the left is the large **German Cemetery** of Maissemy. On the gentle slope, the main path is lined with stones bearing the arms and crests of many

In death all men are equal. France, so often a battleground for warring nations, provides burial grounds for both friend and foe. This is the vast Soldatenfriedhof at Maissemy, last resting place for the sons of many German towns and villages.

The church tower and the village war memorial at Le Verquier.

The flag of the 2nd Australian Division in Péronne town hall.

The Digger of the 2nd Australian Division Memorial on Mont-St Quentin.

German cities and regions, and 30,478 men are buried in the beautiful greensward or in the mass graves which stretch across the centre. A gaunt chapel encloses the symbolic bronze tomb as the central feature.

Turn left at the next crossroads onto the D57 and at the fork go left on D31 to reach **Le Verquier** in 3 kms. During 1915-16, the German aerodromes in the area were frequent targets of RFC raids. It was captured by the Allies on April 9, 1917, but the village really suffered when it fell in the path of the German Spring Offensive of 1918. Stubbornly defended by 24th Division on March 21-22, it was eventually recaptured in September by the Australians. The church tower at Le Verquier is in fact a **memorial to the 24th Division**, given by them and dedicated in October 1926. Alongside is the rather unusual **village war memorial** which in addition to bearing the names of its own heroes includes mention of the 24th Division losses in their village.

Take the D577, rue du 24ème Division immediately opposite the church, to arrive at **Vendelles** in 4 kms and by the D121 to the left in 5 kms return to **Vermand**, turning right onto N29. All this region was in the Fifth Army area in March 1918. In 7 kms, at **Estrées-en-Chaussée**, turn right on D44 for Péronne (10 kms).

Péronne is an ancient town located at the confluence of the Somme and Cologne rivers. It fell into German hands in 1914 and remained a most useful base, protected as it was by the artillery on Mont-St Quentin, about 2 kms to the north. This hill was strongly fortified with subways and deep trenches to give support and shelter for the guns. On its forward slopes, many observa-

tion posts were set up commanding extensive views over a very wide area. This formidable fortress was the cause of the French Army's inability to advance in July and August 1916, although they reached Biaches, 1½ kms to the west of the city. In March 1917, the Germans evacuated Mont-St Quentin when they retreated to the Hindenburg Line but, before doing so, destroyed both the fortress and the town. A year later, they were back in possession of both, capturing many valuable supplies. During the Allied advance, the 2nd Australian Division took the fortress on August 31, and Péronne itself was captured on September 2, 1918.

Completely ruined, the town has been rebuilt around the large square, the Place du Commandant Daudré. The Renaissance **town hall** has been rebuilt in its old style. In the foyer hangs the original **flag of the 2nd Australian Division**.

In August 1992, a new, high-prestige museum was opened in Péronne, the **Historial de la Grande Guerre**. The modern building, built into the rear of the restored medieval château which stands in the middle of the town, was designed by H. E. Ciriani. Set up by the Département of the Somme and sponsored by Paris and the European Community, the museum ambitiously aims to present an international perspective of the war by giving equal attention to all parties, concentrating on the daily lives of the soldiers and civilians, and endeavours to explain the social and economic consequences of the war. To do so, the museum has collected some 12,000 objects, 200 works of art and over 50,000 posters, newspapers and documents. The set-up of the museum is completely trilingual, everything being

explained in French, English and German. In four spacious exhibition halls, the war is presented chronologically, with as much attention for its outbreak and its aftermath as for the years of struggle themselves. Uniforms and equipment are exhibited in a very unusual way, laid out flat in square recesses in the museum floor which, despite its clinical cleanliness, conjures up a striking vision of 'death on the battlefield'. Large-scale use is made of audio-visual material: throughout the museum, there are videos to illustrate a particular subject or theme, in most cases three monitors being stacked on top of each other with French, British and German footage running simultaneously, something which very effectively brings across the national differences and similarities, both in ways of warfare and propaganda images. There are several dozen monitors and, in all, they add up to a total viewing time of over 3½ hours! In a central hall are displayed war drawings by the famous German artist and war veteran Otto Dix which convey the horror and waste of war in all its gruesomeness. In a separate hall, a film is shown which tells the story of the Somme through the personal experience and memories of one British veteran, Harry Welsh of the 12th Northumberland Fusiliers (who died in 1987). The museum has a documentation centre, a bookshop, cafeteria and restaurant. It is also the starting point for a Somme battlefield tour which is signposted as 'Circuit de la Mémoire' and described in an excellent booklet for sale at the museum. The museum is open 10 a.m. to 6 p.m. every day from May to September; 10 a.m. to 5.30 p.m. every day except Monday from October to April (closed December 20 to January 3).

The new Historial de la Grande Guerre museum at Péronne aims to give a comprehensive picture of the Great War in all its aspects. **Set in the rear of the medieval château** (above left), **its displays** (above right) **are imaginatively set out.**

The Foch statue at Buchavesnes-Bergen.

The British Cemetery at Rancourt, with the French chapel and cemetery behind.

Leave Péronne by N17, climbing up **Mont-St Quentin** (3 kms) where proudly stands a bronze Digger — the **Memorial of the 2nd Australian Division**. This statue, mounted on a square plinth, replaced the one erected here originally but destroyed by the Germans during the Second World War. It was one of the very few which suffered this way, but exception was taken to the symbolism of the Digger stabbing the German eagle with his bayonet. On each face of the plinth, which was not destroyed, bronze plaques depict infantry and artillery in action and the list of battles fought by the division. Behind the statue is a bronze **plaque** with a map in bas relief, another one of those sculpted by Ross J. Bastiaan and unveiled by the Australians in 1993 — here is a wide view of the valley where so many Aussies fought.

Drop down to cross the **Canal du Nord**, climbing up and over another ridge, and descend to the village of **Buchavesnes-Bergen** (4 kms). This was the location of a storming attack by the French Army in September 1916; and, in March 1918, there was heavy fighting as the enemy prised apart the Third and Fifth British Armies. In nearby Marlière Wood, South African units of the 9th Scottish Division held out until their

ammunition was exhausted and only a hundred men remained unhurt. The village itself was retaken on September 1, 1918, at the end of the first phase of the British advance. On the left of the road is a fine **statue of Maréchal Foch** presented in 1924 by Mr Haakon J. Wallem of Bergen, Norway. The addition of the name Bergen to the village is in honour of their Norwegian benefactor. The **Rancourt group of cemeteries** is just 1½ km further up the N17. The large **French** one with its chapel is on the right; the small **British** one on the left; the **German** one being about ½ km down the D20 Combles road.

Turn round on the N17, returning through Buchavesnes, and in 2½ kms take the D149 right for **Cléry-sur-Somme**, 3 kms distant over the rolling country. In the village where the 35th Division tried to stem the flood in March 1918, and which the Australians took in September (the French having captured it in September 1916), take a right turn onto the D938 and in 2¾ kms, having crossed the motorway, turn left on the D146 to descend into Hem-Monacu and cross the Somme into **Feuillères**, where, by using improvised bridges, the 5th Australian Brigade crossed the river en route for Mont-St Quentin in August 1918.

In 3 kms **Herbécourt**. Turn right, then left onto D71 for **Dompierre-Becquincourt** in 2 kms, going through the village. As we turn right onto D164, on the right-hand side of the road, is one of the **only remaining stretches of narrow-gauge track** dating from the First World War. It is still in use, a tourist train

being run from a small railway museum at the other end of the line at Froissy, 7 kms away. There used to be a terminal at this end of the line too, near the large sucrerie at the crossroads, but now there is only the one at Froissy. For the first 2 kms, the line runs parallel to the D164, then crosses to the other side to skirt Cappy and end at Froissy.

Cappy, up to March 1918, had been behind the Allied lines but, after the German advance, the aerodrome became one of Richthofen's bases. The **airfield** is on the D1, east of the town, and the **château** used as the Officers' Mess by the Geschwader is on the left, hidden on the old road by an avenue of trees, right at the edge of the town. Today, it appears much as it did in April 1918. Cappy was finally captured by the Australians in August 1918. Thus it was a well-known base for all.

Crossing the Somme onto the D1, **Bray** is reached in 2½ kms. This town, built on the northern steep banks of the river, was the junction between Third and Fifth Armies in March 1918 and was recaptured on August 24-25 in a moonlight attack by the Australians. The **3rd Australian Division Memorial** stands 10½ kms west of Bray on the D1, at the crossroads north of **Sailley-le-Sec**.

The narrow-gauge railway still runs from Froissy to Dompierre.

Cappy château was used as an Officers' Mess by von Richthofen's Geschwader.

The 3rd Australian Division Memorial stands on the D1 near Sailly-le-Sec.

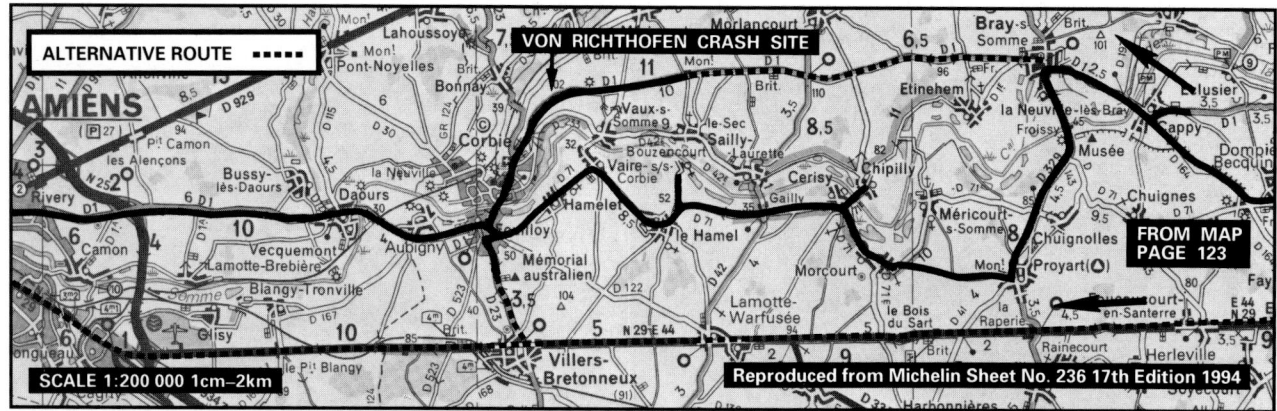

From Bray, the D1 is the direct road to Corbie on the north bank of the river, crossing open country with few villages. It was the route of the retreat in March 1918, but there are few signs of the battle today. Alternatively, from Bray, the D329 goes south to **Froissy**, back across the Somme and its marshes, with the **narrow-gauge railway museum** and the **terminal** of the Froissy–Dompierre line just beyond the bridge on the left, to **Proyart** (6 kms). The village is notable for the stand made by the 39th Division in the March 1918 retreat, and for its enormous village **war memorial**, a miniature Arc de Triomphe complete with Poilu. The Australians took the village in August 1918.

Turn right onto D41, then right again after 100 metres onto a small unclassified road which leads westward to Morcourt where it joins the D71 in 3½ kms. Thence left along the pretty river to Cerisy and Chipilly (3 kms). On the **Chipilly** side of the river, near the church, is the **Memorial to the 58th London Division** — an artilleryman with his wounded horse. The division fought here as part of III Corps in the 1918 Battle of Amiens. Whereas the Australian and Canadian Corps in the centre reached most of their objectives on the first day, August 8, the French in the south and the III Corps in the north had difficulty securing theirs. However, the 58th Division captured the important Chipilly Spur on the second day.

Back on the D71, in 5½ kms Le Hamel is reached. Just before it, 1 km down the road on the right to **Bouzencourt** (C7), on the left roadside, stands a lone broken column. This is the **Memorial to Captain Francis L. Mond**

and Lieutenant Edgar E. Marty of No. 57 Squadron, RAF, whose plane crashed here on May 15, 1918.

From **Le Hamel** to Corbie the road is never far from the river. Before we reach the latter town, a left turn at Fouilloy (7½ kms) onto D23 leads to Villers-Bretonneux and the Australian National Memorial (*see below*). However, joining the D1 and crossing the Somme once again, we enter the quiet market town of **Corbie** with its huge church of St Pierre. This old abbey church, with its massive twin towers, was badly damaged in 1918 but the towers survived and the rest of the building was repaired in the original style.

Corbie was also a headquarters of the Army Graves Registration Service and, later, the Imperial War Graves Commission which was responsible for the work on the cemeteries. Even during the war, these were in many cases quiet flower gardens where the troops went for a peaceful hour. Corbie was a busy forward town during the Battle of the Somme.

In **Corbie Communal Cemetery** lies Major William (Billy) La Touche Congreve, VC, DSO, MC (Plot I, Grave F35), the son of Lieutenant-General W. N. Congreve, VC, who died at Longueval in the action which won him the VC on July 20, 1916. In Corbie's abbey church there is a **memorial** to him.

On the left of the D1 a few hundred metres north of Corbie, is **Baron Manfred von Richthofen's crash site**. He fell to Allied guns, either those of Captain Roy Brown of No. 209 Squadron or the Australian machine gunner serving with the 53rd MG Company, on April 21, 1918. From here, it is also only some 5 kms back east along the D1 to the 3rd Australian Division Memorial near Sailley-le-Sec.

From Corbie, the D1 recrosses the Somme and follows the south bank into **Aubigny** and then recrosses the river to reach Amiens in 12 kms.

ALTERNATIVE ROUTE

If time does not permit the deviation from Estrées-en-Chaussée to include the Péronne-Somme valley, keep straight on along the N29-E44 through **Villers-Carbonnel** (12 kms) and over the front line of 1917. This flat plain with gentle slopes was excellent tank country and, in the 1918 advance, they were used with great effect in the capture of the many positions around here.

Pass through **Warfusée-Abancourt** in 22 kms and, 5 kms further on, we reach **Villers-Bretonneux**. As the village is entered, a **Demarcation Stone** will be seen on the left. Most of this small industrial and agricultural town lies south of the road. Before April 1918, this sleepy town was well behind the British lines, with an RFC aerodrome on its outskirts. Among the squadrons stationed here were Nos. 11, 25 and 27.

As the Germans advanced in April 1918, it is probable that they had visions of repeating their victory of November 1870 when they defeated the Armée du Nord and went on to capture Amiens. However, the Australian Corps with the 8th, 18th, and 58th Divisions stood in their way across the main road. The town fell to the Germans on April 24, and the battles that day were notable for the presence of German tanks and, for the first time, some light British Whippet tanks. The Australians and the 18th Division counter-

The dramatic 58th Division Memorial at Chipilly commemorates the division's part in the 1918 Battle of Amiens, in particular the capture of the Chipilly Spur on August 9.

The plaque on the village school at Villers-Bretonneux, *above left*. The town was taken by the Germans on April 24, 1918, in a renewed attempt to break through to Amiens, but retaken by the Australians that same night. Four months later, it was the starting point of the Fourth Army assault of August 8, 1918, led by tanks and low-flying aircraft, which marked the beginning of the final march to victory. The Sir William Leggatt Museum, better known locally as the Franco-Australian Museum and situated in the attic of the school *(above right)*, is dedicated to the memory of the Australian Corps.

attacked in the night and during the 25th the Australians regained the town. For the next four months, a static war existed in this area with both sides digging in, and trenches were constructed in the woods south of the town.

On August 8, the Allied advance commenced with Fourth Army making a surprise attack with the Canadians and Australians and III Corps together with over 400 tanks (342 Mark Vs and 72 Whippets) and low-flying aircraft. They advanced eastward over the rolling downs and through the woods, completely dislodging the German 2. Armee of General von der Marwitz. Tanks and cavalry played important rôles in the advance on the Somme itself and, within a few days, Villers-Bretonneux was well behind the lines.

In 1975, the **Sir William Leggatt Museum** (better known locally as the Franco-Australian Museum) was opened in the school building on rue Victoria which had been given to the children of Villers-Bretonneux by the Australian children whose fathers and brothers (1,200 of them) had lost their lives in the defence of the town. This museum is run by the Franco-Australian Welcome Committee and gives a very good record of the part that the Australians and the villagers played in the battles. In 1992, the exhibition in the school attic was completely renovated and enlarged and a small video theatre added. The museum is open on Wednesdays and weekends, or by application to the Hôtel de Ville.

High on the hill north of the village, soars the tower of the **Australian National War Memorial.** The **British Military Cemetery** lies before it. It is reached via the D23 road to Corbie. An orientation table is incorporated in the lantern at the top of the tower, which gives magnificent views of the battle area. In the spring and autumn, the outlines of the old German trenches can be clearly seen as chalk slicks through the brown tilled fields to the east. To the west, on a fine clear day, the view extends to Amiens, with the spire of the cathedral clearly in sight. To the north is Corbie, and to the south Villers-Bretonneux on its ridge. Beyond the slopes, out of sight, is the location of the old aerodrome. Further still are the woods of **Hangard** and **Démuin** — scenes of very heavy fighting. To the left of the memorial green stands a bronze **relief map**, one of those erected in 1993 under the Ross Bastiaan project.

Each year a special ceremony is held on Anzac Day to recall the April and August battles, services being held at the memorial and celebrations in the town itself.

Continuing westward from Villers-Bretonneux along the N29, the road skirts the **Bois d'Aquenne** where the Whippet tanks made their initial appearance. We then pass the **Bois de l'Abbé** and away to the left is **Bois de Blangy**. Soon after Blangy Cabaret and Petit Blangy — a mere hamlet — are passed, on the right **Glisy Aerodrome** comes into view. Sometime back, a **memorial to von Richthofen** was erected in the airfield precinct. Then, 17 kms from Villers-Bretonneux, Amiens is entered.

Amiens, the capital of Picardy, makes a good centre for visiting the Somme battlefields. Amiens has had a long history of contact with the English since the reign of King Edward III. There, in 1550, Edward VI and Henri II of France signed a peace treaty and, in 1597, an English force assisted Henri IV to capture the city from the Spaniards. In 1802, the Treaty of Amiens brought a short respite in the Napoleonic wars.

In August 1914, Amiens was the first base for the troops arriving from the UK but, on the 30th of that month, the rapid advance of the Germans necessitated the evacuation of the city. For 12 days, until September 11, it was occupied by a German force which, after making demands for money, supplies and seizing 12 hostages, withdrew as the French Army under Général d'Amade arrived and drove them back to Fricourt. The French remained in the city until it was taken over by the British in 1916. Thereafter, the town bustled with Allied soldiers. It was a centre for all manner of depots and facilities for the army, hospitals and recreation centres and, of course, for the railway to the coast and Paris. Trains from Le Havre brought in reinforcements and took away the injured. In 1918, it came within range of the German artillery until some of the large guns were captured on the Plain of Santerre, east of Chaulmes.

In the Second World War, Amiens was again badly damaged but today a modern city has been re-born with many new buildings. The **Picardy Museum** includes a large art gallery and collection of material relating to the history of the city. In 1966, the **Maison de la Culture** was opened in an attempt to bring together theatre, conference and exhibition halls. In the magnificent **cathedral**, there is a **Memorial Plaque to the Armies of Britain and Ireland**; also several interesting **memorials to the Allies**, including the **Australian Imperial Force**, the **New Zealand Division**, the **Newfoundland Contingent**, the **Royal Canadian Dragoons** and the **US 6th Engineer Regiment**; nearby, on the wall, are a **plaque to Lieutenant Raymond Asquith**, the son of the Prime Minister, Herbert Asquith, who was killed on September 15, 1916, and lies buried at Guillemont; and a **plaque to Général Débeney**, the commander of the French 1ère Armée.

The Australian National War Memorial in the British Military Cemetery at Villers-Bretonneux. Here too is one of the bas relief maps sculpted by Ross J. Bastiaan. It was here in November 1993 that the remains of an Australian serviceman were brought after being exhumed from Adelaide Cemetery on the N29 just west of Villers. At the National Memorial, they were formally handed over to the Australian authorities for transportation to Canberra to become the Australian Unknown Soldier. The empty grave at Adelaide Cemetery (Grave 13, Row M, Plot 111) is now marked with a special headstone.

127

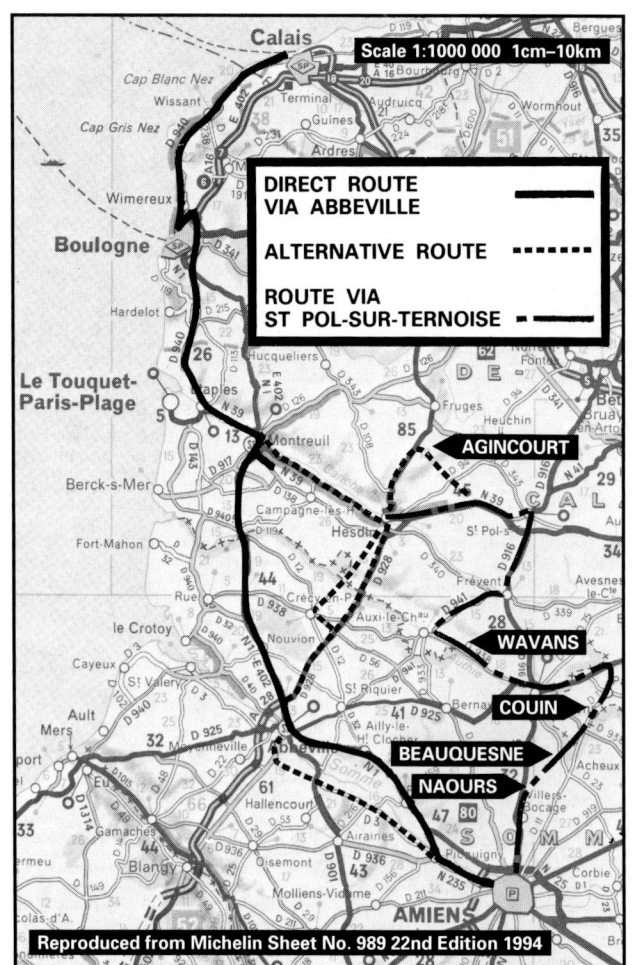

DIRECT ROUTE
VIA ABBEVILLE ———

ALTERNATIVE ROUTE - - - - -

ROUTE VIA
ST POL-SUR-TERNOISE ■ - ■ -

AGINCOURT

WAVANS

COUIN

BEAUQUESNE

NAOURS

AMIENS

Reproduced from Michelin Sheet No. 989 22nd Edition 1994

Château de Beaurepaire, Haig's residence from 1916-18.

· CHATEAU DE BEAUREPAIRE ·
LE MARÉCHAL DOUGLAS HAIG
COMMANDANT EN CHEF DES
ARMÉES BRITANNIQUES DURANT
LA GRANDE GUERRE, FIXA ICI SA
RÉSIDENCE DE FÉVRIER 1916 À
AVRIL 1919, LAISSANT CES
LIEUX EMPREINTS DE SON
· SOUVENIR ILLUSTRE ·

A plaque on the gateway records his stay.

Amiens to Calais

ROUTE 1 via Abbeville

Take the N235 to **Picquigny**, 13 kms, along the south bank of the Somme. Here, the main road crosses the river joining the N1 to reach Abbeville, via **Flixecourt**, in 34 kms. Alternatively, the D3 keeps to the south bank of the river and is probably the more attractive route (34 kms). Both roads travel through the rear areas where training was carried out and concentrations took place before the troops were moved up to the front.

Little of the old **Abbeville**, known to all British soldiers, remains for them or their descendants to visit today, for in May 1940 the town was bombed by Stukas and the entire centre burned out. Not long afterwards, tanks entered the town and the 4ème Division Cuirassée (under the command of a certain Colonel Charles de Gaulle) were in action against German forces which had crossed the river. The defence of Abbeville continued into June with Scottish and other French forces relieving each other until it was finally taken by the Germans on the 4th.

During the First World War, Abbeville, the capital of Ponthieu, was a sleepy market town with cloth-weaving as its main industry. In 1914, groups of marauding Germans entered the town in August and September, but, by the end of that month, it was firmly in Allied hands. On October 8, Field-Marshal French set up General Headquarters here. Later, it became a most-important British base, a centre of communications, supply and transport. There were several hospitals and training areas in the vicinity. The main British base was outside the town and many wooden huts were erected to house the thou-

sands of troops. In 1918, the town and surrounding area was subjected to frequent air raids. Set in very attractive country, and only 20 kms from the sea, it was a much-favoured place by the BEF.

The direct route to Montreuil-sur-Mer is via the N1 and skirts the **Forest of Crécy** for a short distance some 15 kms out of Abbeville. The distance to Montreuil is 44 kms. The longer and more interesting route is via the D928 and Hesdin.

Travel north on the D928 for 16 kms to **Fontaine-sur-Maye**. To visit the **battlefield of Crécy** of 1346, take the left road, D56, at the crossroads. In 2½ kms, an old **cross** on a modern plinth marks the **spot where King John of Bohemia was killed**. The cross is said to be one of the earliest battle monuments surviving in France as it was set up shortly after the battle in 1346.

It is 2 kms to **Crécy-en-Ponthieu**, a small town amid very pleasant country. In the centre of the town is another old **monument** with an amusing English text relating to **Eleanor of Aquitaine** and her sons. Turn right onto the square and leave the town by climbing up the D111 and, on the right, a double-decked wooden viewing tower is close to the **site of the windmill** from where Edward III watched his son, the Black Prince, lead his troops in the battle.

Continue 6 kms to **Dompierre** and turn right onto the D224. Then 7 kms to **Le Boisle** and left on to the D928 to Hesdin (13 kms). **Hesdin** was a 'British' town from 1916 onwards. Various branches of the Staff were quartered here, and there were also hospitals. It was also the RFC headquarters. This attractive town, set amid the hills, made a pleasant leave centre.

From Hesdin, the N39 leads to Montreuil along the marshy valley of the River Canche for 24 kms. **Montreuil** is an old walled town which once was a seaport. The ramparts

encircle the town on its rocky height and within them the streets are narrow, but they lead to the huge market place (Place du Théâtre) and the **statue of Field-Marshal Haig** on his charger, 'Miss Ypres'. The

original was destroyed during the Second World War and, in the 1950s, another bronze was cast from the plaster model, now housed in the Musée des Trois Guerres at Château Diors in Indre.

From February 1916 to April 1919, Montreuil was the British GHQ. Field-Marshal Haig resided in the **Château de Beaurepaire**, some 4 kms south-east from the town on the D138 near **St Nicholas**. A **plaque** on the gateway records his stay. The **military college buildings** at Montreuil housed the administrative staff and it is said that over 5,000 men were attached to GHQ here. In 1918, it was within the range of German bombers and suffered several heavy raids. As a result, at one time the HQ was evacuated at night.

From Montreuil, continue along the N39 beside the River Canche 13 kms to Etaples. **Etaples** was one of the largest centres for reinforcements to the BEF with training depots, hospitals and facilities for 100,000 men. In the sand dunes near the railway was the infamous **'Bullring' training ground**. This is overlooked today by the beautiful **Etaples Military Cemetery** where over 11,000 men from all over the world, friend and foe (there are 657 German graves), lie buried together. The cemetery is 2 kms outside 'Eat-apples' as the Tommy called it, on the D940 to **Boulogne** (26 kms).

On August 14, 1914, the first units of Sir John French's army began to disembark here and, from then on, Boulogne was on the main route for all troop movements from England. This famous old seaport and holiday centre became a bustling British base with hospitals, supply depots and camps being erected on the Camp de Boulogne, built in 1801 as the base for Napoleon's invasion army for England. All around the town, on the hills and coastal downs, camps were built, some semi-permanent hutted camps, others just masses of bell tents.

Except as prisoners-of-war, the Germans never reached Boulogne; the nearest being in 1914 when a few squadrons of roaming German cavalry came within 40 kms. In 1917-18, the town was heavily attacked from the air and much damage was caused both to the town and the base. The Second World War saw the port and coast fortified by the Germans with many blockhouses of the Atlantic Wall, of which quite a few still remain.

In recent years, there has been a great deal of new building and the town has expanded well beyond its 1918 boundaries. But, here and there, the small bungalows, which were brought from England for the use of the camp and later by homeless local population, survive.

The **Colonne de la Grande Armée**, high above the town on the road to Calais, was erected in 1804 to commemorate the nearby Camp de Boulogne. The original statue of Napoleon in a Roman toga was in bronze and was shot off its pedestal by the Royal Navy during the Second War! The head of the first statue can be seen together with other relics in the Boulogne **town museum**.

The direct road to Calais is the A16-E402 motorway (34 kms), built on the line of the old N1. The more interesting road to Calais is the coast road, the D940, on which, in 4 kms, we reach **Terlincthun**. The **British Cemetery** here was one of the first to be completed with the well-known headstones and was visited by the King and Queen.

It is 3 kms to **Wimereux**. All along the coastal downs were hospitals and welfare establishments. Lieutenant-Colonel John McCrae (*see page 33*) is buried in the **British Communal Cemetery**. His headstone, close to the Cross of Sacrifice, is one of those lying

The magnificent vista at Etaples Military Cemetery where flag-bedecked cenotaphs flank the Stone of Remembrance. Over 11,000 men are buried here.

In Wimereux Communal Cemetery, because of unstable ground, the gravestones lie flat around the Cross of Sacrifice.

flat due to the type of ground on which the cemetery is built. This is located behind the town cemetery in the north-eastern part of the village.

Some 5 kms further on, at **Ambleteux**, note the **Portuguese Memorial** on the right, marking the spot where in 1916 the Portuguese Red Cross built a hospital for its country's soldiers.

For the next 31 kms, the road swings up and down just inside the coastal cliffs of **Cap Gris Nez**, through Wissant and up again over **Cap Blanc Nez**, with the **Memorial to the Dover Patrol**, and past the terminal of the newly-opened Channel Tunnel at Sangatte and finally into **Calais**.

At the first traffic circle inside Calais, a left turn from D940 into Rocade Ouest, then in 1½ km a right one across Pont Douaumont, will lead to the complex of **Military Cemeteries**, French, German and Belgian, which lay behind the Communal Cemetery.

The Portuguese Red Cross had a hospital for Portuguese soldiers here at Ambleteux from 1916-18.

The Military Cemetery at Calais has German (foreground), French (centre) and Belgian (distance) sections of graves.

ROUTE II via St Pol-sur-Ternoise

Leave Amiens by the N25 to Poulainville (6 kms) and, in 2 kms, turn left for **Bertangles** (1½ km). Near this village was the RFC aerodrome. The village was also a base for other units including the artillery. Time seems to have stood still, for the village and its magnificent château have altered little since 1918; only the old army hutments and the airfield have gone, replaced by modern villas. The small **communal cemetery** — with one British war grave — is down a lane to the west of the village. It was here that the body of Manfred von Richthofen was buried on April 22, 1918 with full military honours. The **château** used by the British is now open to the public at certain times.

Take the D97 for **Villers-Bocage** (3 kms) and rejoin N25. In 5 kms, turn left onto the D60 to **Naours** (3 kms). The first turning on the right as the village is reached leads to the **Souterrains-réfuges de Naours**. These very extensive underground caves and connecting tunnels can house over 3,000 people and have been used for centuries. They are open to visitors and entry is via the pleasure park and the preserved windmills of Naours.

Return to the N25 and, in 5 kms, we reach **Vert-Galant**. Take the D31, to the right, to **Beauquesne**. Another 1½ km further east along this road is the **Château of Val Vion**,

used by Field-Marshal Haig as a headquarters. The château is on the right up a long tree-lined avenue. Here King George V stayed on his visits to the front. The present building dates only from the post-1945 era as the original house was bombed by the Germans in 1940, killing a party of Belgian refugees. The house was rebuilt almost identically.

The funeral of the Red Baron. The firing party in Bertangles Communal Cemetery, April 22, 1918. His body, transferred to Fricourt Cemetery after the war, was reburied in Berlin in 1925. In 1975, after several years of negotiations with the East Germans, the remains were transferred to the family vault at Wiesbaden. (IWM)

For many years, the plot at Bertangles still bore the outline of the excavated grave.

Take the next left turning at the crossroads, the D11, 3 kms to **Marieux**. Then turn right on to the D938 for 5 kms to **Louvencourt**. On the Acheux road (D938) to the south of the village is a small **British Cemetery**. It was one of the first three to be completed in the early 1920s and was designed by Lutyens. Among those buried here is Lieutenant Roland A. Leighton (Plot III, Grave B20), Vera Brittain's fiancé, who was killed in action on December 23, 1915. There are a number of unusual French grave markers.

Take the small road to the left of the church for **Bus-lès-Artois** (3½ kms). This is one of the concentration areas used for the divisions before July 1, 1916.

On leaving the village by the D176e, which shortly becomes the D25, we enter the Département of the Pas de Calais. The next village is **Couin**. At the junction at the

The French grave markers at Louvencourt Cemetery *(right)* **are of the rare stone type.**

bottom of the hill before the village, note the **notice on the brick wall** on the right. This direction sign for a water point was there in 1916, when the 63rd Division were gathering here, and it is thought to have been placed there by the 94th Brigade. In recent years, parts of the wall on which it is painted have been cut to a lower height but, fortunately, the historic part has been left as it was, although the original sign has obviously been redone with fresh paint.

Continue through **Pas-en-Artois** (4 kms), turning left onto the D6 for **Mondicourt**, another staging area, and then left onto N25 for Doullens (8½ kms). The small road to the left at the traffic circle leads up in 1 km to the **Foch Calvary** from where there are magnificent views. **Doullens** is an industrial town of the Authie valley and the steep hills around it. In 1916, it was the BEF base and concentration area, previously being Foch's HQ. On March 26, 1918, five days after the start of the German Spring offensive, the momentous meeting attended by Lord Milner, Poincaré, Clemenceau, Foch, Haig, Wilson and Pétain was held in the Council Chamber of the **Hôtel de Ville** at which Foch was appointed Supreme Allied Commander. The room, on the first floor, is open to visitors. Today known as the **Salle du Commandement Unique**, it still retains the original furniture, and two large murals vividly depict scenes from the meeting of March 26.

At **Gézaincourt**, a village on the hill to the south-west of the town, beyond the Citadel (3½ kms), is a **British Cemetery** of which there is a model in the Imperial War Museum in London. Two small roads lead up to it from the town and it can also be reached from the N25, signposted through **Bagneux**.

Leave Doullens via the D925 for **Risquetout** (3 kms), then onto the D938 for **Beauvoir-Wavans** (11 kms). A short distance beyond the village and the D117, in **Wavans Military Cemetery**, a small, lonely little graveyard on a narrow road on the right, lies Major J. McCudden, VC, DSO and bar, MC and bar, MM (Grave B10) — after so many

combats killed while taking off from Auxi-le-Petit, not far away.

In 2½ kms, at **Auxi-le-Château**, turn sharply right on to the D941, through the **Bois d'Auxi** and over the plain to **Frévent** (15 kms). Frévent is an industrial town amid hills which was used considerably by the British.

Continue via the D916 to **St Pol** (12 kms). This small bustling town was a British base for most of the war. Third Army had its

Couin. One of the few original signs to be seen . . . and the water-point is still there!

headquarters here in 1916 and it remained GHQ until 1921. The Army Graves Registration Service (later the Imperial War Graves Commission) HQ was here at St Pol. The choice of British Unknown Warrior was made here (in a hut near the **St Pol-sur-Ternoise Cemetery**) by Colonel L. J. Wyatt in 1920 from bodies brought in from various battle areas.

Take the N39 west for Hesdin (22 kms). Some 9 kms from St Pol, a detour can be made from the N39 at **Humières** to go via **Blangy** on the D104 to **Tramecourt** to visit the **site of the battle of Agincourt** (Azincourt) 11 kms. Approaching the village, one of the two **memorials** is passed on the left. A plan of the battle is provided at this and other major positions relative to October 25, 1415, whilst others recall the Tramecourt family, a member of which was present, and his descendants who died in concentration camps in the Second World War. Their **château** is amid the avenues of huge trees. An **RFC aerodrome** was located here from 1916-18. The D71 passes through **Azincourt** village, where there is a **museum** to the 1415 battle, and goes on to the D928 and in 13 kms to **Hesdin**. *(For a description of the route from Hesdin to Calais, see pages 128–129.)*

The Salle du Commandement Unique in Doullens town hall where, in a dramatic Franco-British conference on March 26, 1918, Foch was given sole command of the Allied armies to stop the German Spring Offensive.

Gézaincourt Cemetery clings to the hill above Doullens.

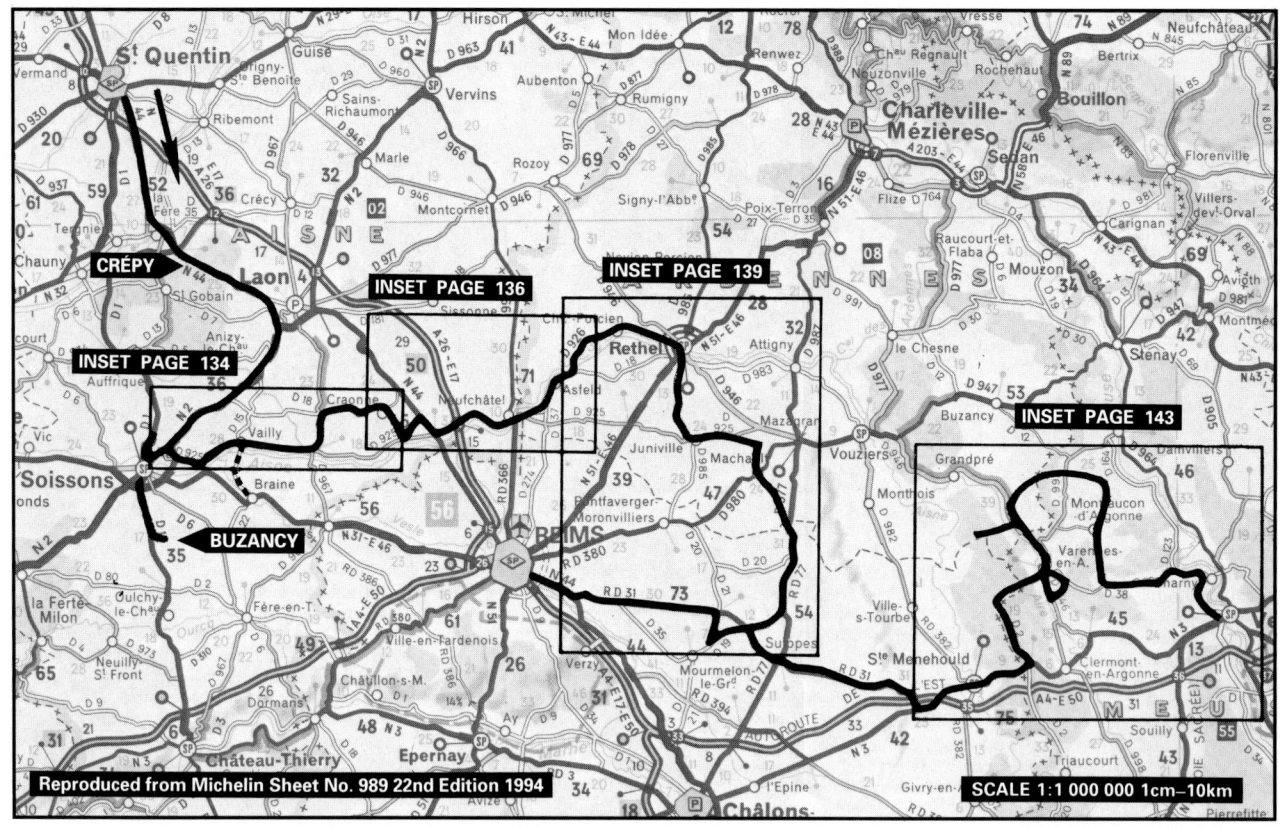

Reproduced from Michelin Sheet No. 989 22nd Edition 1994

SCALE 1:1 000 000 1cm—10km

St Quentin to Reims

This extension to the main itinerary includes the areas of British involvement in 1914 and 1918 in the regions south of St Quentin and part of the American battle-grounds in 1918.

Leave St Quentin southwards via the N44, 21 kms to **La Fère**. Continue on the N44 10 kms to **Crépy**. As the road slopes down towards a bend, take the road on the left, the D267/D26, for 1½ kms. On the left are woods and on the right, a little way from the road, will be seen a cluster of houses on the railway line. This is the **site of one of the huge German guns** which fired on Paris in 1918. The monster, which fired its first round on Paris on March 23 at 7.16 a.m., was hidden amongst the trees in the wood. Four minutes later, the 210mm shell burst in north-west Paris. The distance was 74.12 miles. Today, little remains of the site of the huge railway gun with its three-part barrel, in all some 34 metres in length, weighing over 300 tons. The railway siding can still be traced across the road, along a track to the main line, and into the wood where it becomes a glade through the trees which has rather unusual ridges across it — the sleepers. There are **bunkers** and the mounts for the base plate but nothing more.

Traces still remain, *above,* **of the railway line which carried the Paris guns. Bunkers now used as rubbish tips** *(below left)* **lurk in the undergrowth.**

Return to Crépy and the N44. In 5 kms, the lone hill of **Laon** comes into view and the spires and towers of the old fortress town can be clearly seen soaring 300 feet above the plain.

After another 4 kms, turn right on to the N2. Drop down 9 kms to cross the **Canal de l'Oise à l'Aisne**. Then 5 kms further on, away on the left, are the ruins of the **Fort de la Malmaison** and it is from here that the **Chemin des Dames** — the 25-kilometre-long road (D18) along the ridge between the valley of the Ailette in the north and that of the Aisne in the south — commences. The **calvary** is a memorial to the battles for the fort in October 1917. About 1 km up the Chemin, on the left, is a **Memorial to the**

The calvary at the western end of the Chemin des Dames is a French memorial to the 1917 battles for the Fort de la Malmaison.

French Régiment d'Infanterie Coloniale du Maroc, who battled here on October 23; and a little further up, at the road fork, a **Memorial to the French 38ème Division d'Infanterie**, the regiment's parent formation. Close by is a German Cemetery from the Second World War.

Back on the N2, some 3 kms further along, on the right, is a **Memorial to the French Fusiliers Marins**, a battalion of which had its command post in the cavern which lies behind the memorial and who from here attacked and retook the important **Moulin de Laffaux** position on September 14, 1918. The latter, on the crest 1½ kms further on, was the site of ferocious battles on May 5-6, 1917, in which the French employed a force

The French Fusiliers Marins Memorial below the crest of the Moulin de Laffaux.

The cavern was battalion command post.

The Monument des Crapouillots, to the men of the French mortar troops, is one of several French memorials at the Moulin de Laffaux.

of 48 tanks. There are several **French memorials** here, including one from the Second World War.

It is another 8 kms to **Soissons**. This is one of the oldest cities in France which has been a fortress for many centuries. The Romans were defeated here by Clovis in 486. At the end of August 1914, the BEF, retreating from Mons, crossed the Aisne west of the city. The Germans held Soissons until September 12 before they retired after having blown all the bridges. On September 13, the Battle of the Aisne began. The Germans were dug in amid the hills and quarries on the north bank and the British divisions fought their way back across the river at a number of points east and west of Soissons. The 1st Division crossed at Bourg, the 2nd at Chavonne, the 3rd at Vailly, the 4th at Venizel, the 5th at Missy and the Guards Brigade at Chavonne and at Pont-Arcy. They crossed in boats and rafts, by pontoons, and by using the girders of wrecked bridges. The crossing was successful and the force moved forward only to be checked in the Chemin des Dames region. In October, the BEF were relieved by the French.

Counter-attacks by the Germans were repulsed in 1915 and 1917 but, in May 1918, Soissons fell. On August 2, the city was recaptured only to be ruined further by the artillery bombardment which followed.

The **Soissons British Memorial to the Missing** is just below the cathedral facing the Passerelle des Anglais footbridge. The memorial commemorates the missing of the British IX and XXII Corps which fought during the July and August 1918 battles

alongside the French Army. There are 3,987 names engraved on the panels. The memorial is unique for the sculptural group. Three soldiers in their greatcoats stand shoulder to shoulder, two of them with their gas masks in the alert position. In front of the middle soldier is a rifle butt planted in the ground with a helmet on it. The sculptor was Eric Kennington.

An extension of our route, **Buzancy** lies 13 kms south of Soissons off the D1. This little town clings to the hills which were the scene of hectic fighting in the summer of 1918 and the drive there gives a good idea of the difficulties of the opposing armies. Turn left off the D1 on to D1240. At the junction stands the **US 1st Division Memorial** at the

The US 1st Division Memorial at the foot of the Buzancy heights list all 2,213 men of this division killed here in July 1918.

Eric Kennington's figures, *left*, on the centrepiece of the Soissons Memorial to the Missing, which commemorates the missing of the British IX and XXII Corps.

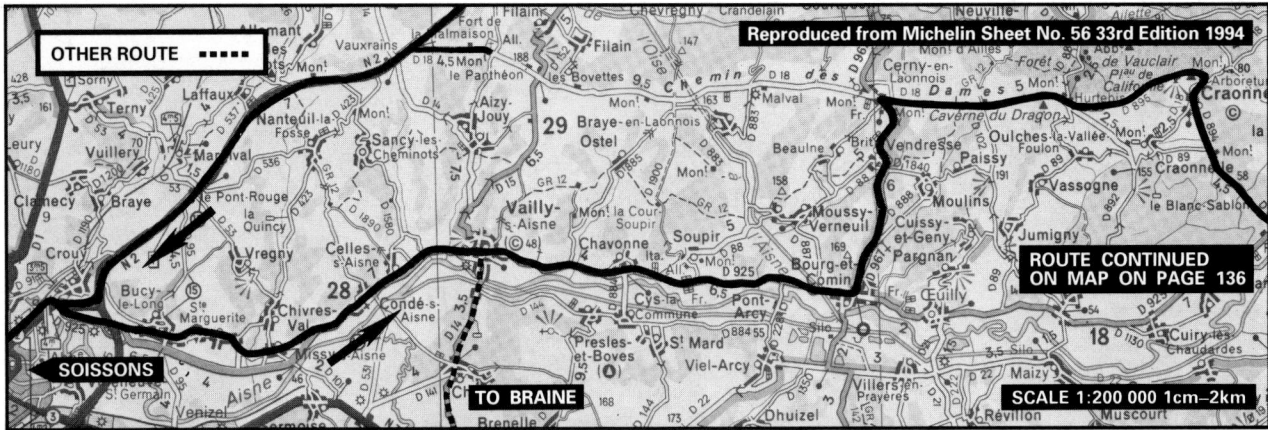

ROUTE CONTINUED ON MAP ON PAGE 136

The 15th Scottish Division cairn in Buzancy British Cemetery.

The dignified Italian Cemetery near Chavonne.

point where this division broke the German lines and assaulted the Buzancy height on July 21, 1918. The memorial lists the names of all 2,213 men of the division killed in this battle. To reach the **British Cemetery**, turn left in the village up a narrow lane. The cemetery was created in July 1918 by the **15th Scottish Division** who fought here with great distinction. Their courage so impressed their French comrades that at the close of the battle they erected a **cairn** to their honour with the inscription (in French): 'Here for all time the glorious Scottish thistle will bloom amid the roses of France'. Some years ago, the rough-hewn cairn was removed to the cemetery for safety.

Return to Soissons and leave the city by the D925, travelling eastward along the pretty banks of the **Aisne river** on the northern side. Views of the area held by the BEF and the places at which they crossed in September 1914 can be seen all along this road: **Missy** (10 kms), **Vailly** (7 kms), **Chavonne** (4 kms) — with the group of **Italian, French and German Cemeteries** along the road 1 km beyond it — and **Pont-Arcy** (3 kms), where there is still an iron bridge similar to that blown by the Germans.

Some 10 kms to the south of our Aisne road, at **Braine** on the N31-E46, Allenby's cavalry fought a delaying action in September 1914, and, in 1918, it was the Americans who were in action here. In the **town cemetery** is a **small British plot** where lies Captain Harry S. Ranken, VC, RAMC, attached to the KRRC (Grave A43). He was mortally wounded at Hautes-Avesnes in the conflict of September 19-20, 1914, suffering ghastly wounds before he would relinquish his task of tending other comrades, and he did not live to know that he had won the decoration announced with the first awards. He was also Mentioned in Despatches and created a Chevalier of the Légion d'Honneur. He died here at Braine on September 25. Braine can be reached via the D14 from Vailly; via the D884/D1320 from Chavonne; or via the D228/D22 from Pont-Arcy.

Continuing eastward on D925 from Pont-Arcy, in 2 kms we reach **Bourg-et-Comin**. At the far end of the village, in a farm barn on the left, is the **Musée du Souvenir**, a private war museum with a surprising collection of uniforms, arms and equipment from the Great War to the present day.

Go back to the centre of the village and turn right (north) onto D967 to climb up the hills to the ridge of the Chemin des Dames. Attractive and beautiful as these hills and valleys are, they show the difficulties the armies must have faced. **Vendresse** is 5 km further on. On the slope above the village is a **British Cemetery**. This is the route of the I British Corps (Haig) in September 1914, and also the sector of the 8th, 21st and 50th Divisions in May 1918.

Pont-Arcy. A bridge still spans the Aisne where the BEF crossed in September 1914.

Both in 1914 and later in 1918, the fighting swept over the wooded slopes at Vendresse as the graves in the cemetery indicate. Over the hill is the Chemin des Dames.

Cerny-en-Laonnois (1½ kms) is a cross-road village on the crest of the ridge of the **Chemin des Dames**. On the left is a tall Greek pillar, the **Memorial of the 1st Bn. Loyal North Lancashire Regiment**; the 1st Brigade of the 1st Division fought here in 1914. In front of you as you reach the cross-roads is the **Memorial of the Chemin des Dames**, a small elegant chapel with a modernistic column *(see right)* before it.

Left: **Two large cemeteries dominate the Cerny-en-Laonnois crossroads, one French and one German. Over the plastic crosses of the former, the grey granite of the latter can be seen.** *Right:* **A striking marble altar in the memorial chapel.**

Rather unusual, the tall grey column at Cerny is a British Memorial to the 1st Bn. Loyal North Lancashire Regiment which fought here in 1914.

Inside the chapel, in gleaming white stone and marble, are the memorials to the French units which fought here. The altar is a striking centre-piece being formed of rows of

crosses in perspective. To the left of the chapel, on the south side of this famous road, are large **French** and **German cemeteries**.

Turn right along the Chemin des Dames, the D18, stretching straight and narrow along the ridge high above the surrounding country. The road owes its name to the daughters of Louis XV as it was constructed to ease their journeys between Compiègne and the Château de la Bôve situated in the upper valley of the Ailette (the river to the north of the Chemin) which belonged to their great friend the Duchess of Narbonne.

The ridge is riddled with caverns and quarries which were used by both armies in the conflict. It is still possible to see the effects of the bombardments on the area in the shell-pocked chalky fields. The French gained a foothold on the ridge in April 1917 during Nivelle's offensive and the Germans fell back to the Ailette river. As with Vimy Ridge, this was considered to be a very strong position and very severe casualties were suffered by both sides in repeated attacks and counterattacks for possession of the ridge.

In 5 kms, on the right, **a group of guns and a 1939-45 tank** come into view with several memorials. They mark the entrance to one of the fortified quarries known as the **Grotte** or **Caverne du Dragon**. The **French memorials** are of the **4ème Régiment de Zouaves**, the **164ème Division d'Infanterie** and the **41ème Bataillon de Chasseurs à Pied** — the last unveiled as recently as May 1982. The

A French field gun and a tank of 1939 vintage at the Caverne du Dragon — which forms a memorial to French colonial regiments.

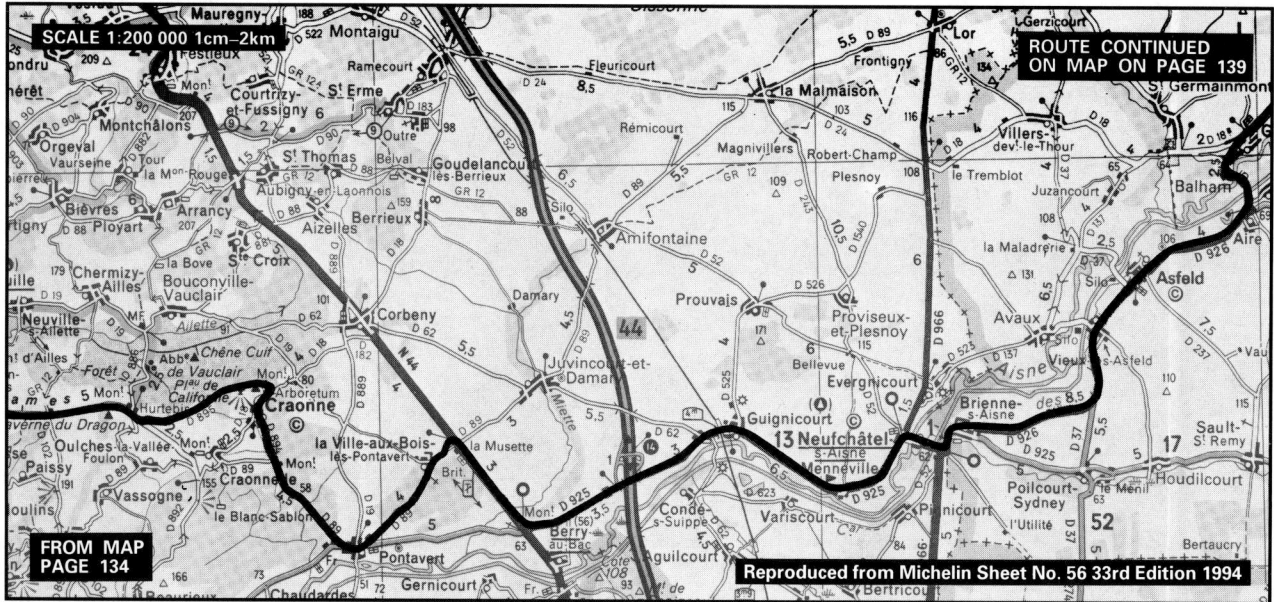

SCALE 1:200 000 1cm=2km

ROUTE CONTINUED
ON MAP ON PAGE 139

FROM MAP
PAGE 134

Reproduced from Michelin Sheet No. 56 33rd Edition 1994

complex, which dominated the French head-lines between April and November 1917, is now a museum open daily during the season. Unfortunately, the collection has suffered from a number of burglaries in the past but new measures have been taken to ensure that this cannot happen again. The entrance is now through a recently-erected building to the left of the steep path down the hillside — decorated with battlefield debris — and in through a foyer decorated with crests and banners of French units and photographs. Access to the underground caverns is via a steep stairway from which the visitor is transported into the chalk rooms and passages. The museum exhibits are displayed in cases representing the men of the French, British and German Armies who fought here. Relics include uniforms and badges, weapons and equipment, and the ephemera of war. In one room, a cinema show is given telling the story of the history of the ridge through the ages. Clever lighting enhances the dread gloom of those who lived and fought below ground. Here, the Germans set up a command post and stores depot for the troops who held the line. They had a huge arsenal and large numbers of men were housed in the various chambers. Water came from a deep well. Lighting was meagre and the modern guides depict the ink-black darkness by blacking out the whole suddenly for a moment and then relighting the area, section by section, in multi-coloured lights. Each time I visit the cavern, I am amazed by the lack of graffiti on the walls, which are all rough and devoid of other markings save the soot from a candle or two. A car park is provided on the north side of the Chemin.

A matter of some hundred metres further along is one of those places which prove the adage 'Once a good battlefield, always a battlefield.' This is **Hurtebise**. A rather striking **group in bronze** commemorates the Battle of Hurtebise Farm in 1814 and the 1914 battles; a **plaque to the 4ème Zouaves** on the wall of the farm recalls their victory here in 1914 and 1917 and another **plaque** the actions of Colonel Charles de Gaulle's **4ème Division Cuirassée** in their armoured battle in 1940.

A little further on along the D18, take the D895 for Corbeny. In this area, there are a number of French memorials relating both to Napoleon's victory over the Allies in March 1814 and to the 1914-18 battles. One is a **statue of Napoleon**, overlooking the battle-field. Around **Craonne** (4½ kms), amid the pine-covered hills, several French positions are indicated, often with car park and picnic areas. Just above the village is the **California**

position used by Napoleon in 1814 and which figured again in 1914 and 1917. An **orient-ation table** is set on the right above the precipitous hill with a magnificent view towards Reims and refers to the 1917 actions.

Towards the end of April 1918, five British divisions were put into the lines between Soissons and Reims to enable them to enjoy a comparative 'rest cure' after the ravages of the German advance on the Lys and Somme fronts earlier in the year, and for them to refit after the tremendous battles. They formed the IX Corps and were to support the

Battles a century apart are remembered at Hurtebise.

French 6ème Armée. To replace casualties incurred in March and April, the units had been reinforced with young and often only partially-trained drafts direct from England. The blow fell on May 27 when the Germans opened the Champagne offensive. The corps was assaulted by a fierce mortar, gas and artillery attack and, with many casualties, fell back across the rivers Aisne and Ardres. On May 28, the Kaiser came to California to view the victory of his troops and is said to have looked out from the site of the orient-ation table at the utter devastation.

The 4ème Régiment de Zouaves fought at Hurtebise in 1914 and 1917.

The California position — used by Napoleon in 1814 and the Kaiser in 1918.

Bois des Buttes — the crumbling trench lines where the Devonshires fought a bitter holding action, virtually to complete annihilation, in May 1918. (RC)

Left: **Their memorial stands nearby in Ville-aux-Bois-lès-Pontavert, its inscription recalling the 'ungrudging sacrifice to the sacred cause of the Allies' and that they 'in the face of an intense bombardment . . . though isolated and without hope of assistance, held on to their trenches . . . and fought to the last with an unhesitating obedience to orders'.** *Above:* **The plaque recording the award of the Croix de Guerre to the 5th (Gibraltar) Field Battery who fought with them, on the wall of the mairie.**

From Craonne, take the D894 and, in 2 kms, rejoin the D89 to descend into the valley near **Pontavert** with its important bridges over the Aisne. Turn left onto D925 and at the far end of the village, just beyond the junction, note the **bunker** next to the cemetery on the right-hand side of the road. Turn back and immediately right. This is again the D89 and, after traversing some open country, the road curves into the notorious **Bois des Buttes**, still threaded with crumbling trenches and shell-holes. Current tree clearance and coppicing of an area marked by warning notices of the danger of flying bullets (from the game hunters) is making it easier to pick out the lines of battle where the 2nd Bn. Devonshire Regiment (50th Division) fought a defensive action until almost being annihilated by a numeric-ally-superior force in the German attack of May 27, 1918. Incidentally, there is a picnic area on the right about ½ km in the wood. Not far from the woods, as they give way to orchards, the village of **Ville-aux-Bois-lès-Pontavert** is reached. There are still a few concrete **bunkers** in the area. The road curves into the village and the simple stone cross of the **2nd Bn. Devonshire Regiment Memorial** comes into view in front of the mairie and church. A **plaque to the 5th (Gibraltar) Battery** of 45th Brigade, RFA, destroyed in the same action, is on the wall of the mairie. The story of the Devons' gallant

Bunker on the edge of Pontavert, guarding the eastern exit road.

battle is graphically told on the plinth of the cross in the words of the commander of the French 6ème Armée, Général Duchène, under whose orders they fought. These words form the citation for the **Croix de Guerre** awarded to them and to the 5th Battery. At the crossroads, turn right to join the N44 in a few hundred metres at **La Musette crossroads** — the original site of the 2nd Devons' memorial before it was moved.

Ville-aux-Bois. Here, the Commonwealth War Graves Commission cemetery contains possibly the greatest proportion of unknown graves to any of those to be found on the Western Front: over 80 per cent of the dead being unnamed. As many such headstones include the regimental badge, this would appear to indicate partial identification from shoulder strap titles or collar badges. Here, too, can be seen graves bearing the Royal Air Force crest — the new service having superseded the Royal Flying Corps on April 1, 1918. Note the nearly-invisible concrete shelters behind the cemetery wall.

The D89 continues straight ahead to **Juvincourt-et-Damary** over part of the old **Berry-au-Bac airfield**, used in both wars by aviators of the French, British and German air forces. Now, it has returned mostly to agricultural land, through which the overgrown runways can be discerned, and one section is maintained as a driving school.

Almost immediately after turning right onto the N44 at La Musette, on the right, is **Ville-aux-Bois British Cemetery** with some **concrete shelters** on the north side of its boundary. The cemetery was made after the Armistice and, to my mind, is one of the most poignant I ever visit. Of the 540 buried here, 413 are unknown. Many are from units of the 8th, 21st and 50th Divisions, the unnamed headstones bearing the badges of several regiments and corps — the Devons, Durham Light Infantry, Middlesex, Machine Gun Corps, Artillery, and so on — who bore the brunt of the German surge forward during the 1918 Battle of the Aisne. The 8th Division alone lost 7,000 out of 8,000 men, killed, wounded, missing or prisoners-of-war. In all, by the time IX Corps was withdrawn in July, it had lost 15,000 dead. The Germans claimed to have taken 45,000 British and French prisoners and 400 guns. Others buried in this cemetery include three airmen: two killed in July 1918 (one of whom is an American who joined the RFC in February 1917) and another, a New Zealander, who died in November 1943.

Proceed south to **Le Choléra crossroads** in 3 kms. On the left is the **Memorial to the French Armoured Forces of 1917-18** and their creator, Colonel, later Général Estienne, while on the right are two examples of more modern **armoured vehicles** and an old crucifix on whose plinth are affixed various **commemorative plaques**. This was the spot from which, on April 16, 1917, French tanks for the first time engaged in a massed attack, on Juvincourt.

Le Choléra crossroads memorial commemorates the French Armoured Forces of 1917-18 and their creator, Colonel Estienne.

Turn left onto D925 for **Guignicourt**, crossing the A26-E17 autoroute to Reims, and in 6 kms reach the latter village on the north bank of the river and canal, carrying on to pass through **Neufchâtel-sur-Aisne** (7 kms). Turn right and take the D926/D18 left to **Rethel**, 34 kms along the pleasant Aisne valley which has a number of hotels — quite a rarity in this area. It is an ancient town which, after the fighting in 1914, was behind

the German line for the rest of the war. It was badly damaged in 1940. It is also hilly and the **ruins of the castle** of the Counts of Rethel are on the high ridge to the north.

South of the Aisne, climb out of Rethel on the N51 and almost immediately take the left fork of the D946 and then the right fork, the D985. The road passes a small airfield as it rises onto the plateau, broken only by the small town of Perthes.

In 15 kms, at a road junction, turn left onto the D925. These are the **battlefields of Champagne** fought over in July 1918 by the Americans.

Just beyond **Mont-St Remy** (8 kms), turn right on to the D23. The road sweeps southward across the rolling plain through **Machault** (4 kms) and **St Etienne-à-Arnes** (5½ kms). Directly after entering the Département of the Marne (4 kms), take the

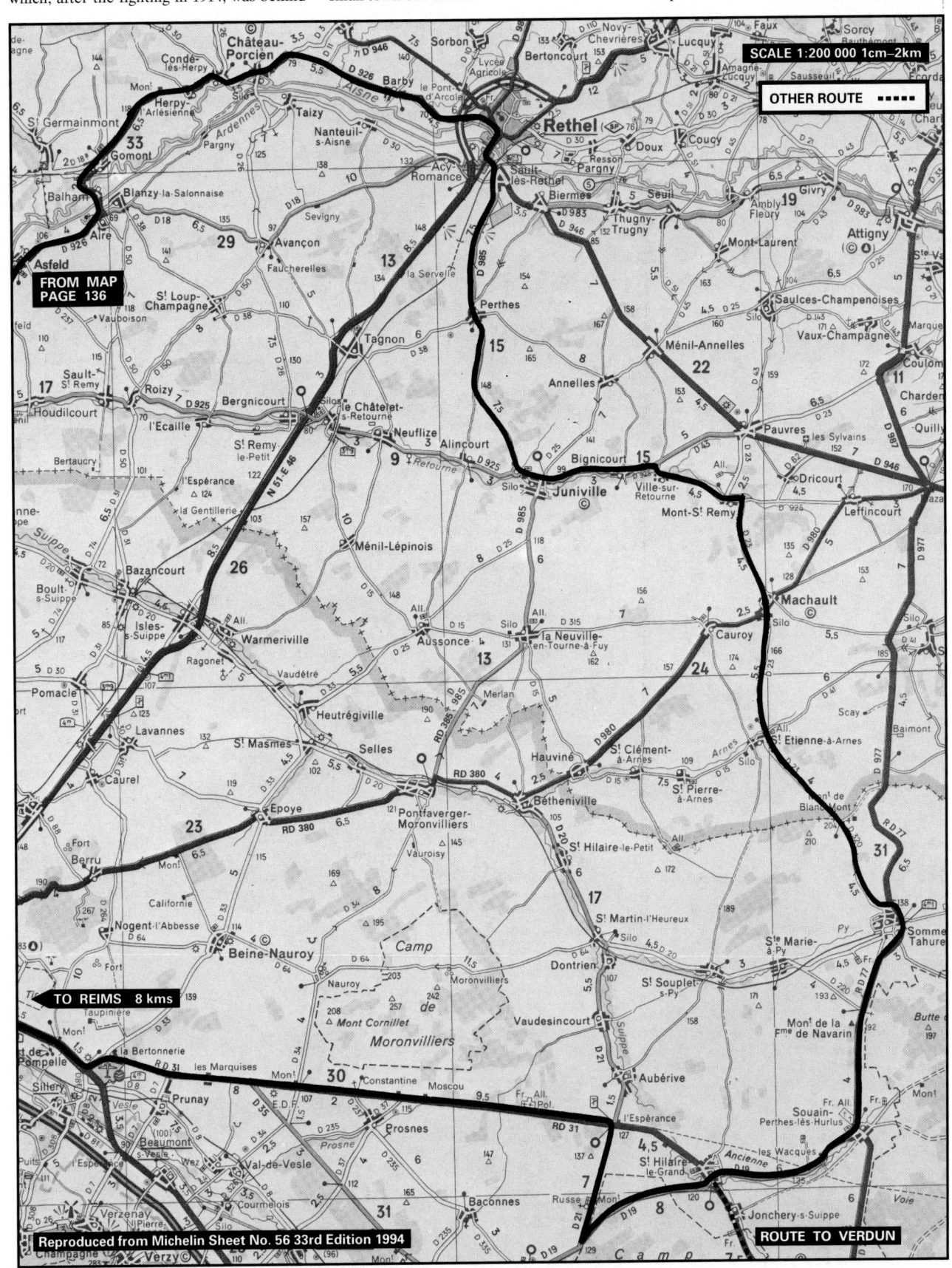

139

Sommepy, where the American Monument now stands, was once a look-out of Kaiser Wilhelm.

Around the Sommepy Memorial, the ground has been left as it was and is complete with grassy trenches and shell-holes.

left-hand road which goes up to the **Blanc-Mont ridge** on which stands the **American Sommepy Monument**. The tall, severe, stone tower rises from the pine-covered crest of a hill attacked and captured by the US 2nd Division in October 1918. All around, there are vestiges of the bunkers and trenches and shell-holes in which they fought. The monument tower is closed on Mondays and Tuesdays. Inside, there is the usual explanation of the operations in the region which one comes to expect from the American Battle Monuments Commission. The outer walls of the monument bear the badges of the divisions which fought in this region in July and September-October 1918 — the 2nd, 36th, 42nd (the 'Rainbow' Division) and the 93rd — together with their battle honours. A stairway leads to the top to give an excellent view of the battlefield.

Take the D320 for **Sommepy-Tahure**. About 3½ kms downhill from the monument, on the right-hand side, stands a lone boulder which is the **US 2nd Division Memorial**. The Indian head on it is the divisional badge.

At Sommepy, turn right onto the RD77. Some 4 kms further south, on the highest point of the road, is the **Monument de la Ferme de Navarin**, one of the principal positions in the Champagne battles of 1914, 1915 and again in 1918. The pyramid is surmounted by a vigorous group of three soldiers. One is an infantryman charging; the second is a

Above: The Ferme de Navarin Memorial of the Battle of Champagne rises above the tomb of Général Gouraud, GOC of the French 4ème Armée. *Below:* With unlimited views over the battlefield, the Navarin memorial marks one of the principal positions in the Champagne battles of 1914-15.

140

machine-gunner with his weapon over his shoulder as he presses forward whilst the third, with his right hand raised, urges them on. This is the work of the sculptor Maxime Real del Sarte and is a memorial to Lieutenant Quentin Roosevelt, the son of President Theodore Roosevelt, and to Général Henri Gouraud, the GOC of the French 4ème Armée. The Général, who died in 1946, is buried in the **crypt**, a small chapel lit by a stained-glass window bearing the likeness of him. In the crypt are many memorial tablets, including a **plaque to the US 42nd Division**, the latter unveiled as recently as April 1992. The Rainbow Division fought under Gouraud in July 1918, helping his army to stifle the German attack of July 15. On the outside of the pyramid, steep steps lead to the foot of the statues from which views of the battlefield are aided by four orientation diagrams. In the immediate vicinity, the ground has been left as it was at the end of the war, complete with trenches and shellholes. Lieutenant Roosevelt was killed in 1918 in the Tardenois battles (*see pages 158 and 159*).

We continue on the RD77 through this huge agricultural plain, passing a **Demarcation Stone** on the left roadside while descending to **Souain-Perthes-lès-Hurlus** in 4 kms. Here, there is a **German Cemetery** containing 13,783 graves. On the right is a **French Cemetery**.

Turn right on the D19 for 6 kms to **St Hilaire-le-Grand**, a small town on the northern boundaries of one of the huge military camps and training grounds associated with this part of Champagne. Take the Mourmelon road, the D19, skirting the edge of a tank training area. (*Note: St Hilaire is also where our itinerary to Verdun branches off—see page 144.*)

In 5½ kms, there is a sharp fork going off on the right, the D21. About 1 km along this road, on a slight incline, can be seen a group of pine trees and on the left, and most unexpectedly emerging from the trees, is the bulbous dome of a tiny **Russian Orthodox church** and beside it a **Russian Cemetery**. Here are buried Russian soldiers who fought for France in both wars with a separate enclosure for civilians. Two mass graves lie in the centre of the military graveyard. Across the road, in a clearing, is a **Memorial to the Russian 2nd Special Regiment**.

The German Cemetery at Souain —sombre like so many of its counterparts.

Set amid the pine trees, the Russian Memorial church stands guard over Russian graves from both world wars.

The memorial for the Russian 2nd Special Regiment sited across the road.

Polish memorial and cemetery west of l'Espérance crossroads.　**Alongside are French and (beyond the trees) German cemeteries.**

Remain on this road for another 3½ kms and, at the **l'Espérance** crossroads, turn left onto the RD31. This highway crosses the battlefields of 1915, 1917 and 1918 as indicated by the **group of French, Polish and German cemeteries** near l'Espérance, and a **memorial to the French offensives of April**

A splendid museum is located in Fort de la Pompelle — still lying in ruins almost as if time has stood still since the last shell was fired at it 1918.

1917 at the junction of the RD31 with the D34.

In 20 kms, the road joins the major highway to Reims, the N44, near an airfield and, on the rise in the ground as we turn right for Reims, the car park for **Fort de la Pompelle** is indicated. Access to the fort from the car park is through a narrow tunnel under the road. One emerges in a shattered landscape of torn chalk with the battered north-east face of the fort on the left.

As one of the forts encircling the city of Reims, it was in the line throughout the war. Bitter fighting took place in and around it, and it changed hands several times but always the French retook it. Today, it is a national museum. A varying collection of artillery pieces and equipment are displayed in front of the fort but most items are in the casemates. The internal galleries are well laid out recording the history of the fort, Reims and the Champagne district. Photographs and documents play a large part. Representative collections concerning Guynemer and

other French heroes and a good selection of the uniforms and equipment of the Allies are displayed. The amazing Charles Friese collection of Imperial German Army headdresses occupies a whole gallery. One subgallery has been filled with battle debris and in another transport is shown. At present, the roof of the fort is being restored, completion of which is expected to take several years.

After another 5 kms, **Reims** is entered. This is a very ancient city which has played many rôles in the history of France, religious and secular, military and political. It is a great industrial centre and famous for its art and learning. Here, in the massive **cathedral**, so badly damaged during the bombardments but now repaired, the Kings of France were crowned.

In September 1914, the Germans occupied the city and ransacked it for a week. On September 15, the German Crown Prince made the **Grand Hôtel** his headquarters. Prince August-Wilhelm was already there

and, shortly, the Kaiser's brother joined them. However, their stay was brief as the French 5ème Armée under Général Franchet d'Espérey arrived and drove them out. For the next four years, the city was in French hands but, always in artillery range, it was constantly shelled or bombed. By 1917, the city was almost surrounded but in 1918 the French gradually forced the Germans back until, in October, the retreat became a rout.

For those interested in the arts, there are several fine galleries; there are collections of Roman remains and of course the priceless treasures of the cathedral which were saved from devastation. The **Porte Mars** is a fine Roman triumphal arch near the Place de la République and, not far from this across the railway, at **Nos. 10-12, rue Franklin-Roosevelt** is the **war room** which is preserved as it was left on May 8, 1945 after General Eisenhower had accepted the German surrender. It is open every day except Tuesday.

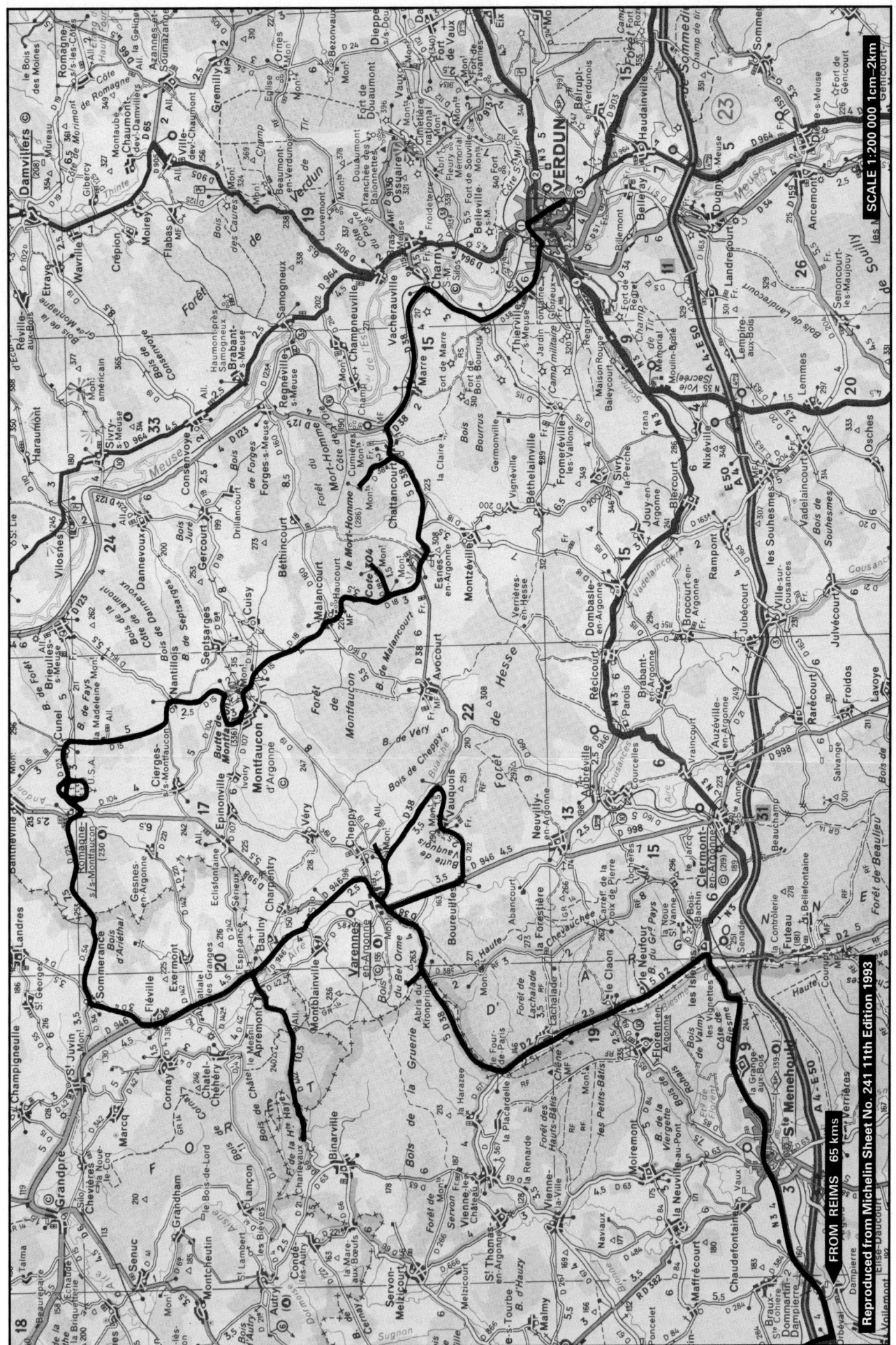

SCALE 1:200 000 1cm=2km

FROM REIMS 65 kms

143

The Verdun Battlefield

ROUTE I   Reims to Verdun

Beyond Reims lies the most sacred battlefield of France — Verdun — and the regions of the greatest American contribution in 1918 — the Meuse, Argonne and Château-Thierry fronts. This is a route for visiting those areas east and south-east of Reims. The southern and south-western region is covered in the final itinerary.

Leave Reims by the N44, branching off to the left onto the RD31 after passing Fort de la Pompelle. Traversing the huge plain of almost uninterrupted grain fields, among which are occasional **forts and military establishments**, in 8 kms we pass a **memorial to the French offensives of April 1917** (at the junction of the RD31 with the D34) and, 7½ kms further on, a **group of war cemeteries** of France, Germany and Poland. In the latter is also a **Polish memorial**. This route, incidentally, is also part of the **Voie de la Liberté**, the Liberty Road marking the US Third Army's advance through France of 1944, and its distinctive kilometre stones are seen on the roadside. After 42 kms, **Suippes** is reached.

In 23 kms, at **Orbéval**, turn left onto the N3 and travel 8 kms to **Ste Menehould**. This ancient fortress town on the western edge of the huge **Argonne Forest** was occupied by the Germans in September 1914 and great destruction was wrought before they were driven out. Thereafter, the town was a busy French HQ in the Argonne front battles.

In another 9 kms, we reach **Les Islettes**. Turn left on the D2. In 7½ kms, at **Lachalade**, on the right opposite the church, is the site of the **former cemetery of the Italian Garibaldi Legion**, initial burial place of those Italians who fell in the Argonne in the winter of 1914-15, and an **Italian Memorial** to Constante and Bruno Garibaldi, descendants of the great patriot-general, who were killed fighting with the legion.

Some 2½ kms further on, at **Le Four-de-Paris**, turn right onto the D38 for 5½ kms through the **Bois de la Gruerie**. A small road on the left makes a sharp turn into the forest; it is straight and has a good surface for approximately 1 km. Where it peters out into a number of mud tracks, a small fenced-off knoll will be seen on the right not many yards off the road, marking the **Abri du Kronprinz**. This unusual concrete shelter, built into a deep trench, was erected for Crown Prince Wilhelm in 1915 and was used by him for quite a time. It has a front portal and large windows but is gradually disintegrating. Four other large shelters are located nearby. Much of the surrounding woodland is cordoned off by barbed wire and entry into the trenches is forbidden.

Return to the D38 and continue to the left to **Varennes-en-Argonne** (4 kms). Before 1914, when the town was captured by the Germans, Varennes was only remembered in the history books as the town where Louis XVI and Marie-Antoinette were arrested to be taken back to Paris and the guillotine. Now, the town is dominated by the **Pennsylvania State Memorial** to her sons (most of whom served in the **US 28th and 80th Divisions**) who died in the battles to recapture this region in September 1918. The memorial, which is on the left as we enter Varennes on the D946, consists of a double colonnade surrounding a paved courtyard with a central monument in Grecian style. In the hillside below are a number of **bunkers and concrete shelters** which originally led into subways.

To the left of the monument is the modern **Musée d'Argonne** where there are ethnographical and art collections, documents relating to the arrest of Louis XVI in June

The memorial to the two Garibaldis who died in the Argonne Forest serving with the Garibaldi Legion. It stands in the field which was the Legion's initial burial ground in 1914-15.

The somewhat elaborate entrance to the Abri du Kronprinz, headquarters dugout of Crown Prince Wilhelm. It is surrounded by other large shelters in the Bois de la Gruerie.

The memorial to the men from the State of Pennsylvania, most of whom served in the US 28th and 80th Divisions.

Bunker entrance still visible today beneath the Pennsylvania State Memorial at Varennes-en-Argonne.

The imposing memorial lantern to 'Les Combattants' amid the barbed wire on the summit of the Butte de Vauquois.

1791, and the **Museum of Mine Warfare** with some interesting dioramas showing how mines were bored and blown. There are many relics of the American activities in the region and the personalities who fought here, including Harry S. Truman.

The road past the memorial leads down into the town where sites relevant to the historic night of 1791 are marked by explanatory signboards. We remain on the D946, leaving the town by returning past the American monument for **Boureuilles**, some 3½ kms to the south. There, turn left on D212 for **Vauquois** and the famous **Butte de Vauquois**.

To visit this mine-riven hill, 290 metres high, requires a short steep walk from the car park. This was once the site of the village of Vauquois, but now it is a grassy desert of barbed wire and mine craters. The village was completely destroyed in the struggle, which lasted from October 1914 to October 1915, sinking almost without a trace into the earth. Only as one reaches the top does one realise that the hill has in fact been completely hollowed out by the mine warfare, and the sight is one of the more dramatic of our entire tour. On the summit is a **memorial** to those who died and close by is one of two excellent **orientation tables**. A map shows a route recommended for a comprehensive visit and each salient position is identified. A **German trench and tunnel entrance** was restored in 1991 and, down the slope on the French side, another tunnel — identified as the **French engineers' command post** — is under restoration. Guided tours are given from the car park every first Sunday of the month at 10 a.m.

Recent work at Vauquois uncovered a German and a French tunnel entrance.

The Angel of Victory surmounts the US 35th Division Memorial near Varennes.

German Cemetery at Apremont and memorial to Landwehr-Regiment 27.

Memorial marking the position of the 'Lost Battalion' beside the D242/D442.

Return to the modern village at the foot of the butte and take the D38 to the left to return to **Varennes** (8½ kms). On the way, note the **Memorial to the US 35th Division and the Men of the State of Missouri**, some 300 metres down the D19 on the right. Captain Harry S. Truman commanded an artillery battery in the 129th Infantry of the 35th Division. On September 26, 1918, Colonel George S. Patton, his tanks lost, won a DSC in this area, fighting with the infantry of the 35th Division.

In Varennes, turn right onto D946 and **Apremont** is reached in 7 kms. From here, a detour into the forest along D242/D442, with the **German Cemetery** on the hillside, will in 7½ kms arrive at the **ravine** where the **Lost Battalion** disappeared for several days having become cut off from their comrades of the US 77th Division between October 2-7, 1918. A marker on the roadside up the hill indicates the valley down very steep slopes.

Return to the D946 and continue north to reach **Fléville** in 4½ kms. Take the D4 to **Sommerance** and, in 3 kms, the D54/D123 to **Romagne-sous-Montfaucon**, 8 kms away, driving through more of the American battle zones to the **Meuse-Argonne Cemetery and Memorial** on the far side of the town. In this huge peaceful park, over 14,000 men lie buried on the gentle slopes of the valley. The administrative block looks out over gleaming white crosses, lawns and trees, to the memor-

The central avenue of the American Meuse-Argonne Memorial and Cemetery.

ial chapel on the opposite crest, in the wings of which 954 missing are commemorated.

Leave the park by the Cunel road. In 2 kms, take the D15 right to **Nantillois** (5 kms), with the squat **Memorial Chapel of the 315th Infantry Regiment** (US 79th Division) on the right-hand side of the village street, and the **US 80th (Pennsylvania) Division Memorial** at the far end of it. Soon, the **Butte de Montfaucon** is in sight and is reached in 4 kms. This outstanding ridge is capped with

Hill 336 from which rises the elegant Doric column of the **American Memorial** marking the US First Army's Meuse-Argonne offensive of September 26-November 11, 1918.

Shallow steps lead to the entrance, and an internal and very graceful stairway up to the observation balcony below the Statue of Liberty from where the view is spectacular. This was the site of an ancient monastery and hamlet which the Germans heavily fortified after its capture in 1914 and it was used

Nantillois has two American unit memorials: a chapel for the 315th Infantry *(left)*, and the US 80th Divisional Memorial *(right)*.

A German OP in the ruins of Montfaucon monastery, *right*, is overlooked by the American monument, *above*.

French 69ème Régiment d'Infanterie memorial outside Malancourt *(above)*. The memorial *(right)* on Côte 304 was paid for by the veterans of 21 French divisions.

thereafter as an OP, particularly in 1916. They built some 17 bunkers in the ruins. In 1914, the Crown Prince had his HQ on this prominence. It fell to the Americans of the 313th Infantry (79th Division) on September 27, 1918 in their attack on the **Kreimheide Line** which ran east to Grandpré.

Leave by D15/D18 for **Malancourt** (5 kms) where, at the far side of the village, there is a bunker with a **Memorial to the French**

69ème Régiment d'Infanterie, a unit which was annihilated in the 1916 defence of the village. Then, in 3 kms, the D18a on the left leads up to **Côte 304** with its **monument**. Over 10,000 men were killed fighting in this hilly wooded area in 1916-17. Survivors of 21 different French Divisions erected the memorial in 1934. All around, the ground is still shell-pocked like a lunar landscape and criss-crossed with trenches.

Return to D18 and continue south, passing the **Memorial to the French 173ème Régiment d'Infanterie** when joining the D38 to the left for **Esnes-en-Argonne** (3 kms) and **Chattancourt** (5 kms).

An apt memorial, *below*, erected by the French 69ème Division d'Infanterie on the summit of Côte 295, Mort-Homme: 'They Have Not Passed'.

French 173ème Régiment d'Infanterie memorial near Esnes-en-Argonne *(above)*.

147

The memorial of the French 40ème Division d'Infanterie on Côte 295.

The infamous hill of **Mort-Homme** is reached by taking the D38bis at the approach to the village. **Côte 295**, the highest in the **Forêt de Mort-Homme,** was the scene of intensive tunnelling by both sides, particularly by the Germans. Their longest subway, named after the Crown Prince, was some 3,000 metres long and others were of 1,500 to 2,000 metres. These connected the three most important hills in the neighbourhood and provided support for the mine warfare, a predominant factor in this region. Mort-Homme has a very sombre memorial on its summit. Known as the **Monument du Squelette**, it was erected by the veterans of the **French 69ème Division d'Infanterie**. Nearby is the **Memorial of the French 40ème Division d'Infanterie**.

From Chattancourt, take the D38 for Verdun via **Charny-sur-Meuse** in 15 kms.

Verdun is a city with a violent history and, despite the terrible destruction of 1916 and the attacks in the Second World War, still retains the atmosphere of an ancient town. There are many monuments recalling its struggle for survival, being the hub of a circle of forts built in the surrounding hills after the war of 1870. In 1914, Général Sarrail saved the city and its military establishments from capture although it was frequently under fire. In February 1916, the Germans made fierce attacks on the fortifications and Fort de Douaumont fell on the 25th. Fort de Vaux held out until June when it also was overwhelmed. The next nearest fortress at Souville almost followed but, although completely ruined, the garrison held out and the city was saved. In July, the German attacks eased as the Battle of the Somme began. In the autumn, Général Mangin's massive offensive regained all the ground lost and Verdun was relieved.

Before visiting Verdun itself or the surrounding battle zone, a call at the excellent **Tourist Office** (Syndicat d'Initiative) is advised. Literature is available in several languages, including compact little guide books and leaflets outlining tours. Also for sale are the excellent ING maps 3212 Est (Verdun) and 3212 Ouest (Douaumont) issued in the 1:25,000 scale by the Institut Géographique National and indispensable for anyone wanting to make an in-depth visit to the Verdun battlefields. The old 'all-in-one' ING map 'Forêts de Verdun et du Mort-Homme — Champs de Batailles de Verdun' is unfortunately no longer in print. The office is in the Place du Nation across

The foreboding statues of French military leaders glare down at passers-by with the Vauban ramparts forming the appropriate backdrop.

Above: **Plaque in honour of Général Mangin whose army finally secured Verdun from enemy attack in December 1916.** *Below:* **Symbolised in stone on the Monument to the Fallen at Verdun — the graven figures representing five different arms of service of the French Army.**

the River Meuse from the handsome **Porte Chaussée**. From the bridge, the Avenue Général Mangin emerges and, opposite the Tourist Office, is the impressive **Monument to the Fallen** — five figures represent the different corps of the French Army standing shoulder to shoulder above the columns of names. On either side are fragments of old fortifications landscaped into public gardens; a **memorial plaque for Général Mangin** is on one wall. Verdun has many very fine memorials and buildings of interest but the **Victory Monument**, which towers over the rue Mazel and Avenue de la Victoire, dominates all. In the crypt are kept the Golden Books recording the many medals awarded to the city. The memorial, up steep steps, is flanked by two Russian guns.

Near where the N3 enters the town from the west, an **avenue of huge statues of the Maréchals and Générals of France**, beneath the Vauban ramparts, leads to the Porte du Secours entrance to the **Citadel** on Avenue du 5ème RAP. As Verdun is still a major garrison, the Citadel remains active but certain sections are open to visitors below its

The Victory Monument, with its two Russian guns, towers over the martyred city.

imposing walls and ramparts. Much of the fortress is underground — in fact there are 4,000 metres of tunnels which were of vital importance during the war. In one of the large chambers, the selection of the French Unknown Soldier was made from eight bodies. A new 'living exhibition' was opened in 1992 in the underground galleries, the **Citadelle Souterraine**, the entrance of which is on Avenue du 5ème RAP. Known as **Expérience 1914-18**, it conducts visitors in

automatically-driven carts through the pitch-dark galleries, past several dioramas which are made to come alive by means of high-tech audio-visual techniques.

There is another **museum in the Hôtel de Ville**, an Italianate Louis XIII-style building, once a small palace, where documents and decorations and flags are shown. Four old cannon flank the zero-kilometre borne and a large shell or two can be seen in the Court of Honour through which access is gained to the museum.

In the **cathedral crypt**, the capitals of a number of the pillars represent various aspects of the Battle of Verdun, the sculptor,

Le Bourgeois, depicting scenes of trench life and horrors in a simple, realistic style. There are many statues and memorials in the city but perhaps one of the most evocative is the

A diorama in the 'living exhibition' in the Citadelle Souterraine recreates the selection of the French Unknown Soldier which took place here.

The four guns at the town cemetery where the ones not chosen now lie.

Statue of Victory by Rodin which is to be found in front of the **Porte St Paul** in the Place Vauban. It was presented to the city by the Dutch nation. There are numerous hotels in the city and nearby towns such as Etain and several camp sites provide for battlefield visitors.

ROUTE II   The French Battlefields

Leave Verdun by the Etain road (N3) pausing perhaps in 1 km to visit the **Cimetière de Faubourg Pavé** — the military cemetery where lie the seven unknown soldiers not chosen. It lies on the edge of the town on the left-hand side of the road. Note also the group of captured **field guns** in the entrance park.

In 5½ kms, turn left onto the D913 and enter the woods of the Verdun memorial parc. Most of the historic sites in this large wooded area — the main Verdun battlefield — are now under the care and control of the Association Nationale du Souvenir de la Bataille de Verdun et la Sauvegarde de ses Hauts Lieux (ANSBV) which is based at the Mémorial de Verdun at Fleury. In many of the clearings in the forests, and at numerous salient positions, the ANSBV have installed boards with good explanatory notices, plans and orientation tables and indicating interesting walks and drives. The whole region is signposted well, and places where it is not wise to penetrate are clearly shown. The paths are labelled and the trees are marked with the relative plot number in strategic spots. All are shown on the 1:25,000 ING maps 3212 Est (Verdun) and 3212 Ouest (Douaumont), for sale at the Verdun tourist office and, within the parc, at the Mémorial de Verdun and the Douaumont Ossuary shop.

In 1½ kms, take the right fork for **Fort de Vaux**, 2½ kms up the wooded slopes. Halfway up is the **Monument des Fusilés de Tavannes** for members of the Resistance executed here in 1944. Fort de Vaux was the north-eastern bastion and one of the many which surrounded Verdun. Externally, it is a battered crumbling heap of stones and the advent of thousands of visitors has ruined the immediate area and thus given the fort an even more desolate appearance. The iron turrets still crown the grassy cover above it. Internally, the galleries, which are open to visitors, drip with damp and present a very sombre and chilling aspect of the life of the men who lived and died here during the bombardments. It was gallantly defended but eventually the garrison was overcome in June 1916. However, the fort was recaptured again by the French in November 1916. A **memorial to the pigeon** which succumbed to the effects of gas after carrying the last message from Commandant Raynal is to be found with others on the outer walls.

A tall cross rises above the seven Unknown Warriors in Verdun Cemetery; the eighth lies in Paris, beneath the Arc de Triomphe.

Fort de Vaux *(above)* **withstood days of continuous attack by flame-thrower and poison gas. Weakened by asphyxiation and lack of water, the garrison surrendered on June 7. Not long before the end, on June 4, a carrier pigeon arrived at headquarters with the last message from the commander of the besieged fort. The bird died on arrival from gas poisoning. A plaque on the fort** *(below right)* **recalls her sacrifice.**

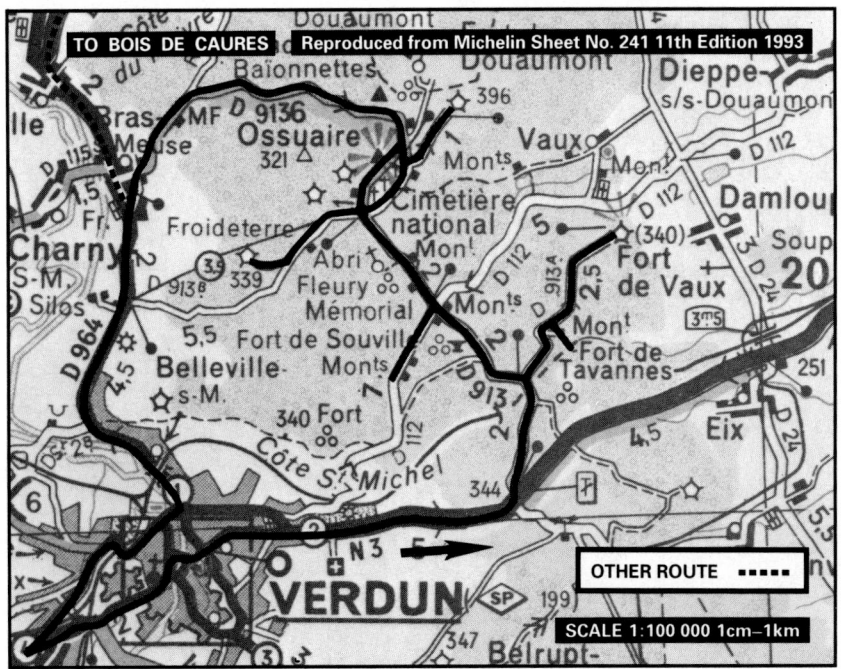

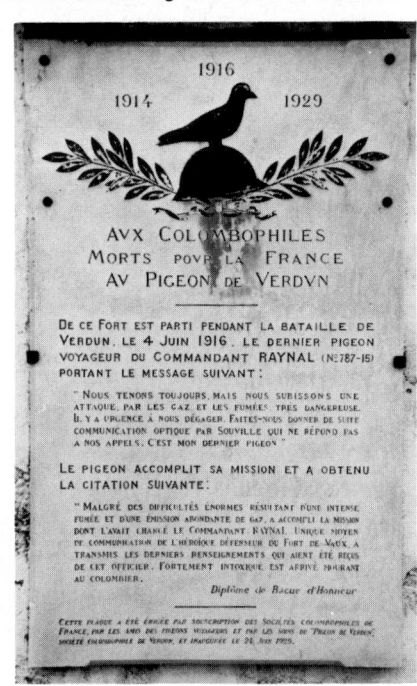

A monument to André Maginot, once a sergeant in the 44ème Régiment d'Infanterie Territoriale, near Fort de Souville.

The Lion Memorial at the Chapelle Sainte Fine crossroads commemorates the French 130ème Division and its allies.

After visiting the fort, return to the D913 and turn right, arriving in 2 kms at the crossroad of **Chapelle Sainte Fine**. The road to the left, the D122, is the direct one from Verdun; within ¾ km, it passes **several monuments** including the **Memorial for André Maginot**, Minister of War responsible for the famous line of forts which bears his name. He fought at Verdun as a sergeant.

The **Lion Monument**, which commemorates the **French 130ème Division d'Infanterie** in particular, but in addition honours ten other divisions and the garrison of the Fort de Souville, also marks the limit reached by the Germans. **Fort de Souville**, attacked by the Germans on July 12 but staunchly defended by the French, lies in the trees behind the lion, a ruined heap amid the craters.

Proceed straight ahead to Douaumont. In a short distance, on the site of the old railway station of **Fleury**, one of the nine villages obliterated by the battles and now marked only by name boards and a chapel, stands the **Mémorial de Verdun**. This is a magnificent

museum where the history of the battle is fully explained in well-designed displays of documents, photographs, exhibits of battle-field equipment and relics found in the region. Captions are in three languages as are the excellent guide books. All the displays are set around a life-size representation of a sector of the battlefield beneath a huge animated map. Films are also shown continuously during opening hours.

Across the forest can be seen the tall tower of the **Ossuary of Douaumont** and, although there are many memorials and monuments in the region, this is the dominant one. The **Jewish Memorial** is on the left as the Ossuary is reached. A large car park is behind the building. The Ossuary was built between 1922 and 1932 and contains the remains of over 130,000 men, both French and German.

Another 15,000 identified dead lie in the **French National Cemetery** in front of it. The building, which is 137 metres long, was inaugurated by Président Lebrun in August 1932. There is a small chapel under the tower and the long aisle is divided into 18 sections or chapels, each dedicated to a different département or city of France with other apses for the Allied nations. Services are held regularly in the chapel and the tower itself can be visited. The exterior of the building is decorated with the crests of the towns of France and others overseas which contributed to the cost of this enormous memorial. At the rear of the building, the bones of the unknown can be viewed through ground-level windows. Temporary exhibitions are staged from time to time in rooms at the rear.

The memorial to the destroyed village of Fleury — one of nine villages obliterated in the Battle of Verdun.

Towering above the French Cemetery at Douaumont is the great ossuary.

The Mémorial de Verdun on the site of Fleury railway station.

The Jewish volunteers memorial near Douaumont Ossuary.

151

A path from the car park leads to the ruins of **Fort de Thiaumont**. Resume your journey by turning left when leaving the car park and skirt the huge cemetery to take the D913b on the left for Fort de Douaumont. At the roadside is the recumbent figure of **Le Soldat du Droit**, the memorial to André Thome who was killed in March 1916.

Fort de Douaumont on **Hill 388** was the most important of the arc of forts built in the last century. Although the keystone to the Verdun defences, it was manned only by an elderly artillery guard and about a dozen men, and it fell without a struggle on the fifth day of the German attack, February 25, 1916. The exterior is similar to Fort de Vaux with untidy paths and grassy tufts covering it. Here again the turrets remain and there is also an observation post looking out over the panoramic view. The German attack came from the region of the military camp to the north. Inside the fort, groups are conducted through the galleries and casemates, although most of the guides only speak

André Thome — the Soldat du Droit.

Battered Fort de Douaumont surmounted by steel cupolas.

French or German. English visitors are given typed translations.

Another interesting complex to visit is the Froideterre fortification on Côte 345. It is reached from the Ossuary by the D913b beside the Jewish Memorial. About 1 km down through the forest, the road first passes the **Abri Caverne des Quatre Cheminées** on the slope which falls away to the left of the road. This bunker was linked with others at Command Posts 118 and 119 near Thiaumont.

Then, just past the Four Cheminées complex, the approach road to the **Ouvrage de Froideterre** on **Côte 345** climbs up on the right. Froideterre was in action right through the Battle of Verdun, was subjected to heavy

bombardments, and was partially occupied by Bavarian troops of Infanterie-Regiment 10. However, the garrison ejected the invaders, due in no small part to the effectiveness of the 75mm turret and its machine

guns. Along the D913b and the fort road the trees have been cleared so that one can see the incredibly shell-torn ground, hitherto completely hidden. However, new trees are already growing up.

The Ouvrage de Froideterre on Hill 345. Designed by the French army engineer Laurent in 1895, it withstood prolonged shelling during the Battle of Verdun.

The Quatre Cheminées shelter below Hill 345 is named after the four ventilation shafts protruding from the slope above.

The successful defence of the Froideterre Casemate de Bourges was largely due to the turret-mounted 75mm cannons which were able to give covering fire to the flanks in concert with the strong point at Charny.

Return to the D913 and turn left before the Ossuary to visit the **Tranchée des Baïonnettes** which is on the right of the road a little way down the hill. The entrance is through a massive gateway with intricately-carved heavy metal doors. Beyond, after passing the recently-restored **Memorial of the French 137ème Régiment d'Infanterie** up on the right, the great bulk of the concrete canopy and pillars enclosing the famous trench comes into view. This was a front-line trench of the Ravine de la Dame sector in which were buried men of the 137ème Régiment as they struggled through the trench. They were found in 1919 when it was noticed that a line of rusting bayonets and rifles was protruding from the ground in an area where men of the regiment were known to have disappeared. Today, there are few bayonets or rifles visible; in fact, every time I visit the monument, I see a difference. Only 17 unknown soldiers remain buried here, marked by the wooden crosses. The other 40 who were identified were reburied in Fleury Cemetery.

The D913 winds down into the Meuse valley to reach **Bras** in 6 kms. From here, Verdun is 7½ kms south on the D964. Alternatively, a detour can be made northwards to visit the **Bois de Caures**, made famous by the resistance of Lieutenant-Colonel Driant and his Chasseurs à Pied. Turn right on to the D964 to **Vacherauville** (2 kms) and then take the D905 6½ kms up into the woods to the junction with the D125. Around this junction are the regimental and individual memorials to the gallant colonel and his 1,200 men who held up the German 21. Infanterie-Division for the first two days of the attack, February 21-22, 1916: on the left is the **Memorial of the 56ème and 59ème Bataillons de Chasseurs à Pied**, both virtually annihilated in the action; across the road, a glade leads to a memorial marking the **site where Colonel Driant fell** on February 22 and, a bit deeper into the forest, the **site of his field grave**; and on the far side of the

Rusty bayonets emerge *(below left)* beneath a concrete canopy — the infamous Tranchée des Baïonnettes at Douaumont. Only 17 unknown soldiers remain buried beneath the bayonets; the other 40 who were identified were interred in Fleury Cemetery. The men buried alive in the trench belonged to the 137ème Régiment d'Infanterie. Its memorial *(below right)* stands close beside the entrance *(above)*.

junction, to the left of the D125, is his **command post bunker**. Colonel Driant, who was the Deputy for Nancy, was the author of the bill which culminated in the institution of the Croix de Guerre.

Memorial to the 56ème and 59ème Bataillons de Chasseurs à Pied and their commander Colonel Driant, who resisted the Germans in February 1916 in the Bois de Caures *(above, below and left)*.

The spot where Colonel Driant was mortally wounded and the site of his field grave are both marked by memorials.

The bunker used by Driant as his command post still standing in the Bois de Caures.

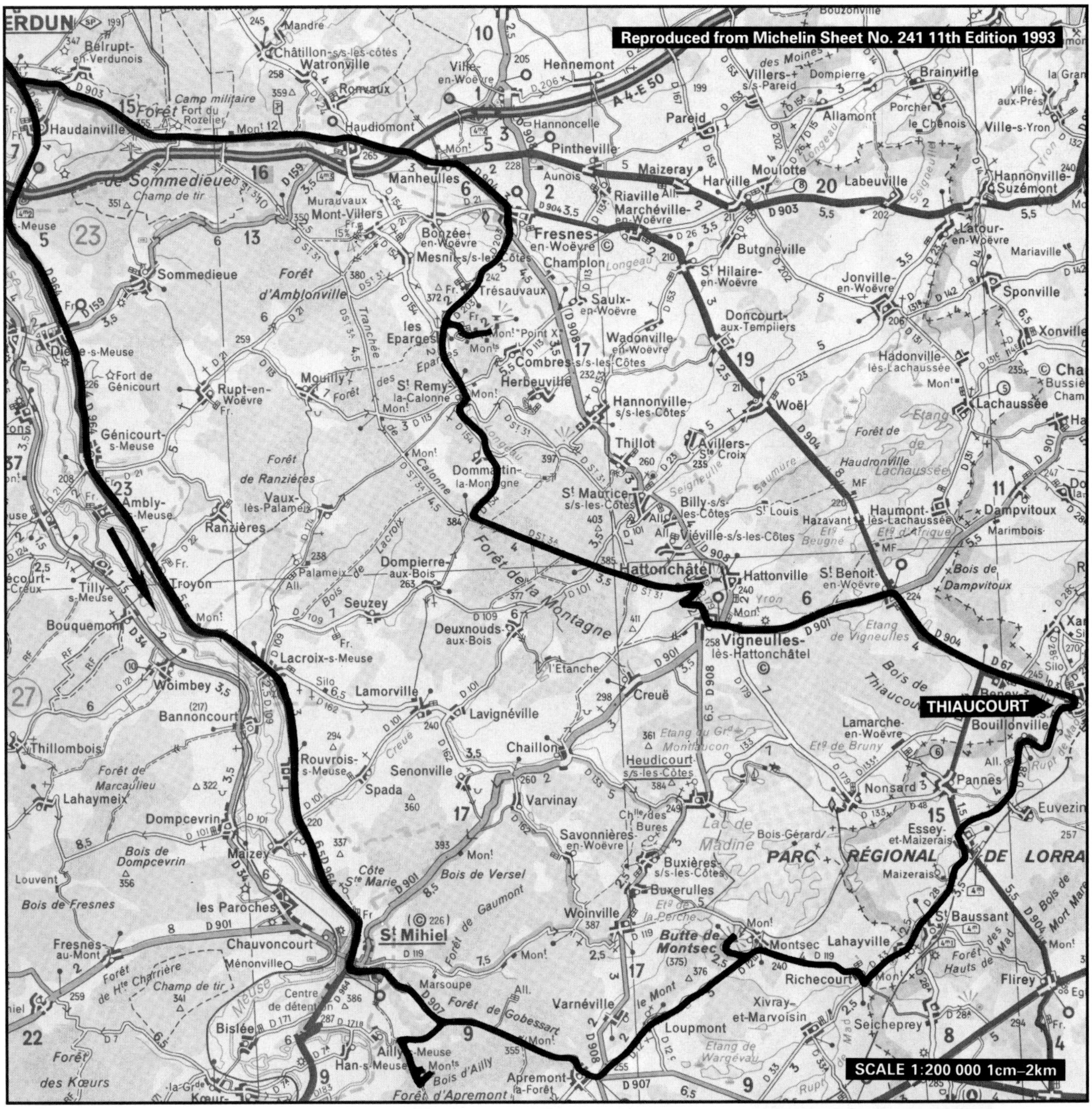

SCALE 1:200 000 1cm–2km

ROUTE III The American Battlefields

Take the D903 out of the city and then branch off to the right on D964. This pleasant road follows the valley of the **River Meuse** and the hills which surround it. At intervals, signposts point to the various forts such as **Fort de Géniecourt** (1 km south of Dieue) and **Fort de Troyon**, 2 kms south of the village of that name.

After 35 kms, we reach **St Mihiel**. The Germans captured this pleasant town in September 1914 and the St Mihiel salient was formed. In September 1918, French Colonial troops with General Pershing's US First Army made attacks on the flanks. Within three days, they had reduced it, taking thousands of prisoners, many guns and much equipment, capturing 200 square miles of enemy-held territory.

Take the D901/D907 towards Apremont-la-Forêt and the Forêt de Gobessart. In 4 kms, a small road on the right leads up to **Ailly-sur-Meuse** from which, in 2 kms, the **Bois d'Ailly** and the **Monument of the French VIIIème Corps d'Armée** is reached. It is down a narrow, tree-lined path to the left of the road, just where the road begins to skirt the wood. Hidden in the woods behind

At the Bois d'Ailly, a path leads from the obelisk of the French VIIIème Corps (left) to the Tranchée du Soif (above).

The memorial of the 172ème and 372ème Régiments d'Infanterie who held out in the Tranchée du Soif in May 1915.

A typical bunker entrance — one of several to be seen in the Tranchée du Soif system of defences.

this monument is an extremely interesting and extensive trench system, known as the **Tranchée du Soif**, the Trench of Thirst. It has many bunkers and concrete shelters, some of which, no doubt, once led into subways. It is wise to keep to the path as subsidence has created gaping holes into the underground workings. The paths themselves can be very muddy too. About 300 metres down the meandering trench trail, and a little to the right, one discerns the **Tranchée du Soif Memorial**, dedicated to the men of the **172ème and 372ème Régiments d'Infanterie** who, though surrounded, held out here for three days, during May 20-22, 1915. It can also be reached by taking the trail leading left into the woods where the surfaced road peters out.

Return to the D907 and, in **Apremont**, take the D908 left, then the D12 right to **Montsec** (6 kms) and climb up to the **American Memorial** on the crest of the **Butte** by a well-made road which ends at the wide stairway to the colonnade. The circular memorial can be seen for miles around and provides a good lookout point for the Meuse battle area. Within the pillars is a large bronze **relief map** of the region and orientation points between each pair.

The imposing American Memorial on Montsec.

In September 1918, the US First Army eliminated the St Mihiel salient, a thorn in the side of the French since 1914, in a two-day pincer attack. The memorial of the US 1st Division is at Vigneulles-lès-Hattonchâtel where the pincers met.

St Mihiel American Cemetery and Memorial — 4,152 men are buried here.

Return to the valley and, in Montsec village, take the D119 to **Richecourt** (4 kms) and there turn left onto D33/D28 to **Essey-et-Maizerais** (6 kms). Cross the D904 and head for **Bouillonville** and **Thiaucourt-Regniéville** (7 kms). Turn left on the D67 and, on the outskirts of the town, the **St Mihiel American Cemetery** is located. The dominating monuments in this cemetery of 4,152 graves are a large eagle sundial, a chapel and a museum connected by a graceful colonnade. There is also a handsome statue of a young American officer.

The direct road back to Verdun is the D904 via Fresnes. However, it is interesting to leave this road at **St Benoit-en-Woëvre** (6½ kms), taking the D901 to the left. In 6 kms is **Vigneulles-lès-Hattonchâtel**, an important position in the St Mihiel salient. Just before the village, at the junction with the D179, stands the **US 1st Division Memorial** (of identical design as the one at Buzancy — *see page 133*), Vigneulles being where this division linked up with the US 26th Division on September 13, 1918, thereby cutting in two the St Mihiel salient. On the

155

The monument to the French engineer troops who tunnelled through and mined the Crête des Eparges.

The Monument du Coq, on the rim of a large crater, is the memorial of the 12ème Division d'Infanterie *(right)* on the Crête des Eparges. The division's 106ème Régiment has a separate memorial not far away down the ridge *(above)*.

rocky ridge above is **Hattonchâtel** with an **interesting old church** and a **château**, rebuilt after the war by an American, Miss Skinner. These heights with their extensive views over the region were of great significance as observation posts.

Take the DSt31/Dst3a going west of the village through the beautiful **Forêt de la Montagne** for 8 kms. At the crossroads, turn right on the D154, leaving the long straight **Tranchée de Calonne** ahead. This road, built by Louis XVI, traverses the forest which formed an obstacle in the Eparges sector. **Dommartin** and **St Remy-la-Calonne** are passed and **Les Eparges** is reached in 7 kms. Beyond the village and to the right of the D203 to Fresnes, a road leads up to the **Crête des Eparges** with its **French Cemetery**, several monuments and huge craters. The Les Eparges ridge was an important terrain feature east of the Meuse, and, in the Battle of Verdun, became what the hill of Vauquois *(see page 145)* was west of the river: a heavily-contested piece of ground riven by mine warfare. As one follows the road up the ridge, one first encounters the **Memorial of the 106ème Régiment d'Infanterie** (12ème Division); a little further on is the **Monument du Genie** to the French engineer troops; then, up on the right, on the far edge of a large **crater** formed on February 2, 1915, stands the **Monument du Coq**, which is the memorial of the **12ème Division d'Infanterie**; next, the road passes several other **craters**; and finally, at the head of the spur and overlooking the plain, are the **Memorial of the 302ème Régiment d'Infanterie** and, at what was known as Point X, the **Monument to the Missing**. Signposted footpaths through the woods lead down the south-eastern slope to a **concrete shelter** and, some distance further down, to yet another **Abri du Kronprinz**, this one in a hairpin bend of the D113.

Return to the D203 and turn right for **Fresnes** (5½ kms). Turn left on the D904 for Verdun. Beyond the town, at the junction of the D904 with the D903 (2½ kms) just before **Manheulles**, stands the **Memorial of the US 4th Division**. In the attack on the St Mihiel

salient, the Ivy Division formed the northern pincer together with the US 26th Division and French Colonial troops, and attacked through this area.

Turn left onto the D903. Verdun is 18 kms away.

To return to Reims from Verdun, the fastest way is to take the A4-E50 autoroute, which can be joined 7 kms south of the town on the St Mihiel road (D903/D964) beyond Haudainville. From there, it is 117 kms to Reims.

Alternatively, take the N3 west for 8 kms, when we reach the **Voie Sacrée** turning to the left. This was Verdun's lifeline in 1916 to **Bar-le-Duc** and, 11 kms to the south, it passes through **Souilly** which was Pétain's and later Pershing's headquarters. However, we continue straight ahead along the N3. In 36 kms, we reach **Ste Menehould** *(see page 144)* and 42 kms further on **Chalons-sur-Marne**. Turn right onto the N44 to Reims which is 44 kms away.

The Memorial of the 302ème Régiment d'Infanterie and the French Memorial to the Missing on the summit of the Crête.

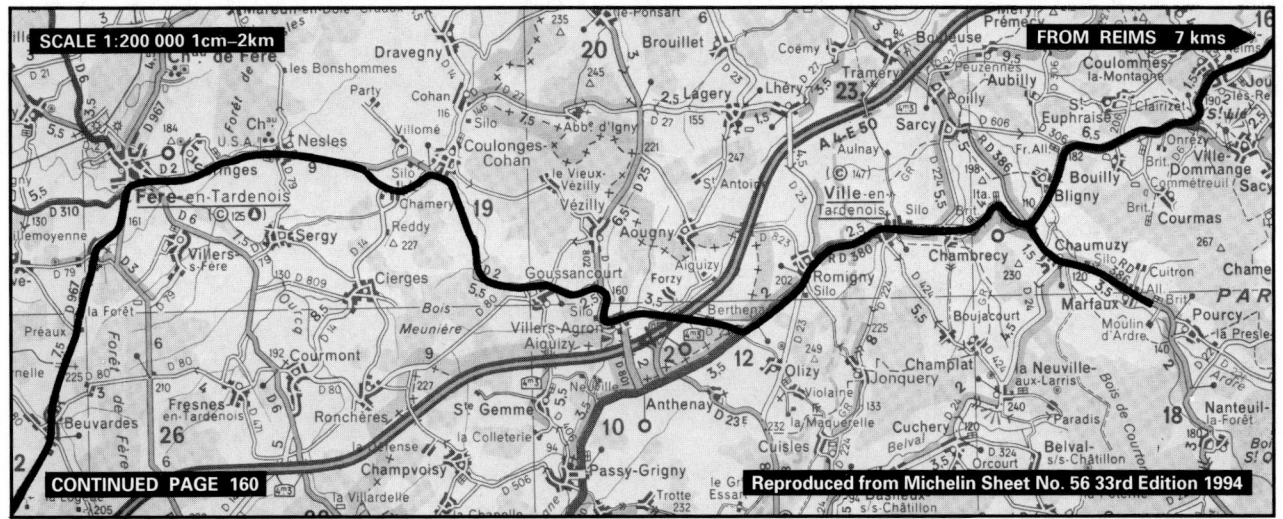

Reims to Compiègne

Leave Reims by the RD380 and, in 17 kms, we are once more in British lines. XXII Corps were in action in this region in July 1918 and the 9th Scottish Division had a fierce struggle in the **Montagne de Bligny** sector in June.

We leave the main road, turning left down the RD386, 4½ kms to the village of **Marfaux**. Here is a small **British Cemetery** containing 1,129 graves and a **Memorial to the New Zealand Missing**. Among those buried here is Sergeant J. Meikle, VC, MM, of the Seaforth Highlanders, killed in action on July 20, 1918 (Plot 8, Grave C1). A **German Cemetery** is adjacent.

Returning to the RD380, we climb up the hill towards **Chambrecy**. On the crest, an **Italian Memorial Garden** lies on the left and an **Italian Cemetery** on the right. These men lost their lives fighting with the French armies in the defence of Reims. In a separate grave lies Generale Ugo Bagnani, killed at Cassel on February 7, 1917, while on a mission in the British sector in Belgium. The broken column in the Garden of Remembrance is a genuine Roman one from Italy.

The road now goes down a steep slope and, almost at the bottom, is the **British**

The shelter at Marfaux Cemetery cloaks the New Zealand Memorial to the Missing in the attacks of 1918.

Grave of Sergeant Meikle, VC, MM, in Marfaux British Cemetery. The German Cemetery lies in the background.

Cemetery of Chambrecy where men of the 9th Scottish, 51st Highland and 62nd West Riding Divisions lie buried.

Ville-en-Tardenois, 2 kms further on, was one of the centres of the British defence in June 1918. About 1 km beyond it, on the right, is a **Memorial to the French 60ème**

Régiment d'Infanterie who fought here in July-August 1918. Some 3½ kms further on, leave the main road taking the D2 to the right to travel across the battle area of both 1914 and 1918. It is a pleasant drive through pretty country with villages typical of the region.

One of two Italian cemeteries in the region is at Chambrecy.

Grave of Generale Ugo Bagnani who was killed at Cassel in February 1917.

Memorial of the 60ème Régiment d'Infanterie outside Ville-en-Tardenois.

After 11½ kms, at the crossroads just beyond **Coulonges-Cohan**, go left on the D14. In exactly ½ km, as the road straightens out, there is a grass track leading up the slope on the left. Should the visitor be interested in the story of First Lieutenant **Quentin Roosevelt**, the son of President Theodore Roosevelt, this is the way to reach his **crash site**. The young man was a pilot in the 95th Squadron, 1st Pursuit Group, of the American Air Service, and was killed on July 14, 1918. Legend has it that not for the first time this short-sighted man was up on patrol and, instead of rejoining aircraft of his own squadron after an engagement, he tacked on to those of the enemy — who promptly shot him down. The actual site is marked by two memorials — one an upright monument, the other a tablet lying on the ground — and is about ½ km from the road, up the track and along under the hedgerow to the right. The monument can just be seen from the village of **Chamery** where there is also a **large fountain** in his memory. This is of cream stone with an ever-flowing water supply, and is near to the farm where the body was brought. He was later buried in the Oise-Aisne American Cemetery but now lies with his brother, Brigadier General Theodore Roosevelt Jr who died in 1944, in the St Laurent American Cemetery in Normandy.

Theodore Roosevelt (a relative of Franklin Delano) was American president from 1901 to 1908. All his four sons fought in the Great War, Quentin being shot down just outside Chamery. This plaque *(above left)* **still marks the spot where his aircraft fell. Nearby** *(above right)* **is a second memorial to him.** *Below:* **'Only those are fit to live who are not afraid to die.' The fountain memorial to Quentin Roosevelt in the village.**

In Chamery, take the right turn — just before the fountain — to return to the D2 and then turn left. In 2 kms, we reach **Nesles** with its rather attractive feudal castle and in another 2 kms, through the front-line area of the US divisions in July and August 1918, approach the **Oise-Aisne American Cemetery**. It is the second largest of the WWI

The Oise-Aisne American Cemetery near Fère-en-Tardenois. Here, 6,012 lie buried in the 36½-acre plot to the north of the D2.

Buildings used as headquarters by three of the protagonists still remain to be seen at Fère-en-Tardenois. *Right:* General John French commanded the British Army in France from the outset until relieved of his command after the Loos battle in December 1915 and replaced by General (later Field-Marshal) Haig. This house was his HQ for a month in 1914.

After the United States declared war on Germany in April 1917, General John Pershing became the American Expeditionary Force Commander. Nicknamed 'Black Jack' after his reputation for stern discipline, he took over this house *(right)* at No. 2 rue du Gres. The German Emperor, Kaiser Wilhelm II, son of Friedrich III and Victoria, eldest daughter of Britain's Queen Victoria, used this room *(above)*, beneath the present Crédit Agricole bank, after the Germans managed to capture the town in 1918. (RC)

American cemeteries and lies on the right of the road with the offices and reception room and car park on the left. On the gentle slope up to the attractive, rose-coloured memorial colonnade, over 6,000 lie buried beneath the glistening marble crosses and the smooth green lawns. Below the avenue of plane trees leading to the memorial are box trees cut into shell shapes. In the chapel, panels record the names of 241 men with no known graves and in the map room the engraved wall map explains the actions of 1918. Above the archways of the colonnade are the insignia of the ten American divisions — the 1st, 2nd, 3rd, 4th, 26th, 28th, 32nd, 42nd, 77th and 93rd — which fought in this region.

Continue 2½ kms to **Fère-en-Tardenois**, a pleasant little country town on the banks of the Ourcq which has a place in history as British GHQ from September 12 to October 8, 1914, when it was moved to Abbeville. The town was then used by the French until they were ousted by the Germans in their May 1918 offensive. It was liberated on July 28 and, soon after, General Pershing established a headquarters here. In 1914, General French conferred with Président Poincaré here and the **house** they used is still today much like it was then. It stands behind a high wall on the far right of the large central square (at No. 22). Years later, it was used by General Pershing as well. He lived on the other side of town at **No. 2 rue du Gres**, having his desk in the bay window of the first floor front room. In the summer of 1918, the Kaiser visited his troops in the area, using the cellar of the bank, Crédit Agricole, at **No. 9 rue des Marchandais**, as his office. The tables he used are preserved beneath the ancient vaulting and are used at meetings held here.

Turn down the D967 to **Château-Thierry** (22 kms). The name comes from the castle on a hill on the northern side of the Marne which, legend says, was built by Charles Martel for the King of the Franks, Thierry IV. The site of the castle is now a public park where the ruined walls are still visible.

On September 9, 1914, a most important date in the First Battle of the Marne (when the Allies began to advance), the British I Corps (Haig) crossed the Marne here and moved forward to Fère-en-Tardenois. Château-Thierry remained far behind the line until the German advance in May 1918. As it had been with the British in 1914, Château-Thierry was to be the scene of the first American offensive. Despite many attacks, the Allied line held and the town, which had fallen to the Germans on May 31, was retaken on July 21, with the American divisions pushing forward into the wooded hills north of the town. Near the bridge over the Marne, to the left as the D967 reaches the river, is the Place des Etats-Unis (a useful car parking area). One of the old buildings salvaged from the destruction of the town in the battles of 1918 was the **Hôtel de l'Eléphant**. This house overlooks the car park and in it was established the Maison Amitié Fraternelle Americaine — the initial letters are on the façade — by the American Methodist Church in 1919. A social centre and school for the benefit of local people, it is still a municipal institution with language and other courses and a good library. Until the bombardment of the Second World War, the façade was decorated by bas reliefs of American soldiers but these have not been replaced. In the courtyard under the balcony are preserved **relics of Lieutenant Quentin**

Roosevelt's aircraft — part of the engine and the propeller — together with **photographs of the battle area**. Dominating the town from the summit of **Hill 204** is the huge **American Memorial**.

To reach the memorial, leave the town by the N3 and climb up a fairly steep hill. In 3 kms, on a corner, the two stone pylons marking the entrance to the memorial will be seen

Quentin Roosevelt was shot down in July 1918. These relics from the machine are now preserved in the old Hôtel de l'Eléphant, now the Maison Amitié Fraternelle Americaine.

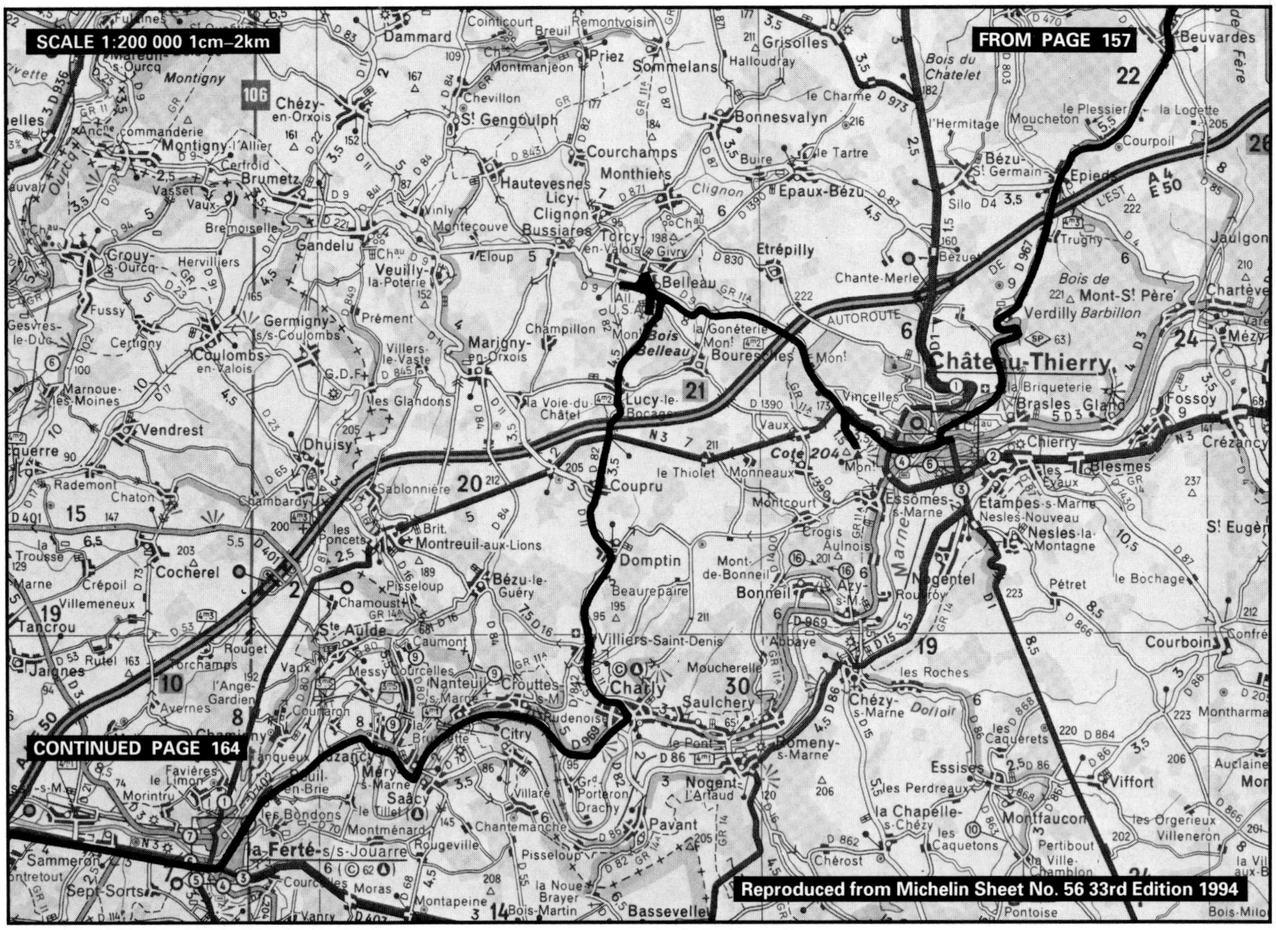

FROM PAGE 157

CONTINUED PAGE 164

The magnificent American Château-Thierry Memorial, *right,* **is set on Côte 204, giving fine panoramic views over the plain below. Château-Thierry was the scene of the first American offensive.**

on the left. The drive up to the memorial is about 1½ kms. The memorial is immense and consists of a double colonnade above a paved terrace framed by an arc of fine trees. On the west face are two heroic figures representing the two countries, France and the USA. On the eastern side, a huge eagle perches above a **map** of the area of the American operations with an **orientation table** on the floor of the terrace.

Return to the main road and, with care, take the road on the far side, the D9 for **Belleau Wood**. When the Germans made their surprise attack along the Aisne river in late May 1918 and advanced to the Marne, Allied reinforcements, including the US 2nd and 3rd Divisions, were hurriedly brought up to stop the enemy progress towards Paris. The 2nd Division, which included the 4th Marine Brigade, was assigned a battle position around Belleau Wood. On June 6, the first of their many attacks on the wood was launched. On the 9th, the occupied parts of the wood were abandoned permitting concentrated artillery fire on German positions. Next day, the wood was again attacked and the former positions regained. The wood was finally captured on the 25th.

In 7 kms, we first reach the village of **Belleau** and the **Aisne-Marne American Cemetery**, with the wood on the high ground behind it. The graves fan out on a curve on either side of a central lawn at the end of a tree-lined drive. Above the slopes of the cemetery is the chapel with its imposing tower. Here, there are 2,289 graves, and the

A demarcation Stone stands opposite the entrance of the American Aisne-Marne Cemetery at Belleau *(right).*

names of 1,060 who have no known grave are inscribed on the walls of the chapel. There is an observation platform high in the tower giving a fine panoramic view. From the chapel, paths lead up into the wood. The one on the left leads to a **ruined chapel** on which is a **plaque of the US 2nd Division**.

Opposite the main gate of the cemetery is the **Demarcation Stone** and the **reconstructed village church**, the work being paid for by the veterans of the **US 26th Division**. Their divisional badge is on the church gatepost. A key to the church is held by the cemetery superintendent. Within are memorials and flags of the 26th Division and other US forces and commemorative stained-glass windows. Down the village street is a **drinking trough**, filled with flowers, the gift to Belleau from the Belleau Wood Memorial Association in memory of the soldiers of Pennsylvania who lost their lives. At the bottom of the street are the **château stables** where the Americans were housed. They are on private property, but access is free. Against the wall opposite the stables, below the château ruins, is another trough with a **fountain** in the shape of a bulldog's head — a gift from the **US Marines** whose badge included such an animal.

The road to the left takes one back to the D9. About ½ km to the right is the large **German Cemetery** where there are 8,625 graves.

The US 26th Division Memorial Chapel at Belleau, with the divisional badge on the gatepost.

The Aisne-Marne American Cemetery at Belleau with its chapel tower inscribed with the names of the missing.

The Belleau drinking trough, used as flower-box, is a memorial to the Pennsylvanians.

The bulldog's head fountain in the grounds of Belleau Château is a gift from the US Marines who were billeted there.

A few hundred metres away from the American Cemetery with its 2,289 graves is the German burial ground containing 8,625 men.

Turn back to Belleau, passing the gates of the American Cemetery, and, immediately beyond, turn right and then right again, thus entering **Belleau Wood** itself. At the entrance to the park, on the right, is a **US 2nd Division boulder stone memorial** (identical to the one near Sommepy — *see page 140*). The park road climbs up to the centre of the wood where there are a flagpole and a **Memorial to the US 4th Marine Brigade**. The memorial states that, by order of the Commanding General of the French 6ème Armée, the wood be officially renamed Bois de la Brigade de Marine. Placed around the clearing are various **artillery guns and mortars** captured by the Marines and in the wood are vestiges of the trenches and craters.

Memorial to the US 4th Marine Brigade in Belleau Wood.

Captured artillery pieces in a clearing in Belleau Wood.

The US 2nd Indianhead Division, of which the 4th Marine Brigade formed part, has three memorials in the Belleau Wood area: a plaque on the ruined chapel in the woods *(above)*; a boulder stone at the entrance to the wood parc *(top centre)*; and an identical stone at Lucy-le-Bocage, on the south side of the wood *(right)*.

Leave the wood via the southern exit road to **Lucy-le-Bocage** (3 kms), where the US 2nd Division first blocked the German drive towards Paris and where, just beyond the church, there is yet another **US 2nd Division boulder stone memorial**. Carry on, passing under the Reims-Paris autoroute and crossing the N3, and take the D82 to **Coupru** and then the D11 for **Domptin** and **Charly** (11 kms). Turn right on the D969 to follow the course of the **River Marne** through very pretty scenery although difficult fighting country. The river winds in large loops between steep banks with hills covered with trees.

In 8½ kms, we arrive at **Luzancy**. Near the entrance to the village, the road crosses the river close to the **site of the weir** over which in 1914 the British infantry crossed as the bridge had been blown. A more modern weir is further up stream.

We then reach **La Ferté-sous-Jouarre** (7 kms), an attractive town at the junction of the Marne and the Petit Morin rivers. The BEF, which began to advance on September 6, 1914, arrived at La Ferté to find the Germans well placed on the northern banks and the bridges blown. The British artillery dealt severely with the enemy guns and the 4th Division Engineers built a floating bridge to enable the left wing of the BEF to cross. This bridge was built close to the ruined one on the main Paris road. At the southern end, today, is the **British Memorial to the Missing** who fell in the battles of Mons, Le Cateau, the Marne and the Aisne 1914. It is best reached by staying on the south bank and turning right at the first traffic circle. The memorial, with the bridge beyond, is then at the next traffic circle (the junction of N3 and D407), on the right.

The names of 3,888 are recorded on the panels of the memorial which stands in a

The BEF crossed the Marne in 1914 between Luzancy and La Ferté.

La Ferté-sous-Jouarre British Memorial to the Missing to those who fell in the battles of Mons, Le Cateau, the Marne and Aisne in 1914 and who have no known grave.

small park presented by the family of Monsieur Bernard de Jussieu. Constructed of white Massangis stone, the monument is surmounted by a sarcophagus on which are laid trophies — ensigns, magazines, bayonets and a tin hat. Four columns stand at the corners of the terrace supporting urns and bearing the arms of the UK. The memorial was designed by G. H. Goldsmith and was unveiled on November 4, 1928 by General Sir William Pulteney in the presence of Maréchal Foch, Field-Marshal Milne and Général Weygand.

On the riverside, by the bridge, the **position of the floating bridge** is marked on each shore by rectangular pylons crowned with the grenade of the Engineers mounted on a circular paving.

From here, Paris is a mere 65 kms along the N3 and it is on this road we leave La Ferté following the river to **St Jean-les-2-Jumeaux** (8½ kms).

In another 11 kms we arrive at **Meaux**. The retreating BEF reached this town on September 3, 1914 and, after crossing the river, blew the bridges and retired to the Fôret de Crécy some 18 kms to the south (on the N36). There they halted and, on the 6th, they began the return march.

One wonders where the connection is in the massive American statue to French soldiery to be seen in a park outside Meaux. This is possibly the most unusual of all war memorials.

The road bridge at La Ferté. The monument records the building of an assault bridge by the 4th Divisional Engineers close to this spot whilst under fire in September 1914.

From Meaux, we turn north on the D405 for 1½ kms. As the road climbs out of the town, there is a park to the right. Soaring above it is a huge group of sculpture which is the **American Memorial to the French Combatants of the Marne**. The figures are massive and are depicted in a fantastic pose. It was erected by the American Friends of France in 1932.

In 1¼ km, turn left for **Chambry** on an unnumbered road and, at the edge of the village, turn left on to the D140 for 1¼ km, then right onto D38 at the crossroads. Here is the **Monument des 4 Routes**. We now pass through the area of the French 6ème Armée of Général Maunoury which, at the height of the 1914 crisis on the Marne, was reinforced by 11,000 men from Paris in taxicabs. Some 3 kms further on, to the right of the junction with the D97 outside **Barcy**, stands the mother-and-child statue of the **Monument of the Notre Dame de la Marne** with the motto (in French) 'You will not go any further (September 1914)'. In 8 kms, the road becomes D51, then D18. In **Reez-Fosse-Martin**, take the D332 for **Betz** (6 kms) across the plateau past one of the French **Memorials to the Army of Paris**.

Take the D332 for **Crépy** (10 kms), occupied briefly by the Germans as they advanced on Senlis on September 1, 1914.

'Tu n'iras pas plus loin' — You will not go any further. Monument of the Notre Dame de la Marne near Barcy.

Memorial to the 'Army of Paris' near Betz celebrating the reinforcement by 11,000 men in Paris taxicabs in 1914.

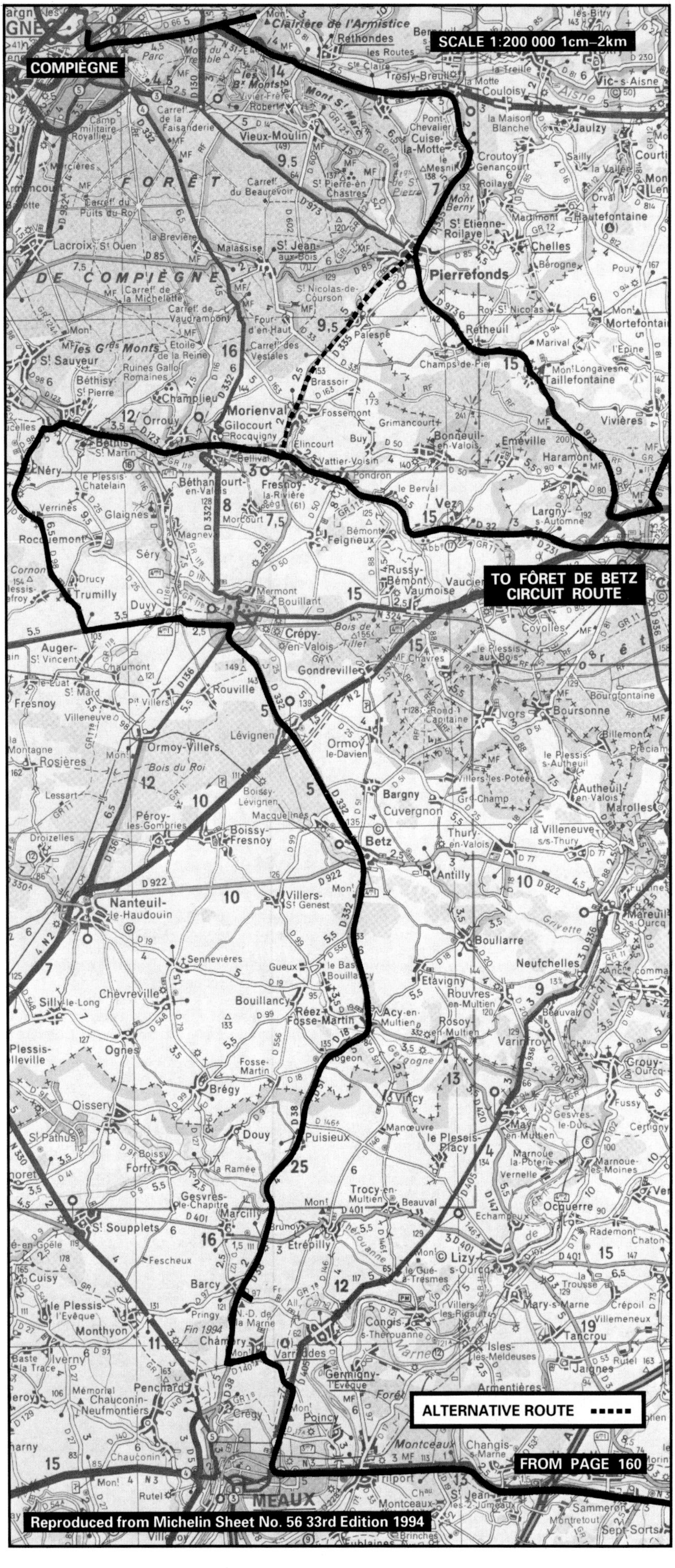

'L' Battery Memorial at the entrance to the village of Néry.

Turn left on the N324 (the Senlis road) and, in 6 kms, turn right on D98 for Trumilly. In 7 kms, turn right again at the junction of D98 and D113 to enter **Néry** 1 km ahead.

In this small village was fought a brief but glorious rearguard action in the mist of the morning of September 1, 1914. 'L' Battery, Royal Horse Artillery, won lasting fame and three VCs when they (and the 1st Cavalry Brigade) were surprised by the advancing German cavalry and artillery. In the action which followed, 'L' Battery lost two guns and their crews and, in a matter of minutes, 5 officers and 49 men were killed or wounded. Five were left to man the one remaining gun: Captain E. Bradbury, BSM G. Dorrell, Sergeant D. Nelson, Driver Osborne and Gunner H. Darbyshire. Captain Bradbury, although mortally wounded, continued to direct the fire until he died, propped up against the gun which Dorrell and Nelson kept firing, supplied with shells by the other two. The 1st Bn. the Middlesex Regiment and the 1st Bn. Scottish Rifles arrived and charged the enemy, recovering the guns and capturing eight of the German field pieces. The **gun position behind the church** is now a tennis court but the **farm**, in which they had sheltered, has probably changed little. In 1984, a **plaque commemorating 'L' Battery** was erected at the entrance to the village, and a **plaque commemorating the 2nd Dragoon Guards** (who with the 5th Dragoon Guards and the 11th Hussars formed the 1st Cavalry Brigade) is on the wall behind it. Twenty-six of those who died — including Captain Bradbury VC — are buried in two plots in **Néry Communal Cemetery** to the north of the village. A **memorial stone** in one of the plots records that five others are buried in the nearby village of Verberie.

Plaque of the 2nd Dragoon Guards who fought at Néry with 'L' Battery.

On the map:

COMPIÈGNE

SCALE 1:200 000 1cm—2km

TO FÔRET DE BETZ CIRCUIT ROUTE

ALTERNATIVE ROUTE ------

FROM PAGE 160

Reproduced from Michelin Sheet No. 56 33rd Edition 1994

Néry church overlooks the tennis court now covering the site of one of the most glorious feats of the British Army *(above left)*. Earning three VCs in almost as many minutes, 'L' Battery of the Royal Horse Artillery fought their famous rearguard action against the German advance on September 1, 1914. The farm which sheltered them remains unaltered *(above right)*. The communal cemetery is the last resting place for most of the casualties *(left, below and right)*.

In 3 kms, at **Vaucelles**, turn right on the D113/D123/D32 for 24 kms and **Villers-Cotterêts** is reached through the attractive Automne valley. The delightful old town is now encircled by a ring-road which relieves the traffic problems in this the birthplace of Alexandre Dumas, which is also an ideal base for visiting the huge **Forêt de Retz**. It was in the forest that the 4th Guards Brigade fought a desperate rearguard action on September 1, 1914, after the Germans had entered the town. They were pushed out and away in the Allied advance ten days later, not to return until June 1918 when they got into the forest some 8 kms distant. In July,

Généraux Mangin and Dogoutte gathered an Allied force in the forest and attacked on July 18, capturing 20,000 prisoners and some 400 guns as they overwhelmed a surprised enemy.

A circuit of the forest is not only very enjoyable but interesting and can be made by taking the D231 out of Villers-Cotterêts, and, almost immediately as the forest is entered, the D80 to the right. After 4 kms **Fleury** and then, after keeping the first railway viaduct to our right and 600 metres beyond the second, turn left along a typical forest road which, by taking the second-left at the multi-forked forest crossroads, leads to

the N2 in 5 kms. In places the forest is really dense and in others the enormous beeches soar over a clear forest floor and it is no wonder that an army could hide here. Cross the double-lane N2, taking the left-hand road on the other side, to once more enter the cathedral of huge trees. In ¾ km, where the beeches seem even more massive, hidden on the right is a track leading up to the **Mangin Memorial** marking the site of his OP. Here, he watched his troops from the eminence of a forest firewatchers' tower.

For a further 2 kms, the road dips and rises and curves through the forest and then descends to join the D811 where there is a

The memorial, *above*, in the Fôret de Retz depicts the firewatchers' tower from which Général Mangin observed his troops going into attack in July 1918.

Left: **Carrefour de la Reine — memorial to Guardsmen who fell in the Forêt de Retz in September 1914.** *Above:* **Guardsmen at rest in a French forest — 98 men out of the 1,114,744 British Great War dead. Casualties from the United Kingdom and Colonies totalled 888,367 (including 412,991 missing); Australia 61,860 (23,397 missing); Canada lost 64,665 (19,507 missing); Undivided India 72,407 (64,518 missing); New Zealand 18,148 (6,299 missing) and South Africa 9,297 (2,815 missing).**

The famous photo taken on November 11, 1918. The signatories descend from the Armistice coach; Admiral Wemyss flanked by Général Weygand (left) and Maréchal Foch (right).

The replica coach today. The original, taken to Berlin after the 1940 Armistice, was destroyed at Jonastal in Thuringia by SS troops, whence it was taken in 1945 from the city. (RC)

private British **Memorial to the Coldstream, Grenadiers and Irish Guardsmen** who fell near this spot. Turn left and soon the Cross of Sacrifice of the **Guards' Grave Cemetery** comes in sight. Here, 98 officers and men of the Guards Brigade are buried in a single grave below the level of the road. The ring-road is gained 2 kms further along. Take the (left) turn for Vauciennes and, after 1 km, turn right onto the D973 for **Taillefontaine** (7½ kms) and **Pierrefonds** (6 kms).

If a visit to Villers-Cotterêts is not required, after Vaucelles turn left off the D32 at **Elincourt/Fresnoy-la-Riviere** (10 kms) and onto the D335 to **Pierrefonds** which is then 9½ kms. The **fairy-tale castle** stands out as the town is approached; it was reconstructed in the 19th Century by Eugène Viollet-le-Duc and is considered the finest example of his work. Turn right onto D335 through the town to turn left onto N31 in 7 kms. Then, 8 kms later, take a right turn onto D546 signposted for the **Clairière de l'Armistice**.

Here is the famous clearing where the Armistice was signed on November 11, 1918, in the Wagon Lits Company coach No. 2419D, which, with another train bearing the German plenipotentiaries, was drawn up on the two sections of railway line from Rethondes. These spurs were originally laid down for heavy artillery firing on Noyon. The two trains stopped there for the first time on November 8 when the terms were put before the Germans by Maréchal Foch and Général Weygand. Admiral Wemyss led the British delegation. They returned on the 11th and the Germans signed just after 5.10 a.m., the cease-fire sounding at 11.00 a.m.

After the war, the marshy area where this event had taken place was transformed and the Glade of the Armistice was laid out in the circular fashion it still retains. The opening ceremony was performed on November 11, 1932 by Millerand and Poincaré. The coach used by Foch had been returned to normal service but it was then taken to the Invalides where it became a popular exhibit. In 1927, it returned to the forest where it was housed in a special shed and the interior laid out as it had been nine years previously.

The Alsace-Lorraine statue to the French soldiers who fought to recapture this disputed border territory was dismantled by the Germans in 1940 as they took offence to the golden sword of the Allies stabbing the German eagle. Found packed in wooden crates at the end of the Second World War, it was re-erected in the 1950s.

The coach shed was also rebuilt after the war as the Germans broke down the end wall to get the original coach out before demolishing the rest of the building.

The statue of Maréchal Foch overlooks the Clairière d'Armistice.

The **Alsace-Lorraine Memorial** to the French soldiers who fought for this contended border territory in 1914-18, an eagle being struck down by a sword, was erected in the avenue and, in 1937, the **statue of Foch** was unveiled.

In June 1940, the coach was brought out of its shed and, amid much pomp and splendour, Hitler reversed the rôles. The Germans then took the coach to Berlin where it went on display. In April 1945, the Germans destroyed the coach by setting fire to it near Jonastal in Thuringia.

On November 11, 1950, the memorials having been repaired and a new shed built (the old one had been destroyed in July 1940 when the Germans defaced the whole area), a **railway carriage**, similar to the original, was run into the shed and fitted out with replicas of the documents, furniture and pictures. The Alace-Lorraine Memorial, which had been smashed in 1940 and taken in pieces to Germany in packing cases, was found after the war, repaired and replaced on its own site. The railway lines into the shed have now been removed just outside the doors to prevent further removal of the coach! The railway carriage museum shed is open daily, 9 to 12 a.m and 2 to 6 p.m.

Armistice at Compiègne. The Armistice Monument, *centre left,* **erected between the wars. The memorial slab** *(left)* **marks the exact spot where the coach stood on November 11, 1918.**

167

The Commonwealth War Graves Commission

The origins of the Commission go back to 1914 when a British Red Cross unit headed by Fabian Ware went to France in September. It was a Mobile Ambulance Unit working with the French Army. In October, Ware visited Béthune cemetery with Dr Stewart, a Red Cross medical assessor. The latter, on seeing a number of British graves with their plain wooden crosses, suggested that although they were adequately marked, there seemed to be no evidence that they had been recorded or registered and that the unit should undertake this work when and where it was able.

From that day onward, the unit searched for, located, identified and registered thousands of graves. Gradually this task superseded the medical side as the Army's medical services improved and the need for the work on graves was appreciated by the authorities. In March 1915, it became the Graves Registration Commission, attached to the Adjutant General's department.

Major Ware, as he had then become, made one of his first tasks that of negotiating with the French government for the permanency of the cemeteries. This led to the passing, in December 1915, of a law that the French nation would acquire the necessary lands and make a free gift of them to the British Empire, in perpetuity, and the British would be responsible for their maintenance.

Early in 1916, a National Committee for the Care of Soldiers' Graves was established with the Prince of Wales as its President. With representatives from the Dominions and India, one of its aims was to deal with the question of permanent memorials to be erected after the war.

In February 1916, the Commission had become the Directorate of Graves Registration and Enquiries and was an integral part of the Army. This Directorate was the sole unit with authority to negotiate between the French military and civil authorities in all matters relating to graves. Similar arrangements were soon made with the Belgians.

In May 1916, Colonel Ware moved his headquarters to London as the horizon of the department widened beyond the Western Front with the huge task of registering, burying and recording the dead. An early result of the work of the Directorate was the introduction of a double identification tag made of compressed fibre in place of the old metal plaque or glazed linen tunic label.

Long before, Colonel Ware had realised the need for photographs of graves for relatives who frequently contacted the unit for information. He organised the systematic photography of the graveyards and, by April 1917, some 12,000 photographs had been sent to relatives. By that date 150,000 graves in France and Belgium, 2,500 in Salonika and 400 in Egypt had been registered.

The horticultural work on the cemeteries began in 1916 when the aid and advice of the Royal Botanic Gardens was sought and plants and seeds from Kew were sent to France through funds supplied by the Red Cross. The flowers and shrubs were chosen with considerable care. The graves at the time were either individual mounds or long trenches, being planted with flowering annuals with grass paths separating them. Characteristic plants from overseas were planted to provide a more local atmosphere for the graves of the men from Canada, Australia and New Zealand. Care was taken with Indian and Chinese graves only to use plants which those nations regarded as sacred and suitable for cemeteries. Nurseries were set up but in 1918 some of these as well as many cemeteries were overrun and all the work was destroyed. In time, this was repaired.

The moral advantage of these almost English gardens was recognised from the beginning as oases of peace and quiet amid the hurly-burly of the battle area or the large base camps and hospitals. Men found the pleasant, colourful graveyards ideal for spending short periods to read letters from home — or to write them.

On May 21, 1917, the Imperial War Graves Commission was created by a Royal Charter with the duties of marking and maintaining the graves of all members of the Services of the Empire who died during the First World War. They were also to construct cemeteries and memorials, to keep registers and records, and to publish them. The principles which guided the Commission all those years ago have been maintained to this day. To quote a recent Commission report: 'That each of the dead should be commemorated individually by name either on the headstone on the grave, or by an inscription on a memorial; that the headstones and memorials should be permanent; that the headstones should be uniform and that there should be no distinction made on account of military or civil rank.'

The whole cost of the work is shared by the partner governments — the United Kingdom, Canada, Australia, New Zealand, South Africa, India and Pakistan — in proportion to the numbers of their graves.

Each headstone bears the badge of the service, corps or national emblem; the name, rank and number and decorations with, at the base, an inscription chosen by relatives. The headstones are 2ft 8in. in height and 1ft 3in. wide. The appropriate religious emblem is also included. Normally the top of the stone is gently curved but variations exist to identify the different nationals or civilians. Headstones of soldiers awarded the Victoria Cross bear the emblem of the decoration in place of any other cross. Until recently Portland or Hopton Wood quarries provided the stone used for headstones but now Botticino limestone is being used as it requires less maintenance. The headstones stand in narrow borders planted, where conditions allow, with roses and perennials offset with lawns, shrubs and trees.

Where some doubt exists as to the exact location of a grave in a cemetery the words 'Believed to be buried in this cemetery' prefix the inscription. In places where the graves were destroyed by later battles, 'Known to be buried in this cemetery' or 'Buried near this spot' are used.

Graves of the unidentified bear the inscription chosen by Rudyard Kipling: 'Known Unto God'. He also suggested the wording inscribed on the Stone of Remembrance found in all but the smallest cemeteries, 'Their Name Liveth for Evermore' (Ecclesiasticus, Apocrypha 44:14). The Stone of Remembrance was designed by Sir Edwin Lutyens and the beautifully proportioned Cross of Sacrifice, found in all the cemeteries, by Sir Reginald Blomfield.

Immediately after the war ended, work on the permanent cemeteries began and, within a few years, these beautiful gardens of rest appeared in the once devastated regions. The first three were completed in 1920 and included two in the battle zones: Forceville and Louvencourt.

The pilgrimages, individual and collective, had also commenced and the Commission began its close contact with the British Legion and with travel agents Thomas Cook which organised cheap trips to the battlefields. Throughout the years the Commission's offices have been offering a first-class service with help and advice to those visiting the cemeteries and memorials.

In the 1920s work commenced on the erection of the memorials to the missing at certain selected sites. These ranged from the gigantic Thiepval Arch and the Menin Gate to the smaller ones such as that at Zeebrugge or Nieuwpoort. The countries of the Empire also had their memorials and, at home, the Naval and Mercantile Marine memorials were erected at the naval ports of Portsmouth, Plymouth, Chatham and on Tower Hill in London.

The Commission also undertakes to care for, on a repayment contract, private Service memorials and certain individual graves of officers and men buried before the Commission came into being.

Almost every cemetery has a small bronze door let into a wall behind which will be found a copy of the cemetery or memorial register. There is also a book for visitors to sign before leaving the cemetery.

In March 1960, the title of the Commission was changed to The *Commonwealth* War Graves Commission and in June 1961 its terms of reference were further defined by a supplemental Charter.

A series of international agreements protect the Commission's work in foreign countries and many Governments have generously purchased land at State expense and given it for perpetual use as cemeteries by the Commission.

Copies of the Registers are published for the Commission by her Majesty's Stationery Office. They can be seen at all the main offices abroad. The area offices in France and Belgium are:

France:
Rue Angèle Richard
Beaurains
62012 Arras, Cedex
Telephone: (21) 230324

North-West Europe:
Elverdingestraat 82
B 8900 Ieper (Ypres)
Telephone: Ypres (057) 200118

The Headquarters of the Commission are at
2 Marlow Road,
Maidenhead,
Berkshire, SL6 7DX
Telephone: Maidenhead (0628) 34221

For further, more detailed reading on the work of the Commission, I recommend *The Unending Vigil*, a history of the Commonwealth War Graves Commission, 1917-1967, by Philip Longworth, published by Constable of London in 1967. A new edition has recently been published.

I cannot, however, close this account without expressing my very deep gratitude for all the advice, encouragement and friendly help I have always received from the Commission over many years.

Addresses of the headquarters of other War Graves Commissions in Europe are:

FRANCE
Secretariat d'Etat Chargé des Anciens
   Combattants et Victimes de Guerre,
139 rue de Bercy, Paris (12c), France.

GERMANY
Volksbund Deutsche Kriegsgräberfürsorge,
Werner-Hilpert-Strasse 2, Kassel 3500,
Germany.

USA (European Office)
The American Battle Monuments
   Commission,
68 rue 19 Janvier, 92 Garches, France.

INDEX

Bedford House Cemetery slumbers under a leaden sky. One of the largest cemeteries in the Ypres salient, it has 5,208 graves.

LOCATIONS